Power, Voice and

A Turning Point for Gender Equality in Asia and the Pacific

Published for the
United Nations
Development Programme

MACMILLAN

Copyright © 2010
by the United Nations Development Programme
Regional Centre for Asia Pacific, Colombo Office
Human Development Report Unit
23 Independence Avenue, Colombo 7, Sri Lanka

ISBN: 978-92-1-126286-5
Assigned UN sales number: E.10.III.B.15

First published, February 2010

Published for UNDP by Macmillan Publishers India Ltd.

MACMILLAN PUBLISHERS INDIA LTD.
Delhi Bangalore Chennai Kolkata Mumbai
Ahmedabad Bhopal Chandigarh Coimbatore Cuttack
Guwahati Hubli Hyderabad Jaipur Lucknow Madurai
Nagpur Patna Pune Thiruvananthapuram Visakhapatnam

MACMILLAN WORLDWIDE
Australia Brazil Cambodia China Egypt France Germany India
Japan Korea Malaysia Nepal Netherlands New Zealand Norway
Pakistan Philippines Russia Singapore South Africa Switzerland
Thailand Turkey United Arab Emirates United Kingdom
United States of America Vietnam and others

ISBN 10: 0230-32919-5
ISBN 13: 978-0230-32919-5

Published by Rajiv Beri for Macmillan Publishers India Ltd.
2/10 Ansari Road, Daryaganj, New Delhi 110 002

Printed at Replika Press Pvt Ltd
310-311 EPIP, Kundli, Haryana 131 028

Team for the Preparation of the
Asia-Pacific Human Development Report
Power, Voice and Rights
A Turning Point for Gender Equality in Asia and the Pacific

Team Leader
Anuradha Rajivan

Core team: Elena Borsatti, Hasna Cheema, Ramesh Gampat, Amaya Gorostiaga, Rohini Kohli, Niranjan Sarangi, Ruwanthi Senarathne, Omar Siddique, Manoja Wickramarathne

Statistics team: Ramesh Gampat, Hasna Cheema, Pradeepa Malkanthi, Niranjan Sarangi, Manoja Wickramarathne

Editor: Gretchen Luchsinger

Designer: Rustam Vania

Publisher: Macmillan Publishers India Ltd.

About the Asia-Pacific Human Development Report

The Asia-Pacific Regional Human Development Report (APHDR) is an important resource and instrument to explore critical development concerns. The Report thus informs policies from a human development perspective, putting people at the centre of development debates. As a regional public good, the APHDR focuses on issues that are of common concern to several countries in the region, have sensitivities that are better addressed at a regional level, or have clear cross-border dimensions.

The APHDR is an independent intellectual exercise developed through a regional participatory process that draws from the contributions of many. The theme for each Report is also selected through consultations that include participants within and outside UNDP. The more nuanced focus of the Report is guided by substantive and diverse inputs that bring together Asia-Pacific stakeholders from governments, civil society, academia, research institutions, the media, the private sector and others. Technical background papers are prepared by eminent experts drawn largely from the Region. An established peer review process contributes to quality and impartiality. The work is enriched by a moderated discussion on the Asia-Pacific Human Development Network, which comprises members from the Region and beyond. Drawing from this rich material, the Report is prepared by the Human Development Report Unit team. The APHDR is disseminated widely, helping to promote dialogue and bring together the people of Asia and the Pacific to accelerate human development.

Foreword

Since their inception in 2003, UNDP's Asia-Pacific Human Development Reports have been stimulating a lively dialogue within the region on a range of important issues. Prepared by experts from Asia and the Pacific, the Reports present an authentic account of human development progress, possibilities, and challenges in this vibrant and fast-growing region.

This year's Report focuses on the critical question of advancing gender equality, as seen through the prism of women's unequal power, voice, and rights. Despite the region's many economic gains, the Report chronicles how in many instances women across the region continue to be held back and disadvantaged. Even as many women have benefited from their countries' improved education, health, and prosperity, they continue to face barriers to the same opportunities available to men.

The Report makes it clear that achieving gender equality promotes human development—not only for women, but for whole societies, and is central to achieving the Millennium Development Goals. Where we see progress towards these goals lagging the most is often where the needs and status of women and girls are accorded low priority.

While recognizing that each country is unique and needs to develop its own responses, the Report calls upon policy makers to correct gender imbalances through a broad "agenda for action" across three areas: supporting the economic empowerment of women, promoting women's political voice, and advancing women's legal rights. Central to undertaking such efforts, the Report argues for unwavering political leadership across the board, and highlights also the need for men and boys to help foster attitudes and take actions to empower women.

Like its predecessors, this is an independent Report commissioned by UNDP to contribute to human development discourse and policy debates in Asia and the Pacific. By highlighting that human development cannot be achieved if fifty per cent of the population is excluded from the opportunities it brings, UNDP hopes that the Report's insights will inspire further discussion, and inform the work of development practitioners and policy makers in the region and beyond as they seek to achieve gender equality.

Helen Clark

Helen Clark
Administrator, UNDP

Preface

The Asia-Pacific region has witnessed remarkable economic progress and rapid development in recent decades, yet gender inequality remains entrenched even through this era of change. The region lags behind on gender parity on multiple counts, despite progress on several other dimensions. While overall indicators for economic prosperity, educational attainments and access to healthcare have improved for the region's population over the recent decades, gender gaps have not closed.

Moreover, the region has seen divergent trends towards gender equality—notably, while East Asia and the Pacific have made significant advances, South Asia's progress on many counts has been slow. A girl born in South Asia today still has very different life chances compared to her counterpart in East Asia in terms of health status, educational attainments or employment opportunities. All countries face challenges—even those performing well on the income, health and education indicators. People, particularly women, continue to confront discrimination in jobs, disparities in power, voice and political representation, and laws that are prejudicial on the basis of their gender. This Asia-Pacific Human Development Report (APHDR) interrogates how some countries in the region have succeeded in narrowing gender disparities more than others. It does this by engaging three arenas where public policy can make a difference by:

- Building economic power
- Promoting political voice
- Advancing legal rights

The Report engages these three areas to understand the persistence of gender inequalities in the public domain, and pinpointing barriers that hold people back from realizing their potential as equal members of society. This report is not a document embodying a Utopian wishlist – instead, it provides concrete interventions in three specific domains, where public policies have demonstrated their potential.

The proposals are timely—we have a few years left to push for the achievement of the Millennium Development Goals, and the recent global economic crises has forced policy makers to review what they consider conventional wisdom. Indeed, the global economic crisis and rapid development offers new opportunities to benefit both women and men, as governments search for economic growth drivers and seek to mobilize all available resources. Persistent gender inequality continues to deprive the region of a significant source of human potential, and remains a barrier to progress, justice and democracy.

This Report comes at a time when the Asia-Pacific region is at crossroads. The global economic downturn, climate change and persistent crises in many countries threaten to further marginalize the vulnerable. In this context, gauging the overall picture of gender inequality in the region presents a picture largely skewed to the disadvantage of women.

The Asia-Pacific region as a whole, especially South Asia, ranks near the worst in the world—often lower than sub-Saharan Africa—on basic issues such as protecting women from violence or upholding their rights to property, as well as on indicators in such key areas as nutrition, health, education, employment and political participation.

Sub-regional disparities are striking. Overall, East Asia is pulling ahead of South

Asia on progress toward gender equality. In the Pacific, a complex brew of customary laws, practices and constitutional provisions represents a key factor behind the subordinate status of women.

Thus, the failure to realize equality on the basis of gender translates into fewer choices, increased human poverty and lower human development for everyone—both men and women.

The APHDR suggests a vision for prosperity for the region that can be shared by all could arise from unleashing the potential of a hugely underutilized resource—women—to seize new opportunities amid the global economic downturn. Both men and women could then find innovative pathways to revitalize their economies and better their lives. Neglecting gender inequalities puts the region's progress towards the MDGs at peril—while focusing on gender interventions now will fast-track efforts towards achieving the MDGs.

The Report argues that gender equality is a right, gender equality is good economics, and gender equality promotes democracy. The ways of translating these into concrete pathways are through building economic power, promoting political voice and advancing legal rights.

Piecemeal efforts will not do: nor will gender equality automatically come about without sustained, comprehensive efforts and long-term commitment. A focus on achieving gender equality must be retained over time. Policymakers need to consider far-reaching systemic and institutional changes in addition to changes in mindsets. Without conscious efforts in these three areas, however, inequalities in the region are likely to widen.

Building women's economic power requires removing discriminatory barriers to assets, prioritizing investments in health and education, expanding paid employment and making mobility safe for women.

Promoting women's political voice can be achieved by instituting quotas for women representatives, training first-time leaders to improve the quality of participation, recognizing the 'women's vote' in political parties and adopting gender-friendly budgets.

Legal equality for women can open the door to transformation in other spheres. Discriminatory laws should be changed and gaps filled, backed by diligent enforcement. Access to justice must be broadly available, whether that means taking justice to people through mobile courts or providing free legal aid.

Bringing equality within reach requires political will and leadership. Greater capacity for effective policymaking is key. Progress must be rooted in local contexts.

In line with the solution orientation of APHDRs, the Report recommends an agenda for action that requires transforming institutions, changing attitudes and strengthening assessments. This multi-pronged agenda for action in economic, political and legal spheres includes: implement international commitments; craft economic policies to support gender equality; make the content of education, as well as access to education, more gender-equal; boost political participation; pursue gender-equitable laws; address legal discrimination and close gaps between laws and legal practice; collect better data and strengthen capacity for gender analysis; and foster new attitudes.

The publication of this Report is especially timely as we have crossed the 30th anniversary of the Convention on the Elimination of All Forms of Discrimination against Women (CEDAW). The widening of equal choice and voice is the greatest enabler for fairness and quality of life. The Report provides an opportunity for the region as a whole to reflect on what has been accomplished for gender equality and, more importantly, what remains to be done and how to achieve it. It aims to catalyze discussions by providing the human development perspective with possible solutions from Asia-Pacific countries. Particular solutions will depend on every country's specific circumstances.

The APHDRs have been engaged by a wide cross-section of partners and stakeholders contributing to their analyses, messages and usage. These reports are products of the robust process of galvanizing Asia-Pacific expertise, including consultations with stakeholders from all the three sub-regions—South Asia, East Asia and the Pacific—and preparation by an independent team. This imparts the report with its independent voice and anchors it with its regional ownership. This is a Report 'for Asia-Pacific by Asia-Pacific'. We would like to thank all individuals and institutions from across the different countries who have helped to bring this flagship work to fruition. In particular, I would like to thank the core Human Development Report Team under the

able leadership of Anuradha Rajivan for their commitment and dedication in preparing the Report. The Report benefitted from substantive contributions from Asia Pacific experts. Stakeholders were generous with their time and ideas. Lively debate on the AP-HDNet provided much food for thought. And finally, we are indebted to Helen Clark, Administrator, UNDP for her leadership and support. May the culmination of efforts trigger fruitful debate on how to reach the turning point for gender equality in the Asia-Pacific.

Ajay Chhibber
*Assistant Secretary General and
Assistant Administrator,
Director, Regional Bureau for Asia
and the Pacific, UNDP*

Acknowledgements

The Asia-Pacific Human Development Report is the result of an intensively collaborative process with contributions from people too many to name individually. A wide cross-section of regional stakeholders contributed to this Report: experts, academia, the media, private sector, governments, Civil Society Organizations (CSOs), UNDP Country Offices from Asia and the Pacific, and colleagues from the UNDP Regional Bureau for Asia and the Pacific and the UNDP Bureau for Development Policy in New York. Individuals who have been instrumental in shaping this Report are acknowledged below. The list is so long that we can only hope that no one is inadvertently omitted.

Contributors

Numerous background papers, drafts, special contributions and notes covering a wide range of issues have informed the Report. The principal contributors were Sunila Abeysekera, Bina Agarwal, Elena Borsatti, Lekha Chakraborty, Revati Chawla, Hasna Cheema, Ramesh Gampat, Amaya Gorostiaga, Angela Hawken, Kirsty Hayes, Imrana Jalal, Rohini Kohli, Marina Mahathir, Marlon Manuel, Yoriko Meguro, Rajini Menon, Kalyani Menon-Sen, Arup Mitra, Gerardo L. Munck, Ranjani K. Murthy, Sohela Nazneen, Michaela A. Prokop, Anuradha Rajivan, Geeta Ramaseshan, Bernadette Resurreccion, Preet Rustagi, Niranjan Sarangi, Ruwanthi Senarathne, Omar Siddique, Hyunjoo Song, Sanjay Srivastava, Pawadee Tonguthai, Amaryllis T. Torres, Yvonne Underhill-Sem, Ali Wardak, Manoja Wickramarathne, Muhammad Yunus and Baige Zhao.

Technical Consultations

The Report also draws on the ideas, feedback and opinions expressed in regional technical meetings as part of the Report preparation process. David Abbot, Patricia Alexander, Suki Beavers, Kiran Bhatia, Elena Borsatti, Neil Buhne, Winnie Byanyima, Hasna Cheema, Amita Chetty, Ajay Chhibber, Jean D'Cunha, Ramesh Gampat, Cherie Hart, Rohini Kohli, Pramod Kumar, James Lang, David Lockwood, Deodat Maharaj, Roohi Metcalfe, Koh Miyaoi, Isiye Ndombi, Omar Noman, T. Palanivel, Anuradha Rajivan, Nicholas Rosellini, Chandra Roy, Rahul Roy, Niranjan Sarangi, Anuradha Seth, Omar Siddique, Surekha Subarwal, Pawadee Tonguthai, Lenka Tucek, Claire Van der Vaeren, Manoja Wickramarathne, Caitlin Wiesen, Garry Wiseman and Yumiko Yamamoto were the participants.

Stakeholder Consultations

The Report benefited from rich and fruitful interactions with a wide cross-section of stakeholders in sub-regional (Asia and the Pacific) consultations. Stakeholders came from academia, governments, the media, private sector, CSOs, think-tanks and UN entities. Participants were Shamim Ahmad, Shamima Ali, Rosa Au, Laisa Bale-Tuinamoala, Wame Baravilala, Suki Beavers, Lee Bong-Mi, Shipra Bose, Yiping Cai, Manel Chandrasekara, Pema Choden, Anna Collins-Falk, Sri Danti, Richard Dictus, Faiza Effendi, Ingrid Fitzgerald, Ramesh Gampat, Samuel Grundler, Cherie Hart, Fezeh Hosseini, Gina Houng-Lee, Wan Nur Ibtisam Wan Ismail, Henry Ivarature, Imrana Jalal,

Akanisi Kedrayate, Naeemah Khan, Rohini Kohli, Jacque Koroivulano, Edwina Kotoisuva, Joanne Lee Kunatuba, Toily Kurbanov, Tom Kalo Langitong, Ana Laqeretabua, Grace Leban, Laura Wai Yi Lee, Brian Lenga, Margaret Leniston, Kuini Lutua, Aye Lwin, Myo Lwin, Lia Maka, Solo Mara, Helder Godinho Martins, Badrossadat Mofidi, Duangsuda Muangwong, Noelene Nabulivou, Asela Naisara, Isiye Ndombi, Gayle Nelson, My Linh Nguyen, Rae Nicholl, Omar Noman, Sivou Olsson, Polotu Fakafanua Paunga, Chansoda Phonethip, Ruth Pokura, Anuradha Rajivan, Michelle Reddy, Kim Robertson, Charmaine Rodrigues, Lorna Rolls, Sharon Baghwan Rolls, Sunita Saxena, Julia Scott-Stevenson, Faga Semesi, Melina Seyfollahzadeh, Zulaikha Shabeen, Thomas Shanahan, Benita Sharma, Omar Siddique, Tanya Smith, Laurentina Domingas Soares, Aishath Raniya Sobir, Hyunjoo Song, Surekha Subarwal, Gloria Suluia, Abdurrahman Syebubakar, Crossley Tatui, Lupe Tavita, Sainmili Tawake, Amgalan Terbish, Linda Yim Peng Tham, Neeta Thapa, Claire Thoms, Richelle Tichel, Nuntaake Tokamaua, Pawadee Tonguthai, Amaryllis T. Torres, Davaadulam Tsegmed, Lenka Tucek, Janet Tuhaika, Patrick Tuifagalele, Susana Tuisawau, Giulia Vallese, Tosaka Vitayaki, Stuart Watson, Garry Wiseman, Yumiko Yamamoto and Sin Joan Yee.

Statistical Work

The statistical team was led by Ramesh Gampat and comprised Hasna Cheema, Pradeepa Malkanthi, Niranjan Sarangi and Manoja Wickramarathne. Comments provided by Elena Borsatti, Amaya Gorostiaga, Rohini Kohli, Anuradha Rajivan, Ruwanthi Senarathne and Omar Siddique greatly benefited the team.

Reviewers

The technical background papers as well as the draft Report were peer reviewed internally and externally at various stages by Meena Acharya, Patricia Alexander, Elena Borsatti, Winnie Byanyima, Hasna Cheema, Sealing Cheng, Ajay Chhibber, Arpita Das, Randi Davis, Ramesh Gampat, Vu Cong Giao, Heather Gibb, Amaya Gorostiaga, Arjan de Haan, Indira Hirway, Sara Hossain, Binod Khadria, Rohini Kohli, Amitabh Kundu, Achie Sudiarti Luhulima, Kamal Malhotra, Marlon Manuel, Roohi Metcalfe, Koh Miyaoi, Tanni Mukhopadhyay, Pamela Nilan, Agnes Quisumbing, Shirin Mehta Rai, Anuradha Rajivan, Vimala Ramachandran, Geeta Ramaseshan, Chandra Roy, Niranjan Sarangi, Babar Sattar, Ruwanthi Senarathne, Benita Sharma, Rhonda Sharp, Omar Siddique, Anushree Sinha, Margaret Thomas, Manoja Wickramarathne, Kshanika Weeratunge, Yut-Lin Wong and Yumiko Yamamoto. The Report benefited greatly from feedback provided by UNDP Regional HIV and Development Programme for Asia and the Pacific.

AP-HDNet Contributors

Stimulating and focused discussions on the AP-HD Network were held from September 2008 to April 2009, which enriched the Report. We are very grateful to James Chalmers who moderated the network discussions. The contributors were: Sara Ahmed, Ramya Solang Arachchige, Fayyaz Baqir, Radhika Behuria, Elena Borsatti, Alexander Broom, Winnie Byanyima, James Chalmers, Lekha Chakraborty, Manel Chandrasekera, Revati Chawla, Hasna Cheema, Gang Chen, Lanyan Chen, Rea Abada Chiongson, Arpita Das, Argyo Demartoto, Mike Donaldson, Kevin Evans, Ramesh Gampat, Amaya Gorostiaga, Rachel

Hackwill, Kirsty Hayes, Difei (Vivian) Hu, Taimur Khilji, Rohini Kohli, Kuntala Lahiri-Dutt, Myo Lwin, Roohi Metcalfe, Manisha Mishra, Annalise Moser, Ranjani K. Murthy, Pamela Nilan, Anuradha Rajivan, Iyavoo Ramachandran Ramasamy, Geeta Ramaseshan, Sunitha Rangaswami, Udoy Saikia, Niranjan Sarangi, Julia Scott-Stevenson, Ruwanthi Senarathne, Benita Sharma, Omar Siddique, Gurpreet Singh, Anushree Sinha, Lionel Siriwardena, Hyunjoo Song, Sanjay Srivastava, R. Sudarshan, Sumitra Sundram, Kalpagam Umamaheswaran, Chatrini Weeratunge and Manoja Wickramarathne.

The Asia-Pacific Gender Community of Practice (Gender CoP) cross-posted the AP-HDNet discussion.

Drafting and Communications Retreat

A significant milestone in the Report's progress is the preparation of the zero draft. Apart from the Human Development Report Unit, participants at the two-part drafting and communications retreat at Mount Lavinia, Sri Lanka and New Delhi, India contributed to shaping the Report. We are thankful for inputs from Hakan Bjorkman, Deirdre Boyd, Ajay Chhibber, Randi Davis, Cherie Hart, Meenakshi Kathel, Gretchen Luchsinger, Ritu Mathur, Roohi Metcalfe, Manisha Mishra, Omar Noman, Paola Pagliani, Nicholas Rosellini and Surekha Subarwal.

UNDP Country Offices

The following Country and Multi-Country Offices provided feedback and support: Afghanistan, Bangladesh, Bhutan, Cambodia, China, India, Indonesia, Islamic Republic of Iran, Lao People's Democratic Republic, Malaysia, Maldives, Mongolia, Myanmar, Nepal, Pakistan, Papua New Guinea, the Philippines, Republic of Korea, Sri Lanka, Thailand, Timor-Leste, Viet Nam Country Offices and Fiji and Samoa Multi-Country Offices. We are also grateful to UNDP Tokyo Office and the UN Country Teams in India and Sri Lanka for their valuable inputs.

Other

We express our gratitude to the students of University of Agder, Norway, for their useful discussions and feedback. We are also thankful to Georgina Bonin, Stephanie Lawson, Noumea Simi and Morgan Tuimalealiifano for feedback and information on Samoan historical stories on women. Thanks to Mohammad Sediq Orya for sharing Afghan folk tales. James Chacko, Kamal Malhotra, Subinay Nandy, Toshiya Nishigori, Xiaojun Wang and Yumiko Yamamoto are gratefully acknowledged for facilitating Special Contributions for the Report.

Production

UNDP Regional Centre for Asia Pacific, Colombo Office Business Services Unit provided critical administrative support and management services. We thank Anusuiya Ainkaran, Walter Burke, Anula Harasgama, Gayathrie Ranasinghe, Nalini Vaithyanathan and Angeline Vijayakumar. Thanks to Dishan Nanayakkara for developing the website. Charmalee Jayasinghe, Rohini Kohli, Manisha Mishra, and Tiruni Yasaratne are thanked for contributing to the website. The team at Macmillan Publishers India Limited; Suresh Gopal, Jyoti Mehrotra and Raj B. Prasad are gratefully acknowledged for layout and production.

Advocacy and Dissemination

Kay Kirby Dorji, Rohini Kohli, Manisha Mishra and Ruwanthi Senarathne with advice from the regional communications and advocacy team of Cherie Hart and Surekha Subarwal handled advocacy and dissemination for this Report. Kay also provided additional editorial guidance.

Overall

We gratefully acknowledge the support, guidance and advice of Ajay Chhibber, Director of the UNDP Regional Bureau for Asia and the Pacific. His interest and very specific inputs helped in refining the content. Nicholas Rosellini was always available and supportive during the process on small and big issues. Winnie Byanyima has been instrumental in supporting the entire process. Tanni Mukhopadhyay facilitated the review of the final draft, and was generous with her time. The work reflects the strategic guidance and dedication of Anuradha Rajivan, without whose leadership this Report would not have been possible.

O. Noman

Omar Noman
Chief of Policies and Programmes
UNDP Regional Centre for Asia Pacific
Colombo Office

Contents

Abbreviations

AIDS	Acquired Immune Deficiency Syndrome
ALP	Australian Labour Party
BWHC	Bangladesh Women's Health Coalition
CAPWIP	Centre for Asia-Pacific Women in Politics
CEDAW	The Convention on the Elimination of All forms of Discrimination against Women
CEE	Central and Eastern Europe
CIRI	The Cingranelli-Richards
CIS	Commonwealth of Independent States
CPR	Conflict Prevention and Reconstruction
CSO	Civil Society Organization
DDC	Deccan Development Society
DFID	UK Department for International Development
EZ	Economic Zone
FAO	Food and Agriculture Organization of the United Nations
FSM	Federated States of Micronesia
GDI	Gender-related Development Index
GDP	Gross Domestic Product
GEM	Gender Empowerment Measure
GGI	Gender Gap Index
HDI	Human Development Index
HDRU	Human Development Report Unit
HIV	Human Immunodeficiency Virus
ICESCR	The International Covenant on Economic, Social and Cultural Rights
ICRC	International Committee of the Red Cross
ICRW	International Center for Research on Women
IDEA	Institute for Democracy and Electoral Assistance
IIAS	International Institute for Asian Studies
ILO	International Labour Organization
IPU	Inter-Parliamentary Union
KIMA	Kawasan Industri Makassar (The Makassar Industrial Zone)
LDP	Liberal Democratic Party (Japan)
LINA	Acehnese Women's League or Liga Inong Aceh
LTTE	Liberation Tigers of Tamil Eelam
MFI	Microfinance Institutions
MP	Member of Parliament
NGO	Non-Governmental Organization
PIAS-DG	Pacific Institute of Advanced Studies in Development and Governance
PIFS	Pacific Islands Forum Secretariat
PRIA	Participatory Research in Asia

RRRT	Regional Rights Resource Team
UN	United Nations
UNDAW	United Nations Division for the Advancement of Women
UNDEF	United Nations Democracy Fund
UNDP	United Nations Development Programme
UNESCAP	United Nations Economic and Social Commission for Asia and the Pacific
UNESCO	United Nations Educational, Scientific and Cultural Organization
UNIFEM	United Nations Development Fund for Women
UNINSTRAW	United Nations International Research and Training Institute for the Advancement of Women
UNRISD	United Nations Research Institute for Social Development
USP	University of the South Pacific
WEDO	Women's Environment and Development Organization
WHO	World Health Organization
WUTMI	Women United Together Marshall Islands

Power, Voice and Rights
A Turning Point for Gender Equality in Asia and the Pacific

Overview

In every country across Asia and the Pacific, pervasive gender inequality remains a barrier to progress, justice and social stability, and deprives the region of a significant source of human potential. Inequality persists despite robust growth and progress, and cuts even deeper for poorer or otherwise excluded groups. It is time to catalyze change by focusing on institutions in three arenas—economics, politics and the law. Deliberate public policy choices, combined with attitudes and assessments that favour social justice can foster progress towards gender equality.

Today, Asia-Pacific is at a crossroads. Whether gender equality is pushed aside or pursued with greater energy, amid economic downturn, depends on actions taken or not taken now by governments and other stake-holders in the region. A conjunction of forces is throwing up opportunities and challenges—progress in the economic, social, health and gender realms; rising inequality; some gender equality reversals; a growing young population that is witnessing the bridging of education gaps; a bulging middle class with significant spending power; further economic liberalization and globalization amid the after effects of the recent global economic downturn. Although the effects of the global economic crisis in particular are high on current public policy agendas, this should not be seen as an excuse to delay gender equality; but rather, as an opportunity to promote long term progress and stability.

This Regional Human Development Report makes clear that gender inequality limits choices for women, men and people with other gender identities; such inequality puts a brake on human development. The

Report focuses on institutions in three arenas —economics, politics and the law—that can usher in far-reaching change. Each involves distinct challenges. But deliberate public policy choices, combined with attitudes and assessments that favour social justice, show these 'windows of opportunity' can accelerate rapid progress towards gender equality.

Where Asia-Pacific Stands on Gender Equality

In viewing gender equality through the 'lens' of human development, the Report finds that many Asia-Pacific countries have made formal commitments to this key development goal. In the region as a whole, women now live longer and are better educated. In a few countries, girls are outperforming boys in education, with a widening gap in favour of girls in tertiary schools. The gap in labour force participation is narrowing as a higher percentage of women goes to work. A handful of countries are also above global averages in women's political participation. Of equal importance, discriminatory laws have been discarded in some cases and national policies adapted to systematically pursue gender equality.

Despite these achievements, Asia-Pacific lags on some aspects of gender equality in relation to other developing regions of the world—and in terms of where it could be with the right attention and political commitment. Large disparities exist between subregions: While East Asia and the Pacific are pulling ahead, progress in South Asia has stalled on important issues. Indeed, South Asia's rankings for many gender gap indicators—health, adult literacy, economic participation—are often close to or lower than those in sub-Saharan Africa. At the same time, Asia has the highest male-female sex ratio at birth in the world, with sex-selective abortion and infanticide leaving a trail of 96 million 'missing' women in some countries. Women comprise 51 per cent of the population in most regions worldwide, yet they account only for 49 per cent of the total population in Asia-Pacific.

Women in the region are also more vulnerable to poverty than men, not simply because they have lower incomes, but also because their ability to access economic opportunities is constrained by discriminatory attitudes that restrict their mobility, limit employment choices and hinder control over assets. In its rates of women's political participation, Asia-Pacific still falls short of all other regions except the Arab States. A large number of countries in the region have no laws on domestic violence. Even where domestic violence laws exist, legislation is not effectively implemented.

Why Isn't Asia-Pacific Closer to Achieving Gender Equality?

Asia-Pacific is behind the curve on gender equality because the efforts of individual countries have not yet been broad, deep, sustained or serious enough to undercut the severe forms of discrimination that persist. In particular, sufficient focus has not been given to the systemic economic, political and legal changes that could make progress take root on multiple fronts.

Women's chronic under-representation in economic, political and legal institutions across the region has produced deficits in power and voice, which in turn allow inequalities to go unchallenged. Lack of knowledge contributes in no small measure to power deficits. In many countries, women may have literacy rates on par with those of men, but they may not be aware of their rights or, for various reasons, cannot exercise those rights. Many policy decisions also are still made by men; these decisions might not be the ones many women, or even some men, would make.

Unquestioned attitudes shape laws, policies, public institutions and their operation, even those commonly viewed as 'gender-neutral' that are designed to uphold equal citizenship. Where notions of women's second-class status remain entrenched, they become a steep barrier to change, often despite public policy measures and commitments. A

Asia-Pacific Often Ranks Low on Gender Indicators

Legend: EAP, SA, SSA, World

Categories (left to right): Ratio of F/M life expectancy at birth, 2007; Ratio of F/M adult literacy rate, 2007; Ratio of F/M secondary enrolment rate, 2006; Ratio of F/M adult labor force participation rate, 2007; Ratio of F/M proportion of seats held in national parliaments, 2008

Note: EAP – East Asia and the Pacific, SA – South Asia, SSA – Sub-Saharan Africa.
Source: World Bank 2009b.

seemingly 'neutral' entity also can function in a prejudicial way because of institutional blindness to distinct gender needs. Making institutions responsive to these needs would improve both functioning and delivery.

Thus, Asia-Pacific has persistent gender deficits in both capabilities and opportunities. Women acquire fewer capabilities than men across much of the region; they still have less education and much poorer health, for example. But even when they do have capabilities, they face shortfalls in opportunities; such as when well-educated women end up in jobs that do not use their skills, as is often the case. The two deficits tend to reinforce each other, since capabilities are required to obtain opportunities which in turn help build capabilities. Too often, a piecemeal approach is taken to policies that could advance gender equality. This occurs in part because the issue of gender is conventionally perceived as being 'just about women.' But gender concerns not only women, but also men and people with other gender identities and sexual orientations. While the large gaps in the status of women in Asia-Pacific justify an intensive focus, achieving gender equality involves assessing *all* gender norms and gender perceptions, and how these may operate in preventing people from pursuing genuine choices and opportunities.

Why Do More For Gender Equality— and Why Now?

The case for gender equality is often pitched as a human rights or social justice argument, but a growing body of evidence reveals that gender equality is good economics as well. For instance, over the last 10 years the increase of women workers in developed countries is estimated to have contributed more to global growth than has China's remarkable economic record. Reaching the same level of women's labour market participation in the United States—over 70 per cent—would

boost GDP in countries, for example, by 4.2 per cent a year in India, 2.9 per cent in Malaysia and 1.4 per cent in Indonesia. The gains would be greater where current female participation rates are the lowest.

Gender equality appears as a win for women and a loss for men only if it is narrowly understood as just granting expanded benefits to women. However, if a more inclusive approach is taken, men also stand to benefit from investigating the gender norms that govern their lives. Questions can be raised about why men dominate certain hazardous forms of employment, or are more likely to die violently. Some men are more suited to relationships based on cooperation, but live in societies where they are expected to be dominant over women. These confining patterns can place tremendous strains on men, leading many to make choices in conformity with social protocols, not based on what they may genuinely want and need.

Integral to respect for human diversity, gender equality supports true long-term social stability and harmony, not just a surface calm. The route to achieving cohesion can be marked by questioning, resistance and turbulence in the interim. Over time, however, this expands the space for people with all gender identities to interact and negotiate on fair grounds, providing opportunities and choices for people to pursue what they value in life and to fulfil their aspirations. It supports the cultivation of strong and healthy families, and gives each child the opportunity to be born, grow and develop into adulthood. It removes sources of injustice, oppressive traditions, disaffection and dissent. As an intrinsic good, equal rights confer dignity, foster freedom and provide opportunities and choices for people to live lives they value. Democratic societies, grounded in the principle of equal citizenship and equal rights, ensure people share responsibilities and benefits. Restricting women's participation and voice is inconsistent with democracy.

Asia-Pacific is now better positioned than ever to make rapid progress towards gender equality. Change is in the air, in no small part because more and more people are experiencing the benefits of development, seeing that change is possible, and demanding more of their leaders and themselves. Demographic dynamics—the large share of young people combined with a growing, consumer-oriented middle class—are powerful forces that can change attitudes, nullify constricting norms and accelerate gender equality. The closing male-female gap in school enrolments, and examples of women outnumbering men entering universities, also provide fertile ground for inter-generational change. Institutions have improved, more resources are available, political commitment has grown, and potential for changing attitudes is far greater than before.

Above all, making greater progress towards gender equality in Asia-Pacific will require a number of deliberate policy steps, as this Report makes clear. Gender discrimination will not decline on its own, and may not be automatically corrected in the course of development. No single policy intervention will be the 'magic bullet' that ends gender discrimination. The three areas chosen by the Report—economics, politics and the law—must be considered in terms of how they relate to each other and how they play out across the different arenas where gender discrimination occurs. Three broad directions further frame the Report's analysis: Institutions have to be right, attitudes have to be in tune so that institutions function as intended, and assessments have to be continuous to reveal gaps and monitor progress.

Building Economic Power

All human beings, irrespective of gender, must have equal opportunities to seek out economic opportunities. People access resources and livelihoods for survival and sustenance. But beyond that, economic power helps them acquire capabilities that enlarge choices for satisfying and creative lives.

As noted above, a growing body of evidence shows that gender equality is good economics. Lack of women's participation in the workforce across Asia-Pacific costs the region an estimated US $89 billion every year. Another estimate, using long-term data from 1960 to 2000, suggests that a combination of gender gaps in education and employment accounts annually for a significant difference of up to 1.6 percentage points in per capita growth rates between South Asia and East Asia. Over that period, East Asia made long leaps in life expectancy and education for women, while pulling a record number of them into the workplace. In turn, this sub-region grew faster than all others worldwide.

Gender equality has not progressed rapidly in Asia-Pacific in part because serious barriers continue to restrict women's full entry into the economic arena. In the ownership and control of assets and the ability to earn incomes, two fundamental pathways to economic well-being, women still lag far behind men in much of the region—and Asia-Pacific as a whole lags behind much of the rest of the world.

Leveraging Assets

Two dimensions—ownership and control—need consideration for assets to make a meaningful contribution to gender equality. It is not enough for women to own an asset and then be unable to determine how it is used. Control without ownership may provide some short-term benefits, but can be a tenuous position over a longer period. In general, assets are critical to rectifying development imbalances. Certain assets—land, housing, livestock, common property resources, businesses, health, finances—are critical because they can be leveraged to acquire other assets, sustain enterprises or diversify livelihoods. The poorest people, however, may have only health as an asset, plunging into destitution when this is weakened through hunger, illness or accident.

Women's overall access to a variety of assets across Asia-Pacific is poor compared to other regions. The Food and Agriculture Organization has found that in most regions of the world women headed 20 per cent of farms; in Asia-Pacific, the figure was a mere seven per cent. Interestingly, in contrast, for as recently as 2007 more than 65 per cent of female employment was in agriculture in South Asia, with more than 40 per cent in East Asia.

Patterns of ownership and control over land and other assets are diverse within the region; reflecting the fact that many practices, particularly those related to property, extend far back in time and custom. Some have arisen as part of complex social arrangements. For the most part, patterns of asset ownership and control make men more likely to inherit, own and manage larger stretches of land, while women's activities remain confined to small household plots. At the same time, women are more likely than men to start businesses out of need than to seize entrepreneurial opportunities.

Severe gender inequality is also giving rise to heightened HIV vulnerability among women. The proportion of women among people living with HIV in Asia is growing, from 19 per cent in 2000 to 24 per cent in 2007. In South Asia, for example, more than 60 per cent of over one million HIV-positive youths aged 15-24 are women. The impact of HIV is most evident at the household level in Asia. Women as care givers, workers and surviving spouses, generally bear the brunt of the consequences. Severe household impacts from HIV often forces women into distress situations, including sexual exploitation, that heighten their vulnerability to HIV. Most of the women living with HIV in Asia have been infected by their partners. On the death of the husband the woman is often blamed and, in the worst instances, deprived of rights to land and housing. Equal inheritance and property rights can critically improve women's ability to help prevent and cope with the impact of HIV/AIDS especially when coupled with appropriate social security schemes.

Multiple ways exist for women to acquire and use assets, including through direct purchase, marriage and kinship ties, and inheritance. Yet they confront difficulties with each method: Direct purchase requires resources that many women do not have, along with supportive social norms that encourage women's ownership. Inheritance and marriage customs tend to protect the continuance of male ownership and control over assets, and may be tolerated or endorsed by legal systems.

The benefits of asset ownership and control begin with economic options and extend across many other aspects of women's empowerment and well-being. Expanding access can therefore spur progress towards gender equality on multiple fronts. Women who own land, for example, have greater say in household decision-making than women without land. Asset ownership also influences fallback positions in times of crisis, whether that involves divorce, sickness, domestic violence or natural disaster.

In some cases, women already play major roles in managing assets, but this has been mostly obscured by a lack of attention. Public policies that recognize these roles might build on them, both to achieve gender equality and reap economic benefits through unleashing potentials for greater productivity. Despite obstacles to credit and capital, for example, the flow of women into business in Asia-Pacific is steady; up to 35 per cent of small or medium enterprises in the region are headed by women.

Paid Work Opens Doors

In recent decades, high economic growth rates and changing social norms in Asia-Pacific have brought women into the paid workforce in record numbers. Paid work is important to women for income—and because it can help them cultivate new capabilities and develop a greater sense of autonomy. When paid work takes place outside the home, it can bring women into contact with new people and ideas and break restrictive social conventions.

Assumptions about women's role in the labour market, reflected in the policies of many Asia-Pacific countries, however, may not actually benefit women. One assumption is that paid work of any kind can be the path out of poverty. This has fed a heavy emphasis across the region on deregulation to boost the creation of jobs, with much less focus on social protection or even the quality of employment. It has helped obscure the fact that the labour market is rife with gender inequalities, so that women in Asia-Pacific consistently end up with some of the worst, most poorly paid jobs—often the ones that men don't want to do, or those assumed to be 'naturally' suited to women.

Where these biases go unchecked, policy-making remains partially blind to the potential of women in the paid workforce, as well as to the principles of fairness and equal opportunity. It may also overlook associated economic costs. East Asia, the most successful sub-region in Asia-Pacific in terms of growth rates, has the smallest gender gap in the world in the employment-to-population ratio, and lower segmentation of jobs by gender.

A number of factors catalyze women's entrance into paid work. Improved literacy and school enrolment rates are coupled with shifting attitudes towards women's work, including growing social acceptance of women employed outside the home. Women's work can be an economic imperative for survival for individuals or families, or part of aspirations for a better life. Nonetheless, on the whole, women still fall short of men in the region in their employment rates, pay and job opportunities. Most employed women in Asia-Pacific are in vulnerable employment—broadly defined as self-employed or own-account workers and contributing family workers. These trends hold despite considerable variations among countries.

Gender also affects the types of employment women can choose. In countries where men are migrating from rural areas to seek opportunities elsewhere, a growing number of women are expected to remain behind to run family farms. Recent trends show that more women from Asia-Pacific are making the move to new areas. Mobility broadens women's employment and life choices; remittances, as a source of foreign exchange, contribute significantly to developing economies. But women migrants can be highly vulnerable to HIV, for example, among Asian women working in parts of the Arab States. This stems from the vulnerabilities they face at different stages of the migration cycle. The isolated nature of household work in unfamiliar and harsh conditions, combined with inadequate local labour laws, put domestic workers in particular at greater risk to verbal, physical and sexual abuse. Migrants found to be HIV positive are often dismissed from their jobs and summarily deported. Strengthening the rights and conditions under which women move is essential to their health and well-being, and critical for job opportunities.

Throughout Asia-Pacific, more women than men enter the service sector, possibly because of job preferences and the lower requirements for job skills compared to manufacturing, where men predominate. Service jobs also encompass many forms of employment that conform to stereotypes about women's capabilities, such as nursing and care work. Still, women workers in the manufacturing industry are increasing in low-paid and subcontracting jobs. While these jobs can provide opportunities, workers are also vulnerable to the growing competitiveness faced by export-based industries such as garments.

Despite laws guaranteeing equal pay for equal work, women still earn only 54 to 90 per cent of what men earn in Asia-Pacific countries. Wage gaps arise from women's predominance in lower-paid positions; interruptions in their work life, often related to family concerns; and the lower valuation of typically female occupations. Other obstacles include biases of some employers and women's generally weak bargaining power. Gender wage gaps vary across countries and economic sectors and change over time, persisting not only in marginalized informal activities, but also in professions such as computer programming, accounting and teaching. For example, female computer programmers make 80 per cent of what men do in Singapore, and 90 per cent in the Republic of Korea.

Several factors combine to keep women in low-paying and vulnerable urban jobs. They use informal networks of neighbours, friends and relatives to find employment, often close to where they live. But neither the networks nor the location may offer diverse choices. Women in low-paying jobs also often do not have the means to build capabilities that might allow them to move to a higher level. In comparison, male workers' contacts as well as mobility are greater.

In the after effects of the economic downturn, gender disparities are now also apparent in the disposability of female workers. Employers have reportedly pressured women to waive severance, leave and social insurance benefits, knowing they may not understand their rights or have the means to protect them.

While women's paid work can make important contributions to women's empowerment, it cannot be looked at in isolation from the work that women perform at home, such as childcare, cooking, cleaning and shopping. This is usually unpaid and under-recognized, but a tremendous absorber of time and energy. Domestic care work continues to be considered women's responsibility, even when women work long hours outside the home. Some feminist economists in Asia-Pacific and elsewhere have argued for calculating the value of women's unpaid domestic work to validate women's economic contributions.

Development for All

The obstacles to women's equal participation in Asia-Pacific economies need to be overcome as a matter of justice, and to benefit women, societies, and economies at large. The barriers are not insurmountable. Progress is coming from many directions, fueled at times by growing recognition of the potentially huge economic contributions women can make. Further steps can direct and speed up this process.

Promoting Political Voice

Access to the political arena is essential for men and women to articulate and shape solutions that unleash progress for themselves and society at large. Gender equality in political participation is socially just and basic to the notion of democracy.

In Asia-Pacific, women have demonstrated the political contributions they can make. They have been vibrant voices in formal political institutions such as legislatures and local governments, along with civil society activism. They have led countries, political parties and ministries. They have been part of the impetus behind political crisis and conflict, as well as processes to forge peace and social transformation. Women scholars have contributed cutting-edge research into critical public policy questions; this is changing the way politicians and governments approach basic tasks such as budgeting.

Nonetheless, despite women's desire and proven abilities to contribute in political forums, and despite rapid gains in basic human development parameters, only 18.2 per cent of legislative seats in Asia and 15.2 per cent in the Pacific are held by women. This is below the global average of 18.4 per cent. The Pacific sub-region alone has four of the six countries in the world that have no women legislators at all.

Social, political, economic and, in a few cases, legal barriers hinder women's participation in formal and informal politics, as well as in higher levels of government. These are expressed in different ways in the private and public spheres. Husbands and families convey the message that women cannot be leaders, but instead belong at home. Political parties avoid female candidates because they may come with fewer campaign resources and links to influential constituencies. In some cases, religion is used as a basis for gender-based restrictions.

Quotas: Boosting the Numbers

Quotas for political participation aim at providing a 'quick fix' to counter historical disadvantages, raising numbers in a relatively short time. Only about a third of Asia-Pacific countries have some kind of gender quota system in place for political participation. In countries without quotas, the women's participation rate in elected offices is around 14 per cent, rising to 20.4 per cent in countries that have them. Quotas should be considered for elected offices, as well as for the civil service, judiciary and other critical public leadership positions where the gender gap is wide, and growing.

Despite indications of their value for improving women's political participation, quotas remain controversial across Asia-Pacific—even illegal in some countries. The reasons for this are linked to social norms around gender, as well as political traditions and ideology. Fundamentally, quotas quantify sudden shifts in political power that stir resistance among those who perceive they will lose out. On the surface, quotas seem to contradict the principles of democracy and equal opportunity for all. They can be read as leading to the election of candidates based on gender, not qualifications, and as preventing the election of more qualified candidates.

Arguments favouring gender quotas include the idea that quotas are not a form of discrimination but a way of compensating for the steep barriers that keep women out of office, especially at the higher levels. Women in some Asia-Pacific countries have contended that when political parties are freely allowed gender-biased choices in nominations, this in itself is undemocratic and blocks the full exercise of voters' rights.

Laws are an important initial step in determining how successful a quota can be. In general, if constitutional or electoral provisions require parties to field women as a condition for access to seats, they are more likely to do so, particularly when sanctions for non-compliance are enforced. When quotas for political parties are too small or parties are allowed to adopt voluntary quotas, however, only those with an ideological commitment to gender equality are likely to comply. The numbers bear this out: In Asia-Pacific, the average number of women elected under constitutional quotas for parliaments is 23.4 per cent and 21.1 per cent under electoral regulations. Tokenism in party quotas has meant that women have about the same chance of being elected with or without them.

The ingredients for effectiveness of quota systems include sound laws, well-designed quotas that match electoral systems and build on political incentives, clear guidelines and timeframes, countermeasures for backlash, and sanctions for non-compliance. Another aspect entails equipping women with the knowledge and training to understand the political process and make it work for themselves and their constituents. This helps improve the quality of governance and minimize complaints about the competency of 'quota candidates'.

Not Often Invited to the Party

Political parties are the gatekeepers to the political system in most Asia-Pacific countries. They provide funds, mobilize voters en masse, produce and advocate for party platforms, and transmit an image that may have broad public recognition. Candidates who affiliate with a party essentially step into an apparatus that generally has experience in how to campaign and win.

Because parties are intended to consolidate and gain political power, much of their behaviour is oriented around this objective. Parties may view women as risky candidates, perhaps because there is a limited history of women in office and women bring fewer resources and political connections to the table.

Women candidates tend to benefit from clearer party rules that make some attempt at treating individuals alike, regardless of gender, or that go a step further to compensate for exclusion. This is possible not only through active quota systems, but also rules to position women candidates in rankings on party lists where they can be elected or agreements that women should comprise a percentage of the members of party nominating committees. Because finance is increasingly a determinant of entry to political systems, campaign financing patterns also should be reviewed both within parties and by electoral management bodies, not just in light of women's inequitable access, but also for cleaner political processes.

Women's growing track record—both as elected politicians and as voters—can also be an argument for parties to take them more seriously. In some cases, the perceptions of voters on the value of women in politics may be further ahead than those of mainstream politicians. Yet both inside and outside political systems, women need to see that they can and should participate, aim for high positions and make a difference that is meaningful to them and their societies. Supporting women's knowledge, capacity and interest in public positions can come through high-quality mentoring programmes or other opportunities to build their skills. Encouraging men's involvement could also expand political support for women.

Achieving More Inclusive Elections

Electoral systems operate within a complex web of their own rules, along with social norms and political practices. Electoral rules are considered easier and faster to change in favour of gender equality than cultural norms that hold women back, although both must be addressed. Parties can make more funds available to women and adjudicate how money can be raised and spent. Controls on campaign financing can also cut patron-client relationships where elected politicians end up dishing out favours, typically at public expense, for large donors. As a general principle, men, women and societies as a whole benefit from well-managed elections that are more inclusive and prevent factions from using violence or corruption for political benefit. Election rules can facilitate efforts of civil society or educational groups to advocate around gender equality in a politically neutral way—through voter education or training on gender equality for male and female candidates and parties from all backgrounds.

Women Participate in War and Contribute to Peace

Women play surprising roles during and after

conflict—surprising because their presence is large and mostly ignored. In non-state armies they face living conditions and risks similar to those of men. Conflict can intersect with the issue of women's political participation in several ways, including challenging traditional norms. Women may have specific insights into the causes of conflict, its resolution and moving towards peace. Many of the skills they acquire in war can be transferred to good use in peacetime.

Post-conflict periods offer opportunities for peacetime political agreements that disrupt past patterns of dominance, often by select groups of men. They have the promise of more egalitarian representation for both women and men. Women survive specific forms of violence that need to be considered in reconciliation processes, but their needs are frequently overlooked. This threatens the stability of communities, especially when large numbers of men have been killed. It also hinders prospects for national recovery and long-term development.

Some post-conflict countries have made laudable efforts to expand women's political role, starting with high-level positions in peace processes. Peace agreements offer opportunities to advance an agenda of inclusiveness, democratic reform and gender equality, including through the demonstration effect of women's participation. Initiatives designed to reach them can include psychological support and help them transfer their wartime capabilities into marketable and socially productive skills.

Transformation Through Participation

Asia-Pacific's record on women's political participation falls short of its development achievements and ambitions. A handful of countries can claim significant progress at national and local levels, but again, the region as a whole lags behind much of the world.

Women's political participation should be part of a broader aim for societies that are democratic, stable and grounded in genuinely equal citizenship. If a wide cross-section of women can come to the political table, they will bring new perspectives, talents and interests to decision-making. Politics and policy-making might become more responsive to a more inclusive array of public concerns—and more complete in decisions about the use of public resources. At first this may not be easy. But by deepening democracy, it can lead to transformation for citizens at large.

Advancing Legal Rights

Asia-Pacific now has more laws that support the advancement of women than at any other point in its history. This achievement deserves to be recognized and is the foundation for continued progress. At the same time, not nearly enough has been done. More than half the countries of East Asia and the Pacific and over three-fourths of South Asian countries are marked by medium to high levels of discrimination in economic rights. The social rights situation is even worse—and deteriorating.

Most legal systems in Asia-Pacific have been buffeted by competing influences—from colonialism to domestic demands to international human rights standards. This explains in part why many have ended up with contradictory or archaic statutes and discriminatory practices. But in the drive towards human development, and in the embrace of modern societies grounded in the principle of equal citizenship, more attention needs to be paid to how the law holds women back and how this can constrain further advancements for women, men, and societies at large.

The region falls far short of where it could be on basic issues such as protecting women from violence, upholding entitlements to property, or even allowing people to divorce in an informed and reasonable way. Two barriers are in place: The first comes from the construction of laws themselves, which may be overtly discriminatory, full of gaps or contradictory. The second barrier is restricted access to the legal system and to justice within it. This involves all the reasons that women—because they are women—may not go to police or the court or other mechanisms for justice, or may not find equal treatment even if they do.

Shortfalls in the Substance of the Law

All legal systems draw on certain basic principles. Three principles outlined by the Convention on the Elimination of All Forms of Discrimination Against Women (CEDAW) are particularly relevant to gender equality and have been articulated in most Asia-Pacific constitutions; these are State obligation, the principle of equality, and non-discrimination. When these principles are poorly or generally defined, as is the case in many of the constitutions, they give court systems wide latitude in interpretation, including ways that can perpetuate discrimination.

One result is gaps in legal systems on issues related to women and gender equality. An area in Asia-Pacific where gaps in laws are wide and longstanding is violence against women. In South Asia, nearly half of the countries have no law on domestic violence; in the Pacific the situation is even worse, with more than 60 per cent of countries without relevant legislation. In East Asia, meanwhile, more than three-fourths of countries have drafted legislation on domestic abuse, some within the past few years. Still, many countries lack sanctions for gender-based violence or narrowly define the circumstances under which it may take place.

Discriminatory laws are often justified as stemming from gender differences. Sometimes this is the case with protective labour legislation that attempts to steer women away from jobs deemed unsafe for them. Some are unconscious holdovers from the past; others

reinforce ongoing gender stereotypes about a woman's physical or mental ability, or simply her capability to work outside the domestic sphere.

Some Asia-Pacific countries have statutes that single out women in different communities that may follow their own personal laws, mainly influenced by religion. Family, property and inheritance laws are among those most prone to following diverse legal paths. This lack of standardization explains in part why Asia has more reservations to CEDAW related to 'compatibility with traditional codes' than any other region in the world. By comparison, Central and Eastern Europe and the Commonwealth of Independent States, along with Latin America, have no reservations on these grounds.

Access to Justice Depends on Gender

A variety of factors come into play in reducing women's access to judicial systems. Courts may be far away, and transportation is often less available to women. Sometimes social conventions dictate that women should not leave their homes or travel or be active in public spheres. Because women at large are responsible for a disproportionate share of household tasks, they may be less able than men to take time for complicated legal processes and repeated meetings with lawyers. If they work for wages, as noted, they will generally be paid less than men and confront poorer working conditions. This, in turn, likewise reduces the affordability and raises the risks of spending time on legal matters.

Women may face physical threats, including violence, if pursuing a legal remedy involves challenging their husbands, other family members, or even the broader status quo. They may fear losing children or economic sustenance. They themselves may have internalized discriminatory norms that insist on women remaining quiet and suffering in silence, and that define women as being less and deserving less.

Women across Asia-Pacific who do find the means to turn to judicial mechanisms to resolve disputes—whether state courts, the police, lawyers, or local resources—still face obstacles. Judicial practices are also subject to discriminatory social norms that do not acknowledge women's rights or concerns, or treat them seriously or fairly.

Legal complexities that require onerous court proceedings represent one reason that women fail to obtain justice. For example, beyond the fact that men's reasons for divorce are often taken more seriously than women's, most countries in Asia-Pacific have a fault-based divorce system. This requires a process of proving charges such as adultery, desertion for a required number of years, willful refusal to consummate the marriage, habitual cruelty and so on. The parties must hire lawyers, file court cases and bring witnesses to court to provide supporting evidence—a tremendous burden, particularly for poor and rural women.

Throughout the region, the stark reality of economic inequality appears when women struggle to obtain custody of their children during divorce. Some countries follow the principle of acting in the 'best interests of the child,' often interpreted in terms of financial advantages that mostly belong to men. Women typically start out at a financial disadvantage because they have less education and access to jobs and assets, or may have been economically dependent on the men they want to divorce.

Court systems continue to carry out procedural indignities that can leave women doubly victimized. While more countries in the region are moving to non-public trials for sensitive issues such as rape and domestic violence, women may still be expected to narrate their experiences in great detail, including to male personnel in cultures with strong taboos against public discussion of sexual acts. Discriminatory rules for trial procedures and evidence diminish or distort women's voice in court in a number of Asia-Pacific countries.

One of the most obvious ways in which courts fail women is when they are reluctant to uphold judgments or pursue crimes against women. This tendency appears in a lack of human and financial resources for enforcement; a lack of sanctions against judicial personnel who make overtly biased decisions, including those that unnecessarily stretch or even contradict the law; and the absence of training for police and court officials on gender and the specifics of gender-based crimes.

Use the Law to Tear Down Gender Barriers

For women to have equal access to opportunities for human development, including those that come through political and economic power and voice, they must enjoy equal rights and protection under the law. This is not currently the case in any Asia-Pacific country. Even those states that have tried to remove overtly discriminatory statutes still have gaps in laws and legal practices that fail to check gender biases. Divorce, inheritance, gender-based violence, labour rights, rules of evidence, citizenship—the list of legal issues that deserve immediate attention is long and worrisome.

Yet the gaps can be narrowed and at some point eliminated, as some countries are beginning to demonstrate. Recognizing that the law cannot claim to be fully impartial is an important step forward. The law deeply influences development in different ways and also shapes the outcomes of many non-legal interventions. The legal process and the law thus need to be crafted in ways that genuinely advance gender equality.

Laws and legal practices, *de jure* and *de facto* alike, need to be designed and implemented in ways that tear down gender barriers. This does not imply a kind of legal favouritism for women and other marginalized groups. But it requires acknowledging, at the minimum, that if people cannot even get to court or will be judged mainly on their gender, then justice is not being served. Legal reform cannot be limited to fixing the laws when compliance cannot be taken for granted.

Countries in the region have made commitments to equality before the law and to banning discrimination through their constitutions, the supreme law of the land. Progressive legal initiatives, both judicial and legislative, testify to intended advances in gender equality. The promise of these milestone legal achievements should be upheld, as in the end that is what matters.

Towards Equal Power and Voice

Thus, Asia-Pacific finds itself at a defining moment. Many more people today are aware of the benefits of gender equality, for individuals and societies. It is time to catalyze this change by moving beyond partial attempts to achieve it. This calls for deliberately strengthening policies and programmes on women's empowerment, including by embedding gender analysis as a routine requirement for framing them. Full political and legal backing then can make them central to—and transformative of—the broader mainstream.

In this process, institutions require transformation because they govern patterns of exchange that determine who has power and voice. Many institutions in Asia-Pacific maintain discriminatory patterns because they are acceptable, invisible or against the interests of powerful groups. Transforming institutions goes beyond traditional gender mainstreaming exercises, which have often had little impact because they have simply treated gender as an 'add-on' to existing institutions that do not, in the end, genuinely serve the cause of gender equality. Transformational mainstreaming implies looking at the places where power, wealth, knowledge, capabilities and rights intersect, and aligning these with principles of equality and justice rather than allowing the status quo to go unchecked.

For transformation to be sustained, attitudes also must change, both within institutions and in society at large. As long as women continue to be viewed as somehow less than equal citizens, progress will be limited. Assessing gaps and change through measurement is part of both transforming institutions and changing attitudes because it reveals what is actually taking place. Many gender equality issues have been simply obscured because they are not measured.

An Agenda for Action

While individual Asia-Pacific countries have their own choices and needs in pursuing gender equality, some overarching strategies are common to all. The following eight recommendations summarize broad directions for action across the three areas covered in the Report.

1. *Make international commitments a reality.* Countries should ratify and use international conventions that promote human rights, respect for diversity and equality for all. The Universal Declaration of Human Rights provides a foundation that was made specific to gender equality in CEDAW. Particular attention should be paid to removing the region's high number of reservations to CEDAW, paving the way for bringing domestic legislation in line with it. Both protective and empowering measures should be integrated into policies and practices.
2. *Craft economic policies to support gender equality.* Too often, the gender-blind nature of economic policy-making results in choices that deny women opportunities, even if they are not intended to do

so. A more deliberate focus on gender and how it affects women's economic options is required—particularly in targeting poverty interventions to provide equal opportunities for women and men. Governments should ensure that fiscal and monetary policies help unleash women's leadership and entrepreneurship. Monetary policy can be attuned to be more supportive of inclusive growth and human development—for example, through directed lending to poor women for productive purposes. Fiscal policy should include gender-based budgeting, covering revenues and expenditures across all budget categories.

3. *Make the content of education more gender-equal*. Because education systems still perpetuate gender stereotypes, national and local governments should develop awareness of gender in such systems, such as through teacher training. Civil society groups and gender experts can be brought in to guide the assessment and development of textbooks and question materials that overtly enforce stereotypes or do so by omission. Schools should promote female leadership and active decision-making, in part, to provide positive role models to girls.

4. *Boost political participation*. Legislatures, political parties and political leaders should recognize the importance of women's political participation to democracy and equal citizenship. Special actions to boost the number and quality of female representatives and women in upper echelons of government might include quotas, political party reform, gender-orientation and capacity development. All these measures need to be approached in the spirit of genuine change, avoiding tokenism or manipulation for political gain. National and sub-national political leaders should assure better gender balance in leadership

across all aspects of crisis management, whether involving natural disasters, conflicts or a sustained economic downturn.

5. *Pursue gender-equitable laws*. Parliaments can benefit from reforming gender discriminatory laws and making new ones where needed. This should include ironing out discrepancies between customary and formal laws that perpetuate discrimination, as well as gaps between laws and constitutional principles. Countries should have gender-specific constitutional provisions on equality and non-discrimination. This will narrow the wide latitude of interpretation currently enjoyed by courts and law enforcement agencies. Legal systems should be subjected to an overall gender equality review of national legislation, as some countries have done, including for CEDAW compliance.

6. *Address legal discrimination and close gaps between laws and legal practice*. The justice system should ensure that legal practices are consistent with laws on the books and that access to justice is broadly available. Professional training for lawyers, judges, magistrates and police should include an orientation around the needs of marginalized groups. Crimes against women should not be treated lightly.

7. *Collect better data and strengthen capacity for gender analysis*. National statistical systems should strengthen capacities to collect, report and analyze sex-disaggregated data, especially in overlooked areas such as the prevalence of gender-based violence and male-female gaps in asset ownership. Systematic and ongoing assessments should feed into policy efforts to close disparities.

8. *Foster new attitudes*. Civil society, the media, academic institutions, religious organizations, businesses and other groups involved in shaping social

attitudes should be enlisted in influencing them to support gender equality. Concrete advocacy tools can be developed and new channels of advocacy and communication explored. A strong push should be made to include men in the understanding of gender equality and steps to achieve it, recognizing their transformative role.

Making Change Take Root

Piecemeal implementation of this gender equality Agenda for Action in Asia-Pacific will not be adequate. Instead, progress towards gender equality requires deep, concerted efforts within each of the eight focus areas. This agenda for change needs to be put in place simultaneously on the economic, legal and political fronts, bearing in mind connections among the three, and maintained over time. Boundaries need to be pushed so that changes take root and begin to generate their own momentum.

Increased gender equality is central to achieving human development in the region, so that people at large can make choices and have access to capabilities and opportunities to lead fulfilling lives. These should never be taken away or diminished solely on the basis of gender. Human development rests on the principles of equality and participation. It is the only route forward that is efficient and sustainable—and extends justice to all.

1

A Case for Gender Equality

She Dared to Dream

Rokeya Sakhawat Hossain, 1880-1932

Ladyland: an imaginary country where gender roles are reversed in the dream of Sultana, a fictional woman. Contemplating the idea of 'mardana', a space for the confinement of men, instead of 'zenana', where women are traditionally secluded, jolts the reader out of simply accepting prevailing customs. Space opens to think differently. The 1905 story about Ladyland, 'Sultana's Dream', features elements of science fiction, the use of renewable energy, and a land free of violence. Where did the author, Rokeya, a woman born in 1880 into a Muslim family in a small village in present day Bangladesh, get her ideas? How did she dare dream of challenging entrenched inequalities?

Rokeya's life is as interesting as her writing. Though married at just 16 and raised in purdah, she was able to transcend the limitations of prevailing society. She not only learned Bengali and English herself, but also educated other women. First her brother and then her husband supported her in this endeavour.

Apart from her fiction, Rokeya is also known for her collection of humorous essays on the extremes of female seclusion, 'The Secluded Ones'. Her social concern is evident from her writing, where she artfully wields imagination, wit and sarcasm to challenge women's oppression. Writing, for her, was an instrument of activism. After her husband's death, Rokeya started a school for Muslim women in his memory, using a sum he had earmarked.

Based on 'Sultana's Dream' written in 1905 by Rokeya Sakhawat Hossain in 'The Indian Ladies Magazine', Madras, and her essay, 'The Secluded Ones' translated into English in 1988.

A Case for Gender Equality

Gender inequality limits choices for women and men, and puts a brake on human development. Pervasive gender inequality in Asia and the Pacific deprives the region of a significant source of human potential. The case for gender equality, though often viewed as a human rights or social justice argument, is also good economics. Gender equality promotes prosperity and enhances the well-being of societies.

In every country across Asia and the Pacific, pervasive gender inequality remains a barrier to progress, justice and social stability, and deprives the region of a significant source of human potential. In fact, there is hardly any country of the world[1] where women have the same or better opportunities overall as men. Inequality persists despite economic, political and social changes, rapid globalization and robust growth—and cuts even deeper for poorer or otherwise excluded groups. It is a global challenge flagged by the Beijing Declaration and Platform for Action 1995 and embedded in the Millennium Development Goals (MDGs). With the world only five years away from the 2015 deadline for reaching the goals, and a 15-year review of the Beijing initiatives in progress, achieving gender equality is more relevant than ever.

Yet today, Asia-Pacific is at a crossroads: Whether gender equality is pushed aside or pursued with greater energy, amid the after effects of the recent global economic downturn, depends on actions taken or not taken now by governments and other stakeholders. A conjunction of forces is throwing up opportunities and challenges—progress in the economic, social, health and gender realms; rising inequality; some gender equality reversals; a growing young population that is seeing the bridging of education gaps; a bulging middle class with significant spending power; and further economic liberalization and globalization. While the economic downturn is especially high on public policy agendas, it should not be seen as an excuse to delay gender equality, but rather as an opportunity to promote long term progress and stability. Women, in particular, face increased hardship during such periods, and the present one is no exception: The 'down' phase of economic cycles constricts policy space even more tightly and reduces available resources, with significant implications for women and other disadvantaged groups. But over the long run, consistent support for reversing gender inequalities can reduce these groups' vulnerability to economic distress.

This Regional Human Development Report makes clear that gender inequality limits choices for women and men, and puts a brake on human development. The Report responds to demands from within Asia and the Pacific for current analysis exploring links between gender and human development, and for considering how this can be far better reflected in public policy-making.

Gender encompasses all aspects of life, but the following chapters deliberately focus on institutions in three arenas—economics, politics and the law—that can usher in far-reaching change. Each of these involves distinct challenges. Under the direction of deliberate public policy choices combined with pro-justice attitudes, these 'windows of

Asia-Pacific is at a crossroads: A conjunction of forces is throwing up opportunities and challenges

opportunities' can unlock rapid progress towards gender equality.

Throughout history, women have struggled for equality. By the 20th Century, aspirations for a range of freedoms were enshrined in numerous international conventions and declarations, which have established norms and obligate States Parties to promote equal rights for women and men. For example, Article 2 of the 1948 Universal Declaration of Human Rights reads: 'Everyone is entitled to all the rights and freedoms set forth in this Declaration, without distinction of any kind, such as race, colour, sex....'[2] The international Convention on the Elimination of All Forms of Discrimination against Women (CEDAW) links the equality of opportunities, secured by a framework of laws, policies and institutions, with the equality of outcomes.[3]

The empowerment of women is not a 'Western' notion, foreign to Asian and Pacific cultures. Nor is it the result of recent globalization. Historical records and folklore from the region show that women exercised power and influence, and demonstrated intelligence and creativity, much before feminist ideas came into the global political discourse.

Is There a Common Understanding of Gender Equality?

The concept of equality in general, and gender equality in particular, is complex. Numerous debates have taken place on how to define and achieve equality. This Report advocates that equality is based on fairness in freedoms and choices and is inherent to the idea of human development.

Gender equality does not imply that all women and men must be the same. Instead, it entails equipping both with equal access to capabilities, so that they have the freedom to choose opportunities that improve their lives. It means that women have equal access to resources and rights as men, and vice versa.

The concept encompasses the notion that all people are inherently valuable, and that historical disadvantage, unequal access, social position and discrimination based on gender need to be taken into account in policies, plans and programmes.

Gender-based inequalities are sometimes justified on grounds of maintaining a given 'order'. In other contexts throughout history, prioritizing 'order' over justice has been used to limit basic capabilities for some people. This has led to grave injustices – 'untouchability' based on caste, colonialism, apartheid and slavery are extreme examples. Centuries of human experience show that 'order,' which does have a value, cannot be sustained unless it is grounded in fairness. Yet modern states, based on ideas of equal citizenship, cannot envisage second-class citizens or sub-citizens. If something is a human right, it should be a legitimate right for all. The decision about conferring such a right should not be made by any nation, society, community or family—it is inherent to being human.

Societies cannot successfully pursue human development in the absence of gender equality; such an approach is not sustainable, equitable, just or morally defensible. Limiting participation based on gender leads to partial information and incomplete solutions. Overall public good is undermined, even when some in privileged positions reap advantages. Gender equality is essential to advancing the lives of women and other people marginalized by gender, but it also benefits society as a whole.

Every society can improve its record on gender equality by embedding appropriate steps in its legal, political and economic institutions. Yet results are often mixed; entrenched attitudes, hardened values and historical privileges can all stand in the way.

Public policy-making has taken several approaches. Narrowly interpreting equality as 'non-discrimination' means treating males

Equality is based on fairness in freedoms and choices and is inherent to the idea of human development

Toward Better Outcomes: Japan's Gender Policies

Dr. Yoriko Meguro

Whatever the form and wherever it may take place, gender inequality cuts across all countries, regardless of the level of economic development. It is a critical concern for all from the standpoints of human rights and human security, and Japan is no exception.

Legal and institutional framework. The present Constitution, enacted in 1946, liberated Japanese women from the pre-World War II patriarchal institution. Two major institutional landmarks in Japan's quest for gender equality are ratification of the CEDAW in 1985 and the enactment of the Basic Law for Gender Equal Society in 1999. In addition to these, the country has also taken legal measures to mitigate domestic violence and facilitate parental leave, for example. Revisions have been made in existing laws, such as the Equal Employment Opportunity Law and the Act on Improvement of Employment Management for Part-Time Workers, with a stronger encouragement for the private sector to eliminate gender discrimination. As one of the so-called top recipients of trafficked women, the Japanese Government has taken steps to cope with this trans-border gender issue in 2004. In the following year, the Protocol to Prevent, Suppress and Punish Trafficking in Persons, a protocol to the Convention against Transnational Organized Crime, was ratified.

The Gender Equality Office was upgraded to the Gender Equality Bureau in the Cabinet Office in 2000, serving as Japan's national machinery and institutional mechanism for the promotion of gender equality. To implement the Basic Law for Gender Equal Society, the Bureau formulates a Plan of Action every five years to be approved by the Cabinet. In accordance with the Basic Law, 22 per cent of Prefectures (provinces) adopted their own ordinance and 57 per cent of the local government authorities have adopted action plans to promote gender equality. 95 per cent of all Prefectures have public centres for women or for gender equality. Furthermore, the government has established a system that provides services to victims of domestic violence and gender discrimination at the work place.

Achievements and challenges. Japan has been an active member of the UN Commission on the Status of Women and an eager participant in the past four World Women's Conferences and the Special Session of the General Assembly: Women 2000. The documents from these meetings have been instrumental in shaping Japan's policies for promoting gender equality. The mandatory nature of national reporting to the CEDAW Committee has kept the government and NGOs sensitized to the progress made and the challenges that remain.

It is fair to say that Japan has made a considerable advancement in building the legal and institutional frameworks for promoting gender equality prior to the turn of the century. The Gender Equality Bureau, however, has expressed its concerns over Japan's Gender Empowerment Measure ranking by UNDP, Japan being 58th among 108 countries in 2008, while it was the 8th on HDI (out of 179) and the 12th (out of 157) on GDI scales. What is there to bring such a large gap between HDI and GEM? It is now clear that economic development is not necessarily a precondition for gender equality. Interestingly Japan's ranking on GEM shows a downward trend since 2001, but its values have slightly increased. This means that those countries which made statistical data available for GEM calculation in the past decade had higher values than Japan. Although women's full access to education has long been achieved, particularly on the primary and the secondary levels, higher education has not generally prepared women to enter career tracks and professional paths. The Japanese Government admits that the pace of advancement towards gender equality by the international standard has been slow and that latecomers advanced faster in a short period of time.

Japan's ranking on the Gender Gap Index (developed by the World Economic Forum) is 98th among 130 countries in 2008. Critical variables used in both GEM and GGI are extremely low for Japan in comparison with many other countries. These are as follows: 1) the estimated earned income; 2) the ratio of female professional and technical workers, legislators, senior officials and managers; and 3) women in parliament and in ministerial positions. Japan obviously lags greatly behind other countries despite the impression that women's visibility in society has increased over the years.

What are the reasons for continued gender gaps in economics and politics? The main reason for gender gap in the labour force participation is the disrupted work career of women owing to childcare. Surveys on the pattern of women's labour force participation have shown a continued trend of the so-called M-shaped curve, indicating a distinct drop in women's labour force participation among those in the child-rearing age brackets. The number one reason for women disrupting their careers and leaving the work is 'childcare'. Despite the high rate of women workers using their legal rights to take the parental leave, particularly in the private sector, many of them do not or can not return to the same job they left behind because of the work conditions and the corporate culture, but also the shortage of support for childcare. It is hard for women with small children to get husband's support partly because some men and their parents still believe that mothers are responsible for childcare, and partly because of long work hours particularly of men who are in the life stage of parenting small children. Even if the young fathers are willing to share the childcare responsibility, they have little time to spend at home. Therefore, women who wish to continue the work career may reluctantly avoid the risk of having more than one child, if any. Those who have a choice of continuing their work and going up the ladder for higher positions are single or childless or are regular employees who are able to find resources for childcare. This is possibly one reason why women make up only 10 per cent of those in managerial positions today. Income is related to the duration of work career and the position at work. Underlining these facts is the strong gender norm defining men as breadwinner/producer and women as housewife/caregiver.

Only 11 per cent of seats in Parliament (the Lower House of the Diet) are held by women in 2008. The culture of political parties, the electoral system, the perception of the voters, and limited resources—including a lack of training accessible by women to run for public offices—all contribute to the low participation of women in public decision-making.

Overcoming gender passing and gender bashing. The majority of the country's population does not understand the concept of gender equality. Therefore, flagging 'gender equality' as an in-depth and serious concern would not gain positive reactions easily at this point in time. Indifference or 'gender passing', so-to-speak, could take place. On the other hand, when anti-gender-equality minded people took over the leadership positions, there were tormenting waves of 'gender bashing' against gender-related policies.

Under these circumstances, it helps to pay attention to the government's policy priorities. One is 'violence against women and children' and the other is 'work and life balance.' There are two different kinds of thought and rationale for the general acceptance of these gender-related policies. The first is a type of paternalism which evokes a sense of sympathy towards the victims. This is not a rights-based approach, but it is a successful case of bringing a private issue to a public domain of national concern. The second is an utilitarian rationale which advocates gender equality as an instrument to achieve another goal which is a major policy matter specific to the country. The need to balance work and life are voiced by women, men and some business sectors for different reasons, but measures are taken with support from the business sector. There are pitfalls in the above cases in which benefits for women may be situational and temporary, but they may lead to other steps forward. If, however, the government is to speed up the process in bringing effective outcomes of gender policies, we need to consider more direct approaches such as affirmative actions including 40/60 rule in all decision-making areas, public support for political education and trainings, and building gender sensitive budget systems on national and local levels. It is essential to recognize that gender-neutral policies are gender discriminatory and this recognition should be extended to Japan's ODA policies.

Dr. Yoriko Meguro specializes in gender studies and sociology, and is Professor Emeritus of Sophia University, Tokyo. She serves as the Japanese Representative to the UN Commission on the Status of Women.

Without adequate attention to wide gaps in outcomes, males and females can face very different circumstances

and females the same. This requires legislation that is gender-neutral. Here the focus is on equal treatment, but without adequate attention to wide gaps in outcomes and the fact that males and females can face very different circumstances. For example, policies aiming at equal enrollment of boys and girls in schools may not guarantee the same level of participation, performance or completion. Restricted female mobility, the burden of unpaid household work, or norms about female segregation can lead to large gender gaps.

The 'protectionist' approach acknowledges male-female differences and qualifies different treatment based on gender. This approach emphasizes gender-based social values, often considering women as weak and subordinate and men as strong and domineering. While the weak certainly require protection in all societies, policies should not systematically *create* the 'weak' by limiting capabilities for one gender and then endeavouring to protect them. Such policies may be well-intentioned; nevertheless, perhaps unconsciously, they penalize women or reinforce stereotypes about their capacities. Prohibitions on night work or restrictions on overseas employment opportunities are examples.

The 'corrective' approach to gender equality recognizes that different genders can experience the same institutions differently. Laws, policies and budgets, for example, affect men and women in dissimilar ways. The 'corrective' approach is concerned with equality in institutions, but focuses much more on outcomes. It aims to ensure that imbalances are progressively redressed.[4]

This Report advocates the 'corrective' approach to gender equality, aiming for justice by recognizing that people's development options are related to their gender. It argues against development exclusion identifiable along gender lines. People who make and influence policies must argue on behalf of recognizing current circumstances as well as historical disadvantages. No society can be fair and just—regardless of culture, history, ethnicity or religion—if freedoms and choice for all people are not a reality. This can only be accomplished if men, women and those with other gender identities can take equal rights for granted. This position is, of course, difficult to maintain and pursue in countries where men have been privileged historically, and where traditional practices continue to be invoked to keep women tied to conventional roles.

Where Asia-Pacific Stands on Gender Equality

In viewing gender equality through the lens of human development, the Report finds that many countries in Asia and the Pacific have made formal commitments to this key development goal that has spurred progress. In the region as a whole, women now live longer and are better educated. In a few countries, girls are outperforming boys in education, with a widening gap in favour of girls in tertiary schools. The gap in labour force participation is narrowing, as a higher percentage of women are now going to work; some, as migrant workers, have begun making huge contributions to remittances, which are important for both their families and national economies. A handful of countries are above global averages in women's political participation. Of equal importance, discriminatory laws have been discarded in some cases and national policies adapted to systematically pursue gender equality.[5]

Yet despite these achievements, Asia-Pacific lags behind on several key aspects of gender equality in relation to other developing regions[6]—and in terms of where it could be with the right attention and political commitment. Large disparities exist between sub-regions as well. While East Asia and the Pacific are pulling ahead, progress in South Asia has stalled on some important issues. More data will be presented throughout the following chapters, but some highlights suggest where the region stands on basic capabilities required for gender equality and human development. Overall, women remain hindered by barriers in many areas of daily life. In the region, South Asia's rankings for many gender gap indicators are often close to or lower than those in sub-Saharan Africa, such as health, adult literacy and economic participation (Figure 1.1). Political participation of women shows the largest gaps.

Females cannot take survival for granted: Asia has the highest male-female sex ratio at birth in the world, with sex-selective abortion and infanticide leaving approximately 96 million missing women in seven

Asia-Pacific lags behind on several aspects of gender equality—East Asia and the Pacific are pulling ahead, progress in South Asia has stalled

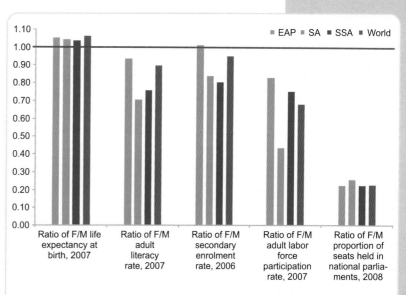

Figure 1.1: Asia-Pacific Often Ranks Low on Gender Indicators

Note: EAP – East Asia and the Pacific, SA – South Asia, SSA – Sub-Saharan Africa.
Source: World Bank 2009b.

countries.[7] In most regions, women comprise 51 per cent of the population, but only 49 per cent in Asia-Pacific.[8] The longevity gap between men and women in South Asia is 2.8 years, only slightly above the figure for sub-Saharan Africa and well below the global average of 4.2 years.[9] All this is particularly troubling when the region is purportedly making sustained gains in economic growth.

Parts of Asia-Pacific still fare poorly in female adult literacy rates and malnutrition. East Asia and the Pacific have made rapid progress in nearly closing enrolment gaps between girls and boys in primary, secondary and tertiary education. But South Asia remains at par with sub-Saharan Africa in girls' enrolment in all three levels,[10] with disparities growing from primary to tertiary. Half of South Asian women still cannot read.[11]

With about 60 per cent of the world's poor living in the region,[12] women of Asia-Pacific remain more vulnerable to poverty than men—not just because they have lower incomes, but also because their ability to access economic opportunities is constrained by discriminatory attitudes that restrict their mobility, limit employment choices and hinder control over assets. Across the region, women head only seven per cent of farms, for example, compared to around 20 per cent in most regions of the world.[13] Women in East Asia and the Pacific, at 66.7 per cent, are above the global average labour force participation[14] rate of 52.7 per cent.[15] But South Asian women are far behind, at 35.7 per cent, a statistic that has remained almost unchanged since 1995.[16]

Asia-Pacific also remains short of almost all other regions in rates of women's political participation, and higher only than the Arab States. Women in South Asia enjoy higher rates of parliamentary participation than those in East Asia, which is at par with sub-Saharan Africa. The Pacific has four of the six countries in the world with no women legislators.[17]

Large numbers of women in Asia-Pacific are among the four billion people who are globally excluded from access to justice.[18] Many countries maintain different evidential requirements for men and women, including on corroborating sexual offences. Nearly half the countries in South Asia and more than 60 per cent of those in the Pacific have no laws on domestic violence, despite the widespread prevalence of this stark violation of women's rights.[19] Even in countries where domestic violence laws exist, they are not effectively implemented. Laws and policies to operationalize CEDAW also are not taken seriously.

Why Isn't Asia-Pacific Closer to Achieving Gender Equality?

Asia-Pacific is behind the curve on gender equality because the efforts of individual countries have not yet been broad, deep, sustained or serious enough to undercut the severe forms of discrimination that persist. In particular, sufficient focus has been lacking on the systemic economic, political and legal changes that could make progress take root on multiple fronts. Several factors explain the shortfall.

Deficits in Power

Throughout Asia and the Pacific, women's movements initially found inspiration, energy and resources from women's significant participation in the independence and freedom movements during de-colonization, which brought large numbers of them into public life as political actors and participants. Often, this engagement evolved into a struggle for equal rights. As with all democratic gains, however, both advances and reversals have occurred.

Women's chronic under-representation in economic, political and legal institutions across the region has produced deficits in power and voice, which in turn allow inequa-

Asia-Pacific is behind the curve on gender equality because the efforts of individual countries have not yet been broad, deep, sustained or serious enough

lities to go unchallenged. Lack of knowledge contributes in no small measure to power deficits. In many countries, women may have literacy rates at par with those of men—but they may not be aware of their rights or, for various reasons, cannot exercise those rights. For example, a woman physically abused by her husband may not seek redress if she is unaware of domestic violence legislation in her country. Moreover, even if she is aware, social pressure and stigma may prohibit her from exercising her rights.

Resistance to women's advancements comes from many sources, from women as well as men, and takes many forms. Patriarchy represents a dominant source of such resistance, where systems of social organization are fundamentally structured around the idea of men's superiority.[20] Many policy decisions and choices are still made by men. These decisions might not be the ones many women, or even some men, would make.

Gaps in Capabilities and Opportunities

As with deficits in power, Asia-Pacific experiences persistent gender deficits in both capabilities and opportunities. Women acquire fewer capabilities than men across much of the region—they still have less education and much poorer health, for example. But even when they have capabilities, they face shortfalls in opportunities, such as when women face opportunity barriers to paid work or when well-educated women end up in jobs that do not use their skills, as is often the case. The two deficits tend to reinforce each other, since capabilities are required to obtain opportunities and opportunities help build capabilities. Deficits in opportunities may benefit from immediate interventions to widen the scope for engagement in productive activities; deficits in capabilities require a longer time-frame to build the sets of competencies necessary for a satisfying and meaningful life. From the human development perspective, once people acquire basic capabilities, they should be able to use these by having access to economic resources, a meaningful political voice and equal legal protection of their rights.

Gender Is Not Just About Women

Too often, a piecemeal approach is taken to policies that could advance gender equality. This occurs in part because gender is conventionally perceived as being 'just about women'. Typically, the issue is shunted off to a women's ministry or department, with few resources and limited visibility, and ignored in mainstream policy frameworks.

But gender concerns women, men and people with other gender identities and sexual orientations.[21] This wide range includes heterosexual and homosexual men and women; people who adopt the dress and mannerisms of other gender identities (transsexuals); people who choose to change their sex (transgender people); and intersex persons, i.e. those born with atypical genitalia. All should be full and equal partners in the process towards human development.[22] While the large gaps in the status of women in Asia-Pacific justify an intensive focus, achieving gender equality involves assessing all gender norms and perceptions, and how these may operate in preventing people from pursuing genuine choices and opportunities.

Can Some Things Not Change?

One common understanding of gender is that it is 'static', or set at birth, based on male or female genitals and chromosomes.[23] This leads to policy-making that either enshrines notions of biological difference or ignores possibilities for intervention because 'things are the way they are'. Interestingly, some parts of the region seem to have an opportunistic view of gender, holding one view or the other as convenient—for example, feminism

Gender concerns women, men and people with other gender identities and sexual orientations

*Unquestioned
attitudes shape
laws, policies and
public institutions,
and render them
blind to distinct
gender needs*

is criticized as a 'Western import', even as sports such as cricket are soundly embraced. Then some traditions accept no other gender identities besides male and female, which are fixed based on biological sex assigned at birth.

Yet, while biology plays a role in who people are and what they may do, gender encompasses notions constructed by societies and individuals, beyond biological sex. Even if these are deeply rooted in social norms, they can—and have—shifted over time as people explore new human possibilities and freedoms. Both the tendency to hold on to traditional attitudes and the desire for exploration are evident in Asia-Pacific today. Some countries in the region are opening to the voices of people from a broader spectrum of gender identities, giving them space to air views and demands.

Social Norms and Attitudes

Numerous influences have shaped attitudes towards gender across Asia and the Pacific, along with the policies and public institutions that perpetuate gender equality gaps. Diverse sources of tradition, including those expressed through religion, both support and constrain gender equality. Some date back thousands of years. These traditions coexist, uneasily at times, with the remnants of colonial systems of law and politics, and with today's imperatives of globalization and rapid change. Conflict, natural disasters and climate change add other elements—globally, the region is home to the greatest incidence of natural disasters.

Every society, regardless of where it has come from or where it hopes to go, has ideas about what men and women should be and do. Some of these support gender equality, some do not. They can be firmly embedded in history and tradition, and intertwined with notions of perceived order, family and survival. They can be valuable to social cohesion,

but hard to discard even with evidence that they may be harmful or unsuited to present ways of living as defined by diverse societies.

Unquestioned attitudes shape laws, policies and public institutions, including those commonly viewed as 'gender-neutral', and render them blind to distinct gender needs while erecting steep barriers to change. Where notions of women's subordinate status remain entrenched, they become a steep barrier to change, often despite public policy measures and commitments intended to support gender equality. A seemingly 'neutral' entity can also function in a prejudicial way because of institutional 'blindness' to distinct gender needs. Making these institutions responsive to these needs would improve both functioning and delivery.

Countries in Asia and the Pacific are rife with examples of how this works: Laws perpetuate gender inequalities through specific discriminatory provisions or by omission, and at times run counter to anti-discrimination clauses in constitutions. Inheritance practices upheld by custom and/or law prevent women from gaining ownership of land and other assets. Education systems encourage girls to go to school, but then may teach them, including in state-approved curricula, that they are most suited to stereotypically 'female tasks' that tend to pay less and be more insecure. Barriers to political participation, such as resource-intensive election campaigns, are maintained despite the fact that the level of women's representation is not even halfway to their presence in populations overall. Yet making all these laws, policies and institutions more responsive to gender needs would improve their functioning and delivery.

Why Should Asia-Pacific Do More For Gender Equality?

Equality Is Good Economics

'*The challenge of increasing the economic growth of a country is … to a considerable extent linked to the role played by women in the society. The costs of discrimination towards women in education and employment not only harm the women concerned, but impose a cost for the entire society.*[24]

The case for gender equality is often pitched as a human rights or social justice argument, but a growing body of evidence reveals that it is good economics as well, promoting prosperity and enhancing the well-being of societies. In turn, rising income can affect gender equality and human development.[25]

Put another way, societies and economies pay a high cost when they maintain discriminatory attitudes and limit freedom, choices and opportunities for women and other marginalized groups. Low levels of female participation in a country's workforce constrain its growth potential. These linkages and feedback effects need to be understood if Asia-Pacific is to continue on its trajectory of rapid economic growth and development.

Several studies using both microeconomic and macroeconomic data confirm that narrowing gender differentials in education and health have positive social and economic effects. Recent research has concluded that reducing the gap between male and female educational attainment will boost growth.[26] Higher female educational attainment also lowers fertility rates,[27] which decreases infant mortality rates and raises life expectancies.[28] Many studies have concluded that increased schooling of mothers is good for child health, schooling and productivity. These benefits are higher for additional schooling for mothers than fathers.[29]

Meanwhile, if the labour supply is artificially reduced by discrimination against women, the average ability of the active workforce is reduced.[30] Women with decent work and earnings also have greater bargaining power in their homes, which can improve their status and lead to other growth-enhancing effects, such as increased savings rates, higher investments in children's health and education, and greater credit repayment.[31] Commercial interests have already recognized the purchasing power of women, as demonstrated by growing diversity in products, services and advertising.

Overall, rising income can contribute to reducing gender inequality, but with limitations. Growth does not automatically lead to gender equality: The Asia-Pacific region has several high-income countries, such as Japan, that score poorly on indicators of women's empowerment.[32] This leads to a larger point: No single measure itself is sufficient to take on entrenched and persistent gender inequalities. Policies to stimulate growth must be accompanied by measures to change norms that block women's progress.

The Millennium Development Goals (MDGs) make these interrelationships obvious. The third Goal, fostering gender equality and empowering women, is monitored through tracking the ratio of girls to boys in education, the share of women in non-agricultural wage employment and the proportion of seats held by women in national parliaments. This Goal is in fact central to the attainment of all other MDGs, as countries aim to end poverty and hunger, universalize schooling, ensure better child and maternal health, combat HIV/AIDS and achieve other core development objectives. Genuinely equal access to opportunities and resources, regardless of gender, is key.

Equality Benefits Both Women and Men

If gender equality is only narrowly understood as granting expanded benefits to women, it appears as a win for women and a loss for men. But if a more inclusive approach is taken, men also can investigate gender norms that govern their lives. Questions can be raised about why men dominate certain hazardous forms of employment, for example, or are more likely to die violently. Some

The case for gender equality is often pitched as a human rights or social justice argument, but it is good economics as well

men are more suited to relationships based on cooperation, but live in societies where they are expected to be dominant over women.

These confining patterns can place tremendous strains on men, leading many to make choices that conform to social protocols, not based on what they may genuinely want and need. Similar considerations apply to homosexuals and people with other gender identities.

Benefits to men from an inclusive gender equality agenda might include more time spent with their families, less pressure to be the sole breadwinner, and a reduction in harmful and violent behaviours and attitudes. Ultimately, relationships could improve, producing happier and less fractious families—and societies.

Equality Promotes Social Cohesion

Integral to respect for human diversity, gender equality supports true long term social stability and harmony, and not just a surface calm. But the route to achieving cohesion can be marked by questioning, resistance and turbulence in the interim. Over time, however, this expands the space for people with all gender identities to interact and negotiate on fair grounds, and provides opportunities and choices for people, regardless of sex or gender, to pursue what they value in life and fulfil their aspirations. It supports the cultivation of strong and healthy families, and gives each child the opportunity to be born, grow and develop into adulthood. It removes sources of injustice, oppressive and archaic traditions, disaffection and dissent.

In the Asia-Pacific region, which continues to face widespread conflict, a high number of natural disasters and economic crisis, gender equality can be part of the 'glue' that helps countries recover more quickly from such upheaval. When women are more prone to abuse and discrimination during crises, as is often the case, some may resort to high-risk behaviour, such as sex work, in order to survive and care for their children.[33] In doing so, they cannot contribute effectively to strategies for recovery.

Equality Is a Right

Equal rights are an intrinsic good. They confer dignity, foster freedom and provide opportunities and choices for people to live lives they value. Democratic societies grounded in the principle of equal citizenship and equal rights ensure people share responsibilities and benefits. Restricting women's participation and voice is inconsistent with democracy.

In an unequal world, the principle of equal rights can seem abstract. But important historical reference points can be found in the elimination of slavery, colonialism and apartheid.[34] Once a critical mass of people understand that certain practices are morally untenable and harmful to their standing in a globalized world, they will agitate against them. Changing institutions and attitudes, recurring themes in this report, are thus of cardinal importance in the struggle against gender inequality.

The Time Has Come

'I'm not afraid of people, and I'm not afraid to speak the truth. There is too much corruption in this country. There are women in villages living in caves. There are boys killing for the Taliban. Someone has to talk about the real problems.'[35]

— Shala Attah, a psychologist and legislator who left her husband and five children in the United States to return to her native Afghanistan to run for president

'After all the attempts to block the passage of the Magna Carta of Women, the Filipino women have finally emerged victorious. This is a by-product of women's continuous struggle for equality and serves

as a gateway in support of women's legitimate concerns,'[36]

– Liza Maza, Gabriela women's party representative from the Philippines

Asia-Pacific is now better positioned than ever to make rapid progress towards gender equality, pushing past the deficits catalogued so far. Change is in the air, in no small part because more people are experiencing the benefits of development, seeing that change is possible, and demanding more of their leaders and themselves. Demographic dynamics—a large share of young people, combined with a growing, consumer-oriented middle class—are powerful forces that can change attitudes, nullify constricting norms and accelerate progress towards gender equality. The closing male-female gap in school enrolments, and examples of women outnumbering men entering universities in some countries, are also providing a fertile ground for intergenerational change. Institutions have improved, more resources are available, political commitment has grown, and potential for changing attitudes is far greater than ever before.

Better Institutions, More Resources

Prosperity, modernization and better education mean that many parts of the region have more effective institutions in place to respond to diverse needs of citizens, including women and other disadvantaged groups. In countries that have successfully capitalized on the global economic surge of recent decades, more resources are available to invest in human development, including gender equality. And despite the current global downturn, the region as a whole may continue its stronger economic growth compared to other parts of the world.[37] Even if public spending choices tighten, gender equality must remain a crucial element in any strategy to foster long-term growth, improve economic

resiliency and promote 'larger freedoms' for all.[38]

Greater Political Commitment

The push towards gender equality is much more than a technical fix—it is fundamentally a political process.[39] Political commitment in this regard may have been spotty in individual countries, but it has gained momentum overall. Discussions on the issue can now be found in political party platforms and election debates. Some countries are making systematic attempts to inject gender equality into policy-making so that discrimination becomes visible and is addressed; for example, Asia-Pacific has pioneered initiatives to assess public budgets in terms of how they may differently affect men and women.

Numerous countries have passed legislations to guarantee women's political and economic rights, such as through quotas reserving seats for women in legislatures. A handful of these countries, typically but not always through quotas, have reached the global upper echelons of women's participation in national legislatures. Political commitment also may come about through bottom-up pressures for governments to take a more proactive stance for change. Building support for this can be done via mechanisms such as the media and civic engagement.

Growing Public Awareness

Awareness of and expertise on gender issues has grown, championed in some cases by influential men and women. Women themselves have become a force as advocates and in voting booths—and some politicians and parties have changed their campaign platforms to appeal to this influential constituency.

Special impetus for achieving gender equality now comes from the growing number

Institutions have improved, political commitment has grown, and potential for changing attitudes is far greater than ever before

of people in the region, women and men, who want and expect a more just society. These comprise families who take pride in the educational attainments of daughters, women who appreciate the autonomy of an independent income, and men who enjoy being an equal participant in raising their children.

These shifts in attitudes are in a nascent phase in much of Asia and the Pacific. But they are there and flourishing, cultivated to different degrees by the media, advocacy groups, rising literacy rates, political movements, consumer aspirations, population demographics and rapid exchanges of information made possible by technology.

Moving Forward Faster

'It cannot be forgotten that discrimination is the antithesis of equality and that it is the recognition of equality which will foster dignity of every individual.'[40]

– From the 105-page judgment of the New Delhi High Court in overturning a 150-year-old ban on homosexual acts as discriminatory and a violation of fundamental rights

Gender discrimination will not decline on its own and may not be corrected automatically in the course of development, as the mixed record on gender equality in some developed countries suggests. Making greater progress towards gender equality in Asia-Pacific will require a number of deliberate policy steps, as this Report makes clear.

No single policy intervention will be the magic bullet that ends gender discrimination. The three areas chosen by the Report—economics, politics and the law—must be considered in terms of how they relate to each other and how they play out across the different arenas where gender discrimination occurs. Economic policies that bolster gender equality will not come about without political will. A woman may have the right to vote and speak her mind, but without decent employment she may be too absorbed in the struggle to survive to participate in any meaningful way in the life of her country or community. On all issues, what is needed is a combination of freedom of action and freedom of thought, including the ability and willingness to question habitual attitudes.

Three broad directions further frame the Report's analysis: Institutions have to be right, attitudes have to be in tune so institutions function as intended, and assessments have to be continuous to reveal gaps and monitor progress.

Institutions: Transforming the Mainstream

Too often, gender mainstreaming is treated as an 'add-on' to existing policies, rather than as a process of transformation from within—a process that should touch all aspects of development, and involve women, men and people with different gender identities. Increasingly, gender issues are informing the policy space; recognition of the vulnerabilities of men and boys, and increased sharing of unpaid and paid work between men and women, are a few examples. But the questions on 'how to' continue to be contemplated.

Gender mainstreaming offers a possible way forward. It constitutes a critical strategy in implementation of the 1995 Beijing Platform for Action as a way to achieve overall advancement of women. Within this framework, it calls for 'removing all obstacles to women's active participation in all spheres of public and private life, through a full and equal share in economic, social, cultural and political decision-making'.[41] Mainstreaming involves addressing concerns and experiences of women and men alike, integral to design, implementation, monitoring and evaluation of all political, economic and societal policies and programmes so that everyone has equal access to benefits, regardless of gender.[42]

Increasingly, gender issues are informing the policy space. But the questions on 'how to' continue to be contemplated

Ideally, mainstreaming is comprehensive and innovative in digging deep to uproot gender discrimination by 'embedding gender-sensitive practices and norms in the structures, processes and environment of public policy'.[43] Awareness raising, technical training and gender statistics are among the tools widely used. Specific plans, budgets and indicators are developed according to how they affect women and men differently. The region has varied models of national mechanisms on gender, from high-level commissions in Lao People's Democratic Republic and the Philippines to full ministries in Malaysia and the Republic of Korea.

However, further efforts are required to ensure effective implementation of mainstreaming practices. In the Beijing + 10 Review of 2005, the Commission on the Status of Women evaluated the progress of mainstreaming 10 years after the Beijing Platform for Action. One major finding was a continued lack of understanding of gender equality and gender mainstreaming among national governments. The review cited inadequate financial and human resources, the lack of political will and commitment, insufficient sex-disaggregated data, and marginal links to civil society as persistent barriers.[44]

In many Asia-Pacific countries as well, attempts to adopt gender mainstreaming have run into problems typically related to an overly narrow and/or unfocused interpretation of the concept. For example, growing female labour participation in export-oriented industries is sometimes cited as an example of successful mainstreaming, even if women in the sector mainly end up with poor-quality jobs.[45]

Mainstreaming, if applied well, should shift attention away from reactive attempts to satisfy individual and group needs that already exist, some of which are defined by gender norms. It must involve a proactive analysis of systems and patterns that give rise to these needs, and to advantages and disadvantages in fulfilling them.[46] From a human development perspective, this entails asking questions not just about existing conditions, but also about the processes that determine who has access to acquiring capabilities, how and why. Beyond access, this involves questions of quality and links to empowerment. Meaningful progress cannot be made if the worst scraps from the table continue to be overallocated to those who are poor and female. Capabilities must be considered through their links to opportunities that strengthen the power, voice and rights of excluded women and men, and that loosen—not maintain—entrenched patterns of discrimination.

Changing Attitudes

Attitudes must be examined for institutional and policy reforms to be initiated, and to ensure they succeed. Without deliberate attempts to shift deep-seated attitudes that fuel gender discrimination, even if reforms take place they will largely remain on paper, since people will not be convinced to implement them.

Efforts to change attitudes can best be tackled through sites that tend to perpetuate them, such as the media, schools and religious institutions. These may encourage individuals to embark on change in their own lives, and/or tap into changes in attitudes and behaviours that are already occurring. In general, attitudinal changes happen at both the individual and collective levels, although typically one triggers the other (Box 1.1). Leaders and role models can inspire people to adopt new ideas, as can new legislation and advocacy campaigns.

Attitudes to gender can be positive or negative. They can produce immediate results, such as reducing gender-based violence. They may deepen poverty and deprivation—for example, when people think

Capabilities must be considered through their links to opportunities that strengthen the power, voice and rights of excluded women and men

THE FLUIDITY OF GENDER: INCREASING RECOGNITION IN PUBLIC POLICIES

A starting point for our understanding about, and attitudes towards, gender is that gender is a culturally constructed concept, which, as a result, is different across societies and time. For example, in the past, Western notions of the 'exotic' Orient viewed the women there as 'sexually free' in contrast to 'Victorian' women in Europe. This has now changed to a stereotypical understanding of Asian women as oppressed and Western women as 'liberated'. The colonial legacy in the Asia-Pacific influenced ideas about what were considered appropriate male and female gender roles. Transgender individuals—in many societies accepted as a 'third sex'—were marginalized by lawmakers' insistence that there were only two legal sexes: male and female. Colonial rule has come to an end, but many of the laws and related legal codes of practice still exist. Nevertheless, there are signs of change—in no small part due to advocacy efforts of civil society organizations, which became more vocal and effective with resources springing from growing concerns around HIV. Thus, policy makers must continue to increasingly recognize the fluidity of gender definitions and sexualities.

In 2009, the Delhi High Court in India declared as unconstitutional the colonial era Section 377 of the Indian Penal Code, which criminalizes homosexuality. Directly responding to accelerating HIV prevalence rates among men who have sex with men in China, the National Center for AIDS/STD Prevention and Control worked directly with civil society to design and launch a national programme to reduce HIV among men who have sex with men. In India and Nepal, new passport forms allow for a third gender category besides 'male' and 'female'. In 2006, the National Conference on Women's Movements held at Kolkata, for the first time featured discussions about transgender people and the participation of transgender women. And, in Thailand, a school in Sri Sa Ket province opened separate toilet facilities to accommodate their many transgender students in continued efforts to provide a safe space for all their students.

Despite these signs of progress, instances of stigma and abuse of sexual minorities (including transgender) continue, directly increasing their vulnerability to HIV. Sexual orientation and gender identity continue to be ruled by socio-cultural attitudes that emphasize conformity with majority (heterosexual) norms, especially in rural areas. Negative family and community attitudes can lead to low self-esteem which, combined with the need for intimacy and the desire for sex, can lead males to engage in unsafe sex, potentially jeopardizing their well-being. Removing punitive laws, discriminatory and stigmatizing policies and practices and enhancing social protection allows men who have sex with men, including gay and transgendered persons, to contribute to society, as fully accepted and productive citizens.

Sources: Das 2009; International Gay and Lesbian Human Rights Commission 2009; Mernissi 2001; Sky News 2008; South Asia Citizen's Web 2006; Srivastava 2009a; UNDP 2008b; UNESCO 2004.

---

change is not possible or that some groups 'deserve' poorly paid jobs. Poverty can also act as a trap preventing people from learning and thinking in new ways, or from experimenting with new ways of doing things.

In the long term, if attitudes harden to the point of assigning people preconceived roles, they distort access to opportunities and limit choice. A more positive alternative comes when attitudes are understood as being connected to core principles of equality and changeable in ways that support these ends. With the speeding up of change, however, comes the risk that too much change too fast will be perceived as threatening, particularly among groups who feel they are losing out. People's self-interest needs to be explained and fairly connected to capabilities and opportunities, so that all see the benefits of more gender-equal societies for themselves, their families and communities.

Assessing Gaps

In its many proposals for reaching gender equality, the 1995 Fourth World Conference on Women in Beijing stressed measurement, indicators and sex-disaggregated data.[47] This emphasis recognized that many gender issues go unnamed and unaddressed because they are poorly defined – and thus remains invisible even to policy-makers otherwise supportive of gender equality. Choosing to assess gender disparities through concrete measures is a critical step to reducing these disparities.

In general, measurement and analysis of gender inequality across the region remains selective or absent in many areas. Very little

Measurement and analysis of gender inequality across the region remains selective or absent in many areas

has been done, for example, to assess the full extent of violence against women, to understand how gender norms affect men, or to investigate the different status of men and women in households, given that many forms of discrimination begin at home. The gender angles of issues such as trade, taxation and capital flows also are comparatively under-researched, while the tracking of asset ownership by gender remains almost non-existent. Data are better only in areas such as microcredit, where the link to feminized poverty has been officially recognized, or in conventional sectors such as education.

Despite these shortfalls, increasing emphasis has been given to production of sex-disaggregated data and indicators since 1995. Some Asia-Pacific countries, such as India, have conducted time-use surveys, recognizing the fact that many women's activities take place at home and in the informal sector, outside more conventional data-gathering systems.[48] These surveys encourage better-quality gender analysis and improve the accuracy of forecasting potential policy outcomes.

Several countries also are adopting gender budgeting tools, which can assess and reveal gender differences in the raising and spending of public funds. Some research is being devoted to developing economic and public policy models to systematically measure and anticipate gender impacts. One study on labour segmentation, for example, concluded that women face lower wages during periods of economic reform. Flanking policies may be necessary to mitigate their exclusion from potential benefits.[49]

Contours of the Report

The following chapters examine how deficits in women's power, voice and rights in three areas—economics, politics and the law—entrench patterns of discrimination that hinder progress towards gender equality in Asia and the Pacific. Policy choices can set the course for change in all three areas. These areas are all strategic, as shifts within them can influence other spheres. The Report assesses both the challenges in the region and positive steps being taken to address them.

Chapter Two. Gender discrimination stands in the way of the assets and livelihoods that women need to acquire capabilities and opportunities. This chapter proposes ways to remove institutional and attitudinal barriers in accessing assets, expand paid employment, foster gender equality in education and make migration safe for the growing number of women relocating to pursue new livelihoods.

Chapter Three. Participation in political decision making is integral to the notion of democracy, but women's voice is far from being even half-representative. This chapter looks at why the numbers of women in office are still so low and explores mechanisms for greater state accountability to women, such as legal quotas and gender budgets.

Chapter Four. Despite promises of equal citizenship and equality before the law, gender norms mean that women and men experience the same legal systems differently. This chapter analyzes deficits in laws and legal practices that prevent women from accessing justice. Reforms will depend on making the legal system more responsive overall to gender.

Chapter Five. From the analysis of the Report, this chapter distils an eight-point agenda for change.

WHERE THE REGION STANDS: A SNAPSHOT
Major Indicators of Gender Gaps

The Asia-Pacific region has made much progress in advancing gender equality in life expectancy, school enrolment and labour force participation, with the most rapid gains occurring in East Asia and the Pacific. In South Asia, by contrast, large gender gaps remain, even in basic capabilities such as education, health, nutrition and employment opportunities. To place the region in a broader context, this snapshot compares Asia-Pacific sub-regions to other regions[50] of the world on several indicators for survival, capabilities and empowerment (Appendix Table 1.1 and Figures 1.1 to 1.13). These selected indicators and figures also assess where the region is with regard to international commitments on gender equality, such as achieving the Millennium Development Goals (MDGs) and implementation of the Beijing Declaration and Platform for Action 1995.

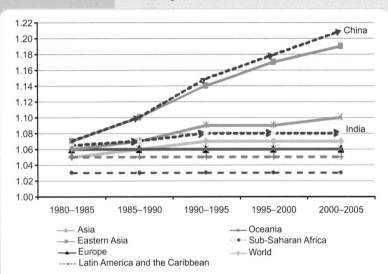

Figure 1.2: Many More Baby Boys than Baby Girls
Male-to-Female Sex Ratio at Birth, 1980-85 to 2000-05

Source: UN 2009b.

The Male–Female Sex Ratio Widens

More boys than girls are born in Asia as a whole than in any other region of the world. And the divide is increasing over time. East Asia has the highest male-to-female sex ratio at birth—119 boys for every 100 girls. This exceeded the world average of 107 boys for every 100 girls during the 2000-2005 period (Figure 1.2). The high sex ratio indicates a strong preference for male children and the deliberate use of certain means to achieve it— a form of gender inequality that begins even before birth.

Large Numbers of Missing Women

Close to 100 million women in Asia are estimated to be 'missing',[51] having died because of discriminatory treatment in access to health and nutrition or through pure neglect – or because they were never born in the first place. China and India each has about 42.6 million missing women (Figure 1.3). The numbers seem to be increasing in absolute terms.[52]

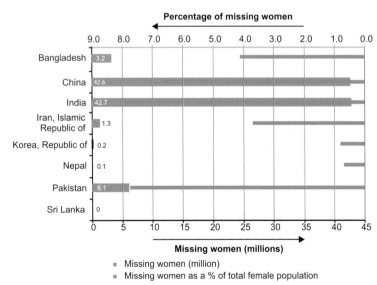

Figure 1.3: Two Countries Have the Greatest Shortfalls
Estimated 'Missing' Women in Asia, 2007

Source: Based on Klasen and Wink 2002.

Mixed Progress in Education

In primary school enrolment, East Asia and the Pacific are closest in the world to eliminating the gender gap. They are ahead of South Asia in enrolment at all levels, and completion rates at the primary level (Figures 1.4 and 1.5). South Asia and sub-Saharan Africa are the poorest performers in the world at all levels. The entire Asia-Pacific region lags behind the global average of more women than men enrolled in tertiary education.

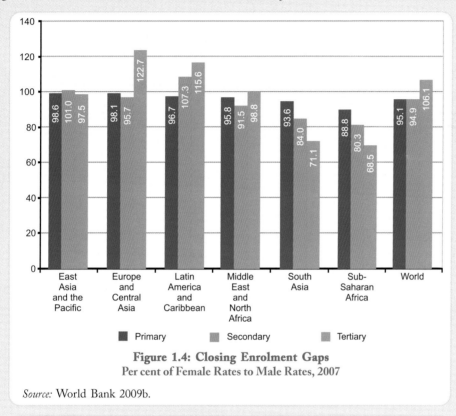

Figure 1.4: Closing Enrolment Gaps
Per cent of Female Rates to Male Rates, 2007

Source: World Bank 2009b.

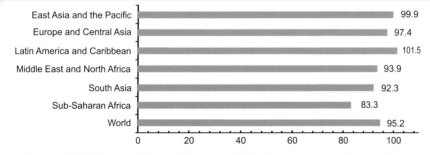

Figure 1.5: Worst and Best: Female-to-Male Primary Completion Rates
Per cent of Female Rates to Male Rates, 2006

Source: World Bank 2009b.

Data between 1990 and 2000 show that less than half of the adult women in South Asia were literate. This progressed to just above half by 2007—still the lowest percentage in the world (Figure 1.6). The rates in East Asia and the Pacific are higher than the world average.

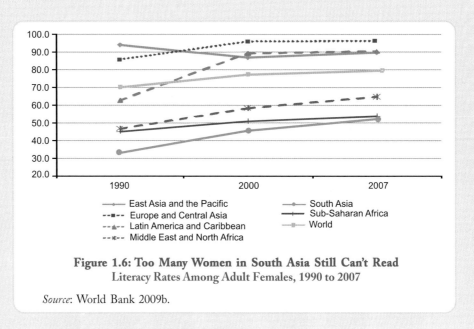

Figure 1.6: Too Many Women in South Asia Still Can't Read
Literacy Rates Among Adult Females, 1990 to 2007

Source: World Bank 2009b.

Health and Nutrition: East Asia Pulls Ahead

Female life expectancy (at birth) has steadily risen in all Asia-Pacific sub-regions. Progress has been greater in East Asia and the Pacific, though gender gaps still remain. Women in East Asia and the Pacific now live longer than the world average and are short of the high performers such as, Europe and Central Asia and Latin America and Caribbean (Figure 1.7). South Asia, while behind East Asia, is now ahead of sub-Saharan Africa. By 2007, female life expectancy in South Asia fell short of the world average by just five years compared to ten years in 1980.

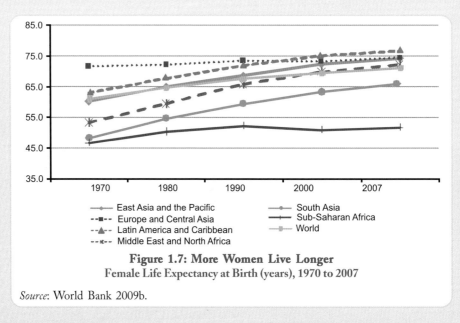

Figure 1.7: More Women Live Longer
Female Life Expectancy at Birth (years), 1970 to 2007

Source: World Bank 2009b.

Since the 1970s, increases in the ratio of female-to-male life expectancy in all Asia-Pacific sub-regions have confirmed that, over time, females are living much longer than males, a trend that is well-established in developed countries. South Asia, which was persistently lower than sub-Saharan Africa on this indicator, is now ahead. But the sub-region remains far behind other regions and below the world average (Figure 1.8).

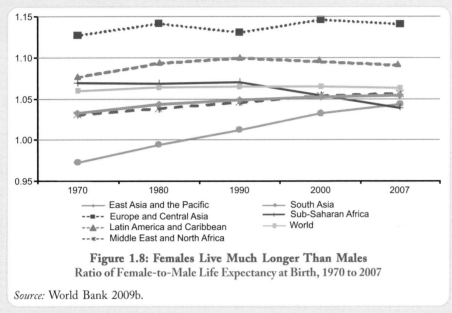

Figure 1.8: Females Live Much Longer Than Males
Ratio of Female-to-Male Life Expectancy at Birth, 1970 to 2007

Source: World Bank 2009b.

South Asia had the highest prevalence of malnutrition rates in the world in 2007. More than 41 per cent of the children in this sub-region were underweight, compared to less than 27 per cent in sub-Saharan Africa (Figure 1.9). Malnutrition remains prevalent in East Asia and the Pacific, though at rates lower than the world average.

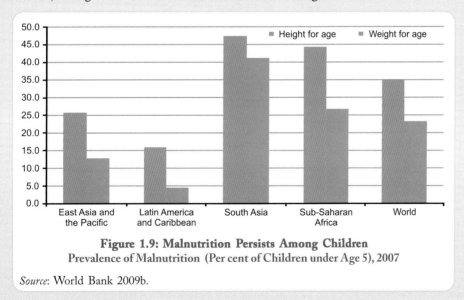

Figure 1.9: Malnutrition Persists Among Children
Prevalence of Malnutrition (Per cent of Children under Age 5), 2007

Source: World Bank 2009b.

More women die in childbirth in South Asia—500 for every 100,000 live births—than any other part of the world except sub-Saharan Africa. The maternal mortality ratio in sub-Saharan Africa was 1.8 times higher than South Asia in 2005 (Figure 1.10). In the latter, it was more than three times higher than in East Asia and the Pacific.

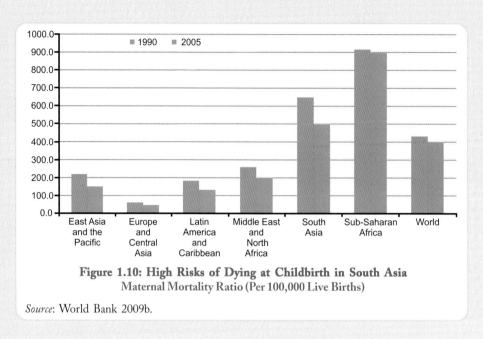

Figure 1.10: High Risks of Dying at Childbirth in South Asia
Maternal Mortality Ratio (Per 100,000 Live Births)

Source: World Bank 2009b.

Employment Opportunities: Best in East Asia and the Pacific

The female labour force participation rate is the highest in East Asia and the Pacific among all regions in the world. In South Asia, the female labour force participation rate of 35.7 per cent in 2007 was much lower than that of sub-Saharan Africa at 59.9 per cent, as well as the world average of 52.7 per cent (Figure 1.11).

Worldwide, the male-to-female ratio for labour force participation is lowest in East Asia and the Pacific, while South Asia lags behind all regions except for the Middle East and North Africa (Figure 1.12).

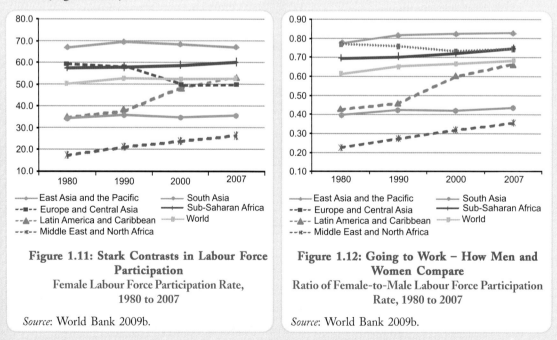

Figure 1.11: Stark Contrasts in Labour Force Participation
Female Labour Force Participation Rate, 1980 to 2007

Source: World Bank 2009b.

Figure 1.12: Going to Work – How Men and Women Compare
Ratio of Female-to-Male Labour Force Participation Rate, 1980 to 2007

Source: World Bank 2009b.

A Lack of Legislation Against Domestic Violence

Nearly half of the countries in South Asia and more than 60 per cent of the countries in the Pacific do not have laws on domestic violence. East Asia has made more progress in enacting such legislation (Figure 1.13).

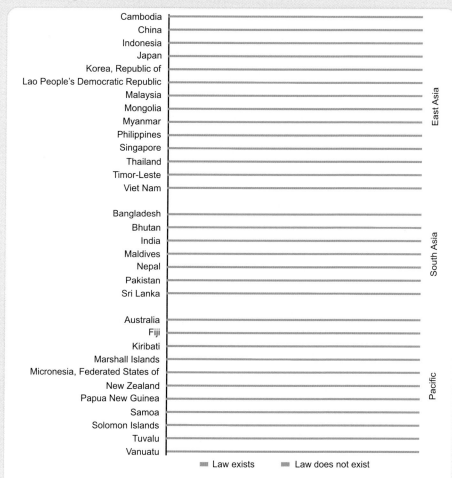

Figure 1.13: Legislation Against Domestic Violence: A Spotty Record in South Asia and the Pacific

Note: Reports of State Parties to the UN CEDAW Committee were not submitted for Afghanistan and Brunei Darussalam. In July 2009, a presidential decree was signed on the Elimination of Violence Against Women in Afghanistan, which for the first time criminalized sexual violence against women, including rape (Civil-Military Fusion Centre 2009). The National Assembly is considering a Bill on the matter (UNAMA and OHCHR 2009).

Source: Statistical annex Table 19.

Gender Inequalities Cut Across Development Levels

The Gender-related Development Index (GDI) assesses the impact of gender inequalities on human development by adjusting the Human Development Index (HDI) for differences in male-female income, life expectancy and education—the three dimensions on which the HDI is based. The value of the GDI is typically less than that of the HDI for all countries

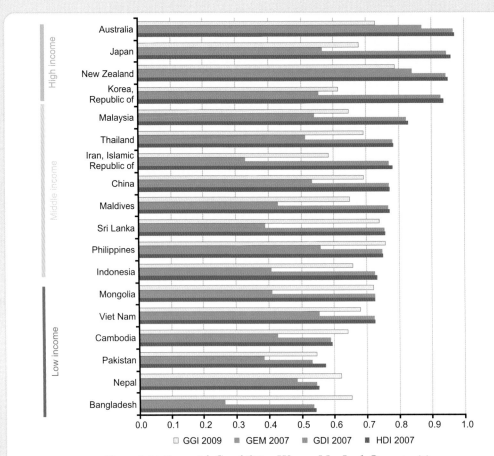

Figure 1.14: Even with Capabilities, Women May Lack Opportunities

Notes: Countries within each income category have been ordered by HDI value. The HDI ranges between 0 (minimum) to 1 (maximum). Higher values indicate high human development. The GDI ranges between 0 (minimum) to 1 (maximum). Higher values indicate greater gender equality. The GEM ranges between 0 (minimum) and 1 (maximum). Higher values indicate greater gender equality. The GGI varies between 0 to 1. Higher values indicate greater gender equality.

HDI, GDI and GEM values are from the global indices (UNDP 2009). While many countries have national human development reports (NHDRs), only global indices have been presented in the interest of cross-country comparability.

Sources: UNDP 2009; Hausmann et al. 2009.

regardless of development levels as measured by GDP per capita, because of differences in the achievements of men and women.[53]

Further, the Gender Empowerment Measure (GEM), which reflects the economic and political opportunities women have, tends to be lower than the GDI. This suggests that even when women have capabilities, they may not have adequate opportunities to use them.[54]

Based on a wider set of indicators than the GDI or the GEM, the World Economic Forum's Global Gender Gap Index (GGI) calculates gender gaps on the basis of 14 indicators grouped around four dimensions: economic, political, education and health. The GGI shows no significant association with levels of development (Figure 1.14 above).

These broad indices aside, it needs reiterating that economic growth by itself does not automatically translate into gender equality.

GENDER GAPS BY REGION

	Year	East Asia and the Pacific	South Asia	Europe and Central Asia	Euro area	Latin America and the Caribbean	Middle East and North Africa	Sub-Saharan Africa	World	World best (Earliest 1960; latest 2008)	World worst (Earliest 1960; latest 2008)
Education											
Ratio of female-to-male primary enrolment rate (%) (MDG)	2006	98.6	93.6	98.1	..	96.7	95.8	88.8	95.1	Europe and Central Asia (1991); East Asia and the Pacific (2006)	South Asia (1991); Sub-Saharan Africa (2006)
Ratio of female-to-male secondary enrolment rate (%) (MDG)	2005-2006	101.0	84.0	95.7	..	107.3	91.5	80.3	94.9	Latin America and the Caribbean (1991 and 2005-2006)	South Asia (1991); Sub-Saharan Africa (2005-2006)
Ratio of female-to-male enrolment in tertiary education (%) (MDG)	2007	97.5	71.1	122.7	..	115.6	98.8	68.5	106.1	Europe and Central Asia (1991 and 2007)	Middle East and North Africa (1991); Sub-Saharan Africa (2007)
Primary completion rate, female (% of relevant age group)	2005	97.8	76.5	92.2	..	100.1	87.7	53.3	84.0	Euro area (1991); Latin America and the Caribbean (2005)	Sub-Saharan Africa (1991 and 2005)
Primary completion rate, male (% of relevant age group)	2005	97.8	82.9	94.7	..	98.6	93.4	64.0	88.2	East Asia and the Pacific (1991); Latin America and the Caribbean (2005)	Sub-Saharan Africa (1991 and 2005)
Ratio of female-to-male primary completion rate (%)	2005	99.9	92.3	97.4	..	101.5	93.9	83.3	95.2	Latin America and the Caribbean (1991 and 2005)	South Asia (1991); Sub-Saharan Africa (2005)
Literacy rate, adult female (% of females aged 15 and above)	2007	89.7	52.1	96.3	..	90.3	64.5	53.8	79.4	East Asia and the Pacific (1990); Europe and Central Asia (2007)	South Asia (1990 and 2007)
Literacy rate, adult male (% of males aged 15 and above)	2007	95.8	73.8	98.9	..	91.7	81.8	71.1	88.4	East Asia and the Pacific (1990); Europe and Central Asia (2007)	South Asia (1990); Sub-Saharan Africa (2007)
Literacy rate, youth female (% of females aged 15-24)	2007	97.6	73.6	98.6	..	97.4	85.8	67.4	86.8	East Asia and the Pacific (1990); Europe and Central Asia (2007)	South Asia (1990); Sub-Saharan Africa (2007)
Literacy rate, youth male (% of males aged 15-24)	2007	98.1	83.7	99.3	..	96.6	92.5	77.4	91.3	East Asia and the Pacific (1990); Europe and Central Asia (2007)	South Asia (1990); Sub-Saharan Africa (2007)
Health and Nutrition											
Life expectancy at birth, female (years)	2007	74.0	65.9	74.4	83.3	76.4	71.9	51.8	70.9	Euro area (1960 and 2007)	Sub-Saharan Africa (2007); South Asia (1960)
Life expectancy at birth, male (years)	2007	70.3	63.1	65.3	77.4	70.1	68.1	49.8	66.7	Euro area (1960 and 2007)	Sub-Saharan Africa (1960 and 2007)

Contd...

Contd...

	Year	East Asia and the Pacific	South Asia	Europe and Central Asia	Euro area	Latin America and the Caribbean	Middle East and North Africa	Sub-Saharan Africa	World	World best (Earliest 1960; latest 2008)	World worst (Earliest 1960; latest 2008)
Health and Nutrition											
Maternal mortality ratio (per 100,000 live births)	2005	150	500	44.3	5.3	130	200	900	400	Euro area (1990 and 2005)	Sub-Saharan Africa (1990 and 2005)
Malnutrition prevalence weight for age (% of children under age 5)	2007	12.8	41.1	..	..	4.4	..	26.6	23.2	Latin America and the Caribbean (2007)	South Asia (2007)
Malnutrition prevalence height for age (% of children under age 5)	2007	25.8	47.3	..	..	15.8	..	44.3	34.7	Latin America and the Caribbean (2007)	South Asia (2007)
Employment Opportunities											
Labour force participation rate, female (% of female population aged 15 and above)	2007	66.7	35.7	50.1	48.2	53.0	26.2	59.9	52.7	East Asia and the Pacific (1990 and 2007)	Middle East and North Africa (1990 and 2007)
Labour force participation rate, male (% of male population aged 15 and above)	2007	80.3	82.1	67.2	64.8	79.9	73.8	80.0	77.6	South Asia (1980 and 2007)	Euro area (1990 and 2007)
Unemployment, female (% of female labour force)	2004	..	6.0	9.6	10.4	11.5	18.4	..	..	South Asia (2004)	Middle East and North Africa (2004)
Unemployment, male (% of male labour force)	2004	..	5.1	10.0	8.1	6.9	10.4	..	..	South Asia (2004)	Middle East and North Africa (2004)
Share of women employed in the non-agricultural sector (% of total non-agricultural employment) (MDG)	2000-2002	..	17.3	47.6	44.6	41.3	16.7	..	36.3	Euro area (1990); Europe and Central Asia (2000-2002)	South Asia (1990); Middle East and North Africa (2000-2002)
Political Participation											
Proportion of seats held by women in national parliaments (%) (MDG)	2008	18.3	20.3	14.9	25.2	22.4	8.8	18.1	18.5	East Asia and the Pacific (1990); Euro area (2008)	Middle East and North Africa (1990 and 2008)

Source: World Bank 2009b.

APPENDIX TABLE 1.2

ESTIMATES OF MISSING WOMEN IN SOME ASIA-PACIFIC COUNTRIES

Countries	Missing women (percentage in select years, Klasen and Wink 2002)	Missing women (millions, Klasen and Wink 2002)	Total female population (millions, 2007, World Bank 2009b)	Missing women (millions, 2007 estimates by the HDRU using columns 2 and 4)
1	2	3	4	5
Bangladesh	4.2 (2001)	2.7	77.4	3.2
China	6.7 (2000)	40.9	636.5	42.6
India	7.9 (2001)	39.1	540.9	42.7
Iran (Islamic Republic of)	3.7 (1996)	1.1	35.0	1.3
Korea (Republic of)	0.7 (1995)	0.2	24.2	0.2
Nepal	0.5 (2001)	0.1	14.2	0.1
Pakistan	7.8 (1998)	4.9	78.7	6.1
Sri Lanka	0.0 (1991)	0.0	10.1	0.0
Total		**89.0**		**96.2**

Sources: Based on Klasen and Wink 2002; World Bank 2009b.

2

Building Economic Power

Talented in Business, Generous at Heart

Kim Manduk, 1739-1812

Born in 1739 on Jeju Island, south of mainland Korea, Kim Manduk was orphaned at thirteen. Though her uncle had her registered as a kisaeng, a professional entertainer, that was not what she wanted to be. She took charge of her life and approached the local authorities, including the Governor of Jeju, and had her name removed from the register. Married by the age of twenty, she was soon widowed. Despite her early troubles, she developed a talent for business, setting up an inn and commercial services for merchants in the island's busy harbour city. Eventually, she diversified into trade in textiles, ornaments and local specialties like tangerines, even buying her own ship as business prospered.

But a great famine hit Jeju in 1794. Manduk used her wealth to buy five hundred sacks of grain to contribute to relief, surpassing all other donations. When the news reached the King in Seoul, the capital city, he ordered the Jeju Governor to fulfill any wish of lady Manduk, however difficult. But Manduk only asked to visit Seoul to see the King's palace, and to travel to the beautiful Kumgang (diamond) Mountain. Although women were forbidden to leave Jeju at that time, the King granted her wish. He even provided her with an official position so that she could meet him and the Queen face-to-face, a privilege otherwise not allowed to commoners.

In Seoul, the King honoured her with gifts, and people flocked to make her acquaintance. The Prime Minister wrote her biography. Scholars composed verses on her actions. At Kumgang Mountain, she saw the magnificent twelve thousand summits and a golden Buddha statue. All her wishes fulfilled, Manduk returned to Jeju and died at the age of 74. She is still remembered today for her virtue and generosity.

Based on 'Chung Hyo Ye: Tales of filial devotion, loyalty, respect and benevolence, from the history and folklore of Korea'.

Building Economic Power

All human beings, irrespective of gender, must have equal opportunities to seek out economic opportunities. People access resources and livelihoods for survival and sustenance. But beyond that, economic power helps them acquire capabilities that enlarge choices for satisfying and creative lives. This is the promise of human development.

In Asia and the Pacific, gender discrimination continues to stand in the way of women acquiring capabilities and opportunities, even after decades of discussion. It is a conundrum that the region has raced so far and fast in expanding its economies but has extended only a limited share of the benefits to women and other disadvantaged groups. A time of economic crisis in particular, where all available resources must be mobilized, calls for understanding that gender equality is both an issue of social justice and economic pragmatism.

A growing body of evidence shows that gender equality is good economics. For instance, over the last 10 years, the increase of women workers in developed countries is estimated to have contributed more to global growth than has China's remarkable economic record.[1] Reaching the same level of women's labour market participation in the United States, over 70 per cent, would boost GDP in countries, for example, by 4.2 per cent a year in India, 2.9 per cent in Malaysia and 1.4 per cent in Indonesia.[2] The gains would be greater where current female participation rates are the lowest.

Lack of women's participation in the workforce across Asia-Pacific cost the region an estimated US $89 billion every year.[3] Another estimate, using long-term data from 1960 to 2000, suggests that a combination of gender gaps in education and employment accounts annually for a significant difference of up to 1.6 percentage points in per capita growth rates between South Asia and East Asia.[4] Over that period, East Asia took long leaps in life expectancy and education for women, while pulling a record number of them into the workplace. In turn, this sub-region grew faster than all others worldwide.[5]

In the ownership and control of assets and the ability to earn incomes, two fundamental pathways to economic well-being, women still lag far behind men in much of the region—and Asia-Pacific as a whole lags behind much of the rest of the world. This results in lost opportunities for economic growth and fairer societies that can build upon the advantages of human diversity.

When women have equal opportunities to obtain assets and earn incomes, their overall social and economic standing improves, leading to an expanding circle of opportunities, such as in politics. They also develop a stronger position to bargain and negotiate within their homes, which means that male relatives are no longer the sole reference point for decisions they make. This frees women to make possibly different choices—including getting out of oppressive situations—that can improve their own welfare as well as that of their children and families. Incomes and assets also leave women much better equipped to cope in times of crisis, supplementing the major role of social protection systems.

In the ownership and control of assets and the ability to earn incomes, women still lag far behind men in much of the region

Across Asia and the Pacific, achieving equal opportunities to own assets and earn incomes depends on new approaches to economic policy-making that make this a basic and systematically pursued objective, rather than something assumed to trickle out of growth. Political will and legal protections, the subjects of the next two chapters, are crucial elements to broaden the reach of these commitments.

Good education also has clear economic returns for individuals and societies. Learning linked to job opportunities opens up remunerative employment options. At a more basic level, a woman who can read with understanding is better able to decipher a land deed and will know if she is being cheated of her entitlements. But the economic benefits of education are not automatic. Transformative potential depends on the level, content and quality of education, opportunities to use the knowledge for productive purposes, openings for continual learning, and exposure to different ideas, experiences and ways of doing things.

Mobility also is strongly linked to the freedom to pursue new choices. Increasingly, women are seeking economic benefits through migration, although marriage remains a driver as well. The outcome of migration is not always positive, but a record number of women in Asia-Pacific are moving from the country to the city, or from their own countries to others, often on their own. In the process, many are acquiring incomes and assets. Some gain a new sense of confidence about their ability to make choices and manage their lives. Collectively, their efforts make an enormous economic contribution through remittances, which for some Asia-Pacific countries now rival or exceed sums from foreign direct investment.

Migration hints at how powerful an economic force women can be—and how capable many women are in carving out new opportunities. On their own initiative and supported by public policy, women can strengthen their capabilities, make informed choices and invent new roles, unobstructed by gender constraints.

Leveraging Assets

Assets come in many forms—from land and livestock to knowledge, pension plans, businesses and good health. Men and women around the world use economic assets[6] as the building blocks for better lives. For many women, other disadvantaged groups and poorer men, assets serve as a means to overcome discrimination. Women who can acquire, retain and control assets—and by themselves, not just through husbands or relatives—rise in social and economic standing. This can translate into greater bargaining positions in households and a stronger voice in public affairs.[7]

Two dimensions—ownership and control—need consideration for assets to make a meaningful contribution to gender equality. It is not enough for women to own an asset and then be unable to determine how it is used. Control without ownership may provide short-term benefits but can be tenuous over a longer period. In general, assets are critical to rectifying development imbalances. A measure of the gender asset gap could be an effective indicator of progress towards MDG 3 on achieving gender equality.[8]

Certain assets—land, housing, livestock, common property resources, businesses, health and financial assets—are critical because they can be leveraged to acquire others, sustain enterprises or diversify livelihoods. The poorest people, however, may have only health as an asset, plunging into destitution when this is weakened through hunger, illness or accident.[9] This Report considers all these types of assets except financial assets, due to a lack of data for the region.

Women who can acquire, retain and control assets rise in social and economic standing

Diverse Practices, Consistent Shortfalls

Despite the basic importance of assets to gender equality, women's overall access to a variety of assets across Asia and the Pacific is poor compared to other regions. Land ownership data are not available by gender regionally, but surveys in individual countries provide some inkling of the imbalances. A 2001 household survey in Pakistan found that women owned less than three per cent of plots.[10] According to the 2001 Population Census in Nepal, 'only 11 per cent of households reported some land under female legal ownership', but around 90 per cent owned less than one acre.[11]

The agricultural census of the Food and Agriculture Organization from 1989 to 1999 gives another indication. It found that in most regions women headed around 20 per cent of farms: in Asia-Pacific, the figure was a mere seven per cent (Figure 2.1).[12] Interestingly, in contrast, for as recently as 2007 more than 65 per cent of female employment was in agriculture in South Asia, with more than 40 per cent in East Asia.[13]

Patterns of ownership and control over land and other assets are diverse within the region, reflecting the fact that many practices, particularly those related to property, extend far back in time and custom. Some have arisen as part of complex social arrangements. In many parts of South Asia women can inherit land, but do not actually do so. A study in Gujarat, India, for example, shows that women commonly refrain from claiming land in favour of their brothers, whom they see as a source of social support.[14] Asset patterns are also affected by current laws and economic pressures and by the distribution of power within households, communities and political systems. Most societies in the Pacific islands, for example, are patrilineal. In some communities, like Gaua in Vanuatu, the land inheritance practices have swung back and forth between customary matrili-

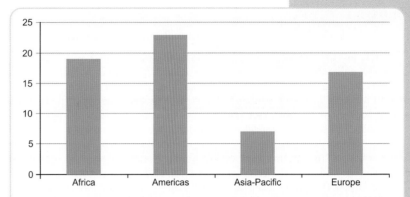

Figure 2.1: Hardly Any Women Farm Owners in Asia-Pacific
Per cent of Farmland Owned by Women

Source: FAO n.d.-b.

neal and patrilineal systems (Box 2.1).[15] When colonial laws were introduced in Fiji, Tokelau, Solomon Islands and Vanuatu, they contradicted communal approaches by enforcing private, often male, ownership. More recently, women have lost access to land from interaction with outsiders (immigrants), who tend to engage primarily with men based on the assumption that men own the land.[16]

Yet, not all practices of asset ownership and control work against women in the region. In Bhutan, 60 per cent of rural women hold land registration titles; the law provides equal inheritance rights to men and women.[17] While Islamic law traditionally favours inheritance for men, a few Muslim communities in Sri Lanka practise a system of matrilineal inheritance where women inherit land and men have rights to use it.[18]

For the most part, however, patterns of asset ownership and control make men more likely to inherit, own and manage larger stretches of land, while women's activities remain confined to small household plots. Men tend to harvest and sell timber, while women collect wood for fuel and non-wood forestry products sold for smaller profits. Men own cattle and larger, more valuable animals; while smaller animals, such as goats and poultry kept near the house, are women's domain. Women are more likely than men to

Patterns of asset ownership and control make men more likely to inherit, own and manage larger stretches of land, while women's activities remain confined to small household plots

WOMEN REASSERTING RIGHTS OVER MATRILINEAL LAND

Historically in the Republic of the Marshall Islands, land was owned collectively by lineage groups (the *bwij*). Their basic tenets were matrilineal dominance in land, a two-tiered system with varying levels of usufruct rights, and flexible customary practices. Women possessed authority and influence directly connected to their matrilineal rights to land, with men having a complementary role as lineage heads in the public sphere, acting on behalf of the group. Men of the chiefly *(irooj)* class were *iroojlaplap* and women were *lerooj*, but the basic chiefly duties were left to the junior male relatives. In the exercise of power and duties, consultation with the *lerooj* was critical. Female and male chiefs sat in equal numbers in the Council of *Irooj* (Chiefs). The *alap* was the lineage head of the *bwij*, responsible for the overall productivity of land and for being a liason between the *irooj* and others. The *alap* was traced through the female line but both genders could be *alap*.

Marshallese women today have a critical political power base because of matrilineal heritage, and they have direct power in decision-making over land. Nonetheless, there is an emerging political power structure dominated by men. Tensions have sprung up around the legitimacy of females to be *alap* and to participate in the public and political spheres. In 2005, the Republic of Marshall Islands High Court, with the concurrence of the Traditional Rights Courts, decided in favour of two female plaintiffs claiming *alap* and senior *rijerbal* rights on Kwajalein Atoll (where the Ronald Reagan Ballistic Missile Defence Site is located and which brings huge income to traditional land owners). Subsequently, two male senators of the Parliament introduced Bill 84 to codify Marshallese customary law so as to define the term *alap* only as a male elder person.

Women United Together Marshall Islands (WUTMI), a woman's NGO, mobilized to defeat Bill 84. They conducted a strategic campaign relying heavily on the media, using especially the voices of the female *lerooj* in newspapers and radio. Community petitions targeted elected members of the *Council of Irooj* as the government monitors of custom. The lobbying effort was successful and demonstrates the extent of female authority in custom, as many women saw themselves not as radicals, but as traditionalists protecting Marshallese *manit* (custom). That said, WUTMI conducted a very modern, smart, strategic and media effective campaign, reminiscent of modern feminist campaigns to either pass or defeat proposed law.

Source: Stege et al. 2008.

start businesses out of need than to seize entrepreneurial opportunities.[19] Female economic activity and asset utilization in Asia-Pacific is primarily driven by subsistence activities and survival strategies.

Access to assets may be changing. One source of change is the law (Box 2.2), as also explored in Chapter 4. Trends in wealthier countries suggest that women's home ownership will eventually rise with employment income. According to a Housing and Land Survey by the Ministry of Internal Affairs and Communications in Japan, home purchases by men declined between 1998 and

A LONG CAMPAIGN USHERS IN SWEEPING PROPERTY RIGHTS REFORMS

Women's activists in Nepal conducted a long advocacy campaign to secure legal recognition of women's property rights, finally achieving this aim in 2002 through the passage into law of the Eleventh Amendment of the Country Code Bill. The statute is sweeping in its scope, overturning a series of discriminatory laws. It is backed by sanctions for non-compliance.

Among its provisions is the equal right to ancestral property for daughters and sons by birth. Previously, only unmarried daughters who had reached the age of 35 were entitled to this right. An earlier requirement that a widow could claim her share of property only after attaining the age of 30 and living separately was replaced with the right for a widow to claim her share when she requires, even if she gets remarried.

Wives now have immediate rights to a share of the husband's property after marriage, without the previous waiting period. Property must be partitioned between husband and wife at the time of divorce, with alimony set on the basis of the husband's property and earnings. New maintenance rights for daughters cover food and appropriate education and health.

More recently, the Supreme Court of Nepal issued a directive to ensure gender equality against the legal requirement that daughters must return property upon marriage. The Act to Amend Some Nepal Acts for Maintaining Gender Equality, 2063 (2006) states that, 'the unmarried girl, married women or a widow living separately may enjoy the movable and immovable property on her own'. Married women don't have rights to ancestral property, however. So unless they have acquired it before marriage, discrimination prevails.

Sources: Legal Aid and Consultancy Center n.d.; An Act to Amend Some Nepal Acts for Maintaining Gender Equality, 2063, 2006.

2003 by an average annual rate of 1.5 per cent, while those by women increased by a rate of 2.2 per cent.[20] A survey by the Institute for Research on Household Economics in 2004 found that among married women, the higher the annual income and education level, the higher the ratio of those who have housing in their own names.[21]

Why Assets Remain Out of Women's Reach

Multiple ways exist for women to acquire and use assets, including through direct purchase, marriage and kinship ties, and inheritance. But they confront difficulties with each method. Direct purchase requires resources that many women do not have, along with supportive social norms that encourage women's ownership. Inheritance and marriage customs that tend to protect the continuance of male ownership and control over assets[22] may be tolerated or endorsed by legal systems.

Historically, land ownership in particular has been skewed towards men in much of Asia-Pacific, as in other regions, because many societies have defined agriculture as a male activity—even if this is no longer technically accurate in many places—and because land is so closely associated with economic and political power. Different systems of customary laws still remain deeply embedded in traditions that are, in some cases, hundreds or thousands of years old.

In India, for instance, Hindu inheritance practices are detailed in ancient texts such as the *Mitakshara*.[23] It defines two types of property: joint family property—which is jointly held by the family, and separate property—such as land that is self-acquired. While the rights of male heirs differ between the two types, women are prohibited from fully inheriting either. Widows and unmarried daughters are entitled to inherit a limited income from a joint estate. From an independent property, widows can inherit if there is no son or grandson, but only for her lifetime. She cannot sell, mortgage or gift the property. For a daughter to inherit her father's land, there should be no son, grandson or widow.

These concepts were codified in the 1956 Hindu Succession Act until a landmark amendment in 2005 finally defined a Hindu woman's right to inherit land as equal to that of a Hindu man. All daughters have a stake in *Mitakshara* joint family property,[24] and they have the same rights as sons, whether they are married or not, to reside in or seek partition of the family dwelling house.[25]

Some Muslim countries continue to follow Islamic principles of inheritance, which stipulate that women inherit a smaller share than men.[26] In Indonesia, for example, Article 176 of the Compilation of Islamic Law (Presidential Instruction No. 1 of 1991) states that where there is one son and one daughter, the inheritance ratio is two to one.[27] Other barriers to the acquisition of assets can be found in Indonesia's Civil Code. Article 108 prevents married women from entering into contracts on their own behalf and from receiving any payment from individual business activities. Banking practices also restrict women's access to loans to advance their businesses. Married women were using their husband's tax number,[28] although this has changed.

Marriage customs and laws that continue to make women subordinate to men pose other hindrances. Women are typically expected to move to their husband's locality, which may be distant from their own, reducing the chances that they will be able to maintain control over property they already own. Even women in matrilineal cultures can face pressure to marry from within a kinship group and remain in the ancestral village so the family can retain control over her land.

In South Asia, although women may continue to own land and other assets brought to the marriage through dowry, husbands

Multiple ways exist for women to acquire and use assets, including through direct purchase, marriage and kinship ties, and inheritance. But they confront difficulties with each method

may have the liberty to sell, mortgage or give these away without a wife's approval. Among the Hindu Tamils of Jaffna, Sri Lanka, daughters receive dowries from their mother's property that are established in their name, but disposition still requires the husband's consent.[29] Critically, divorce laws across Asia-Pacific still continue to strip women of assets, even when that means they will end up in poverty.

With or without laws or customary practices, more general social pressures discourage women from aspiring to acquire assets or asserting their rights over them. Afghanistan provides limited inheritance entitlements under Islamic law, yet women are likely to turn away from these because of social conventions that brothers are expected to care for their sisters in times of need.[30] When women follow traditions such as purdah and female seclusion, they have little ability to use land or other assets outside the household.

Ideas about what topics women and girls 'ought' to study partly explain why education systems equip women with fewer technical or business skills to manage assets. These deficits are compounded by financial and business practices that favour well-established men. Women can find it difficult to become part of all-male networks that can be critical to starting and expanding a business.[31] Institutional credit that drives investments in existing or new assets is not easily available

Women can find it difficult to become part of all-male networks

---

SPECIAL CONTRIBUTION

WOMEN'S COMMAND OVER IMMOVABLE ASSETS: A VITAL KEY

Professor Bina Agarwal

The past decade has seen a growing global recognition that women's command over immovable assets, such as land and homesteads, can be critically important for theirs and their children's economic and social well-being and overall empowerment. *Command* over such assets—implying both access and control—adds significantly to livelihood options, economic and social security and poverty alleviation.[32] It also increases the likelihood of children surviving, attending school and receiving health care;[33] and reduces the risk of families falling into poverty and destitution following widowhood, spousal desertion, protracted family illness, or husbands dying of HIV/AIDS.[34]

Recent research also suggests significant links between women's ownership of a house or land and a reduced risk of marital violence. In a study in Kerala (India), for instance, 49 per cent of the property-less women reported long term physical violence by spouses relative to 18 per cent and 10 per cent of those owning land or a house respectively, and seven per cent if they owned both.[35] These assets deter violence by visibly signaling the strength of a woman's fall-back position and tangible exit option and also provide an escape route should violence occur. Access to land or a house thus provides both physical and economic security. More generally, immovable assets increase women's bargaining power and hence their ability to negotiate a better distribution of goods and tasks within the family, and more status and voice in the community.

Apart from gains in welfare, equity and empowerment, women's command over productive assets, especially land, could prove key to reviving agricultural productivity and enhancing food security. Across Asia, increasingly, farmers have a female face. We see a growing feminization of agriculture, with more men than women moving to non-farm work. In India, in 2004-2005, 65 per cent of female workers relative to 49 per cent of male workers were confined to agriculture.[36] In Nepal, the relative percentages were 98 for women and 89 for men.[37] In Asia as a whole, women constituted 45 per cent of all farm workers in 2006, with percentages as high as 55 in Cambodia, 52 in Bangladesh, 49 in Viet Nam and Lao People's Democratic Republic, and 48 in China.[38] These percentages have been growing in recent decades. To revive and sustain agricultural growth, as well as adapt to or mitigate climate change, the role of women farmers will be central. How effectively they can contribute, however, will depend crucially on their having secure rights in the land they cultivate, as well as access to credit, technology, information and infrastructure.

To what extent do women have command over assets such as land and house? Few countries collect comprehensive data, but existing evidence indicates substantial gender gaps in most of Asia. In Nepal, only 16.3 per cent of rural women own land or a house.[39] In India, the proportions are likely to be similar.[40] In rural China, women constitute an estimated 70 per cent of those without access to their own land under the family land use allotment system.[41] There are, however, significant regional variations in women's command over immovable assets across and within countries. The gender gap is much larger in South Asia than in South-East

Asia; and in the northern belt of South Asia (northwest India, Bangladesh, and Pakistan) than in south India and Sri Lanka.[42] Underlying these regional variations are differences in laws, culture (especially post-marital residence and the ideology of female seclusion), ecology (e.g. women's work contribution is more visible in rice farming systems), ethnic and religious diversity, political freedoms and overall development. In Sri Lanka, for instance, historically all communities, irrespective of religion, recognized women's land claims, and the country's favourable social indicators (90 per cent female literacy, gender balanced sex ratios) cannot be delinked from women's historical advantage there in command over productive assets.

How can women gain immovable assets? Mainly from three sources: the family (via gift or inheritance), the state (via land transfers) and the market (via purchase or lease). Access via families depends especially on inheritance laws and their implementation. Such laws are gender equal in several countries (e.g. Bhutan, Viet Nam, most communities in the Philippines and Sri Lanka), and are moving in that direction in many others. In India, for instance, the 2005 amendment of the Hindu Succession Act made inheritance laws gender equal for 80 per cent of Indian women who are Hindus.[43] There are, however, substantial gaps between *de jure* and *de facto* rights in most Asian countries, due to poor legal implementation and social barriers, including male bias in bequeathing property within families.[44] Exceptions include Bhutan, where women own an estimated 70 per cent of the land,[45] and Sri Lanka where most women from landed families inherit some land, even if in amounts unequal to men.[46] The effective implementation of laws will require not only transforming social norms and attitudes but spreading legal literacy, providing legal aid, and gender-sensitizing land registration officials and the judiciary. The media and civil society organizations can play a significant role in this.

The state and the market are important additional sources of immovable assets for women. At present, agricultural and homestead land distributed by governments under their anti-poverty, land reform or resettlement schemes goes largely to men, and limitedly to women—either individually or jointly with husbands. Land titles transferred solely to women could go some way towards compensating for male bias in inheritance. Governments can also facilitate women's market access to land and housing through subsidized grant-cum-credit schemes.

In both State and market-related efforts, however, a *group approach* in increasing women's access to land and housing can prove more economically effective and socially empowering than transfers to individual women or joint titles with spouses. Although untried for housing, a group approach has been used successfully for increasing women's land access, albeit in small pockets. Catalyzed by the Deccan Development Society (DDS) in Andhra Pradesh (south India), for instance, poor, low-caste women, organized into groups of five to 15, have leased in or purchased land in groups, through various government schemes providing subsidized credit and/or grants. The women are now farming these lands in groups in some 75 villages.[47] Working together has enhanced their ability to survey land, hire tractors, share labour, meet government officials, buy inputs and market the produce. Group members report improvement in family diets, healthcare and children's education, reduction in spousal desertion and violence, and enhanced social status in the community. Group farming is also being undertaken by women elsewhere in India, such as through a UNDP-Government of India project involving 50,000 women in three states,[48] as well as in Bangladesh. There are examples too of women undertaking pisciculture collectively in many regions, and of Bangladeshi women's cooperatives acquiring minor irrigation equipment and rights to sell water to male farmers.[49] A recent evaluation by IFAD-funded projects in Bangladesh also pointed to the potential of poor women working in cooperative arrangements if provided with adequate credit.[50]

Basically a group approach, if promoted by governments and civil society organizations, can help women gain access to land or other productive assets through the market, which they can rarely do as individuals. It can also help them retain and use more productively the assets they obtain directly from, say, families and governments.[51] The geographic spread and reach of such innovative approaches, however, needs to be increased. One promising route lies in encouraging women's micro-credit and self-help groups, which at present are largely confined to family-based enterprises, to take up joint enterprises including group farming. India alone has 2.2 million self-help groups, many constituted into federations through horizontal and vertical linkages, and these could provide a basis for such collective ventures.[52]

All said, women's command over immovable assets such as land and housing is a vital key for promoting welfare, equity, efficiency and empowerment. This would also help agricultural revival, improve food security and fulfil better the millennium development goals of gender equity, ending poverty and improving maternal and child health. For women to acquire immovable assets, retain control over them and use them productively, however, we need to go beyond individual-oriented approaches to try out a mix of innovative institutional forms of asset ownership, control and use. A group approach could prove to be a particularly effective means of enhancing women's command over significant assets, for their economic and social advancement.

Bina Agarwal is Professor of Economics and Director of the Institute of Economic Growth, Delhi. She is the author of the path-breaking, multiple award-winning book – A Field of One's Own – which had a catalytic effect in promoting the cause of women's land rights, worldwide.

to women, especially those without a track record or network of support. Agricultural extension services rarely acknowledge that men and women may use agricultural assets differently and therefore require targeted forms of assistance.

Some barriers to assets have come through policy and development processes that fail to recognize the impacts that gender can have. Women have lost traditional land rights during procedures that deliberately issue titles to male heads of households. States that have assigned plots as anti-poverty measures for poor households have seen these go mainly to male heads of household, unless there are deliberate attempts to ensure joint ownership rights.[53]

In India, community forestry programmes have been designed to provide spaces for poorer people, including women, to access and manage forest resources. But these have sometimes run into strong male resistance within communities where public decision-making is traditionally the realm of men.[54] One lesson has been that simply including women in this kind of programme may not be enough without efforts to address underlying gender norms.

The Benefits of Expanded Access

The benefits of asset ownership and control begin with economic options and extend across many other aspects of women's empowerment and well-being. Expanding access can therefore spur progress towards gender equality on multiple fronts. A number of surveys from South Asia have found that women who own land have a greater say in household decision-making than women without land.[55] According to field research in Nepal, when women control the income from livestock, they can make decisions independently on managing these assets.[56] Asset ownership also influences fallback positions in times of crisis, whether that involves di-

vorce, sickness, domestic violence or natural disaster[57] (Boxes 2.3 and 2.4). It opens opportunities for political participation, as women begin to feel more confident in expressing their demands, and for health and education, since women have more control over financial resources.

With all the positive potential, the relationship between assets and gender-based violence is not always straightforward. When formerly powerless persons start to assert themselves, pre-existing power structures can feel threatened. In situations of changing power dynamics, such as through policy action, civil society encouragement or otherwise, male backlash can contribute to increase in gender-based violence. These complexities do not always come out clearly in studies, but would benefit from explicit recognition in policies.

In some cases, women already play major roles in managing assets, but this has been mostly obscured by a lack of attention and data defining their contributions. Public policies that recognize these roles might build on them both to achieve gender equality and reap economic benefits through unleashing potentials for greater productivity.

Despite obstacles to credit and capital (Table 2.1), for example, the flow of women into business in Asia-Pacific is steady. According to a survey of Global Entrepreneurship Monitor (GEM),[58] across the region up to 45 per cent of women are owners of businesses.[59] Up to 35 per cent of small or medium enterprises in the region are headed by women.[60]

In a region which has 86 per cent of the fishers and fish farmers worldwide, women in some countries perform the bulk of fish processing, either in their own cottage-level industries or large-scale industries.[61] The Philippines has produced several examples of innovations by women, including highly successful technology and methods that have helped the shrimp hatchery industry to grow. Both have driven up production yields.[62]

Asset ownership also influences fallback positions in times of crisis, whether that involves divorce, sickness, domestic violence or natural disaster

Microenterprises in particular have become an important way for poor women to build assets.[63] Nine out of 10 enterprises in the Philippines are microenterprises—and among microentrepreneurs, women outnumber men two to one in the trade and repairs sectors, for example.[64] Women also operate nearly 20 per cent of the 14,560 registered small and micro-businesses in Fiji,[65] as well as a third of enterprises employing between one and 21 people in Mongolia.[66]

The microcredit programmes that often fund these initiatives were pioneered in Asia-Pacific and have spread throughout the world. Globally, Asia has the largest number of microcredit borrowers and the highest percentage of poor women borrowers— 98 per cent of the total in 2006, compared with 66 per cent in Africa and 62 per cent in Latin America.[67] Overall, outcomes of microcredit include improved individual and household well-being, better nutritional status and increased education for children.[68] Employment rises as well—50 per cent of women borrowers from Grameen Bank in Bangladesh (and almost seven per cent of men) were unemployed before joining it.[69] The average borrower also works more days, as additional employment is generated.

In Afghanistan, Parwaz, a microfinance institution, has been successful in promoting business activities among women and catalyzing women's mobility. Women clients are now venturing to the market themselves, negotiating with male store owners for an appropriate rate for the merchandise, taking orders and delivering the items.[70]

Yet despite the success stories, issues are emerging in more mature microfinance markets and require attention—such as microfinance 'bubbles' through oversaturation of the market, as in parts of southern India, where competitive pressures have started pushing multiple micro-loans onto women regardless of the stability of their businesses. This has resulted in indebtedness and backlash.[71]

BOX 2.3

ASSETS CAN PROTECT WOMEN FROM VIOLENCE

Everywhere in the world, women from all social and economic backgrounds can be vulnerable to gender-based violence. But in some cases, assets like houses and land can play a critical role in protecting them from violence within the home.

The Indian state of Kerala, for example, has high levels of women's literacy and a generally egalitarian environment for women. However, according to a survey in one part of Kerala conducted in 2001, violence against women is pervasive even there. Though it is difficult to get accurate data on this issue, up to 35.7 per cent of women reported having experienced at least one incident of physical violence after marriage. According to the National Family Health Survey (NFHS-3), in 2005-2006, 16.4 per cent of ever-married women experienced spousal violence in Kerala.

The risk of physical and psychological violence appears to decrease if women have control over assets, as discussed in the special contribution by Bina Agarwal in this Report. Other factors reducing risk may include social support from family and neighbours, and the household's economic status; both are negatively correlated to violence.

Sources: ICRW 2006; IIPS and Macro International 2008; Panda 2006; Panda and Agarwal 2005.

BOX 2.4

MORE AT RISK FROM DISASTER

During the 1990s, more than two-thirds of the deaths from natural disasters globally occurred in Asia, which was also the continent most frequently hit by this kind of crisis.

In societies where the socio-economic status of women is low, they are more likely than men to die as a result of disasters. Existing patterns of discrimination that render women more vulnerable to fatal consequences are exacerbated. In one eastern coastal district of Sri Lanka, after the tsunami, female mortality rates were twice those of men.

Mobility restrictions especially disadvantage women when a disaster occurs. A disproportionate number of women died in the 1991 cyclone in Bangladesh because of cultural norms restricting them to their homes. They were less likely than men to know how to swim and had few chances of escaping from the affected areas. More women than men died in the tsunami in Sri Lanka because they did not know how to swim or climb trees.

Disasters disrupt economic activities and land ownership and use patterns by killing land titleholders, destroying land records and erasing boundaries. Determining and redistributing land ownership promptly and equitably after natural disasters is an important step in the transition from short-term humanitarian relief to the long-term reconstruction of livelihoods and communities.

Sources: Brown and Crawford 2006; Neumayer and Plümper 2007; Nishikiori et al. 2006; Sachs 2007, cited in World Bank et al. 2009; WHO 2002.

A growing rationale for expanding women's access to assets comes from the threat of climate change. Women with less

TABLE 2.1

GENDER POSES OBSTACLES TO CREDIT

Institutional Level	Individual	Household	Community/National	Constraint
Embeddedness	• Lack of education and skills • Lack of information and experience with obtaining credit	• Traditionally limited role of women in decision-making within household	• Customs restrict women's ownership rights • Constrained women's mobility • Perception that economically independent women ruin families	Religious/ cultural/ Traditional
Institutional environment	• Women are not aware of or lack confidence in claiming their rights	• Lack of protection (statutory and customary) of women's rights to jointly owned assets	• Women's equal rights to assets for collateral are not defined or implemented • Banks do not see women as potential market • Formal rights to land ownership are lacking/weak	Political/ legal
Governance structure	• Women undertake activities that produce low returns • Lack of access to credit from banks in their own right • Limited monetary support from informal credit	• Unequal access to and control of land, labour and inputs • Gender division of labour (domestic, agricultural and manufacturing)	• Women are locked in low-paying jobs • Stereotypes of economic role of women in society • Perception that men control money/men decide • Women borrowers/entrepreneurs not taken seriously	Economic/ transactional
Resource allocation	• Lack of control over own income • Decision-making on allocations of money for businesses or family	• Men decide on how household money is allocated • Household credit channeled to husband	• Few community credit resources available for women borrowers	Resource

Note: The downward moving arrows signify influence from the higher level going down. The upward moving arrows signify feedback from the lower level going up.

Sources: Adapted from Johnson (n.d.) and Williamson (2000), cited in Hampel-Milagrosa 2008.

Women have knowledge about natural forestry and other environmental resources that may be valued locally, but otherwise goes unrecognized in broader strategies to respond to climate change

control over assets and fewer coping mechanisms will be among those most affected by natural disasters and declines in energy, water and food resources. But through the use of assets, they may also have an impact on the course of climate change, for better and worse. When property rights are weaker for women, they may have less capacity and fewer incentives to practise conservation and protection—particularly if they are struggling to make a living. Crops that can be quickly grown and harvested, even if they lead to soil erosion, will take precedence over long-term options, such as slow-growing trees needed for reforestation.[72]

In a number of Asia-Pacific societies, women have knowledge about natural forestry and other environmental resources that may be valued locally, but otherwise goes unrecognized in broader strategies to respond to climate change. Women also often have more ready access to common resources in forests than to agricultural land. Independently, they acquire knowledge of forestry in gathering wood for fuel, and of non-wood forestry products for food, medicines, construction materials and resources to sell for income. Around 80 per cent of people in developing countries rely on these products to meet nutrition and health needs.[73]

THE TRANSFORMATIVE POTENTIAL OF MICROFINANCE

Professor Muhammad Yunus

We achieve what we want to achieve, change what we want to change: it is our vision or lack of vision which makes things happen or not happen. We can build the world according to our liking only if we decide what is it that we actually like. People are not born just to somehow survive until death, but rather, to explore their potential, to unleash their energy and unshackle their creativity. All human beings, women and men, should get a fair chance to do so without the hindrance of social and economic deprivation. Poverty compromises human rights. Our 1976 experiment in Jobra village, Bangladesh, unshackled a force that makes it possible for women and men to share in economic prosperity, participatory democracy and live in dignity.[74]

Grameen is no longer a word restricted to its Bengali language meaning 'of the village'. Going beyond Bangladesh, beyond South Asia, it has become a symbol of progress and empowerment of the poor, particularly women. Transformed into a formal bank in 1983, by mid-2009 the Grameen Bank operates in around 84,000 villages of Bangladesh with a total of 7.87 million borrowers, an overwhelming 97 per cent of whom are women.[75] Group-based, collateral-free lending reduced the monopoly power of moneylenders in informal rural credit markets and provided the poor access to financial services. The past two decades have seen a huge growth of microfinance institutions (MFIs) in developing countries of Asia, Africa and Latin America. Ironically, with the success of MFIs, formal financial institutions have also incorporated microfinance in their portfolios. Demonstrating that the poor are bankable, Grameen Bank and similar organizations have helped to change mindsets in the formal banking system. According to the Microcredit Summit Campaign, more than 106 million of the world's poorest families received a microloan by 2007, surpassing the goal

of 100 million set ten years earlier. Notably, between 1997 and 2007, the number of microloans has grown from eight million to 106 million very poor women worldwide.[76]

Increase in women's incomes and assets. Globally, microfinance has had a strong female client base. Grameen Bank focuses on women because 'giving loans to women always brought more benefits to the family'.[77] The positive impact on income generation and entrepreneurship has been widely studied around the world.[78] Overall, women's access to financial services has indeed led to individual and household economic empowerment.[79] In the case of Grameen, 68 per cent of borrower families who have been with Grameen Bank for more than five years crossed the poverty line.[80] Under Grameen Bank's housing loan, 640,000 homes have been financed and legal ownership is with the women themselves.[81] Studies from Bangladesh also show that credit to women increased women's non-land assets.[82] Another less recognized aspect is savings in women's own names, which contribute to economic security. Savings is a key product of Grameen Bank. Borrowers' total deposits amount to around US $539 million.[83] A critical point is that beneficiaries are also shareholders in Grameen: they own the bank.

Increase in social and public participation. Going beyond the family, microfinance has enlarged the exposure of poor women to different public institutions, increased their mobility, social networks, and interaction with government officials at the local and national levels. A number of studies have found positive impacts not just in Bangladesh, but also in other countries such as India. For example, one study noted that membership matters in attending *panchayat* (a local governance institution) meetings for those previously socially excluded.[84] In a study in Tamil

Nadu,[85] India, significant differences between members and non-members were noted: in the past five years members visited more places together, increased their circle of friends and made friends from other castes or communities. The study also found that 95 per cent of members voted during the last *panchayat* elections; many of them discussed the pros and cons of candidates during group meetings. Studies in Bangladesh showed positive impacts on women's access to government programmes, voting in national and local elections and accurately naming the local level elected woman representative.

Transformative potential: changing male attitudes. Microfinance has catalyzed mindset changes among men as well – particularly significant in strong patriarchal societies. Women have benefited from greater voice, participation and support in the home and community. Impact studies have noted that women are empowered, not only through the process of making independent decisions on loans and enterprise profits, but also by participating much more actively with their husbands and other household members in joint economic decisions.[86] In countries where microfinance is predominant, there are signs of transformation from within in terms of lower fertility rates, better health and nutrition and higher literacy rates for women. For example, in Bangladesh loans to women positively influenced children's education and contraceptive use, in addition to the more obvious economic benefits.[87] Positive effects on individual women and on households were observed in India where men have also supported women's activity.[88] In remote areas with difficult market access, men's support has contributed to the sustainability of women's income generating activities.

Let's make poverty and gender inequality history. Though there are limitations to

Health is an Asset

Health is wealth, in the most literal sense for the poorest of the poor, who count it as their only productive asset. Good health and access to health care ensure that economies have an efficient labour supply and that individual men and women can develop their capabilities and improve their well-being.

Despite the obvious rationale for basic health care for all, patterns of gender disparities exist in most Asia-Pacific countries. Because of better health services, life expectancy has improved for both men and women,[89] especially in South-East Asia.[90] But the ratio of female-male life expectancy is below the world average of 1.06 in several countries in the region, defying the biological advantages of women at birth.[91] This discrepancy stems from a lifetime of gender discrimination, starting from the deliberate abortion of female foetuses and extending through nutritional shortchanges in the distribution of food.

In some cases, gender norms also disadvantage men's health, particularly through stress on aggression and risk-taking. Men have higher rates of injury, including traffic accidents. In the mining sector in China and Thailand they suffer from high rates of respiratory infections and mercury poisoning, and have a lower body mass index than people of other occupations.[92]

Since good health is a condition for earning a livelihood, gender inequalities in health care also limit women's abilities to

work and move up the economic ladder. Loss of potential or actual income results, further undercutting what may be an already limited ability to pay for health care. Across Asia-Pacific, women work longer hours than men and still spend a significantly higher proportion of their time on household chores. Being indoors longer than men, they are more likely to have an acute respiratory infection due to their exposure to pollutants from cooking and heating.[93]

The heavier workload also leads to greater musculoskeletal problems, including during pregnancy, and less time to access health care services.[94] In Nepal, a study conducted among Tamang women indicated that their heavy workload produces a high incidence of uterine prolapse soon after delivery. One of their main tasks is to collect heavy wood loads, and they start working from the third day of delivery.[95] Women in the garment industry in Fiji, who are required to sit in the same position as men, suffer from body pains, obesity, and bladder and kidney problems.[96]

Severe gender inequality is also giving rise to heightened HIV vulnerability among women. The proportion of women among people living with HIV in Asia is growing, from 19 per cent in 2000 to 24 per cent in 2007.[97] In South Asia, for example, more than 60 per cent of over one million HIV positive youths aged 15-24 are women.[98] The impact of HIV is most evident at the household level in Asia. Women as caregivers, workers and surviving spouses, generally bear the brunt of the consequences. Severe

Gender inequalities in health care also limit women's abilities to work and move up the economic ladder

household impacts of HIV often forces women into distress situations, including sexual exploitation, that heighten their vulnerability to HIV. Most of the women living with HIV in Asia have been infected by their partners.[99] According to a study in India, female victims of intimate partner violence show higher incidence of sexually transmitted infection or HIV prevalence. Abused wives face increased HIV risk based both on the greater likelihood of HIV infection among abusive husbands and elevated HIV transmission within abusive relationships.[100]

Women affected by communicable diseases associated with stigma, particularly HIV/AIDS, tend to lose jobs. Concentrated in the urban informal sector, subsistence farming or lower-paid jobs in the formal sector, they have little security in terms of income, insurance or social protection. Loss of income from an ill partner can force women without education and skills into hazardous occupations, including sex work, which further increase their vulnerability. On the death of the husband the woman is often blamed and, in the worst instances, deprived of rights to land and housing.[101] In India, despite constitutional guarantees and legal safeguards, a study[102] shows that as high as 79 per cent of HIV positive widows were denied a share in their husband's property. More than 90 per cent of the HIV positive widows had stopped living in their marital homes after the death of their husband.

Labour and health laws lag behind desirable standards in much of the region. Anti-discrimination legislation mostly does not cover men and women with HIV, and laws have little to say on coverage of the health needs of sexual/gender minorities. Indonesia is one of the few countries to pass legislation on the right to health.[103]

Asia-Pacific has few mechanisms to hold either public or private market institutions accountable for providing basic health care or ensuring gender equality in that process. The shift towards private health care has meant rising medical costs that affect poorer men and women most.

Although no regional data exist on gender biases in health care expenditures, some studies show that biases within households reduce women's access to care. Particularly in homes with scarce resources, spending on women's health may receive low priority, as seen in many parts of South Asia. A study in Bangladesh observed that rural girls suffering from diarrhoea are less likely than boys to receive an antibiotic, and in urban areas are less likely to be seen by a licensed allopath.[104] In rural China, women are more likely than men to go blind as a result of cataracts, corneal opacity and glaucoma, all of which are treatable.[105] In parts of South Asia, an important health issue is the lack of female health professionals; women and girls are prevented by customs to seek treatment from male health professionals. Lack of awareness, combined with reliance on faith-based cures, can contribute to the poor health of women in particular.

Paid Work Opens Doors

In recent decades, high economic growth rates and changing social norms in Asia-Pacific have brought women into the paid workforce in record numbers. Paid work is important to women for income—and because it can help them cultivate new capabilities and develop a greater sense of autonomy. When it takes place outside the home, it can bring women into contact with new people and ideas, and break restrictive social conventions. As is the case with assets, it may be an avenue for greater participation in public life, including through collective bargaining or broader political processes, as women acquire a sense of the value of their voice and contributions.[106]

In Bangladesh and India, studies of the impact of outside work on the domestic

High economic growth rates and changing social norms in Asia-Pacific have brought women into the paid workforce in record numbers

balance of power have found a move away from decisions based on norms that favour male control. Decisions become joint, rather than a male prerogative.[107] Bangladeshi women working outside the house in formal jobs have higher levels of savings, greater mobility and a lower incidence of domestic violence,[108] though the number of women in formal-sector jobs is low.

But women's entry into the labour market can also undercut a central aspect of masculine gender identity: the position of men as provider-protectors. Studies show that men can experience shame at perceived 'failure' to provide for their families. High expectations around such predefined gender roles can be a source of strain on men, who often face social pressure to demonstrate virility among male peers.[109] This can result in depression, which is high among unemployed men. Crisis situations can trigger extreme reactions, such as farmer suicides and gender-based violence.

However, assumptions about women's role in the labour market, reflected in the policies of many Asia-Pacific countries, may not actually benefit women. One such assumption is that paid work of any kind can be the path out of poverty. This has fed a heavy emphasis across the region on deregulation to boost the creation of jobs,

with much less focus on social protection or even the quality of employment. It has helped obscure the fact that the labour market is rife with gender inequalities, so that women in Asia-Pacific consistently end up with some of the worst, most poorly paid jobs—often the ones that men don't want to do, or those assumed to be 'naturally' suited to women.

Where these biases go unchecked, policy-making remains partially blind to the potential of women in the paid workforce as well as to the principles of fairness and equal opportunity. It may also overlook associated economic costs. By contrast, East Asia, the most successfully growing sub-region in Asia-Pacific, has the smallest gender gap in the world in the employment-to-population ratio, and lower segmentation of jobs by gender.

Not Enough: Participation, Pay, Opportunity

A number of factors catalyze women's entrance into paid work. Improved literacy and school enrolment rates are coupled with shifting attitudes towards women's work, including growing social acceptance of women employed outside the home.[110] Women's work can be an economic imperative for survival or part of aspirations for a better life (Box 2.5). Nonetheless, on the whole, women

---

BOX 2.5

A 'JOB FOR WOMEN' GAINS IN VALUE

The province of Sayaboury of Lao People's Democratic Republic is located along the Thai border. It is home to many women who take part in both cross-border trade as well as the manufacture of the traded goods. The province has long been an entry point to Thailand, a role that was severely curtailed during the Viet Nam war (1964-1973). In the early 1990s, a policy of trade and border liberalization resulted in the opening of checkpoints to allow the movement of people and goods, including at Sayaboury in 1996.

While there is a long history of weaving and trade in woven cloth involving women in many villages in Sayaboury province, the war severely disrupted this aspect of the community's life. Since the mid-1990s, however, weaving and trading in material have once again returned as an important source of cash-income in an economically impoverished area.

The government has also played a role in introducing weaving as a source of income among groups that did not have a history of it.

The effect of the revival of weaving upon women's social position is interestingly linked to the ways in which weaving is perceived as a *gendered* activity. So, in villages with a previous history of weaving, it continues to be regarded as 'woman's work' that can be conducted when women have 'free time' on their hands. In villages where the activity has been newly introduced, there are few preconceived notions attached to it. Weaving is considered a major source of income. In the 'new' weaving villages, men have been much more willing to share in domestic work as well as excuse women from other work such as collecting forest produce.

Sources: Kusakabe 2004; Srivastava 2009b.

still fall short of men in the region in their employment rates, pay and job opportunities. These trends hold despite considerable variations among countries.

In 2007, women's labour participation rate was less than 35 per cent in India and Pakistan, for example, compared to some 70 per cent or more in Cambodia, China, Papua New Guinea and Viet Nam (Figure 2.2). Even so, men's participation rate was higher in all of these countries. Nearly 70 per cent of women had paid employment in East Asia in 2007 compared to 58.9 per cent in South-East Asia and the Pacific and only 37.4 per cent in South Asia.[111] The corresponding figures for men were 83.1 per cent, 87.8 per cent and 86.4 per cent, respectively.

Female labour force participation reflects only partially women's contribution to the wider economy. Official statistics miss unpaid economic activities, such as work on family farms and enterprises and contribution to the care economy, which have many larger societal benefits.

Women have a higher unemployment rate than men in every Asia-Pacific sub-region, except East Asia. In South Asia, South-East Asia and the Pacific, the differences between male and female unemployment figures in 2008 were twice the global average.[112]

Despite laws guaranteeing equal pay for equal work, women still earn only 54 to 90 per cent of what men earn in Asia-Pacific countries.[113] Women also participate less in the labour market. The two factors contribute to lower earnings by females on average. The ratio of female-to-male estimated income in 2007 (in Purchasing Power Parity terms) is less than one for all countries in the region, varying from 0.18 for Pakistan to 0.87 for Mongolia[114] (Figure 2.3). Wage gaps arise from women's predominance in lower-paid positions; interruptions in their work life, often related to family concerns; and the lower valuation of typically female occupations. Other obstacles include biases of some

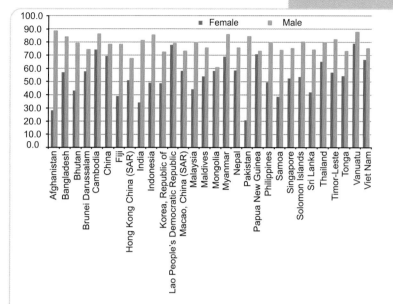

Figure 2.2: Fewer Women Than Men Participate in the Workforce
Labour Force Participation Rates of Women and Men, 2007

Source: Based on ILO 2009b.

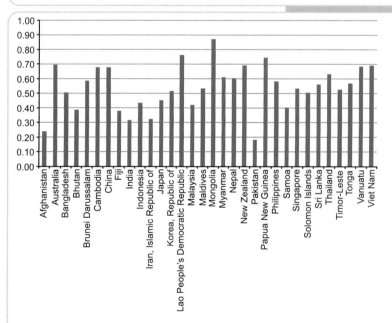

Figure 2.3: Women Earn Less than Men
Ratio of Female-to-Male Estimated Earned Income in Asia-Pacific, 2007, US $ PPP

Source: Based on UNDP 2009.

employers and women's generally weak bargaining power. Gender wage gaps vary across countries and economic sectors and change over time, persisting not only in marginalized informal activities, but also in professions such as computer programming, accounting and teaching. For example, female computer programmers make 80 per cent of what men do in Singapore and 90 per cent in the Republic of Korea.[115]

Gender also affects the types of employment women can choose. In countries where men migrate from rural areas to seek opportunities elsewhere, a growing number of women are expected to remain behind to run family farms. In South Asia, the agricultural sector comprised more than 65 per cent of all female employment in 2007, the same level as in sub-Saharan Africa.[116] Across Asia-Pacific, more women than men enter the service sector, possibly because of job preferences and the different requirements for job skills compared to manufacturing, where men predominate (Figure 2.4). Service jobs also encompass many forms of employment that conform to stereotypes about women's capabilities, such as nursing and care work.

Provisions for maternity leave vary and are frequently absent, although some encouraging steps have been taken. In China, the Methods for Maternity Insurance of Enterprise Workers provides for public pooling of insurance resources. Enterprises surrender maternity premiums, calculated according to a fixed percentage of a worker's wages, to designated insurers to establish a maternity insurance fund. Maternity benefits consist of a maternity allowance, leave with pay and health care. By presenting their maternity certificates, women workers may obtain allowances from the designated insurers and have maternity-related health care expenses reimbursed. The pay for women workers on maternity leave is fixed at the level of the enterprise's monthly average in the previous year and disbursed by the fund.[117]

Women's Work Involves Poorer Terms

Across all job sectors, women's labour has certain common characteristics. Women workers are often in demand after available supplies of male labour are exhausted, or because women are willing to accept low wages and poorer work conditions. Most employed women in Asia-Pacific are in vulnerable employment, broadly defined as self-employed or own-account workers and contributing family workers.[118] In 2007 this definition covered 61.4 per cent of women in East Asia, 66.2 per cent in South-East Asia and the Pacific, and 85.1 per cent in South Asia. The respective figures for men were 51.1 per cent, 58.9 per cent and 74.3 per cent. All these numbers are above the global averages of 53 per cent of women and 49 per cent of men.[119]

In the region as a whole, wage and salary employment is higher for men than women. Usually wage and salary employment increases through growth and development over time, although this is not consistently the case in Asia-Pacific. While many countries do not collect this data, numbers from the Maldives and Pakistan suggest that wage and salary employment may be dropping. Sri Lanka has also registered a slight decline.[120] For women facing this tendency plus the barrier of fewer marketable skills, self-

In South Asia, the agricultural sector comprised more than 65 per cent of all female employment in 2007, the same level as in sub-Saharan Africa

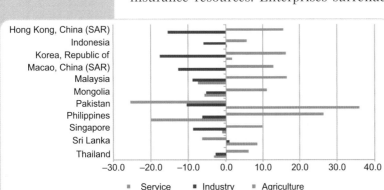

Figure 2.4: More Men than Women are in Industry, But Not in the Services
Female-Male Differences in Job Sectors, 2007

Note: Bars represent differences between the percentage share of total female workers and total male workers engaged in agriculture, industry and services in 2007.

Source: Based on ILO 2009b.

employment—normally on highly insecure terms—is often the only option.

Certain industries in Asia-Pacific have drawn obvious benefits from women's work, which is considered labour par excellence for highly competitive, labour-intensive sectors such as making clothing and processing fresh produce.[121] Much of this labour has been free of fixed costs for benefits associated with male employment in the organized sector. Low pay is justified by the notion that men are the real breadwinners, perceived to be the heads of households, and 'deserve' to earn more. But segregated job markets not only limit women's employment options, but also reduce the wages they can expect to earn.[122]

Women have also become an essential source of labour in export-processing zones, a major source of new jobs in Asia-Pacific. Yet women working there face a series of well-documented problems. Many jobs offer only low-paying piece-rate work, at wages less than those earned by men and under poor working conditions. Sexual harassment can be common.[123] Labour organizing is discouraged.[124]

Women workers in the manufacturing industry are increasing in low-paid and sub-contracting jobs. In India, for instance, the share of women in manufacturing in a subsidiary capacity (not as the perceived principal activity of the women concerned) has been increasing since 1987-1988, currently accounting for 11 per cent of all women employed in manufacturing.[125] An important reason for this is the growth of home-based sub-contracting for exports as well as domestic manufacturing. Pay is often poor and on a piece-rate basis and such work is not incorporated in employment statistics. This may explain the paradox that even while women's share of recorded employment in manufacturing has not increased much, the dependence of the sector on the productive contributions of women may well have increased. In 2004-2005, there were just under 15 million women workers in the informal sector. More than half of them were women involved in home-based work for different industries, mostly on a piece-rate basis.[126] While these jobs can provide opportunities, workers are also vulnerable to the growing competitiveness faced by export-based industries such as garments.

In the midst of the after effects of the global economic downturn, gender disparities are also now apparent in the disposability of female workers. More than half of the 40,000 jobs lost in the Philippines were in export-processing zones, where 80 per cent of workers are women. By February 2009, Cambodia and Sri Lanka had shed 30,000 mostly female garment industry jobs. In addition, employers have reportedly pressured women to waive severance, leave and social insurance benefits, knowing they may not understand their rights or have the means to protect them.[127]

Informal Employment is Often the Only Option

Tremendous population shifts have occurred in much of Asia-Pacific through the explosive growth of cities and migration away from rural areas. For millions of people, livelihood strategies have changed from eking out a living on a small plot of land to earning an income in urban service, business or industry.

New employment options have opened up, but the nature of work is frequently insecure, with little fallback available. The share of informal employment in India exceeds 90 per cent of total employment, for example; in Sri Lanka, the figure is two-thirds.[128] Informal work is one of the factors driving more people in the region to pursue diversified livelihoods, piecing together various sources of sustenance to make ends meet.

Diverse factors influence the nature of informal work in urban and rural areas, but common to both is that gender norms

Women have become an essential source of labour in export-processing zones, a major source of new jobs in Asia-Pacific. Yet women working there face a series of well-documented problems

determine how people are positioned to manage. Women's more tenuous employment paths, limited skills and restricted mobility help explain why they comprise more informal-sector workers than men in most countries (Figure 2.5). In India and Indonesia, nine out of every 10 women working outside agriculture hold informal-sector jobs, as do half or more of non-agricultural workers in parts of East Asia.[129]

In urban areas, evidence from some Asia-Pacific countries suggests that men and women are about equally engaged in informal work.[130] Even so, women dominate certain segments – such as income activities based in homes. These are often statistically invisible. Fully counting them would likely increase both the share of women in informal jobs and the share of informal workers in the work force.[131]

Home-workers typically produce garments, fashion accessories, toys and handicrafts for domestic and export markets, frequently under exploitive and unstable conditions. Many live in cramped quarters, with detrimental effects on their own and their children's health.[132] Some women choose such work because of the flexible hours, greater compatibility with family responsibi-

lities and relative ease of entry. But for many, no other opportunities are open; even as they confront growing pressure to contribute to family incomes.[133] They end up struggling with job and income insecurity and a real risk of marginalization in the labour market.

A study of slum dwellers in New Delhi, India, found that several factors combine to keep women in low-paying and vulnerable urban jobs.[134] They use informal networks of neighbours, friends and relatives to find employment, often close to where they live. But neither the networks nor the location may offer diverse choices. Women in low-paying jobs also often do not have the means to build capabilities that might allow them to move to a higher level. In comparison, male workers' contacts as well as mobility are greater.

Despite their drawbacks, urban informal-sector jobs can offer new openings to women. In Taiwan, Province of China, the pattern of industrialization has generated a large and heterogeneous informal sector that draws heavily on married women, for example. In small family enterprises, wives contribute their labour as unpaid workers.[135] A survey of 50 small family businesses in different industries found that men take charge of market relations and outside business contracts, and women manage the businesses from within the firm.[136] Though women are usually subordinate to men in these arrangements, bosses' wives are often in an indispensable position in the family business, which bolsters their bargaining power at home as well as the workplace.

In rural areas, changes in informal work mainly stem from the shrinking position of agriculture in transforming economies.[137] As other sectors leap ahead, rural areas are being left behind, yet this is where about 80 per cent of the poor live. Women's work or management of farms due to male migration are curtailed when men return and take control over marketing crops women have grown. Women also have less access to credit, agricul-

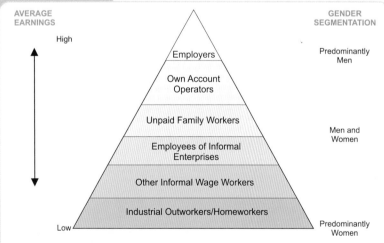

Figure 2.5: Gender Segmentation of the Informal Economy

Source: Chen et al. 2004.

tural extension services and markets.[138] Many are overburdened with the tasks of maintaining the household as well as the farm.[139]

In Cambodia, rural-urban migration appears to be unfolding along the lines of both gender and age. Men and younger women are leaving rural areas, while older women remain. Some evidence suggests that this provides a social safety net of food and care for migrants with risky urban jobs. The willingness of older women to manage farms also frees younger women to work in cities.[140] Yet amid increased female migration, vulnerable forms of employment still dominate.

In some countries, corporate farming is ushering in technological changes and the commercialization of agriculture in ways that have marginalized smaller farms, which women are more likely to own. Women who opt to work on corporate farms have jobs that are seasonal, long, less safe and insecure, and have no scope for advancement.[141] In Punjab, India, about 60 per cent of labourers in corporate tomato farming are seasonal female workers.[142] They earn about 60 to 75 per cent of what men do and face health and safety risks, and sexual harassment.

Factoring in Women's Unpaid Household Labour and Contribution to the Care Economy

While women's paid work can make important contributions to women's empowerment, it cannot be looked at in isolation from the work that women perform at home, such as cooking, cleaning, fetching fuel and water and providing care services. This is usually unpaid and under-recognized, but one which absorbs tremendous time and energy. Domestic care work continues to be considered a woman's responsibility even when she works long hours outside the home. For example, a time-use survey—overall an important tool in gathering statistics on the size and activities of the labour force—found that, on average,

women in the Republic of Korea spend 21 hours more than men per week in unpaid work, and their total working week exceeds men's by almost an hour a day.[143]

At times, the combination of paid and unpaid labour forces women to make choices that may not be ideal for them or their families—or even the broader economy if women's capabilities remain confined or untapped. Women opt to remain outside the paid workforce, or to accept work that is convenient but underpaid, so they have time to keep up with domestic duties, family care and obligations.

Some economists in Asia-Pacific and elsewhere have argued for calculating the value of women's unpaid domestic work. In Fiji, for example, recent research estimates the value of unpaid household work at almost FJD480 million (US $237 million), a figure greater than the income from sugar or tourism, the country's two largest industries. Sums like these have been helpful in drawing attention to women's immense but statistically invisible contributions. They validate women's economic contributions instead of treating their unpaid work as being 'unproductive'.[144]

In 1993 the United Nations Statistical Division extended its System of National Accounts to include unpaid care work in national accounting systems as satellite accounts, a kind of alternative calculation of Gross Domestic Product. This can provide a fuller understanding of not just the economic value of unpaid work, but also how resources and time are allocated. It can further help in monitoring the impact of policies on services critical to welfare that are provided within households or from the market.[145]

Education for People and Economies

Through constitutional guarantees of education as a basic right, targeted reforms and national development plans, a number of Asia-Pacific countries have tacitly recognized

Combination of paid and unpaid labour forces women to make choices that may not be ideal for them or their families—or even the broader economy if women's capabilities remain confined or untapped

the value of education as a social good and a source of human capital. Education has transformative potential for individuals and societies. It helps people make greater economic contributions and gain more benefits through enhanced productivity and earnings.[146] It is part of the process of changing social conditioning that limits the ways people see themselves and their society, including in terms of gender. The returns from educating girls are multiplied by the impact on fertility, which declines, and the schooling of the next generation, which improves.[147]

A seminal 1993 World Bank study demonstrated that high-performing economies in East Asia, such as Indonesia, Malaysia, the Republic of Korea, Singapore and Thailand, had been much more successful—and quicker—than others in eliminating gender gaps in school enrolment. At the regional level, a strong correlation exists between the increase in the number of years the average girl spends in school and the growth of per capita GDP.[148] And in countries with higher initial education, a one per cent increase in the share of adult women with secondary school education may boost per capita income growth by 0.3 per cent.[149]

Shortfalls in Access and Quality

In primary education, two-thirds of Asia-Pacific countries have achieved gender parity. However, South Asia scores much lower on female-to-male enrolment ratios for primary, secondary and tertiary education than East Asia and the Pacific.[150] Its achievements are only marginally higher than in sub-Saharan Africa; girls start out relatively well in schools in South Asia, but start to disappear as education progresses.

At the same time, while there are still fewer women than men in tertiary education across the region, their numbers are steadily growing. The average gender parity index climbed from 0.75 in 1999 to 0.94 in 2006; in some countries, including Mongolia, the Philippines and Thailand, women even have an edge over men.[151] The parity index has climbed to 1.31 in the Pacific.[152] A gender gap favouring men lingers in South and West Asia, though.

Even as Asia-Pacific has moved towards closing male-female education gaps, issues of access and quality remain. Education systems still perpetuate gender stereotypes and fall short of adequately preparing women for the workplace. This can be a handicap in an era when a well-prepared, flexible workforce is key to managing rapid changes in the global economy.

Gender stereotypes in textbooks, for example, commonly underscore that women and men are limited to certain roles. A study on primary Chinese-language school textbooks in Hong Kong, China (SAR), published during 1995 and 2000 found that women and girls are underrepresented overall and rarely appear as main characters. They are more visible in family or household settings, while men and boys are more dominant in public settings. The range of occupations for women is markedly restricted to lower-paid and less-valued occupations. These tendencies persist despite a decline in sexist content over time.[153]

Although the precise causes and consequences of shortfalls in the quality of and access to education vary from country to country, some common constraints include: endemic poverty; the costs of schooling; the burden of household labour; cultural and social practices that discriminate against girls, including early marriage and restrictions on female mobility; gender stereotypes; and limited employment opportunities for women.

The lower immediate economic benefits that families receive from girls' education—since many young women become part of the family they marry into or work in low-paying jobs—are also a deterrent. An old Bengali saying reflects the view that resources invested in a daughter will be lost: 'Caring for a daughter is like watering a neighbour's tree'. It is one of the arguments used to keep girls out of school in Bangladesh,[154] although it produces a self-reinforcing cycle. When women do not acquire skills, they cannot exercise choice or attain better employment.

Stereotypes Curtail Impacts

Given the persistence of gender stereotypes in formal schooling, education does not automatically translate into the best jobs or transform one's social and political standing. In Hong Kong, China (SAR), China, and Thailand in 2005, for example, unemployment was highest for males with only primary education and for females with secondary education.[155]

The political, economic and social climate in a country influences both gender parity in education and the extent to which it translates into more and better employment opportunities. This implies that education is only one element in a strategy to empower women; it is not a proxy for empowerment. Gender discrimination operates on many fronts, so even educated woman may still have limited control over decisions that affect their lives, including basic choices such as where to work and how to spend their earnings.

In Indonesia, for example, girls are almost at par with boys in primary and secondary gross enrolment and are closing the gap in tertiary education. But school-to-work transition surveys show that perceptions of 'appropriate' gender roles and of the division of responsibilities between men and women continue to influence job opportunities for both. Young women are still expected to quit their work after marriage or after the birth of their first child.[156] The ratio of male-to-female employment rates for youth in Indonesia is 1.8, indicating a significantly higher propensity for men to be employed. When women do enter the workforce, as in other countries, they tend to occupy low-paying and low-skilled occupations.

Countries that now have more women than men in tertiary education, such as Mongolia and the Philippines, show women with an edge in service sector jobs. But they still do not match men in the generally higher-paying manufacturing sector. Only 14.8 per cent of Mongolian women's employment was in industry in 2005, compared to 18.9 per cent of men's. Similar patterns hold in the Philippines.[157] In the Islamic Republic of Iran, higher enrolment of women in tertiary education compared to men has increased the number of female teachers, university professors, researchers, health workers, scientists, physicians, artists, writers, poets, filmmakers, lawyers, athletes and journalists whose activities are visible at the local and national levels. Yet even though female labour force participation rates have improved over time, they still stood at 32 per cent in 2007, less than half the male figure of 75 per cent.[158]

Education does not automatically lead to political voice either. In the Islamic Republic of Iran, despite the favourable changes for females in higher education, their level of participation in the political sphere is low.[159] Women held only four per cent of the seats in the national Parliament in 2007.[160]

While education is not the only input into women's economic empowerment, it is a central one. It can provide an unparalleled expansion of choices, more so for those without physical assets. Education equips individuals with basic capabilities to develop intellectually, expand mental horizons and increase livelihood options. It is crucial, therefore, that all levels of the formal education system are gender-equal in access and quality and systematically eliminate all forms of bias. Lifelong learning, the media

Countries that now have more women than men in tertiary education, show women with an edge in service sector jobs. But they still do not match men in the generally higher-paying manufacturing sector

and technology can be other catalytic drivers of information and knowledge. If appropriately used, they can be tools with which individuals can learn and aid transformative group thinking and behaviour.

Making a Move for More Opportunities

Mobility broadens women's employment and life choices; remittances as a source of foreign exchange contribute significantly to developing economies

Mobility broadens women's employment and life choices; remittances as a source of foreign exchange contribute significantly to developing economies. Many families and communities in Asia and the Pacific now survive on the strength of women's ability to earn money abroad.

Migration Trends

Recent trends show that more women from Asia-Pacific are making the move to new countries or new areas within their own country for work, marriage or other reasons.[161] The number of female migrants has risen over the last decade in all sub-regions except South and West Asia, reaching or exceeding the number of male migrants in some countries (Figure 2.6).[162] Indonesia and Sri Lanka deploy more female than male migrant workers—between 60 and 80 per cent of all legal migrants for work. In the Philippines, women migrants began outnumbering men as long ago as 1992,[163] although by 2007 there were roughly equal numbers of men and women migrating.[164] Single migrant workers represent a common phenomenon in the region, as does migration between Asia-Pacific countries and to the Arab States.

Internal migration data are seriously constrained by inadequate official statistical systems. But an overview of research in four Asian countries suggests that migration within Asia is high and has increased during the last two decades.[165] Men and women are on the move from rural to urban areas, usually seeking non-farm employment opportunities. For example, the sharp growth of tourism and manufacturing in Thailand has prompted more than 1.3 million women from rural areas to move to urban, municipal areas.[166]

While the recent global economic downturn is expected to affect international migration and remittances, it is uncertain how severe the impacts will be. Huge job losses have already hit export manufacturing, trimming the ranks of male and female internal migrants from rural areas.[167] Construction jobs have disappeared mainly for men, but impacts on export processing zones and call centres may affect women more, since they are employed in large numbers there. The need for women in caregiving is likely to remain relatively constant, but those engaged as domestic help would be more at risk of job loss.[168] In China's Guangzhou Province, where many women professionals have moved in recent years to find employment, Home EZ Services has reported an uptick in the number of women with higher education applying for domestic work.[169]

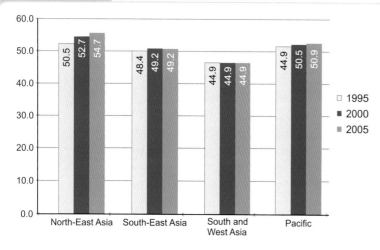

Figure 2.6: Almost Half of Asia-Pacific Migrants Are Women

Female Migrants as Percentage of All International Migrants in UNESCAP Sub-Regions, 1995, 2000 and 2005

Source: Based on UN 2009a.

Restrictions Constrain Choices

Gender norms determine the supply of and demand for women migrant workers, including through their reflection in public policies and laws. As much as economic 'push' factors, social conventions guide whether or not women have the freedom to move to a new place, work in a job of their choice and make choices that will be respected by their family and community (Box 2.6). The major 'sending countries' in Asia-Pacific, Indonesia, the Philippines and Sri Lanka, have relatively open emigration policies for women. In several West Asian countries, however, the approach is more restrictive, compounded by customary practices.

As is true of employment at large, women migrants are dominant in the care and entertainment sectors, where jobs are regarded as 'appropriate' for them, even if they possess different or better qualifications. In South-East Asia, more than two million migrant women are working as domestic workers.[170] Around 90 per cent of the female migrant workers from Sri Lanka are employed as domestic workers, mainly in Kuwait, Saudi Arabia and the United Arab Emirates.[171] Many of these jobs are underpaid and poorly protected, including by laws in recipient countries, which frequently exempt domestic work from labour standards (Box 2.7).

Thailand is the major destination country for migrant workers from Lao People's Democratic Republic; likewise, the main occupation of these women migrants is domestic work. Under labour laws in both countries domestic work is not fully protected, so contracts for domestic workers are not as comprehensive as for jobs in the formal sector. This hinders domestic workers from obtaining visas and permits to stay and work legally, and makes them more vulnerable to exploitation and abuse.[172]

The migration of skilled and professional women has also been on the rise, but again,

---

BOX 2.6

SEEKING FREEDOM, FINDING JUDGMENT

The Makassar Industrial Zone (KIMA) in South Sulwaesi, Indonesia was established in the early 1990s to deepen Indonesia's 'international trade ties'. Many women who came to work in KIMA were motivated by the opportunity for urban life and work to provide a degree of freedom from familial control.

But even as the zone drew in a large number of young women, the Indonesian state was propagating gender norms emphasizing women's roles as supportive wives and dutiful daughters. Instead of being viewed as 'respectable' breadwinners, women workers confronted stereotypes about the zones as sites of loose morality where women could mix freely with men. Bowing to social pressure, many women workers eventually presented their decision to work in the zone as a quest for finding a husband.

Sources: Silvey 2000; Srivastava 2009b.

---

typically to fill traditionally female jobs in education, health and social work. The Philippines supplies the majority of nurses to countries such as the United States.[173] Nurses from Melanesia are increasingly migrating to the Marshall Islands, Palau, New Zealand and the United Arab Emirates.[174] Research by Public Service International has found that these jobs continue to be undervalued. They frequently combine heavy responsibilities with low pay and workplace risks from communicable diseases. Women in these circumstances may face not only gender discrimination but also racial barriers.[175]

Some migrant women enter the sex industry, in addition to those trafficked for that purpose. The risks to health, safety and free-

Women migrants are dominant in the care and entertainment sectors. In South-East Asia, more than two million migrant women are working as domestic workers

---

BOX 2.7

NATIONAL LEGISLATION EXCLUDES DOMESTIC WORKERS

Japan: The Labour Standards Law, 1995 stipulates: This Law applies to the enterprises and places of business listed in each of the items below; provided, however, that it does not apply to any enterprise or place of business employing only relatives living with the employer as family members nor to domestic employees.

Republic of Korea: The Labour Standards Act, 1997 states: This Act shall not apply to any business or workplace which employs only relatives living together, and to a worker who is hired for domestic work.

Malaysia: The Employment Act, 1955 stipulates that the provisions on Rest Days, Hours of Work, Holidays and other Conditions of Service are not applicable to persons engaged as domestic servants.

Source: Ramirez-Machado 2003.

---

dom posed by this profession can be amplified by irregular immigration status and the criminal nature of trafficking. Sex work is largely unregulated and unquantified in Asia-Pacific, but one estimate from the 1990s suggested it was a major economic force, accounting for two to 14 per cent of GDP in four South-East Asian countries.[176] Japan has deliberately encouraged Filipina workers in entertainment establishments by dubbing them skilled workers with special provisions under its Immigration Control Act.[177]

Rewards and Risks

For developing countries with too many workers and not enough jobs, labour migration – especially when it is temporary – can help improve the economy, the balance of payments and the lives of migrants. Remittances can ease families out of poverty and provide more money for health care and education. Migration also benefits host economies by reducing cyclical labour shortages and filling jobs that nationals do not take up. Both sending and receiving locations benefit.

Migration could enable women to find new employment opportunities, higher incomes and recognition of the value of their work. The knowledge of conditions and possibilities elsewhere can have an important liberating effect, stirring momentum for positive social change and gender empowerment over time.

Many women see migration as a temporary means of achieving certain objectives, such as savings to build a home or educate children. These objectives are difficult to achieve in the short term, so women typically stay longer than expected. But delayed returns are not always because of inadequate savings or other constraints. Some migrant women workers start appreciating the autonomy that comes from earning their own livelihood and are willing to continue, even at significantly lower wages than those received by local workers, or under adverse and demanding working conditions.

Some evidence suggests that patterns of economic migration may be changing in ways that reflect women's growing empowerment. The migration of women into Australia used to be dominated by less-skilled women accompanying their husbands or entering as part of family reunification programmes.[178] In recent years, more professional and skilled female entrants are coming on their own. In 1989-1990, women accounted for just over 40 per cent of those classified as 'principal applicants' for settlement. By 2002, the figure had climbed to 52 per cent.

Women migrants may lack recognition and support in both source and destination countries, especially if they run into problems. Legal systems have wide gaps in protections for migrants in general, and more so for workers in the informal sector, where many women end up.[179] Recourse to settle disputes or recoup unpaid wages may be limited. The incidence of sexual assault and violence can be high and access to justice impossible to obtain, for reasons ranging from a lack of understanding of the local language to a fear of being deported.

Women migrants also can be highly vulnerable to HIV, for example, among Asian women working in parts of Arab States.[180] This stems mainly from the vulnerabilities they face at different stages of the migration cycle. The isolated and individualized nature of household work in unfamiliar and harsh conditions, combined with inadequate local labour laws, put domestic workers in particular at greater risk to verbal, physical and sexual abuse. Migrants found to be HIV positive are often dismissed from their jobs and summarily deported.

Studies on internal rural-urban migration reveal similar patterns of positive and negative consequences.[181] While female migrants may work in key revenue-generating industries that enable them to earn more than they

Migration could enable women to find new employment opportunities, higher incomes and recognition of the value of their work

did elsewhere, social experiences of living in the city while working as waste pickers and recyclers, for example, may place them at greater risk.[182]

Taking Action: Towards A Better Balance in Economic Power

The obstacles to women's equal participation in Asia-Pacific economies need to be overcome as a matter of justice, and to benefit women, societies and economies at large. The barriers are not insurmountable. Progress is coming from many directions, fueled at times by growing recognition of the potentially huge economic contributions women can make. Sources of change include political commitments to gender equality, deliberate policy interventions, economic forces generating new sources of wealth and opportunities, and the choices women make to pursue new capabilities and livelihoods. Further steps can direct and speed up this process by freeing access to assets, expanding paid employment, connecting education to new opportunities, investing in women's health, and making mobility safe. All these areas require specific responses, but they have many levels of interconnection that should be considered as well.

Remove Barriers to Assets

Eliminate discriminatory laws and close legal gaps, particularly those relating to inheritance and marriage (Box 2.8). When rights are defined by law and formalized through specific legal procedures that are widely acknowledged and applied, people can be confident that their property will remain their own. They can also enjoy the freedom to use it to pursue other assets, including using it as collateral for loans.

Laws in many cases need to move beyond assumptions about 'neutrality' to address the specific constraints that women face. Despite obvious discrepancies in land ownership bet-

---

BOX 2.8

REFORMS EXTEND WOMEN'S RIGHTS TO OWN LAND

Several South-east Asian countries have attempted land reforms designed to deliberately combat discrimination in land ownership. In Cambodia, traditionally women had equal access to land through inheritance. But when land distribution took place in the 1980s, communal ownership was replaced by private land. This had a negative impact on women, since land was usually registered only in the name of the husband. The land law passed in 2001 aims to strengthen land tenure security, promote land distribution with equity and protect women's rights. The new law has brought changes in land titling. According to a 2007 survey, 20 per cent of titling is now in the wife's name, five per cent in the husband's name and 70 per cent under both names.

But challenges continue to exist. Patterns of gender bias allow men to control decision-making in households, so even with joint titles to land, the principle of joint ownership is not always upheld. One study found that women often need their husbands' permission to include their names on land titles. If men decide to sell land, women are expected to defer to their choices. Women's limited knowledge of the law and the registration process may also reduce their abilities to claim their rights. Half of women farmers are illiterate or have less than a primary school education, compared to 29 per cent of men; 78 per cent of women farmers are engaged in subsistence agriculture.

Lao People's Democratic Republic, with an agricultural labour force that is 53 per cent female, also has a national law stating that men and women are equally entitled to hold property; any property purchased during marriage is regarded as jointly owned. Land owned by a woman prior to her marriage remains hers, as does any land she inherits from her parents.

To help the law take hold, the Department of Lands has collaborated with the Lao Women's Union, which has worked at the grass-roots level on mass campaigns to teach people about women's land rights, helping to bring about a sharp increase in the number of land titles registered in women's names or jointly with their husbands.

Sources: IFAD 2003, cited in UNIFEM et al. 2004; Mehrvar et al. 2008; UNDP 2008c; UN-HABITAT 2007; World Bank et al. 2009.

---

ween men and women in Asia and the Pacific, discussions on formalizing land rights under the law have made few references to these. Formalized rights are assumed to uniformly apply, even as women confront discriminatory inheritance practices and a variety of disadvantages in claiming legal rights, as will be discussed at greater length in Chapter 4.

Improvements in statutes themselves should be coupled with initiatives to change public attitudes that tolerate unfair practices that are illegal. Given long-entrenched customs around asset ownership and control, results can be mixed when limited attention

Laws in many cases need to move beyond assumptions about 'neutrality' to address the specific constraints that women face

is paid to implementing progressive laws. A 1995 survey of property inheritance in Bangladesh revealed that only 25 per cent of widows had received their rightful share from parents and only 32 per cent from their husbands.[183]

One way of recognizing the gender patterns in land ownership is through joint land titling. Typically shared by male and female household members, it can expand women's household bargaining power and provide greater protection from dispossession through abandonment, divorce or death of a spouse. It can be particularly critical in natural disasters, when states issue land as compensation to help people recover. Joint titling is not a panacea, however, as social conventions may continue to assign land-use choices to men.

Review asset-related policies for gender dimensions. Most policies do not yet recognize the different constraints, opportunities and needs of women and men. Very little data is available to guide more informed and effective efforts to tap the proven economic potentials of women as part of a balanced and sustainable approach to human development.

Some countries have started making policy choices to increase women's home and land ownership. In India, to encourage the registration of property in the names of women, states have introduced policies that lower property tax rates for women. The Indira Awas Yojana programme gives priority to widows and unmarried women in constructing houses for poor people in rural areas.[184] The National Housing Policy in Bangladesh also favours extra support for widows, single women and women who head households living below the poverty line. Nevertheless, a gap exists between promises and what really happens in these programmes.[185] Greater efforts and commitment by governments and more vigilant civil society and media can reduce discrepancies.

Granting women assets to correct past exclusion can be an important initial step.

Beyond that, policies might aim to help women grow as economic agents by building on existing assets or acquiring new ones, given their record of success in managing small loans and businesses. More attention could be paid to the ways that different categories of assets might interact to create new opportunities—having a home for many Asia-Pacific women means also having a place to do business, for example. Even marginal assets, such as a flock of poultry or a patch of forest, can be considered entry points, particularly since they may be the only assets that poorer women have.

Economic power, especially acquisition and control over resources, helps reduce the potential for gender-based violence. But transition periods can result in increased male backlash and gender-based violence, where formerly assetless women start to acquire economic power or where public decision-making has traditionally been in the realm of men. These are complexities difficult to measure, as attitudes towards gender and stereotyping of gender roles operate as subtle and explicit barriers. The interconnectedness of the factors that contribute to disadvantages based on gender require that solutions recognize and leverage the synergies.

Increase women's access to the means to acquire and manage assets. Microfinance is one important strategy that can be expanded in the region. Other financial and social protection services should be provided as well, including systems for savings, investment and insurance. Having a national identity card or an independent bank account improves access to such services where they exist. Information also makes a difference, although dissemination processes need to acknowledge potential gender differences in the types of information required and the ability to access it. For women, access to information may be affected by higher illiteracy rates and lower mobility.

In India, the MS Swaminathan Research Institute has introduced community-managed

Internet kiosks, with women managing a third of them. They provide information on prices in different marketplaces so that farmers can find the most lucrative prices. According to farmers, both men and women, earnings have improved by up to 20 per cent.[186]

Provide training and skills development for women. Training and skills development can encompass skills to acquire and manage assets, basic literacy and numeracy, as well as steps to build confidence, and a sense of ability and independence. Providing assets without these skills is not always enough to counter social norms. Studies on microfinance programmes for women across South Asia indicate that women were passing on all or most of their loans to male family members under circumstances that gave them little say over the use of this capital.[187]

Ensure women's meaningful participation in forums that make decisions about assets. Many forums that make decisions about assets exist, both within public institutions and the private sector. While women's participation alone will not guarantee gender-responsive decisions, they should be able to participate as equal citizens, and they may offer diverse perspectives that render decision-making more accurate. Particular opportunities may come in the context of decentralization, where local bodies play a growing role in governance and service provision. If local traditions are strongly patriarchal, women can be shut out of these, requiring a deliberate focus on both inclusion and quality of participation.

Expand Paid Employment

Orient economic policies around the provision of 'decent work'. Tight job markets tend to restrict the number of jobs or dampen the quality of those that are there through lower wages and poorer working conditions. Either way, women tend to lose first and worst.

Countercyclical policies may reduce the possibility of job and income losses during recessions and can be critical in the absence of social protection schemes. Raising the minimum wage level and progressive tax policies are among the options to reduce income disparities and support decent work.[188]

Job creation should be viewed in terms of both quality and quantity and understood as a process that always has gender dimensions. These may correct or deepen inequalities; without a deliberate policy focus, the latter is more likely. Experiences in the region show what happens when a 'race to the bottom' produces more jobs, but under conditions that are not conducive to either gender equality or human development.

Put a legal framework in place for fair employment. The labour market in much of Asia-Pacific is not operating on a level playing field. Basic laws should be adopted and upheld to restrict gender discrimination in hiring, promotion and pay, and to penalize sexual harassment in the workplace.

Support women's work through targeted services and benefits. Safe transportation from home to work, accessible childcare and adequate health care improve women's job prospects. Maternity and paternity benefits acknowledge the importance of reproductive care work and the roles that both men and women have in it.

Extend formal-sector benefits to informal work. Women in the informal sector have few fallback positions; a job loss, cut in income or health crisis can be a devastating blow. The struggle for basic survival also prevents many informal workers from developing the capabilities they need for better employment. Providing health care, maternity/paternity leave, minimum wage guarantees and unemployment insurance to them would ensure a strong social safety net and might encourage movement into better jobs over a long term.

Extend options to acquire job skills and link education to employment. Opportunities to

Job creation should be viewed in terms of both quality and quantity and understood as a process that always has gender dimensions

acquire job skills should be extended to informal-sector workers and women currently outside the labour market. They should be oriented around improving women's labour market participation rate and accessing decent jobs likely to produce upward income mobility.

Strong links between education and employment should be considered in light of the fact that too many educated women in Asia-Pacific are not able to obtain jobs that match their skills. This deprives women of opportunities and is an inefficient use of resources—it is, in effect, a damper on the acquisition of capabilities. It may hinder national or sub-national objectives in achieving a workforce profile consistent with sustained future development. Social conventions around women's employment should be addressed in schools, where they often take root, and in workplaces, where they flourish through skewed hiring and promotion patterns.

Give visibility to unpaid domestic work. This is a first step towards a fair and just distribution of household and reproductive care work between men and women. Time-use surveys can collect data for use by national statistical systems. They can clarify tradeoffs being made in individual households and the larger economy and contribute towards mapping policies to balance paid and unpaid work. Tradeoffs must be looked at through the lens of women's freedom to make choices, given the constraints that may be imposed by limited bargaining power in homes, political forums and the market.

Share domestic work. A more equal distribution of unpaid work at home would earn women leisure and provide them with opportunities to undertake paid work. It would promote balance and emotional health among both women and men. While maternity leave and benefits are important to keep women in the labour force, provision of paternity leave is crucial to recognize and support men's role in childcare. Parental leave can be critical for single-headed households, more so in low-income situations. Sustained media campaigns could foster changing attitudes about sharing care and other unpaid domestic work, including by emphasizing the benefits.

Advocate the value of women's economic role. Public institutions, the media and civil society organizations could highlight the contributions working women make to economies and individual households. Advocacy messages could emphasize that these contributions should be taken seriously and encouraged.

Deepen the Benefits of Education

Extend access to education. Improving educational opportunities for girls needs focused policy attention through prioritizing public expenditure on education. Steps to increase access continue to be needed, especially in South Asia. Higher education should be encouraged in cases where girls start out relatively well but disappear as education progresses. Issues related to the cost of education, physical access and transportation, safety, teacher shortages and attitudes of teachers continue to exist despite improvements. Interventions could be identified in consultation with communities, which can help identify priority needs and constraints. Awards and parental incentives for outstanding girl students and gender-responsive teachers, both male and female, could be considered. Teacher training should be made an essential part of this.

Improve the content and quality of education. High-quality education overcomes gender stereotypes, with positive benefits for parents and children. It makes a contribution to thriving societies and economies, including by opening new employment options for women. Government at national and local levels needs to take the lead in strengthening the content and quality of education, including curriculum reform making it more gender-equal. Civil society organizations can play a role in advocating for high-quality education, revealing gaps, and holding local and national governments and international organizations to their commitments.

Look beyond primary education. Although essential, the completion of five to six years of schooling is far from sufficient for good literacy skills. The economic and social benefits of education may be unattainable with such limited schooling. The increase in the numbers of women in tertiary education across the region is a positive sign. Yet more remains to be done. Labour market policies could be instrumental in providing incentives for women's higher education if it is perceived as instrumental for better economic opportunities. Governments could ensure that higher education policies also receive due attention.

Create incentives for educating girls. Policies, resources and sustained action are visible signs that girls' education has a tangible value. Female stipend programmes in Bangladesh have laid special emphasis on raising female literacy at the secondary levels since 1994. Initially started in targeted areas, the programme has expanded to most parts of the country. It covers monthly tuition fees, stipends, book subsidies and examination fees for female students. There are provisions for discouraging early marriage.[189] Since the health and nutritional status of girls is important for developing cognitive abilities and remaining in school beyond the primary level, food supplements in school and health camps for students represent other important incentives to encourage the poor to send their children, especially girl children, to school.[190] Incentives are especially important for girls from poor families, for whom the direct and indirect costs of schooling can be minimized to enable them to study beyond primary education.

Assess results. The ability to measure learning outcomes can be improved, going beyond the number of students in seats. National outcome measures are an important indicator, but results should also be disaggregated by region, gender, ethnic group and socio-economic status to locate specific areas of weaknesses and address them.

Invest in Women's Health

Prioritize public investments in health. Ill health is directly related to workdays lost, absenteeism and loss of earnings, apart from being a financial drain through treatment costs. Greater public allocations for health care should include increased public expenditure on sexual and reproductive health, in line with women's needs. Special schemes, such as direct nutrition supplements and immunization for pregnant and nursing women and children under 36 months, would help improve gender equality in health among the poor. Provision of essential health services should be encouraged through female-friendly health facilities. Men and women should be counseled about the importance of supporting and seeking health care. Universal social health insurance would represent another positive step.

Value the girl child's birth. Strict actions against sex-selective abortions are required to balance the sex ratio at birth in many countries in the region, specifically those with alarmingly high male-over-female ratios at birth, such as China and India.[191] Even if laws exist against such abortions, their effective implementation remains a challenge. Health professionals, media and civil society have to act as watchdogs and influencers of attitudes. Often preference for sons comes from within the family, making awareness programmes critical for attitudinal changes. Affirmative actions linked with incentives for girl children can also help improve the balance between male and female children at birth.

Labour market policies could be instrumental in providing incentives for women's higher education if perceived as instrumental for better economic opportunities

Invest in girls' health. Intra-household biases against females in health expenditure, care and food lead to higher malnutrition and health risks for women and girls. Attitudinal changes that recognize females as equally valuable members of the household, including in terms of their economic contributions, are essential. Monitoring by governments in areas such as the incidence of domestic violence, malnutrition among boys and girls, and the participation of women in reproductive health decisions would help strengthen corrective actions towards female health. Private-sector health services could also be made more accountable. To challenge dominant norms on masculinity that harm the health of women and men alike, NGOs could campaign for new attitudes among men and boys in households and communities, as well as among community and religious leaders.

Protect women against vulnerabilities to HIV/AIDS. Increasing number of women are HIV/AIDS positive in Asia-Pacific, and their vulnerability mainly stems from the severe gender inequality prevalent in the region. Governments and donors must pay more attention to the health needs of HIV-vulnerable women as well as men, and policies and laws should be aimed at protecting them. There should be no discrimination of job opportunities on the grounds of HIV/AIDS. Equal inheritance and property rights can critically improve women's ability to help prevent and cope with the impact of HIV/AIDS[192] especially when coupled with appropriate social security schemes.

Integrate gender and health with economic interventions targeted at women and sexual/gender minorities. Health insurance, gender and health awareness, and awareness of health entitlements can be added to economic programmes targeted at women, as attempted by BRAC in South Asia. Great potential for doing this exists, given the scale of women's microfinance groups in the region.

Make Mobility Safe

Acknowlege the contributions women make and the threats they face. Women migrants have been overlooked in much official discourse, in both sending and receiving countries. State institutions should have a role in determining the patterns and outcomes of international female migration, keeping in mind the benefits for women, economies and societies when this is a safe process that allows women opportunities to fully use existing and potential capabilities.

Ease the legal barriers constraining women's migration. Sex-specific bans and discriminatory restrictions on the basis of women's age, marital status, pregnancy or maternity status still exist in some countries and should be repealed, along with requirements for permission to travel from a spouse or male guardian. Many laws and policies implicitly assume a male-breadwinner model of migration and overlook independent access and protection for women. Some laws that seem designed to protect women – such as those mandating official emigration clearance for unskilled workers – can create another hindrance and encourage migration through informal and unsafe channels that can put them at even greater risk of exploitation and vulnerability. They need to be adjusted based on women's articulation of their own needs.

Protect the basic rights of all migrants. Within countries, many citizenship rights are residence-based, requiring some paper proof of local residence. This affects not only political rights, such as the ability to vote, but also socio-economic rights, such as labour laws and unionization. Short-term and seasonal internal migrants end up losing these rights, as do cross-border migrants. These problems are particularly acute for women migrants, who require greater support in terms of nutrition and reproductive health services. States should also ensure that laws and labour codes provide the same rights to

Equal inheritance and property rights can critically improve women's ability to help prevent and cope with the impact of HIV/AIDS especially when coupled with appropriate social security schemes

women migrant workers as to all other workers, including the right to organize to defend and further their professional interests and collective bargaining.[193] The legal validity of contracts for women migrants should be assured. Special attention should be granted to occupations where shortfalls in rights are particularly prominent, including domestic labour and sex work. Laws should not create barriers for migrants to accessing health and HIV related services. Discriminatory and stigmatizing systems, policies and practices that violate migrants' rights, such as mandatory HIV testing as a precondition for employment and deportation on the basis of HIV status, should be eliminated. Strengthening the rights and conditions under which women move is essential to their health and wellbeing and critical for job opportunities.

Foster cross-border cooperation. Bilateral agreements between governments of sending and receiving countries should recognize the rights of female migrants and create legal frameworks to protect them. These should focus on safety. The Royal Thai Government and the Government of Lao People's Democratic Republic, for example, have a memorandum of understanding on employment cooperation that sets the legal framework for procedures in labour recruitment and employment between the two countries as well as steps to prevent illegal migration and illegal recruitment/employment networks.[194]

Broaden options for information and support. Both governmental and non-governmental channels can provide free or affordable gender and rights-based pre-departure and returning information and training programmes. These can increase awareness of legal rights and entitlements, job opportunities, the nature of contracts, problems that may arise in the journey or the destination, health related issues including HIV awareness, possibilities for protection at each stage of the migration process and

agencies that provide help. Commercial recruitment agencies should be regulated in terms of their performance in meeting women's needs and protecting their rights. However, they should not be the only source of information and services related to migration; government agencies and NGOs should also play leading roles.

Make remittances easier and safer for women migrants. Women migrants tend to use informal channels for remittances because of inadequate knowledge or lack of public access. Special measures should be taken to provide assistance to women in accessing formal financial institutions and safe money transfer options, at reasonable costs. Women should be encouraged to participate in saving schemes as well as safe and productive investment opportunities.

Make policies, laws and services sensitive to the needs of trafficked women and ensure that their application does not re-victimise them. The complexities of trafficking and the economic forces driving women to migrate need to be borne in mind when designing policies, laws and services to respond. In particular, women should be treated as people with needs, difficulties and aspirations, not as helpless objects. Moralistic judgments and patriarchal attitudes have often crept into trafficking interventions. These should not be imposed upon women, their activities or their future movement.

Improve the legal, social and economic conditions for returning women migrants. Women who wish to return to their countries or places of origin should be able to do so without threat of coercion, abuse or social sanction. Special socio-economic, psychological and legal services can ease women's reintegration. Public advocacy can seek to diminish stereotypes about women's 'morality' in venturing to new places, and encourage people to value women's attempts to seek opportunities to better their lives.

Bilateral agreements between governments of sending and receiving countries should recognize the rights of female migrants and create legal frameworks to protect them

Strengthen urban management policies and programmes. For internal migrants, local governments should strengthen urban management policies and programmes to respond to their specific needs for adequate settlement, both temporary and long-term, and provide access to urban infrastructure and social services such as health and education. Rights as citizens should be recognized, including through the provision of equal access to services and the easing of restrictive and exclusionary residence policies.

Development for All

Asia-Pacific is a fast growing and dynamic region, but women are not benefiting proportionately. Gaps in women's capabilities and economic opportunities, and thus their well-being, have been deep and persistent in much of Asia and the Pacific. Growing capabilities are not translating into equivalent opportunities. Attitudes about who should control resources have continued to relegate women to unpaid work, poor-quality jobs and inferior assets—when they can even obtain them. But if they do have assets and jobs, they may still have little control over them, whether in deciding how to use land or voicing concerns about labour conditions through collective bargaining.

Women and girls face a number of barriers to economic power—visible and less visible—due to continuing barriers to market access. These are synergistically interconnected with gaps in political voice and legal rights, as also with the subtler barriers in attitudes towards women. The latter operate at sites closest to women and girls—the family and community. Attitudes also influence how institutions function. Primary responsibility for unpaid care work, unfair labour regulations, restrictions on labour mobility, corruption that affects women much more than men, and gaps in education and access to justice all result in denying women equal economic opportunities.

This exclusionary tendency coexists with visible and growing proof of the significance of women's economic contributions. Attitudes are slowly changing, in part because rising levels of education and economic liberalization are transforming perceptions about what women can do. Across the region, the dynamo of women's labour has allowed industries to grow and compete in the global marketplace. It is fueling the growth of the small-business sector even as it is maintaining agricultural productivity.

Recognizing these contributions means policy makers can begin to systematically build on them. It is also important to leverage synergies between the interconnected factors that contribute to disadvantages based on gender. Fair development provides room for all human potentials to emerge, regardless of sex or gender. Despite disparities in the region, mounting evidence suggests the time to engender development has come.

Attitudes about who should control resources have continued to relegate women to unpaid work, poor-quality jobs and inferior assets

BUILDING ECONOMIC POWER: TOWARDS A BETTER BALANCE

Inequality in economic power between men and women in Asia and the Pacific thrives on discriminatory inheritance laws, inequalities in job opportunities, unequal pay, gender stereotypes in education, severely inadequate investments in health and a lack of policies for safe migration. Attitudes about women's roles perpetuate the gaps.

A framework for action includes fixing institutions, changing attitudes and undertaking assessments. It should build on synergistic links with political voice and legal rights, and root priorities in local circumstances. Important components include steps to:

Remove barriers to assets. Eliminate discriminatory laws and close legal gaps, particularly those relating to inheritance and marriage ‣ Review asset-related policies for gender dimensions ‣ Increase women's access to the means to acquire and manage assets ‣ Provide training and skills development for women ‣ Ensure women's meaningful participation in forums that make decisions about assets.

Expand paid employment. Orient economic policies around the provision of 'decent work' ‣ Put a legal framework in place for fair employment to restrict gender discrimination in hiring, promotion and pay, and to penalize sexual harassment in the workplace ‣ Support women's work through targeted services and benefits ‣ Extend formal-sector benefits to informal work ‣ Provide options to acquire job skills to informal workers and women currently outside the labour market, and link education to employment ‣ Give visibility to unpaid domestic work ‣ Promote the more equal distribution of household work between men and women ‣ Advocate the value of women's economic role through the media and civil society organizations.

Deepen the benefits of education. Extend access to education and improve educational opportunities for girls by prioritizing public expenditure on education ‣ Improve the content and quality of education, including by removing gender biases from curricula ‣ Look beyond primary education for better economic opportunities ‣ Create incentives for educating girls, especially those from poor families ‣ Assess results to locate specific areas of weaknesses and address them.

Invest in women's health. Prioritize public investments in health, including increased public expenditure on sexual and reproductive health, in line with women's needs ‣ Balance skewed sex ratios through measures to protect the birth, health and survival of girls ‣ Recognize and reduce women's vulnerabilities to HIV/AIDS ‣ Integrate health and economic interventions targeted at women and sexual/gender minorities.

Make mobility safe. Acknowledge the contributions women migrants make and the threats they face ‣ Ease the legal barriers constraining women's migration to discourage the use of informal and unsafe channels ‣ Protect the basic rights of all migrants, including through access to health and HIV-related services ‣ Foster cross-border cooperation between governments of sending and receiving countries ‣ Broaden options for information and support through governmental and non-governmental channels ‣ Make remittances easier and safer ‣ Create policies, laws and services sensitive to the needs of trafficked women, and ensure their application does not result in further victimization ‣ Improve the legal, social and economic conditions for returning women migrants ‣ Strengthen urban management policies and programmes for responding to specific needs of internal migrants.

3

Promoting Political Voice

Leader in war, organizer in peace

Nafanua, circa 16th Century

Stories of women in positions of power are part of traditional history and folklore in many parts of the Pacific. In the Samoan tradition dating back to the 1500s, Nafanua is a warrior priestess acclaimed for her success in war and her skill as a leader in times of peace. An organizer of the chiefly system, she is credited with initiating the inaugural gathering of people with the highest titles in the land, which contributed to unifying Samoa. Nafanua could be the first effective tafa'ifa—a holder of the four chiefly titles for the four extended families of Samoa. Every Samoan can trace his or her lineage to one of these four titles. Under Nafanua, the tafa'ifa honor was formally conferred on Salamsina, also a woman.

There are many stories about Nafanua that extol women's capabilities. She inspired a popular Samoan proverb used every time women outperform men:

> 'E au le ina'ilau a tamaitai ae le au le inailau a ali'i.'
> It means 'women will achieve while men won't.'

The saying comes from a competition Nafanua held where teams of men and women used lava rock to thatch parts of her residence. The competition ended with the women's team completing its side. The men's team did not.

Adapted from a contribution for the APHDR by Noumea Simi.

Promoting Political Voice

Chapter **3**

'We must ask whether the majority of women citizens of Indonesia are truly regarded as citizens or stakeholders in this nation.... Democracy without the involvement of women is not democracy.'[1]

– Professor Chusnul Mar'iyah, University of Indonesia and
member of the Indonesian Election Commission

Political decision-making touches all areas of human development and many aspects of people's daily lives. Access to the political arena is essential for men and women to articulate and shape solutions that unleash progress for themselves and society at large.

Gender equality in political participation is socially just and basic to the notion of democracy. A political system—elected offices, but also other positions that influence public decisions—where half the population cannot participate, defies the meaning of the term. Broad-based participation also has a clear practical dimension—and a development rationale. It supports efficiency: More sources of information and voice make public policies more informed and responsive to diverse realities on the ground. That women are seriously underrepresented in elected offices is now in focus. Assessment of women's low share in other executive positions of government has received much less attention, even though that is where political agendas are operationalized.

Women, as a group, have different experiences than men. While some men may support women's issues in the halls of power, a more typical pattern is that without women expressing their own perspectives, these mostly go unnoticed. This hinders development through the failure to build on all available capabilities and pursue all potential opportunities. Social stability and harmony are further benefits when most people feel they have a voice and a stake in development.

In Asia and the Pacific, women have demonstrated the political contributions they can make. They have been vibrant voices in formal political institutions such as legislatures and local governments, and in civil society activism. They have led countries, political parties and ministries. They have been part of the impetus behind political crisis and conflict, as well as processes to forge peace and social transformation. Women scholars have conducted cutting-edge research into critical public policy questions; this is changing the way politicians and governments approach basic tasks such as budgeting.

Progress has been slow even since the commitments to take deliberate actions to increase women's participation were made by most governments at the 1995 Fourth World Conference on Women in Beijing. At that time global parliamentary representation hovered around 11 per cent; it had increased to just over 18 per cent in 2009.[2]

Despite women's desire and proven abilities to fully participate in political forums, and despite rapid gains in basic human development parameters across Asia-Pacific, the region is behind most of the rest of the world in women's political equality

Gender equality in political participation is socially just and basic to the notion of democracy

(Figure 3.1). When both houses are considered, Asia-Pacific has the lowest percentages of women in national legislatures of any region outside the Arab states.[3] Compared to the global average of 18.4 per cent, women in Asia occupy 18.2 per cent of legislative seats and in the Pacific only 15.2 per cent. The Pacific sub-region alone has four of the six countries in the world that have no women legislators at all.[4]

These shortfalls occur across the region's diverse political systems and ideologies. A quarter of the countries have presidential governments, and most have embraced parliamentary democracies. The rest are constitutional monarchies or one-party states.[5] Still, the results for women are mostly the same: low levels of participation, although political systems with constitutional or electoral quotas do slightly better.

Existing levels of development do not correspond closely with women's political equality. Some of the most developed countries lag far behind—women in the Republic of Korea have attained less than 14 per cent of legislative seats, and women in Japan occupy less than 10 per cent of seats in their lower house.[6] This is not to suggest that having fewer women in politics is somehow good for development. Globally, the most developed countries rank the highest in women's political participation, although only the Nordic states can claim to be close to roughly equal numbers of women and men.[7]

A few Asia-Pacific countries serve as models for what is possible within the region, even with the severe disruptions of conflict and the drain of high levels of poverty. In part because of women activists, Nepal ended up with women in about 33 per cent of its Constituent Assembly seats. In Timor-Leste, women activists and freedom fighters put pressure on the constitutional drafting process after independence to guarantee women's political participation, which helped women capture 29.2 per cent of parliamentary seats. In its 2009 elections, Afghanistan had 342 female candidates at the provincial level and two women running for President.[8] Its quota system guarantees women at least 27 per cent of seats in its lower house of the national legislature.[9]

In the evolution and maturing of its political systems, and in its pursuit of human development, the Asia-Pacific region has come a long way in recent decades. Could it go further with women more equally on board?

Inequality Excludes Women from Public Life

'Fiji's glass ceiling is tough, because our community is driven by both ethnicity and patriarchy. I am a Muslim, Indo-Fijian woman, and the combination of my race, religion and gender is very hard for many people to stomach (...) I have been called

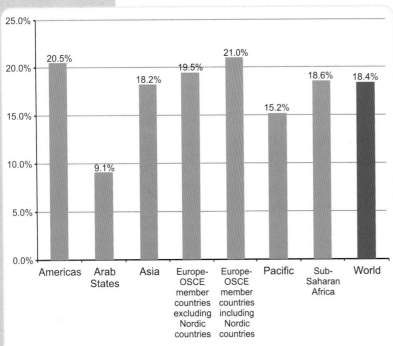

Figure 3.1: Asia and the Pacific Rank Second Worst in the World when it Comes to Women's Representation in Parliament

Per cent of Women Parliamentarians, By Region

Source: IPU 2009.

hostile, spiteful, manipulative, devious, cunning and power-hungry. It is not surprising that many women in Fiji decide that it is too difficult to continue to forge change. For all the rewards attached to my position as an Indo-Fijian female High Court judge, there are an equivalent number of sanctions.[10]

– Justice Nazhat Shameem,
former Judge of the High Court of Fiji

Social, political, economic and legal barriers, in a few cases, hinder women's participation in formal and informal politics, as well as in higher levels of government. These are expressed in different ways in the private and public spheres. Husbands and families convey the message that women cannot be leaders and should stay home. Political parties avoid female candidates because they may come with fewer campaign resources and links to influential constituencies. Political ideologies also define openness to women; some emphasize that individuals need to carve out their own opportunities, others that people who start behind deserve extra support. In some cases, religion is used to justify gender-based restrictions.

Gender Norms Limit Participation

Technically, laws and institutions guide the mechanics of governance and political participation. These may seem gender-neutral, such as when anyone older than 21, man or woman, can legally run for office or seek other executive positions. In reality, they intersect with ideas about the gender roles of women and men that influence their ability to take part in politics. Leadership, for example, is still considered a mostly male skill and prerogative across Asia-Pacific. And because of patterns of gender discrimination, women have less access to education, health care, wealth, mobility and other forms of social capital that allow people to stake a claim in the wider world. People of diverse gender identities have also struggled; although, like women, they are starting to achieve gains in the region (Box 3.1).

Ideas about leadership are set in the home, where men are commonly considered the household head, and then reinforced in the world, where men dominate positions of power. Even when the home is considered a realm in which women take responsibility for the everyday decisions of household management, the administration of the rest of society is left to men. Expectations that women will perform most of the household duties are often cited as well for why more women do not have the time or skills to become involved in public life.

In the Pacific, which has one of the lowest percentages of women in national politics in the world,[11] customary notions about

Social, political, economic and legal barriers, hinder women's participation in formal and informal politics

---

BOX 3.1

DIFFERENT BUT EQUAL: LGBT RIGHTS AND NEPAL'S BLUE DIAMOND SOCIETY

The Blue Diamond Society in Nepal was founded in 2002 as an organization working for the rights of sexual and gender minorities. In the April 2008 elections, founder Sunil Pant gained a parliamentary seat under the Communist Party.

Two developments have fostered the movement for greater rights in Nepal. The first was the significant change in the attitudes of the Maoists towards sexual and gender minorities, such that all three parties vying for elections included lesbian, gay, bisexual and transgender (LGBT) rights in their election manifestos. But the real breakthrough came when Nepal's Supreme Court declared that sexual minorities are 'natural persons' deserving protection against discrimination. The Blue Diamond Society and three other groups had previously brought a lawsuit before the court, challenging a law against 'unnatural' sex, and demanding equal rights and an end to discrimination for LGBT people.

Since the ruling, LGBTs in Nepal have found recognition in many ways. Several organizations, including a private bank, the Education Ministry and the Home Ministry, have added a box for the 'third gender' in their forms. The Home Ministry is also working on a policy that will soon be circulated in the districts to give citizenship identity papers to third genders all over Nepal.

Pant maintains that much remains to be done. He estimates that it will take at least five more years to have effective policies, laws and a Constitution that respects the rights of LGBTs in Nepal, and another 20 years to change the real situation on the ground. But, as is the case with women, the opportunities of participation in governance structures are already apparent.

Sources: Ireland 2008; Larssen 2008; Torres 2009.

women's 'true' position in society may be among the biggest impediments to their political participation. Indigenous Fijian women, for example, are still regarded as the property of their fathers, then husbands.[12] Men continue to construct themselves as fighters and warriors,[13] while women maintain the home and bear many children. Pre-colonial traditions were re-shaped by Christianity, where '[Christian] churches tend to keep women "in their place"'.[14] Women today are the mainstay of the extremely powerful Methodist church in Fiji, for example, but never its local or national leaders.

In Timor-Leste, despite remarkable progress in bringing more women into the national legislature, longstanding conventions about leadership still rule at the local level, where men make the major decisions for their communities. Superstitions about avoiding the wrath of the ancestors by having the 'right' leader (i.e. a man) mean that women generally cannot become traditional leaders, even if they are from otherwise matrilineal clans. Some serve in village councils, but never in senior positions. At meetings, they sit on the sidelines or behind male leaders, and are more likely to be found serving food than participating in discussions.[15]

Indonesia provides an example of how gender norms can be married to political motivations. As part of the project of nation building, Suharto's New Order policies[16] sought to homogenize the diversity of indigenous gender roles throughout the archipelago into nationally promoted, ideal male and female roles, in which women were supposed to be traditional and subordinate to men.[17] The regime enshrined the patriarchal ideology of *Bapakism*—literally, rule by the father. When Megawati Sukarnoputri, the country's first female President (2001-2004), was nominated for Vice-President in 1999, a major objection was that a woman could not, by definition, lead.[18]

Conservative gender norms can clash directly with political conventions. Women throughout Asia-Pacific are more likely than men to live in a constituency area determined by marriage, not birth, a possible disadvantage in building political networks and voter support. In Afghanistan, routine tasks such as delivering speeches, traveling through the countryside and distributing campaign flyers with photos of themselves can put women at risk of violence and backlash.[19] The Afghan Election Commission has debated whether Islamic principles support women's participation and mobility in electoral processes. It concluded that they do, and that men should be supportive of women's political activities.[20]

For many women, gender norms can be compounded by barriers linked to class or, in South Asia, caste and some tribal communities. Being poor and marginalized means not only having more limited resources to run for office, but also being treated as less deserving of a political voice. Due to a reservation system, a record number of women now serve as elected representatives in India's *panchayat* (local government) system, for example. But members are not paid, leaving the system open to corruption and domination by upper-class people who can afford to work for free. This can undercut the ability of poorer women to act effectively for their community or women at large.[21]

One indication of how women in Asia-Pacific are viewed in terms of political leadership comes from the distribution of political appointments to ministerial positions. The region echoes a global pattern in which women are slotted into 'feminine' health and family portfolios rather than 'masculine' finance and defence briefs. But it also has some of the lowest percentages of women ministers across all portfolios. In infrastructure, women in the region hold a mere 1.5 per cent of posts, compared to 10 per cent in Africa and almost 21 per cent in

The region echoes a global pattern in which women are slotted into 'feminine' health and family portfolios rather than 'masculine' finance and defence briefs

Latin America and the Caribbean. Women hold about 13 per cent of social and cultural posts, about half the number in the next-lowest region, Africa.[22]

Women are also poorly represented in other critical decision-making positions that are central to translating laws and policies into practice. Some progress has been made, but no country in Asia and the Pacific has achieved parity between women and men in positions such as ambassadors, judges and heads of universities;[23] most are far behind. The Philippines has appointed women to 31 per cent of ambassadorial posts, but Nepal has no women ambassadors, for example. In Mongolia, the percentage of women judges has topped 41 per cent; Pakistan so far has only reached 2.8 per cent. University leadership reflects similar shortfalls.

Men Set the Political Terms

In politics, men set the norms and women are expected to live up to them. At times, norms are framed as standards of competence. Former Philippines President Ferdinand Marcos once stated, 'The Filipino woman should be intelligent but demure. She can run her husband, but she should run him through the bedroom'.[24] Ideas such as this are unjust, and shut out the rich possibilities for public service that come from diverse experiences and ways of reasoning. Also overlooked is the question of whether or not current norms are desirable. Across Asia and the Pacific, political practices in systems dominated by men continue to emphasize competition over cooperation, violence over negotiation, and depersonalization over empathy.[25] Some systems are notable for corruption, personality politics, clientelism, and a preference for short-term profits over long term social investments.

Current male norms in politics may not even be typical of most men or good for societies as a whole, but once they become entrenched, they benefit men who endorse them and have an interest in maintaining them. They also undercut the willingness of women or men from excluded groups to enter politics, as well as their effectiveness once they get there. Discrimination crops up in many places: The structure of political parties, access to campaign financing, parliamentary responses, and old-boy political networks. In many Asia-Pacific countries, the path to politics still lies through the male-dominated military or the legal profession.[26]

Across Asia-Pacific, even educated women who have functioned well in other spheres of life can have the perception that politics is a dirty, difficult game that contributes little and extracts a personal cost, particularly for those who do not enter it with substantive resources and connections. Many women who have been successful in politics in the region are well-to-do, or shielded by family ties and dynastic politics. At the opposite extreme, women politicians—particularly those with the extra vulnerabilities of poverty or association with marginalized groups—have been killed, raped or faced physical threats for challenging the status quo.

In one Indian state, male *panchayat* members have spread stories that women members were sexually promiscuous, harassed them with obscene phone calls and made sexual innuendoes during meetings. Men have also prevented money from being allocated to women's wards in an attempt to make them unpopular for re-election.[27] In Bangladesh, women in local governments, despite legal definitions of their duties, have in practice been prevented from four basic tasks: Registering births and deaths, examining building designs, assisting in census and demographic surveys, and monitoring law and order. Women also have limited access to office space, transport or other facilities (Box 3.2).[28]

In politics, men set the norms and women are expected to live up to them

WOMEN FACE THREATS TO LIFE AND LIBERTY

Women *panchayat* members in India have faced some huge obstacles to participation—some of which have resulted in tragedy. Forty-eight-year-old Dhoolla Ratnam was burnt to death along with her grandson in the village of Srungavruksham in Andhra Pradesh in 2007. She had dared contest the elections against the upper caste Kapu community, whose members distributed saris, and gold and silver idols to the villagers in order to win their votes.

One of Dhoolla's first assignments, after winning, was to fight corruption by making sure that the fair price dealer in her village did not divert grain rations meant for the poor to the open market. The Kapus retaliated by burning her paddy fields. When this threat failed to deter her, she was killed. R. Sandhu, the Additional Secretary, Ministry of Panchayati Raj, says: 'Initially, many of these women receive support from their family members. But once they get deeply involved in panchayat-related work and executing projects, their family members complain that they are spending too much time away from home.'

Illiteracy remains another major problem. Munna Bai, a village council leader in Raisa district, found herself jailed on charges of embezzling US $100 from the panchayat family welfare fund. She claims she does not know why she has been arrested, as she only put her thumb impression on documents prepared by a block-level officer.

Source: Sehgal 2008.

Discriminatory assumptions about women's rights and ability to compete lead parties to bypass them as candidates

Discriminatory assumptions about women's rights and ability to compete lead parties to bypass them as candidates, even as they use them as lower-level campaign workers and vote-getters to attract women constituents. Women who do get elected may find their concerns overlooked, trivialized or denied. If they fail to be as vocal and expressive as men while in chambers, they can be unfairly rated as 'weak' and ineffectual leaders.[29] One study of the New Zealand Parliament found that women made fewer personal attacks during debates than male colleagues, and were more often the subject of harassing remarks. But they also became more aggressive over time in an effort to adapt.[30]

While some female political leaders have been depicted as strong and authoritative, inordinate attention can still go towards their maternal and familial roles. Past news reports on former President Corazon Aquino of the Philippines and former President Chandrika Kumaratunga of Sri Lanka tended to focus on their parental and marital status, despite their contributions as public officials. Because they were both widows of previous politicians, there was a preoccupation with the theme of bereavement. Women politicians in general face undue focus on their physical appearances, clothes and hairstyles, while their political accomplishments are downplayed.[31]

In 2008, as Rustriningsih campaigned to become Vice-Governor of Central Java, one of the most important parts of Indonesia, she traveled constantly. This was not in keeping with the conventional role of an Indonesian wife and mother (she is both). The opposition campaign emphasized her absence from home and alleged neglect of family duties. Respectable Indonesian women, especially married women, do not work in situations where they must be out at night or working irregular hours in teams of men—which are typical of the working life of female politicians and lawmakers. Rustriningsih successfully fought these stereotypes and won the elections, demonstrating to other women that a viable political career is possible for them too.[32]

Male-dominated political systems have been slow to recognize that women have extra responsibilities for household work and care of children. These do not fit easily with the demands of public service, in the absence of work-sharing at home. But rarely have even rudimentary forms of support been offered, such as childcare facilities in parliamentary or party offices.

Laws and Customs Hinder Women's Presence

'It is good to swim in the waters of tradition but to sink in them is suicide.'[33]

– Mahatma Gandhi

In a general way, legal systems in Asia and the Pacific support women's political participation. A number of Asia-Pacific

THE EXPERIENCE OF THE CHINESE GOVERNMENT ON PROMOTING GENDER EQUALITY

H.E. Dr. Baige Zhao

Since the founding of the People's Republic of China in 1949, equality between men and women has become the government's basic principle in handling gender relations. The Constitution (1954) states 'Women in the People's Republic of China enjoy equal rights with men in all spheres of life, in political, economic, cultural, social and family life'. In 1995, this basic principle gained greater awareness, and was integrated with 'gender' as a concept. Promoting gender equality began to be seen as an essential factor to achieve social development and penetrates all facets of economic and social life. There are three main aspects of the Chinese Government's experience on promoting gender equality:

1. At the national institutional level, a comprehensive public system has come into being to protect the rights and interests of women and promote equality between men and women. Based on the Constitution, the system takes the Law on the Protection of Women's Rights and Interests as its main body, and also encompasses various specific state laws and regulations, local regulations and administrative regulations enacted by various Government departments. In order to ensure women's rights and their social participation, a range of policies and measures have been improved in areas of law, politics, economy, employment, education, resources allocation, right protection, marriage, family and health, striving for eliminating all forms of discrimination against women.
2. At the civil and social level, three types of non-governmental organizations are very active in the field of gender equality. First, the international organizations (such as United Nations agencies, the Ford Foundation, etc.) have entered the field of women and social development in China. In cooperation with the Government and civil societies, the international organizations initiate projects and carry out ongoing cooperation to promote gender equality. Second, Women's Federations at various levels, Population and Family Planning Associations, Chinese Communist Youth League and other social groups serve as a link bridge between the government and public. Third, a variety of non-governmental organizations with different focuses (such as focus on research, service, recreation and other comprehensive interests) are developing rapidly and are playing an important role in social management and services provision.
3. Strategic and special actions have also been taken. In order to better target the goal of improving girls' living environment and promoting gender equality, specific actions have been taken to punish the behavior jeopardizing women's rights and interests. At the public policy level, the central and local Governments have issued a series of specialized public policies since 1986. Those policies strictly prohibit the abuse of the artificial insemination technology, sex identification of foetus for non-medical purpose and termination of pregnancies for sex selection. The drugs of pregnancy termination and of accelerating ovulation are listed as prescription drugs. The Government also resolutely penalizes criminal acts such as drowning, discarding and abusing baby girls and trafficking in women and children. Other illegal acts also include discrimination against and abuse to women giving birth to female babies. Those efforts are made to protect women's right to life and survival. As regards to specific action, the 'Care for Girls' initiative since 2003 has been tackling the issue of imbalanced sex ratio at birth. It is a special national action taken by the Government that includes cash incentives and campaigns in the countryside to address the challenges for girls' survival. Its mission is to take the all-round human development as the core. Its goal is to ensure women and girls' rights to survival, to development, to protection by law, and to participation, and other basic rights and interests. Through the establishment of behavioral constraints mechanism, interest-oriented mechanism and institutional innovation mechanism, we improve girls' living environment, promote the social gender equality, build a harmonious society and provide a favorable population environment for the coordinated and sustainable development of China's society and economy.

The laws, policies and actions mentioned above have played an active role in improving women's living and development environment as well as promoting gender equality in Chinese society.

Dr. Baige Zhao is Vice-Minister of the National Population and Family Planning Commission (NPFPC), Chairperson of the International Council on Management of Population Programmes (ICOMP) and board member of the Chinese People's Institute of Foreign Affairs. She is currently in charge of the administration, international cooperation, information, education and communication in population and family planning. She received her PhD from the University of Cambridge in 1988.

constitutions make a commitment to ending sex-based discrimination or upholding gender equality, with some specifically stipulating affirmative-action quotas to assist women in obtaining political offices. Electoral laws in some countries contain similar provisions. Every woman in the region can now vote, except for those in Brunei Darussalam, where men cannot vote either.[34] In 2008, Maldives finally amended a constitutional provision that used to ban women from serving as President and Vice-President.[35]

But for the most part, these legal promises have not been enough to counter strong gender biases in society and political systems. Most constitutions are vague in defining what sex discrimination and gender equality mean; some bar the passage of legislation that would allow quota systems. Quotas for underrepresented groups are not necessarily backed by sanctions and capacity development, meaning they can easily go ignored. Women continue to face disadvantages from the lack of laws or regulations constraining campaign financing, to which they have less access than men, and the impunity for violence and corruption that characterizes elections in some countries.

The Pacific countries and territories face particular conflicts between customary practices protected under the law and calls for women's equal participation. In Fiji, Republic of Marshall Islands, Samoa, Solomon Islands and Tonga, women do not have equal access to the customary title, chiefly or noble systems, all entry points for eligibility for political representation.[36] The Bill of Rights in the Samoan Constitution specifically prohibits discrimination on the basis of sex[37] and allows for affirmative action, but people who are not members of the traditional *matai* (chiefs) system cannot stand as candidates for the legislature. Because women only hold one out of every 19 chiefly titles,[38] only about eight per cent of parliamentarians are female.[39] Another

challenge comes from the deeply rooted concept of *fa'aaloalo* (respect), which can encourage women to pass titles to male siblings or family members.

Real Participation Means an Equal Say

While sincere efforts to improve women's political participation have occurred in Asia and the Pacific, there have also been activities that suggest tokenism or a superficial endorsement. In Timor-Leste, a decision was made not to employ a quota system for the 2001 elections, since this was viewed as anti-democratic and culturally incompatible. Instead, incentives were offered to nominate women candidates, such as extra media time. A woman headed the Socialist Party, but after her party won only one seat she was removed and the seat given to the next person on the list, a man. While women did remarkably well in the election, garnering just over 25 per cent of the seats, the second-largest party fielded no women candidates at all.[40]

In India, the leading Congress Party has put forward more women candidates than the rival Bharatiya Janata Party. Both parties have female leaders and platforms that make commitments to gender equality. But often women are put into constituencies where they are less likely to succeed[41]— a common practice for parties that want to appear to embrace gender equality without actually having to disrupt the status quo.

Some single-party states have relatively high averages of women parliamentarians: 25.8 per cent in Viet Nam, 21.3 per cent in China and 25.2 per cent in Lao People's Democratic Republic.[42] These achievements are important to recognize, but may be tempered by questions about the extent of voice and quality of participation. Participatory and gender-friendly governance systems, however they are configured, go beyond representation to ensure that women actually have an equal say in shaping policy agendas.

Expanding Women's Voice

In the general transition to greater democracy in Asia-Pacific today, political systems are being buffeted by multiple forces, among them globalization, conflict, rapid economic growth, exposure to new technology and ideas, and the newfound assertiveness of marginalized groups. All these shifts open opportunities for adapting political agendas, including to expand women's participation.[43]

Increasing women's political voice never happens through a single step. It may require a combination of elements such as new laws, voter education campaigns and revised regulation on campaign financing. A handful of common entry points are explored here, mostly applied to the legislative branch since that has received the most consistent attention. They can, as appropriate, be extended to all other aspects of governance. Especially important are the spectrum of higher executive positions that shape the design and operationalization of public policies and programmes, influence social services, including the police and judiciary—all critical for achieving development goals.

Quotas: Boosting the Numbers

'When one applies the principle of democracy to a society characterized by tremendous inequalities, such special protections are only spearheads to pierce through the barriers of inequality. An unattainable goal is as meaningless as a right that cannot be exercised. Equality of opportunities cannot be achieved in the face of tremendous disabilities and obstacles which the social system imposes on all those sections whom traditional India treated as second—or even third-class citizens. Our investigations have proved that the application of the theoretical principle of equality in the context of unequal situations only intensifies inequalities, because equality in such situations merely means privileges for those who have them already and not for those who need them.'[44]

– From a 'Note of Dissent' published after the 1974 meeting of the Committee on the Status of Women in India

Quotas for political participation invite direct attention to the under-representation of particular population groups. They aim to provide a quick fix to counter historical disadvantages, raising numbers in a relatively short time. Experiences globally and within Asia-Pacific suggest that they work best when they are effectively designed and enforced, connected to a meaningful definition of participation, and accompanied by steps to generate political and public support.

An estimated 40 per cent of countries globally have adopted quotas for women in national legislatures, achieving an average participation rate of 22 per cent. In those countries without quotas, the average drops to 14 per cent.[45] Of the 22 countries where women constitute more than 30 per cent of the national assembly, 18 have some form of quota.[46] Quotas at the sub-national level or political party quotas for electoral candidates currently raise the number of countries with quotas to 111.[47]

Only about a third of Asia-Pacific countries have some kind of gender quota system in place for political participation.[48] In countries without quotas, women's participation rate in elected offices is around 14 per cent, rising to 20.4 per cent in countries that have them.[49] Quotas should be considered for elected offices, as well as for the civil service, judiciary and other critical public leadership positions where the gender gap is wide and even growing. The Magna Carta for Women of the Philippines, which was recently signed into law,[50] has re-emphasised this. It calls for a 50-50 gender balance in Government positions to be achieved within the next five years.

Only about a third of Asia–Pacific countries have some kind of gender quota system in place for political participation

GENDER QUOTAS DELIVER RESULTS IN AFGHANISTAN

The Afghan Constitution of 2004 stipulates a quota for each of the two main chambers of its national Parliament. There is also a quota for women to occupy at least 25 per cent of provincial council seats under Afghan electoral law.

The lower house of Parliament, the Wolesi Jirga, consists of 220 to 250 parliamentarians, which is proportional to the population of each of the nation's 34 provinces. The quota provision states that an average of at least two female candidates from each province should become members of the Wolesi Jirga. This guarantees women at least 27 per cent of parliament seats. In case there are not enough women on the list of candidates in a particular constituency, the seat(s) in question remain vacant until the next election.

For the House of Elders, the Meshrano Jirga, a mixed electoral system is used. The President appoints one-third of the members, and the gender quota regulation stipulates that 50 per cent of these should be women. This means women will fill at least 17 per cent of the seats.

After the 2005 elections, women occupied 67 out of 242 seats in the Wolesi Jirga, or 27.7 per cent. In the Meshrano Jirga, women held 22 of 102 seats, or 21.6 per cent. Afghanistan currently maintains one of the higher levels of women's parliamentary participation in Asia-Pacific and the world.

Sources: International IDEA and Stockholm University n.d.-b; European Union Election Observation Mission (EU EOM) 2009; IPU 2009.

Despite indications of their value for improving women's political participation, quotas remain controversial across Asia-Pacific

The Magna Carta also seeks at least 40 per cent women's representation in both membership and leadership positions of political parties, encouraging the integration of women in their internal policy-making structures, appointive and electoral nominating processes. This 40 per cent also holds for development councils and planning bodies from the regional, provincial, city and municipal levels.[51] While the region is far short of a percentage even approximately reflecting the number of women in the population, and while it lags behind most other regions on women's participation in politics and more broadly in public decision-making, quotas seem to be making some difference.

Quotas can be defined in constitutions, electoral laws, party by-laws and in executive recruitments. In South Asia, quotas for women in parliament are a feature of the constitutions of Afghanistan (Box 3.3), Bangladesh, India and Pakistan.[52] The Indian Constitution sets aside 33 per cent of seats[53] for women in rural *panchayats*[54] and local governments and bodies in urban areas. This provision has brought a record number of women into local politics.

The Republic of Korea reformed its Political Party Law of 2000 to include a quota for women. The quota is applied to both its proportional and majority electoral systems for the Lower House. For the party list portion, where 56 deputies are elected to the House of the People, political parties are mandated to present candidate lists with women in 50 per cent of positions. For the majority portion of the election, where 243 representatives are elected in single-member districts, at least 30 per cent of candidates from a party should be women. The law has resulted in the number of women elected rising from 5.9 per cent to 13 per cent in 2004, and then to almost 14 per cent in 2008.[55]

In the Pacific, where women's participation in politics is lower than the Asia-Pacific average, the French Territories stand out because they are subject to the French Law on Parity 2000. It requires all political parties to include women as 50 per cent of their candidates. New Caledonia has a legislature that is 44.4 per cent female and French Polynesia has reached a level of 42.1 per cent.[56] No country in the region as a whole can claim similar achievements.

Pros and cons. Despite indications of their value for improving women's political participation, quotas remain controversial across Asia-Pacific, and even specifically illegal in some countries. The reasons for this are linked to social norms around gender, as well as political traditions and ideology. Fundamentally, quotas quantify sudden shifts in political power that stir resistance among those who perceive they will lose out.

For this reason, quotas can be viewed as socially disruptive or, more blatantly, as artificially reducing the natural prerogatives of men. On the surface, they seem to contradict the principles of democracy and equal opportunity for all. They can be read as leading to the election of candidates based on gender, not qualifications, and as preventing the election of more qualified candidates.[57]

Women themselves have at times rejected quotas because they want to be elected on their individual merits, not as women. In Bangladesh, one of the first countries in the region to adopt a quota system in 1972,[58] the small allotment of seats to women soon became seen as the only way women could get into Parliament; all other seats were 'reserved' for men. Other countries have had similar experiences, with quotas being viewed as a maximum, rather than a minimum.

Arguments favouring gender quotas include the notion that quotas are not a form of discrimination, but a way of compensating for the steep barriers that keep women out of politics, especially at higher levels. Women have the right to equal representation, and their experiences are needed for a political system to fully respond to the concerns and priorities of its citizens, including on key aspects of human development. Women in some Asia-Pacific countries have contended that when political parties are freely allowed to make gender-biased choices in nominations, this in itself is undemocratic and blocks the full exercise of voters' rights.

Quota design. Laws are an important initial step in determining how successful a quota can be. In general, if constitutional or electoral provisions require parties to field women as a condition for access to seats, they are more likely to do so, particularly when sanctions for non-compliance are enforced. When quotas are too small or purely voluntary, only those with an ideological commitment to gender equality are likely to comply. The numbers bear this out: In Asia-Pacific, the average number of women elected under constitutional quotas for parliaments is 23.4

per cent and 21.1 per cent under electoral regulations.[59] Tokenism in political party quotas has produced just under 14 per cent, meaning women have about the same chance of being elected with or without them.[60]

To be successful, quotas should be designed according to the requirements of the system and a substantive notion of women's participation. They should reflect political incentives so that parties and candidates—men and women alike—will reap benefits and be more willing to comply with them (Box 3.4). Clear criteria to guide the selection of individual beneficiaries, the extent of the reservations, and exit points for those ready to face open competition can help reduce public and political resistance.

Quotas can target the pool of potential aspirants for public office, nominated candidates, or a number of reserved seats, either elected or appointed. Globally, more countries are choosing to reserve seats—a trend evident in South Asia as well—and a growing number of women are being elected to them.[61] Seat reservations have the advantage of ensuring that women actually end up in political office. Compliance is easier to measure, particularly in countries that have a lot of political parties and/or a low level of party transparency.

On the other hand, quotas for aspirants or nominated candidates can be more

Quotas should be designed according to the requirements of the system and a substantive notion of women's participation

---

BOX 3.4

An Australian Party Adopts Quotas for Women – and Men

The Australian Labour Party is the only one in Australia to have gender quotas for internal party posts and elected positions at all levels of government. A quota for women was first established in 1981 at 25 per cent for internal jobs. It has since expanded to all positions and risen to 40 per cent.

Now the party, which embraces strong support for gender equality in its platform, has also extended the quotas to men—part of a new wave of quota systems positioned as gender-neutral. Starting in 2012, a 40:40:20 quota will be in place. This means that women are entitled to 40 per cent of positions, men to another 40 per cent, and either men or women to the remaining 20 per cent. It ensures neither men nor women will have more than 60 per cent, while allowing flexibility in choices for party staff and candidates.

Source: Clark 2009.

politically palatable because they imply greater choice in the electoral process, instead of a foregone result. Experiences with party quotas show that unless parties make a deliberate effort to put women candidates in electable positions, however, they end up running for office, but never arriving there. In proportional systems, they may be clustered exclusively at the bottom of the party list, with little chance of securing a seat. In majoritarian systems, they can be sent off to contest unwinnable seats.

One debate over quota systems involves whether to make them temporary or permanent. Temporary quotas are meant to give people a leg up until they can stand on their own. Once people see that women can be effective politicians, they will start voting for them based on their qualifications or political ideas, so quotas will no longer be necessary. Yet experiences show that this process can take a long time and be fraught with obstacles. Bangladesh's provision for quotas for women in its 1972 Constitution, for example, lapsed in 1987. It was reinstituted in 1990, but lapsed again in 2000. The Parliament elected in 2001 had no reserved seats for women, and the proportion of women legislators who took office that year was a meagre two per cent. By 2008, a quota was again in force, stipulating the reservation of 13 per cent of seats for women. The general election resulted in 18.6 per cent of seats going to women.[62]

Preventing backlash and non-compliance. Several countries in Asia-Pacific have had protracted debates about adopting quota systems, underscoring the need for measures to build public and political support. These may need to emphasize that quotas are not just about taking power from some groups to give it to others, but about distributing power more evenly among citizens as part of a fairer and more democratic system of governance.[63]

India has had a long-running, and at times violent, experience with reservations

for people from the scheduled castes. Echoes of this experience could be heard around the adoption of local quotas for women politicians in 1993,[64] with concerns raised about the *biwi* (wife) brigade about to descend on local governments, bringing few skills and acting mainly as proxies for men. While the record since then has proved significantly more mixed, combining both obvious failures and great successes, India has not moved forward on national quotas. Women obtained 10.9 per cent of lower house seats and 9.5 per cent of upper house seats in the 2009 elections,[65] but this is still far below the global average. The Women's Reservation Bill that sought to provide a 33 per cent reservation for women in both houses of Parliament was defeated twice.[66]

The national Bill has in fact encountered another form of backlash related to caste and India's shifting political landscape, where political leaders from traditionally marginalized groups have begun challenging the dominance of elites. At the same time, the Hindutva nationalist movement has underscored caste, class, religious and other divisions. The Bill has been questioned on the grounds of whether or not it would simply provide more room for elite women to gain seats or would encompass women from a range of backgrounds. Political leaders, even from supposedly liberal parties, and the media have tended to present the debate as one of 'gender vs. caste.' Some women's organizations have tried to confine the discussion to 'men vs. women,' without a willingness to explore the complexities of how gender intersects with social and economic standing. The result, so far, has been a standstill.[67]

Debates over quotas occur even after they have seemingly been accepted. A revision of Mongolia's election law in 2005 introduced a 30 per cent quota for female candidates nominated by political parties and coalitions. This was removed by another revision in 2007,[68] just before an election. Despite strong

BOX 3.5

WHERE QUOTAS STUMBLE, PUBLIC AWARENESS STEPS IN: REAL STRIDES IN INDONESIA

Women's representation in Indonesia's parliament has seen its ups and downs, but has improved over time overall (see table below). For some years, the proportion of women in Indonesia's parliament was dismal. Despite affirmative action, it hovered around 10 per cent. With democratization beginning in 1998, however, the movement for women's representation has picked up momentum and visibility. Supporters were able to lobby for the inclusion of a provision in the Election Law passed in 2004 requiring all political parties to apply a 30 per cent quota for women to their candidate list. The provision lacked teeth, resulting in only a few parties adhering to it, but it was considered a historic achievement in Indonesia. It generated an awareness that, as a first step, resulted in increasing the proportion of women representatives in the national parliament by 25 per cent in 2004.

Even more significant results were produced in 2009. The new election law passed in 2008 combined a 30 per cent quota for party lists with a 'zipper' system in which for every three candidates fielded by political parties, at least one had to be a woman. But the Constitutional Court in late 2008 issued a ruling that negated the quota and required the election to be decided wholly by the popular vote. While the decision was meant to curb the power of political parties and transfer it to the voters, it effectively dismantled affirmative action for women representatives. Many women's activists expressed pessimism about any possibility of increasing women's representation.

Amidst this setback, however, the affirmative action debate generated greater interest in the issue of women's representation, and galvanized the efforts of different stakeholders. Civil society organizations launched activities to spread awareness of the importance of having a gender-balanced parliament. These efforts were backed by a number of political parties and some government agencies, such as the State Ministry on Women's Empowerment, the Ministry of Home Affairs, and the General Election Commission. UNDP and bilateral donors also actively supported the efforts of Indonesian stakeholders through civil society voters' education initiatives, media campaigns, and public consultations among political parties, academics and civil society.

The results took even activists by surprise. Many more parties took the 30 per cent quota seriously, even in the absence of legislation. As many as 70 per cent of the 38 parties competing in the 2009 election nominated women for more than 30 per cent of their candidates. The election has considerably increased the number of women in parliament—shattering the 100 seats ceiling in the DPR (lower house).

Though still below the 30 per cent mark that many activists set as their target, women's representation in the two chambers of Parliament has never been higher. The share of women representatives in the DPR has increased by 63 per cent. In the newly constituted upper house, the House of Regions or DPD, where only individuals may be candidates the increase was 77 per cent. This brought women's membership to 27.3 per cent, or just three per cent shy of the 30 per cent target. It suggests that political party reform may be a policy aim.

The Indonesian experience shows that even when the affirmative action quota is removed, once public attention and awareness is generated around the issue, change in attitudes can successfully push the agenda forward by increasing real public support for women's representation. The achievement also reveals that the voters in the world's largest Muslim nation have no qualms about supporting women in politics, thus negating the stereotype commonly associated with Islamic religious belief. Indonesia's strides in this sphere are admirable and deserve support, so that women's share is closer to half in future elections.

Period	Women Members of DPR (Lower House)		Women Members of DPD (Upper House) ****	
	Number	Percentage	Number	Percentage
1955–1960 *	17	6.3	–	–
1971–1977 **	36	7.8	–	–
1977–1982	29	6.3	–	–
1982–1987	39	8.5	–	–
1987–1992	65	13.0	–	–
1992–1997	62	12.5	–	–
1997–1999	54	10.8	–	–
1999–2004 ***	46	9.0	–	–
2004–2009	62	11.3	27	21.0
2009–2014	101	18.0	36	27.3

* The parliament was formed in 1955 as a result of the first free and fair election in Indonesia. It was disbanded in 1960, however, with the introduction of Guided Democracy by President Sukarno. A new parliament was formed but membership was appointed by the President.

** Following the fall of Sukarno, the New Order government was formed under General Suharto. This government formally conducted elections once every five years, but this was generally regarded as less than a free and fair exercise. The first New Order parliament was formed in 1971 and the last one in 1997.

*** After the resignation of Suharto from office in 1998, Indonesia embarked on democratization. The democratic elections in 1999 produced a new parliament, and subsequently elections have been held and parliaments formed every five years.

**** In 2002, the Indonesian Constitution was amended so as to establish another chamber in Indonesian parliament. The House of Regional Representatives (DPD) was meant to function like the Senate in other countries, representing the interests of administrative regions. But in Indonesia's case, the DPD's authority is limited to consultative rather than legislative functions.

Source: UNDP Indonesia 2009.

lobbying by some members of Parliament and women activists, and a veto by the President, the quota was not restored. As a result, the June 2008 election saw a decline in women parliamentarians, from five to three. A draft Gender Equality Law was submitted to Parliament in July 2009; re-introducing the 30 per cent quota is its most-debated provision.[69]

A major obstacle to quotas making a meaningful contribution to women's political participation is non-compliance, particularly when there are no associated sanctions. Indonesia requires parties to field a one-third ratio of women candidates, yet the 2009 elections resulted in women obtaining only 18 per cent of parliamentary seats.[70] It has no legal sanctions for non-compliance and no rules about where women should be placed on parliamentary lists[71] (Box 3.5).

Fulfilling their promise. One part of using quota systems to make a meaningful contribution to women's participation involves the systems themselves. As described above, the ingredients for effectiveness include sound laws, well-designed quotas that match electoral systems and build on political incentives, clear guidelines and timeframes, countermeasures for backlash and sanctions for non-compliance.

But another part of successful quotas entails equipping women who may be new to politics to understand the political process, and make it work for themselves and their constituents. This helps improve the quality of governance and minimize complaints about the competency of 'quota candidates'.

Leaving aside for the moment the reality that many under-qualified men also enter the political arena in Asia-Pacific, it is also true that women start behind men in their access to political competencies through inferior education and less exposure to professional skills. Research on the profile of local women politicians in Asia and the Pacific indicates that they are generally young, low-income

earners, inexperienced in politics and poorly educated.[72] Those with internalized notions of inferiority and submission are often unprepared to assert their independence and may end up under-confident and unable to perform even at the level of their existing capacities. They may be unequipped to manage the expectation that their first responsibility is to their families, leaving little time for the meetings, consultations and study required to take on community and national problems.

Deliberate exercises to cultivate women's capacities have been proven to better prepare women for office and make them more competitive as candidates running for election. These capacities can encompass technical political skills, such as drafting legislation and interacting with constituents; skills related to advancing gender equality, such as through reviewing laws and budgets for potentially different impacts on men and women; and psychological skills to overcome low self-confidence or conflicts between public and personal roles.

Not Often Invited to the Party

Political parties are the gatekeepers to political systems in most Asia-Pacific countries. They provide funds, mobilize voters en masse, produce and advocate for party platforms, and transmit an image that may have broad public recognition. Candidates who affiliate with a party essentially step into an apparatus that has experience in how to campaign and win.

Party configurations vary widely. There may be one party, as is the case in China or Viet Nam, or many. Different parties may operate on local and national levels. They may be highly centralized or completely decentralized, strictly or loosely affiliated with a particular ideology. Parties in presidential systems—common across much of Asia-Pacific—tend to be less structured, since the

Deliberate exercises to cultivate women's capacities better prepare women for office and make them more competitive as candidates running for election

failure to vote with one's party does not threaten to bring the government down. Members may be freer to identify with regional, ethnic, economic, gender or other divisions when considering policy issues or during election campaigns.[73]

Because parties are intended to consolidate and gain political power, much of their behaviour is oriented around this objective. From this perspective, parties may view women as risky candidates, perhaps because there is a limited history of women in office, and women bring fewer resources and political connections to the table. Space for women candidates may be particularly squeezed in unstable or hotly contested political environments, although in any system, if parties are not supportive of gender equality and women candidates, women's representation will be low.

Women in some Asia-Pacific countries have viewed parties with skepticism, seeing them as ineffective in advancing women's participation or campaign promises of gender equality. In Pakistan, women's activists have argued fervently against applying quotas for women through parties, maintaining that this will constrain women to parties with patriarchal structures and that are weak and corrupt in some cases as well.[74] They have demanded direct elections instead. Women's ability to appeal directly to the electorate was clear in Bangladesh's 2008 national election, where 19 of the 64 successful women were directly elected by voters, without assistance from party quotas.[75] In the Philippines, one novel response has been for women to form their own party (Box 3.6).

Despite the reasons for working outside the party system, there may be more reasons for working with parties on a programme or reform from within. Possible steps to build the presence of women in parties include:

Revise party positions and rules to support gender equality. Party positions and rules determine how parties operate, including in the crucial nomination process. They may be stated or unstated, with the latter typically allowing political patronage systems to flourish. Women candidates tend to benefit from clearer rules that make some attempt at treating individuals alike, regardless of gender, or go a step further to compensate for exclusion. This is possible not only through active quota systems, but also rules to position women candidates in rankings on party lists where they can be elected or agreements that women should comprise a percentage of the members of party nominating committees.

In Japan, party leaders of the Liberal Democratic Party chose candidates, rather than the party rank and file. While party leaders can espouse and help spread more progressive perspectives on gender equality, more typically they are the upholders of party traditions which in Japan have consistently kept women's representation low. Women won a total of 26, or just under nine per cent, of the 296 LDP seats in the 2005 elections.[76]

Some positive examples of parties adopting policies to compensate for women's financial constraints come from outside Asia-Pacific but could serve as models for the region. The New Democratic Party in Canada has a provision for child-care support for women candidates. In Nigeria, the People's

Some positive examples of parties adopting policies to compensate for women's financial constraints come from outside Asia-Pacific but could serve as models for the region

---

BOX 3.6

A PARTY WOMEN CALL THEIR OWN

In 1995, the Philippines revised its Party List System Law to provide 20 per cent of seats in the House of Representatives to candidates from excluded groups, including women. Voters chose both a district representative and a 'sectoral' party. GABRIELA, the largest alliance of women's organizations, fielded a candidate in 2001. She won, and was re-elected in 2004. In 2007, GABRIELA earned nearly four per cent of the total votes, enough to ensure it had two seats.

GABRIELA representatives have lost no time in being active on behalf of women and other excluded groups, such as migrant workers. They have been engaged in passing legislation to stop trafficking and violence against women, and active on issues such as fairer divorce, the protection of women and children in conflict areas, and the welfare of female prisoners.

Source: UNIFEM 2008.

Democratic Party has dropped charges for nomination forms for women, leading to a higher number of women contesting and winning elections.[77]

Establish women's party sections. Women who come together as a group within a party can lobby more concertedly for the party to take action on gender equality, encourage the recruitment of more women members and candidates, organize training and provide support systems for women new to the party—as long as there is a conscious and concerted effort to avoid marginalization.

Lesley Clark, a former Member of Parliament from Australia, cautions that while a women's branch or committee can do much to challenge male attitudes and support women entering politics, it should also be treated as a formal part of the overall party structure so that party members as a whole take it seriously.[78]

Recognize that women can win. Women candidates have proven to be remarkably successful even in adverse circumstances. Data from India suggests that even though parties field far fewer women candidates than men, women consistently and in some elections substantially are elected in higher percentages than men.[79]

Make connections with voters. Women's growing track record, both as elected politicians and as voters, can also be an argument for parties to take them more seriously. In Republic of Korea, for instance, the comparative success of women in the 2007 elections led parties to actively recruit women candidates to represent a 'women's agenda' and appeal to women voters.[80]

In some cases, the perceptions of voters may be further ahead on the value of women in politics than those of mainstream politicians (Box 3.7). In Afghanistan, 62 per cent of women and 40 per cent of men agree that women and men should share leadership equally. Half of men but only 20 per cent of women think that political leadership should be mostly for men.[81] In India, political parties have proven more resistant to state and national quotas for women. One survey found that 75 per cent of men and women support quotas.[82]

One question raised about women's voting, particularly when women are assumed to be strongly under the sway of men, is whether they cast their own votes or follow the inclinations of male family members. Since the early 1970s, researchers from the Centre for Developing Societies in New Delhi have asked women voters in India whose advice they seek while casting their ballots. Fewer than 50 per cent of women vote based on what their husbands or male family members have to say. Since women's voter turnout has climbed, this means more and more women are making their own choices.[83]

Achieving More Inclusive Elections

Beyond political parties, the structure and management of electoral systems also

Women who come together as a group within a party can lobby more concertedly for the party to take action on gender equality

---

BOX 3.7

PEOPLE WANT MORE WOMEN IN OFFICE, BUT...

The low numbers of women in political office may not necessarily reflect what the general population would like to see. In Thailand, for example, an opinion poll in 2005 found a contradiction between women's low representation rates and positive public perceptions of women in politics. Women currently have 11.7 per cent of the seats in Thailand's House of Representatives and 16 per cent in its Senate, both below the global average. Local elections tend to produce even lower numbers—at around nine per cent.

The poll, carried out by UNDP and Bangkok University, surveyed 6,000 people in urban and rural areas. It found that 85 per cent of respondents believe a woman would be a good prime minister, and 75 per cent would like to see more women in leading civil service positions and Parliament.

Discriminatory attitudes were also apparent. Thirty per cent said they would choose a man if presented with equally qualified male and female candidates. About a third still did not believe that women are as good as men at making decisions and solving problems.

Sources: IPU 2009; Office of Women's Affairs and Family Development and UNDP Thailand 2008; UNDP and Women for Democratic Development Foundation 2006.

determines who gets into office and how. Global research suggests that in democracies, proportional representation systems help more women enter parliament.[84] The vast majority of the top 20 countries in the world in terms of women's presence in the legislature use proportional representation. The average level of women's representation is appreciably higher in countries with these systems than in countries with plurality/majoritarian systems.[85]

One explanation for this is that women have a greater probability of being included on a party ticket, particularly in larger districts with more than one representative. Parties and voters can hedge their bets, especially if supporting a woman candidate feels like a new and risky experiment. In plurality/majoritarian systems, a woman candidate usually has to compete one-on-one with a cross-section of male candidates, only one of whom will emerge the winner.

In the Asia-Pacific, 15 countries are in the top half of 187 countries ranked by the percentage of women in a lower or single-house legislature. Eight have proportional or mixed electoral systems; seven have plurality/majoritarian systems. Nine countries have some form of quota in place. Those countries that seem to do well without quotas—aside from New Zealand, which is number one in the region—tend to be clustered in South-East Asia. Lao People's Democratic Republic, Singapore and Viet Nam have participation rates around 25 per cent under plurality/majoritarian systems.[86]

From a perspective of women's participation, majoritarian systems that operate without quotas do less well in the Pacific. A survey of 12 countries and territories where women hold less than 10 per cent of legislative seats found that more than two-thirds employ majoritarian, first-past-the-post electoral systems, where the person with the most votes wins. None have quotas in place. This combination of the lack of quotas and electoral systems that tend to perpetuate existing patterns of power has not been enough for women in the region to overcome often-daunting social and economic constraints on participation. Of the six countries in the world that still have no female members in their national Parliaments, four are in the Pacific—Federated States of Micronesia, Nauru, Solomon Islands and Tuvalu. Three use first-past-the-post systems.[87]

Electoral systems operate within a complex web of their own rules along with social norms and political practices. They do not hold all the solutions to increasing women's political voice, but they may contain some and deserve to be analyzed accordingly. For one thing, electoral rules are considered easier and faster to change in favour of gender equality than the cultural norms that hold women back, although both must be addressed.[88] Some possible steps within current structures include:

Implement existing quota provisions. These may need to be better defined, monitored and encouraged through incentives and sanctions, possibly through an election management board or similar mechanism.

Examine rules, codes of conduct and election logistics. Often assumed to be gender-neutral, these should still be reviewed from a gender perspective, considering any specific constraints that women may encounter.

Assess campaign financing. In Asia-Pacific and the rest of the world, elections are becoming more expensive, a disadvantage to women. Parties can make more funds available to women, but electoral systems can also have a role in adjudicating how money can be raised and spent. Public financing and campaign contribution limits can help make access to funds more democratic, for women and men, as can requirements for detailed reports on campaign spending. Controls on campaign

Electoral rules are considered easier and faster to change in favour of gender equality than the cultural norms that hold women back

EDUCATING PARTIES, VOTERS AND CANDIDATES PAYS OFF

In Cambodia's 2007 local and 2008 national elections, a civil society group called the Committee to Promote Women in Politics trained women politicians, convinced political party leaders to support women's leadership and conducted campaigns to educate voters on women's leadership potential. In three of the provinces targeted by the group, the number of women commune councilors successfully contesting the election doubled and tripled.

The committee was active in convincing national party leaders to put women at the top of candidate lists and to adopt a 'sandwich system' of alternating male and female names. These activities helped the overall number of women commune councilors rise from 8.5 per cent to 15 per cent, and the number of parliamentarians increase from 12 per cent to 22 per cent. Polls of voters found that more feel confident that women are good leaders, and fewer believe that men are better leaders than women.

Cambodia has quotas for women's representation at the village level and in the civil service, but not in national politics—so the experience illustrates in part how much can be done by mobilizing people to change their minds.

Source: UNDEF 2008.

Conflict can intersect with the issue of women's political participation in several ways, including challenging traditional norms

financing can also cut patron-client relationships where elected politicians end up dishing out favours, typically at public expense, for large donors. Singapore, for example, allows candidates to spend a maximum of US $12,000[89] on a single election.[90]

Control violence and corruption. As a general principle, men, women and societies as a whole benefit from well-managed elections that prevent political factions from using violence and corruption for political benefit. Women in Asia-Pacific have at times taken public stances against violence and corruption, but may also be more hesitant to enter a campaign where they may be at risk, including being deliberately targeted for gender-based violence. Families and communities may also be more protective—i.e. discouraging—of women trying to compete in an obviously dangerous arena. Corruption disadvantages women in part because they are less likely as a group to have the funds and connections to practise it.

Allow room for advocacy around gender equality. In some countries, election rules can facilitate the efforts of civil society or educational groups to advocate around gender equality in a politically neutral way, such as through voter education or training on gender equality for male and female candidates and parties from all backgrounds (Box 3.8).

Include gender equality in voter and civic education. Where voter or civic education is publicly provided, including in schools, efforts can be made to include information on gender equality, its benefits for society and the equal value of women and men as potential voters and political leaders.

Women Participate in War and Contribute to Peace

'Are we only capable of running the House of Representatives as a speaker from the street but not in the actual House?'[91]

> – A woman activist helping to prepare Nepal's gender-responsive model Constitution

Conflict simmers across the Asia-Pacific region, and sometimes explodes, from the streets of Bangkok to the mountains of Afghanistan and the jungles of the Philippines. The worst of crisis has passed in some places, such as Nepal and Timor-Leste, but the long task of recovery remains.

Conflict can intersect with the issue of women's political participation in several ways, including challenging traditional norms. Armed movements can themselves be a form of political expression, or spark counter-movements that may be violent or attempts to find peace. Post-conflict periods offer opportunities for peacetime political agreements and institutions that disrupt past patterns of political dominance, often by select groups of men. They may promise more egalitarian representation for both women and men.

Women can play surprising roles during and after conflict—surprising because their presence is large and mostly ignored. The participation of women and girls in armed conflicts is observed in Africa, Asia and Latin America. In Asia—Indonesia, Nepal, Sri Lanka, Timor-Leste—females in non-state armies have shared similar conditions and risks as men. Less formal institutional structures and the pressure to utilize every human resource fully can lead to the blurring of traditional gender-roles, with women and girls expected to face risks similar to those of men. Yet they have often been marginalized in post-conflict power sharing, depriving countries of skills and perspectives which have the potential to be used productively in peacetime.[92]

One incentive to recruit women is the perception that they will be more obedient and easier to train, although this notion does not always hold true. In Aceh, Indonesia, female warriors are traditionally seen as heroines of exceptional character, who are noble, fearless and ready to die as a martyr in the interests of society.[93]

Women join for many reasons. Some decide to fight for change. In Nepal, for instance, ordinary village women who joined the Maoist Army learned a new liberation vocabulary that encouraged them to question traditional gender roles. They learned to expect and create change, resist abuse, and demonstrate discipline and resilience.[94] Some women end up as combatants after fleeing abuse or forced marriages at home, or hope for a sense of purpose and being, since even non-state armies can provide an association with leadership and strength—a telling reflection on the conditions females face in society. Other women and even girls are forcibly recruited. Poverty is a driver, along with lack of education or other employment opportunities.[95] Women perform varied roles that include:

Supporters. Women drive trucks, lead army units, carry out intelligence assessments, cook meals and provide health care. They also handle logistics, undertake administrative tasks, repair equipment, carry out propaganda and raise funds. And in so doing they face living conditions and risks similar to those of men.

Combatants. While estimates of female combatants in armed conflicts vary, they range between one-tenth to one-third.[96] In Sri Lanka and Nepal[97] women are estimated as constituting about one third of the combatants.[98] For example, in the Liberation Tigers of Tamil Eelam (LTTE) female cadres were included in all the units of the movement, including, fighting, bombings and suicide missions. Slogans like 'equity for the nation and equality at home' were common. Since women are generally perceived as less dangerous in public places, they were used in carrying out suicide attacks.[99]

Brokers of peace. In formal negotiations and within their families and communities, women have played essential, if mostly unacknowledged, roles in efforts to foster peace. Where they are seen as unaffiliated with the fighting of different factions, they can serve as emissaries to plead the case of peace before different groups, at times crossing lines that would be impossible for men. Around the world, women who have struggled to protect their families and communities have offered a powerful symbol for the greater social good achieved by ending hostilities (Box 3.9). They are also significant in holding together local economies, including by performing tasks ordinarily assigned to men.

As combatants or as advocates of peace, women can pick up a variety of skills and find quick routes to power that might never have been available in civilian life. Their new abilities and knowledge can be brought into the process of social and political trans-

In Bougainville, Settling Conflict and Furthering Equality

A bloody civil war in Bougainville from the mid-1980s to mid-1990s killed or displaced over half the population. Infrastructure and economic activities were destroyed. A series of peace agreements from 1997 led to Bougainville acquiring autonomous status from the National Parliament of Papua New Guinea in 2000. All along, it was clear that for peace to take hold, peacemaking would need to take place both in high-level negotiations and among citizens themselves. Women proved to be essential to both pursuits.

While the conflict was still raging, women organized themselves in church groups to pray for reconciliation. They served as peacemakers in their communities and as go-betweens among warring factions; some went into the bush to bring their sons home. They created humanitarian networks that provided food and medicine to people in areas controlled by both the government and the rebel Bougainville Revolutionary Army. Contacts with women's organizations in New Zealand and Australia did much to bring attention and support from abroad. Peace marches attracted thousands of participants.

In 1996, a Women's Peace Forum brought together women from all parts of the island and sides of the conflict to begin strategizing on how to achieve peace. When the 1997 peace talks got underway, a delegation of representatives from women's organizations was prepared to participate in the negotiations. In an adjoining statement on peace, they said, 'We, the women, hold custodial rights of our land by clan inheritance. We insist that women leaders must be party to all stages of the political process in determining the future of Bougainville.'

Having achieved an opening in the negotiations, women went on to press for gains in political participation in the new Constitution. In 2005, for the first time, 3 of the 41 Legislative Assembly seats were reserved for women. Among the arguments put forward by women for the quota provision: women had been at the forefront of peacemaking and therefore had the most experience.

Source: UNDP Pacific Centre 2009.

---

formation that may follow. Yet women too often are overlooked, or even punished for their newfound independence, especially in heavily patriarchal Asia-Pacific societies that put a premium on women remaining subordinate to men. Three opportunities in particular may be lost:

Room for increasing women's political participation. Some post-conflict countries, such as Nepal (Box 3.10), have made laudable efforts to expand women's political role, starting with high-level positions in peace processes. Peace agreements offer opportunities to advance an agenda of inclusiveness, democratic reform and gender equality, including through the demonstration effect of women's participation. This can set the stage for women to gain experience and visibility that can later be used in peacetime political institutions such as parliaments. As social consensus grows around ideas of equality and wider participation in nation-building, it may foster greater acceptance of concrete steps such as affirmative action measures that can reduce male-female gaps and contribute to stability and development in a relatively short time.

Valuable perspectives on paths to peace. Women experience conflict differently than men. They may survive specific forms of violence that need to be considered in reconciliation processes. They may have particular insights into the causes of conflict and the people fomenting it—including themselves—as well as into what is needed to resolve it and move towards sustainable peace. Women's economic needs, in particular, are frequently overlooked in countries like Afghanistan. This threatens the stability of women, their children and their communities, especially when large numbers of men have been killed, depriving them of other sources of income. It also hinders prospects for national recovery and longer-term development.

Put women's new skills to work. Many of the skills women acquire in war can be transferred to good use in peacetime. But disarmament and reintegration processes typically ignore the re-absorption of female combatants. Post-war rehabilitation efforts that predominantly focus on women as civilians, refugees and other displaced populations, can miss the special needs and potential

Peace agreements offer opportunities to advance an agenda of inclusiveness, democratic reform and gender equality

NEPAL'S PEACE TRANSFORMS ITS POLITICS

Women in Nepal gained 33 per cent of the seats in the 2008 Constituent Assembly elections, an unprecedented achievement for Nepal and South Asia at large. The gains were made by setting a 50 per cent quota for the proportional representation segment of the election. A partnership initiative between local activists, lawyers, parliamentarians and public officials, facilitated by UNIFEM and the UN Democracy Fund, helped contribute to this.

Nepali women, who played prominent roles in the country's Maoist movement during a decade of conflict, have so far found a place in peacemaking. But the focus has also been on what they can contribute to gender equality from that position. Towards that end, the UN partnership has assisted in a review of foreign constitutions, including the Rwandan Constitution, which explicitly refers to equal rights between women and men and establishes quotas for women. Rwanda, which like Nepal has emerged from political crisis, now has the highest percentage of women parliamentarians in the world, at over 55 per cent.

In Nepal, the review led to the production of a draft gender-responsive Constitution that has been discussed in national and local meetings across Nepal. Other activities included assessing political party platforms for their gender responsiveness, and, in the run-up to the election, circulating a list of more than 2,000 women qualified to compete.

Recommendations that emerged from the initiative are similar for both the new Constitution and political party platforms. They include ensuring women's proportional representation in state bodies, ending violence against women, and taking specific measures to increase access to health care and education. While the Constitution will not be finished until 2010, early indications suggest that some of these ideas will be included, along with general provisions for gender equality. Political party manifestos have already shifted – endorsing women's role in political decision-making and efforts to end violence against women. And in November 2008, a woman was elected as Vice-Chairperson of the Constituent Assembly after securing 69 per cent of the vote.

Sources: UNDEF 2009; IPU 2009.

of women who have served in other roles, especially in armed forces and non-state armies. Initiatives designed to reach them can include psychological support for a peaceful transition, and help them transfer their wartime capabilities into marketable and socially productive skills.

Under United Nations Security Council Resolution 1325[100] on women, peace and security, some interesting steps have already been taken. In Liberia, for example, female supporters were identified as 'women associated with the fighting forces' rather than 'camp followers' so as to be included in the disarmament and reintegration process. Women then represented 24 per cent of those demobilized.[101] Some female ex-combatants have themselves taken active steps to carve a place for participation in rebuilding. The Acehnese Women's League (Liga Inong Aceh, or LINA) emerged in 2006 to help female combatants get their dues.[102] Women at the grass-roots level in Afghanistan have also used Resolution 1325 to lobby for participation in peace-building, post-conflict elections and the rebuilding of their societies.[103]

After conflict, the successful reintegration of women and men into normal civilian lives helps individuals be productive, and reduces disaffection and alienation. It means that women and men can make livelihoods, be protected by the law, and have a peaceful political voice to express grievances and aspirations. Treating women involved in conflict as valuable assets heightens the chance of achieving—and maintaining—these gains.

The Difference Women Make in Politics

'Don't think of yourselves as being unfortunate because of having to live through these times. Think of it as fortunate, because you have an opportunity to work for justice and the welfare of other people. This sort of opportunity does not come to everybody all the time.' [104]

– Aung San Suu Kyi

Women participate in politics in many ways. One notable characteristic of the Asia-Pacific region has been the prominence of women in the top positions of executive power, including

Treating women involved in conflict as valuable assets heightens the chance of achieving—and maintaining gains

as heads of state. Women also lead civil society organizations and are an obvious presence at ballot boxes. Political positions have proven to be open to women with resources or family connections; civil society movements to people willing to work for political change and new understandings of development. Where women's political participation has tended to fall short is in the whole range of formal institutions of public decision-making that lie anywhere between the top post and the person on the street.

People intent on discouraging an influx of women leaders often raise the issue of how effective women can be in office. Women have had this debate themselves—but more often it is linked to the effectiveness of the governance system and the capacity of women in leadership positions to support gender equality. In Bangladesh, for instance, the quota system for parliamentary seats was originally designed so that winning parties could nominate 15 women candidates.[105] This led to treatment of the 15 seats as a kind of parliamentary vote bank. The women parliamentarians were both a small minority and completely dependent on the parties, essentially rendering them powerless. The number of reserved seats for women increased in 2004 to 45, which were to be distributed among the parties according to elected representation.[106] Women activists, in many countries, have spent years petitioning for direct election to reserved seats, as is the case on the sub-national level. In Bangladesh's 2008 national election, 19 of the 64 women elected to Parliament were in a direct process.[107]

This experience suggests that women politicians, public executives, activists and voters all need to be engaged in an agenda that promotes fair representation across all levels of government as a right of citizenship. The example also demonstrates that gender equality and democracy should build on all forms of political participation. Politics may never be an easy, straight road. But women and men can work together to make sure it heads in the right directions.

Women's Representation Boosts Effectiveness

The starting point for women's political participation is that it is a matter of fairness and representation. After that, like men, women will be naturally responsive to competing influences such as party expectations, constituent demands and political ideologies. No assumptions can be made about women politicians as individuals, although some general patterns do emerge in two areas:

Issues. A recent global survey by the Inter-Parliamentary Union found that women parliamentarians as a whole tend to emphasize issues such as childcare, equal pay, parental leave and pensions. They highlight reproductive rights, physical safety and gender-based violence, human development, the alleviation of poverty and the delivery of services.[108]

Similar patterns have been found in Asia-Pacific, where they have been studied. In New Zealand, a study carried out over 25 years—as the portion of women in Parliament rose from 4 per cent in 1975 to 29 per cent in 1999—tracked debates on childcare and parental leave. It found that women were far more likely than men to prompt parliamentary debates on these issues, and at times were the only representatives calling attention to them. A decline in discussion of the two issues was noted when the number of women representatives dipped as well. One of the changes that occurred over that time was the acceptance of parental leave provisions for women and men.[109]

It is also true that women representatives helped vote down the 1998 Paid Parental Leave Bill, which would have brought New

Zealand in line with international standards for paid leave. This has been attributed to the embrace of free market ideologies by some women opposed to the content of the bill, as well as to the diversity of women's representation at the time, which undercut the process of reaching political consensus.[110]

In India, studies comparing how local councils function in the states of West Bengal and Rajasthan, show systematic differences between men and women in the complaints and requests they file. More women than men complain about water resource management, for example. The number of drinking water projects was 60 per cent higher in female-led than male-led councils. In West Bengal, female-led councils undertook road-building projects at a higher rate than male-led councils, since the jobs were likely to go to females.[111]

A study by the society for Participatory Research in Asia (PRIA), found that men in local councils in India generally welcomed attempts to meet women's needs arising from the gendered division of labour, such as access to land and water. But when other gender issues were questioned, such as the prevalence of domestic violence, they were resistant. A local woman politician in western Rajasthan reported: 'I was beaten by…when I prevented him from beating his wife… I raised this in the Gram Sabha, and the members said this is not the place to raise personal issues and waste the precious time of the *panchayat*.'[112]

The anecdote illustrates not only how patterns of gender discrimination continue to operate, but also how male-dominated groups find it natural to dismiss or ignore issues that challenge their authority or are not relevant to their concerns. This may explain some of the significant gaps in gender-responsive legislation that are explored in the next chapter. Another indication of this frequently occurs in crisis situations, where women are almost always heavily under-represented in decision-making forums that might make a difference to their survival. Natural disasters that take place in more equal societies, by contrast, have a more even-handed affect on life expectancy.[113]

The 'critical mass' theory has always maintained that enough women need to be in political positions for them to make a difference, and to push back against experiences like the one in Rajasthan. This notion is behind calls for ensuring that women comprise at least a third of political positions. But numbers alone, aside from an equity perspective, are a relatively blunt measurement for the gender equality impact of women's political participation.

Women parliamentarians and civil society groups in Afghanistan fought hard against the April 2009 law allowing the minority Shia community to control women's movements outside the house and prevent married women from refusing sex.[114] Even though Afghanistan has one of the highest percentages of women parliamentarians in the region, however, women across ongoing parliamentary debates have proven to be just as divided as men on the lines of ethnicity, class, language, political affiliations and regions. One review of the first 18 months of the Parliament's operation concluded, 'The discrepancy between women's political presence, and their ability (or indeed willingness) to represent or prioritize their collective 'gender interests' has become evident.'[115]

Leadership and decision-making. Research on diverse groups in general shows they tend to make better decisions, draw on multiple sources of talent and have a better understanding of risks.[116] When women are involved, this does not imply that decisions will conform to gender stereotypes about the style of women's leadership—plenty of examples exist of women leaders in Asia-Pacific who have put to rest notions about

In crisis situations, women are almost always heavily under-represented in decision-making forums that might make a difference to their survival

women automatically pursuing more 'feminine' or 'pacifist' policies.

A survey on local women leaders from Asia-Pacific countries, however, found that many characterize their leadership style as being more inclusive, consultative and collaborative than that of men who traditionally dominate politics. They perceive themselves as more tolerant of different points of view, people-oriented and encouraging of participation, with a focus on issues instead of personalities.[117] In Bangladesh, people report a higher rate of satisfaction with the decisions made by local women representatives in terms of the distribution of public resources and allocation of projects.[118]

Experiences in Cambodia[119] and India[120] suggest that local women leaders are more accessible to women in their communities and thus may have exposure to a broader range of constituents. A study in India revealed that men believed women's participation had led to greater transparency in local governance and women appeared to be more honest and hardworking. Women's success on the local level has led the Assembly in the Indian state of Bihar, among others, to extend reservations for women in the *panchayat* system from 33 per cent to 50 per cent.[121]

Leadership roles also change women. An all-India survey on women in local governments highlights that they have gained a new sense of power, and no longer turn to their husbands to make key decisions. The survey, conducted across 24 states, pointed out that out of 2.8 million male and female *panchayat* members across the country, 37.4 per cent are women[122] and 80,000 women have become *sarpanchs* (chairpersons).[123]

Taking Action: Bolstering Voice, A Gender Equality Agenda

If the initial goal of increasing the number of women in politics can be achieved, it is relevant to reflect on how a more balanced configuration of men and women may be more effective not just in forwarding a gender equality agenda, but also the overarching goal of human development. Gender balance in ministries like finance, public works, commerce, industry, municipal administration, rural and urban development, health, home and education, a gender balance can influence progress towards development goals. Some action points that may contribute to linking progress on women's representation and democracy to advancements in human development include:

Encourage women and men to act collectively on gender. Gender equality is about and stands to benefit both women and men. Both can be involved in advocating for gender equality and may be more and more willing to do so as gender norms become more balanced. Encouraging men's involvement can expand political support. It also helps reduce the impression among some men that for them, gender equality is a zero-sum game designed to strip them of power and privilege. Social, economic and political benefits can all accrue when diverse groups participate in the full exercise of democracy and citizenship.

Make gender equality part of common politics. While often associated with more liberal political philosophies, gender equality can be and has been a point of common ground for people from the full political spectrum. Alliances can form around advancing gender equality, even in the presence of disagreements about other issues.

For Fiji's progressive Family Law Act 2003, the overwhelming majority of female representatives in Parliament not only championed and supported the proposed law during parliamentary debates, but lobbied within their parties for it to be passed across party lines.[124] In an informal coalition, women parliamentarians mobilized along gender and across racial lines—the latter an unprecedented step in Fiji's legislative history. This spurred the building of new alliances, and in the end, only one indigenous Fijian female MP, a high chief, refused to support the new law.[125]

In Viet Nam, the Women's Union is a mass organization that mobilizes women from the grassroots to the Central Committee. It has successfully advocated the adoption of laws, policies and programmes for women's poverty reduction, education and reproductive health care. At the local level, the union nominates women for election to Party committees, the National Assembly and people's councils. It has played a significant role in getting out the vote for women nominees among its constituencies. Union-sponsored training courses equip women nominees with skills to win in the People's Committee elections.[126]

Support women's participation inside and outside the formal political system. Women's movements in the Asia-Pacific region have had long debates about whether it is better to work towards gender equality inside or outside the formal political system. Some activists have chosen to remain outside political systems for some of the same reasons as potential women candidates. They contend politics is male-dominated, overtly discriminates against women or is riddled with 'dirty' political practices. Common alternatives have entailed pursing equal rights through legal means and grassroots mobilization. At the same time, women in a number of Asia-Pacific countries have been strong proponents of increasing the number of women in political offices.

Both approaches have yielded achievements, suggesting they can be mutually reinforcing and should be pursued in tandem. Some evidence shows that women are more effective inside political institutions when they enjoy the support of women mobilizing

outside. Women and others interested in deepening democratic institutions are also active in educating voters, advocating for the passage of laws, creating networks and channelling information about gender equality issues into the political system.

Increasingly, civil society groups have helped prepare women for political positions, especially in local government. In South-East Asia, informal women leaders have become the logical choices of their community associations to represent women's interests in local councils or governments. Other women elected to local legislative bodies may be homemakers, small-scale producers, village teachers or volunteer workers for livelihood, health and nutrition programmes. What they often share is the critical realization that women can improve their circumstances, promote their rights, and enhance the development of their communities and nation.

Inside formal political systems, the menu of options for action on women's political participation includes adopting and implementing well-designed quotas. These should take into account local circumstances and the electoral system, and be backed by legal compliance mechanisms. Constructive public debate around quotas can raise public awareness and political interest, helping to push boundaries where political parties are unlikely to provide more balanced opportunities on their own. Quotas should be considered for elected offices, as well as for the civil service, judiciary and other critical public leadership positions where parity lags behind.

Engaging political parties, along with traditional leaders and bodies, is another important step. They can help extend support for gender equality and minimize possible backlash against a growing political role for women. Gender sensitization training, including through study tours within or across countries, can be conducted for political candidates and leaders before elections, and politicians in office after elections.

Inside formal political systems, the menu of options for action on women's political participation includes adopting and implementing well-designed quotas

As discussed earlier in this chapter, some of the elements for parties in particular include revising party positions and rules to support gender equality, consciously promoting women candidates through higher placements on party lists, and understanding the political benefits that can come from appealing to women and other voters. Since finance is increasingly a determinant of entry to political systems, campaign financing patterns should be reviewed both within parties and by electoral management bodies, not just in light of women's inequitable access, but also for cleaner political processes.

Both inside and outside political systems, women need to see that they can and should participate, aim for high positions and make a difference that is meaningful to them and the societies in which they live. Supporting women's knowledge, capacity and interest in public positions can come through high-quality mentoring programmes or other opportunities to build their skills.

Education systems should also support direct experience of democratic processes as part of schooling. School elections for positions like 'head boy,' 'head girl' or 'prefect' can provide early training on campaigning, voting, accepting and conceding power, and providing a healthy opposition. Future generations would benefit from such exposure, as against teachers picking the most obedient or best-performing students.

Know, use and change the rules. Institutional rules generally dictate the functioning of, for example, a parliament, with impacts on the conduct of parliamentarians and the passage of legislation. Women should learn about these, apply them to their advantage and change them where necessary. If laws or their interpretation inhibit political participation, legal reform can provide all citizens with equal opportunities in public life.

Some areas of focus in terms of gender equality include securing institutional procedures that are gender-friendly, such as provisions for childcare; reviewing committee positions for gender balance; providing on-going support for women entering parliament and serving in leadership positions once they get there; initiating and building political support for legislation that advances gender equality; and parliamentary discourse that routinely integrates and therefore normalizes gender equality as a core component of political debate.[127]

Electoral rules can address barriers such as unsafe campaigning spaces and restrictions on female mobility, opening up more space for women to step forward.

Recognize the value of women as role models for others. Women in public office, especially when they excel, demonstrate to other women that it is possible for them to succeed in public life—and that politics does not need to be about just the usual faces and patterns of behaviour.

If women are proactive or greater in number, they show that women can influence political events, shape and operationalize political voice and introduce issues that are otherwise ignored. New ground can be broken as women interact with new groups of people, acquire the skills to verbalize and address the interests of constituents, and gain confidence as active agents of social change. When women are conscious of their capacity as role models, they can deliberately use this to encourage other women's participation. Systematically tracking information on women in a full range of positions—including in the executive and legislative branches, political appointments, the civil service, the judiciary and non-traditional ministries—can demonstrate the diversity of political opportunities available for future generations of both women and men.

Women's political participation can also shift dynamics within families, extending from there into the community. Studies of the *panchayat* system in India have found that husbands now consult their wives on issues they had not consulted on before, and take on housework. Women are seen as persons in their own rights, rather than in relation to male family members.[128]

Explicitly seek out women's voices in crises and after. Women and men face conflicts and natural disasters, playing varied roles in times of crisis. They share insecurity, poor living conditions and danger. Both may join armed combat. While women and girls are vulnerable in specific ways, such as through gender-based violence and restricted mobility, they make active contributions and have useful inside information. They also pick up a variety of skills in crises, some of which are transferable to normal life, and valuable in formulating policies and programmes for the aftermath.

Women's engagement should be explicitly sought in all relief, early recovery and rehabilitation programmes, as well as across all phases of peace negotiations, disarmament, demobilization and reintegration. Post-crisis initiatives that ignore gender complexities can miss out on women's enormous potential, and the potentially different needs of women and men. Political leadership backed by civil society has the chance to genuinely 'build back better'.

Link political voice to all other human development issues. Women's poorer health, economic standing and education are barriers to political participation. Equally, steps to improve women's standing on these issues should be connected to efforts to ensure that women can hold the political system responsible for sustained progress.

This issue is increasingly relevant to local governments in countries undergoing some variation of devolution or decentralization, given the greater role local officials are playing in the delivery of services. In Bangladesh, advocacy and monitoring by civil society groups led to increases in the number of physicians in 12 sub-districts. Now there are seven to eight physicians, up from two to four, in each sub-district health centre. They include an obstetrician/gynaecologist.[129]

The groups *Mahila Samakhya* (Education for Women's Equality) and *Vanangana* (Daughters of the Forest) have worked in some of the most economically backward regions of India, and among some of the poorest people in these regions, to improve social and economic conditions and enhance political voice. Mahila Samakhya has trained poor lower caste and tribal women as handpump mechanics, sparking a new consciousness among the women about caste, class and gender issues and inspiring in many a deep desire to pursue formal literacy.[130] The two groups have collaborated to directly address deaths related to marriage dowries. Street plays in villages use local idioms and folklore to critique the common notion that sons-in-law must be revered and that parents should 'befriend their daughter at her birth, but not in her fate'—where her fate is her marriage.[131] The performances generate intense debate, with many women in the audiences drawing connections between women's lack of access to resources and their devaluation and vulnerability to violence inside the household.[132]

In the Indian state of Andhra Pradesh, an anti-*arrack* (a type of alcohol) movement was created out of the awareness stirred by the mass literacy campaign of the National Literacy Mission. Most of the groundwork was done locally, with women collectively protesting against *arrack* in their villages. As the movement gathered momentum, political parties became involved. The resulting political pressure changed the state leadership. Overall, the experience demonstrated how women's issues can align with the larger issues of state and society.[133]

Women's poorer health, economic standing and education are barriers to political participation

Gender budgeting goes point by point through the raising of revenues and the allocation of expenditures to ensure that fiscal policies are not gender-blind

Expand mechanisms for accountability. An increase in women's representation, and even the adoption of a gender equality agenda, means little in countries with limited state capacities for implementation and mechanisms to hold politicians to account. Implementation capacities can be a matter of insufficient public resources, but questions also need to be raised about political choices made to disburse funds that are available. Although money is often seen as being gender-neutral, choices about how to raise and spend it have gender dimensions. Many priorities remain set by political patterns that favour powerful men.

One accountability tool now adopted in some form by about half of Asia-Pacific countries is gender-responsive budgeting (Box 3.11). It assesses budgets to see if they have different impacts on women and men. This does not entail the crafting of a separate budget or simply spending more on items specific to women. Rather, gender budgeting, in its fullest form, goes point by point through the raising of revenues and the allocation of expenditures to ensure that fiscal policies are not gender-blind. Allocations to health care may favour urban hospitals to which men have more access than women, for example,

---

BOX 3.11

BUDGETS ARE NOT GENDER-NEUTRAL

Several Asia-Pacific countries have experimented with gender budgeting. The results have varied with the extent of the exercise and political commitment.

India: In 1999, the National Development Council, one of India's highest policy-making bodies, made empowering women and socially excluded groups a specific objective of the Ninth Five Year Plan. The National Institute of Public Finance and Policy subsequently embarked on a comprehensive study of gender budgeting, coming up with an innovative strategy lauded by national and international experts in the field. Among its features is the ability to assess the benefits of budget allocations, and track the link between fiscal policy and gender development.

Based on the study, the Ministry of Finance called upon all government ministries and departments to establish gender budget units and prepare benefit analyzes linked to gender. In 2005, it asked 18 ministries and departments to submit targets benefiting women in their annual reports and performance budgets, and a separate statement on gender and budgetary allocations appeared in the 2005-2006 Union Budget. Over 50 government ministries and departments now prepare gender budgets. The 2008-2009 Union Budget pointed out that gender-specific allocations increased over the previous year from US $3.7 billion to US $5.5 billion.

Nepal: The process of mainstreaming gender into macro policy-making began in 1994 when four different sectors of the Eighth Plan—agriculture, energy, tourism, labour and industry—were analyzed through a gender perspective. A gender-auditing module was incorporated into the Ninth Plan in 1997, after which the process became a gender budgeting exercise covering both taxation and expenditure.

Guidelines on gender budgeting were prepared for ministries to undertake gender budgeting, and revised for

sub-national governments. In 2005, the Ministry of Finance began issuing a Gender Budgeting Statement and instituted a Gender Budgeting Committee. Nepal is now working on a system to score allocations by their impacts on gender, using markers such as increases in women's participation and employment options. In 2008, a Gender Budgeting Statement revealed that 13.9 per cent of the total budget comprises allocations that directly respond to gender issues; 35.4 per cent are indirectly responsive and 50.6 per cent are gender-neutral. More recent gender budgeting statements for 2009 and 2010 reveal improvements: 17.3 per cent, 36.4 per cent and 46.3 per cent respectively.

The Philippines: Gender-responsive budgeting initiatives began in 1995 with a decision to earmark at least five per cent of all departmental expenditures on programmes for women in national and sub-national budgets. This approach proved problematic, resulting in the misallocation or lack of use of earmarked funds. Gender issues became marginalized in mainstream budgeting, as some departments construed floor limits as a spending ceiling. Targeting expenditures based on the identification of appropriate programmes for women or reprioritizing expenditures based on a generic list of appropriate programmes and policies might have been more effective.

A few local gender budgeting initiatives, particularly in the municipalities of Sorsogon and Hilongos, have made attempts to identify specific gender needs before budgeting. They have moved from quota-based gender budgeting to the identification of entry points for results-oriented budgeting. In the process, they have come up with specific targets, such as strengthening the agricultural sector to provide women with more income options and reduce forced migration.

Sources: Chakraborty 2009; Khanal 2009.

even as rural maternal mortality rates remain unacceptably high because women there have no voice or visibility to demand better care.

The depth and effectiveness of gender budgeting depends on it being placed firmly on political agendas, as budgets are a political process. Political leaders need to understand that a gender-sensitive orientation for fiscal policies can lead to more accurate and effective spending choices for both women and men—which can in turn boost human development progress. Ideally, after a gender budgeting exercise, a budget will end up connected both to overall fiscal policy strategies, as is the norm, and to a national gender development framework so that steps towards equality can be deliberately pursued.

Part of the political value of gender budgeting is that it encourages transparency through a process of close scrutiny. This can help protect allocations to support gender equality from disappearing into other uses. When women and men are aware of the choices that have been made—or even involved in helping to shape such choices, as politicians, civil servants or civil society representatives—they can also insist that policy makers keep their promises.

Transformation Through Participation

Asia-Pacific's record on women's political participation falls short of its development achievements and ambitions. A handful of countries can claim significant progress, either at the national or local level, but the region as a whole lags behind much of the rest of the world. The unrest felt in some parts of the region suggests that a groundswell of people is pushing back against limits imposed by political systems that are not participatory, either by design or practice.

Women's political participation should be part of a broader aim for societies that are democratic, stable and grounded in genuinely equal citizenship. If a broad cross-section of women can come to the political table, they will bring new perspectives, talents and interests to decision-making. Politics and policy-making might become more responsive to a more inclusive array of public concerns—and more accurate in decisions about the use of public resources. At first, this may not be easy or straightforward. But by deepening democracy, it can lead to transformation through improved human development prospects for citizens at large.

The depth and effectiveness of gender budgeting depends on it being placed firmly on political agendas, as budgets are a political process

BOLSTERING VOICE: A GENDER EQUALITY AGENDA

Gender equality in political participation is socially just and basic to the notion of democracy. A political system where half the population cannot participate defies the meaning of the term. Broad-based participation also has a clear practical dimension—and a development rationale. It supports efficiency: More sources of information make political decision-making more informed and responsive to diverse realities on the ground. Through access to the political arena, men and women can articulate and shape solutions that unleash progress for themselves and society at large. Progress in political voice and decision-making is therefore critical in shaping issues of economic power and legal rights.

Linking progress on women's representation and democracy to progress on gender equality and human development includes actions to:

Encourage women and men to act collectively on gender. Promote men and women's public involvement in advocating for gender equality ↦ Encourage men's involvement to expand political support.

Make gender equality part of common politics. Support issues of gender equality as common ground for people from across the political spectrum ↦ Form alliances between governments, civil society organizations and others around advancing gender equality, even in the presence of disagreements about other issues.

Support women's participation inside and outside the formal political system. Adopt and implement well-designed quotas in legislatures, political parties, the judiciary and civil service ↦ Back quotas with legal compliance mechanisms ↦ Review campaign financing to ensure equitable access for women ↦ Support women's and civil society groups mobilizing around gender issues, including by educating voters, advocating for the passage of laws, creating networks and channelling information about gender equality issues into the political system ↦ Cultivate women's knowledge, capacity and interest in public positions through high-quality mentoring programmes or other opportunities to build their skills ↦ Make direct experiences of democratic processes part of education systems.

Know, use and change the rules. Provide opportunities for women to learn about institutional rules that dictate the functioning of parliament, parties and other institutions of governance ↦ Promote legal reform when laws or their interpretation inhibit political participation ↦ Address barriers during elections related to security and restrictions on female mobility, opening up more space for women to step forward.

Recognize the value of women as role models for others. Show women the opportunities they may find or the gaps they can fill by systematically tracking information on women in a full range of positions – including in the executive and legislative branches, political appointments, the civil service, the judiciary and non-traditional ministries.

Explicitly seek out women's voices in crises and after. Engage women in all relief, early recovery and rehabilitation programmes, as well as across all phases of peace negotiations, disarmament, demobilization and reintegration ↦ Encourage political leadership to work with civil society to genuinely 'build back better'.

Link political voice to all other human development issues. Factor in women's disadvantages in health, economic standing and education as barriers to political participation ↦ Identify ways to ensure that women can hold the political system for sustained progress to improve women's standing on all issues linked to their capabilities and opportunities.

Expand mechanisms for accountability. Put gender-responsive budgeting firmly on political agendas to ensure the collection and allocation of public funds supports gender equality, and encourage transparency.

4

Advancing Legal Rights

A Brave Voice against Injustice

An anonymous woman, circa 6th Century

More than 1,500 years ago, the cruel king Zanburak Shah ruled in Kabul. All males in his jurisdiction had to work with no pay—their rights compromised—on building a wall around the city to repel invaders. All day the men toiled, bending, lifting and cementing stones. Those who did not or could not work were buried alive in the wall.

Among them was a young man who, although engaged to a woman from the city, was hesitant to ask for leave to marry for fear of being buried alive. His young fiancée heard this. She put on working clothes and joined the workers.

Zanburak Shah visited the site and was surprised to see a woman among the men. When he approached to find out more, she immediately covered her face. The puzzled Shah asked, 'How is it that you veil your face from me but have no problem with these men?'

Angered by the Shah's injustice and the meek obedience of the workers, she answered, 'Among all present here there is only one man—you who so cruelly work these people by force! All these others working here are not even fit to be women!'

Picking up a stone, she flung it at Zanburak Shah. The stone hit him on the head and he collapsed. The young woman's brave act triggered the workers to attack the king, ending his misrule. Thus Kabul society was saved.

As told to Anuradha Rajivan by Mohammed Sediq Orya from Afghanistan.

Advancing Legal Rights

A country's legal system touches every aspect of human development, human rights and gender equality. In regulating rights and imposing duties, the law and legal practices influence how women and men seek opportunities and make choices to better their lives. They affect the capabilities of men and women and determine physical security, relations within the family, workplace conditions and voice in public discourse. The ability to access the justice system also has an impact on whether or not these laws touch people's lived experience.

Despite constitutional provisions on equality before the law, gender norms seep into legal systems unnoticed and unchallenged. This means that women and men experience the same laws and legal systems differently.[1] But should they? Gender equality requires uncovering biases in the legal process, so that both the substance of laws and how they are upheld become powerful tools to advance equality, including by adhering to the principle of the rule of law and applying corrective measures to redress past discrimination.

The alternative, prevalent in much of Asia-Pacific today, is for laws and legal practices to allow—even encourage—discrimination to fester. They can be overtly biased or silent on the imbalances in the social, economic and political standings of women and men, even when these mean that not every citizen has equal access to justice. They may be inconsistent, offering broad protections of rights on the one hand, often in constitutions, while stripping away these guarantees on the other, typically through inconsistent laws or practices within the daily running of the justice system.

Asia-Pacific now has more laws that support the advancement of women than at any point in history. This achievement deserves to be recognized and is the foundation for continued progress. At the same time, not nearly enough has been done. More than half the countries of East Asia and Pacific and over three-fourths of the South Asian countries are marked by medium to high level of discrimination in economic rights. The social rights situation is even worse and deteriorating.[2]

Most legal systems in Asia-Pacific have been buffeted by competing influences, from colonialism to domestic demands to international human rights standards. This explains in part why many have ended up with contradictory or archaic statutes and discriminatory practices. But in the drive towards human development, and in the embrace of modern societies grounded in the principle of equal citizenship, more attention needs to be paid to how the law holds women back, and how this can constrain further advancements for women, men and societies at large.

The region falls far behind where it could be on basic issues such as protecting women from violence, upholding entitlements to property—or even allowing people to divorce in an informed and reasonable way. Two barriers are in place: the first comes from the construction of laws themselves, which may be overtly discriminatory, full of gaps or contradictory. The second barrier is restricted access to the legal system and to justice within

The region falls far behind where it could be on basic issues such as protecting women from violence, upholding entitlements to property

it. This involves all the reasons that women—because they are women—may not go to police, the court or other mechanisms for justice, or may not find equal treatment even if they do.

Too often, gender discrimination in the region's legal systems remains justified on the basis of conventional notions about the needs and capabilities of women and men. These have not always been examined in light of whether or not they truly serve current priorities or a future of human development. Rarely are women themselves consulted about how the law could be a lever for change, rather than a source of deepening inequalities. In April 2009, scores of Afghan Shia women protested against the controversial provisions of the Shia Personal Status Law. They argued that the new law 'insults the dignity of women' and must be withdrawn because it was imposed on them without consultation.[3] The law was passed anyway, containing many provisions that deny women their rights. It grants custody rights for children exclusively to fathers and grandfathers, and stipulates that a woman can leave the house without her husband's permission only if she has 'reasonable legal reasons'.[4]

Legal rights are critical to back gains in economic power and political voice. Legal systems that support gender equality and human development provide consistent guarantees of equality in all spheres: constitutional, civil and criminal, public and private. This implies eliminating overt discrimination, filling gaps and removing contradictions. CEDAW, signed by 35 countries in the region, can be an important reference point. It focuses on substantive equality, which means that all people, regardless of gender, have the same status in respect to specific rights and obligations.[5]

While there is no perfect legislation in the arena of human relationships, this chapter explores how legislation can pave the way towards more balanced interactions between women and men. In doing so, it provides protection and opens new opportunities for both to acquire capabilities and pursue human development.

A Tangle of Legal Influences

People do not make or enforce laws in isolation. Multiple influences, from colonialism to indigenous customs, have shaped the legal systems of Asia and the Pacific—not always in desirable or consistent ways. These factors determine the foundation of the law itself, as well as its evolution and ongoing interpretation.

Varying political, economic, religious, social and cultural reference points with a mixed record on gender equality mean that women in the same country may not be equal before the law. Some are born into communities governed by different laws; others lack the knowledge and economic resources to access the justice system. Examining past and present influences throws light on the roots of legal inequalities, as a starting point for rectifying them. It also reveals signs of progress pointing the way towards further advancements.

Colonial Legacies Persist

Legal systems across Asia and the Pacific still bear the marks of former colonial powers. Archaic 19th Century legal codes permeate laws in many of the former British colonies of South and South East Asia, for example. Three main pieces of British-based legislation—the Penal Code, the Evidence Act and the Code of Criminal Procedure—are the foundation of the criminal justice systems in Bangladesh, India, Pakistan and Sri Lanka, although changes have been made in each country.[6]

Pre-colonial India based its law on sacred religious texts, unlike England where canon or ecclesiastical law gradually disappeared

Archaic 19th Century legal codes permeate laws in many of the former British colonies of South and South East Asia

from the legal system. For Hindus, the divinely inspired Vedas and Dharamshastras —the oldest of which was the Code of Manu believed to have been written during 200 BC to AD 100—contained, among other things, the rules of right conduct. For Muslims, the Quran was the source of legal norms. The function of the state was restricted to enforcing the law. It was not involved in making laws since these were already complete and enshrined in the sacred texts and customs. Legal procedures were not highly institutionalized with formal rules and rituals. A typical legal proceeding in pre-colonial India was likely to be conducted by a village headman or committee consisting of local men of status.[7]

When the British colonialists arrived, they had some input into family law in South Asia, but generally opted not to interfere in this area. Extremely diverse family law systems were maintained, with each community following its own set of rules and regulations and with different kinds of legislative interventions.

The British did leave their imprint on other forms of law, believing that British laws should be the model for other countries, regardless of their values and interests.[8] Prevailing British norms called for protecting the honour of the individual and his or her family, for example, over punishing an injury to a woman. All British colonies also inherited laws criminalizing sodomy and sex work, some of which still remain in force. Rape laws contain narrow definitions, such as excluding marital rape and considering consent from the view of the offender.

The advent of colonization in the Pacific meant that some traditionally matrilineal areas—including in Fiji, Tokelau, Republic of Marshall Islands, Vanuatu and Solomon Islands—gradually became patrilineal. Women no longer had the same rights to assets or inheritance. In Pohnpei in Federated States of Micronesia, German law awarded

'each adult male a piece of land', so land is now commonly transferred from father to son, although daughters can also inherit it.[9]

Customs Can Open the Door to Discrimination

Women and men in different Asia-Pacific societies find strength in traditions, customs and beliefs, including those derived from religion. But these can also be a source of discriminatory gender norms that at times affect systems of justice, even in officially 'secular' or 'modern' societies. They may remain uncodified in laws, but enforced in a *de facto* manner by local leaders or informal courts. They can also be codified and enforced by mainstream courts, or broadly recognized within constitutions so that courts must determine how they fit with other laws. Afghanistan, for example, attempts to strike a balance through legal provisions that require courts to rule in accordance with general custom, provided that the custom does not contradict existing laws or the principles of justice.[10]

This kind of attitude, while intended to respect and accommodate prevailing norms, has not been sufficient in scrubbing out practices that harm women. Since customs and religious beliefs are deeply rooted in the social and cultural ethos, they can enjoy a kind of extra-judicial authority—an exception to the principle of non-discrimination on the grounds of gender, or even the notion of all citizens being equal before the law—so that different communities may end up with different legal rights. Too often, customs and religious beliefs have become a rationale for laws and legal systems to ignore or soft-peddle or even, in the worst cases, justify issues such as discriminatory inheritance practices and the multiple forms of violence that specifically target women.

It is important to debunk the notion that customs or traditions are automatically more regressive than more modern, secular laws. Bhutan's Inheritance Act of 1980, for example, guarantees equal inheritance for sons and daughters, but traditional inheritance practices may also be observed. For most Bhutanese, these stipulate that daughters inherit family land. As a result, 60 per cent of rural women hold land registration titles – a higher figure than anywhere else in South Asia. Inheritance practices favouring daughters also account for the large number of women who own shops and businesses. [11]

In Viet Nam, by contrast, there has been a deliberate attempt to modernize legal statutes, including those related to land. By law, the land belongs to the people; the state leases land and issues land-use rights certificates. The names of both husband and wife must be mentioned on the certificate as stipulated in the revised Land Law 2003.[12] Since the law was amended, 90 per cent of *newly-issued* land use right certificates have the name of both husband and wife. However, existing certificates issued before the revised Land Law still remain in effect and are used in current transactions.[13] The Viet Nam Household Living Standards Survey 2004 reveals that for agricultural land, 15 per cent of those households with land user certificates held them jointly, while 66 per cent were held by men and 19 per cent by women.[14]

At times, customs and religious beliefs can be deliberately mixed with the law to consolidate political, economic and social power to the detriment of less powerful women and men. In Pakistan, a local *jirga* pronounced the judgment of gang rape on a village woman—Mukhtar Mai—in 2002. Her 12-year-old brother had been seen walking with a girl from the more influential tribe. The tribe demanded Mai's rape to avenge their 'honour'.[15]

A few Pacific countries and territories still have archaic laws against witchcraft and sorcery that are couched in gender-neutral language, but applied exclusively to older women. Public killing of those suspected of witchcraft and sorcery is not uncommon. As recently as January 2009, a woman in rural Papua New Guinea was bound and gagged, tied to a log and set ablaze on a pile of tires, possibly because villagers suspected her of being a witch.[16]

Courts in the Pacific struggle to manage a complex brew of customary laws and practices, constitutional provisions, longstanding notions of women's subordinate status and emerging expectations around women's rights to equality. These are reflected in the laws themselves and how they are interpreted. In Vanuatu, the traditional *Malvatumauri* (House of Chiefs), supported by church leaders, attempted to pass a 'new' customary law in 2005 to prevent ni-Vanuatu women from wearing trousers, shorts, pants or jeans. The Vanuatu Women's Centre challenged this with a media campaign saying the dress code was unconstitutional and against their rights. The code was withdrawn, but is still enforced intermittently and informally.[17] In Tuvalu, there is a common practice called *moetolo* where a man creeps into the *fale* (traditional house) and rapes a woman, while others are sleeping or pretending to sleep. If the rapist is taken to court—a long shot, since this crime is mostly unreported—the court may maintain that if a woman was really being raped, someone would have taken action to stop it. This sidesteps the issue of whether the watchers refused to interfere because they believe that women's role is to please men, a belief often shared by judicial officials. In most cases, the man will only be charged with trespassing.[18]

Patterns of social organization, often reflecting religious or customary beliefs, also influence notions about gender that in turn are reflected in legal systems. Patriarchal societies, found in much of Asia-Pacific, are premised on a notion of male superiority. Women are seen as weak, biologically inferior and incapable of decision-making.[19] These attitudes appear in the creation and interpretation of laws when the husband is automatically perceived as the 'head of the family' while the wife is a 'home-maker'.[20] In child custody issues, the father is the 'natural guardian' of the child. Violent behaviour in the home can be treated as a normal male prerogative that does not require the justice system to intervene. In Viet Nam, the Confucian concept that men are responsible for the 'education' of their wives and children underpins acceptance of physical violence. [21]

Politicized Religion Sees Rights as Threats

The politics of religion remains a contentious issue in Asia-Pacific, one that is reflected in laws and legal practices. Provisions for religion in some constitutions have made it a potent legal and political force, with consequences for how women experience the justice system. Fundamentalist voices have raised the spectre of women's rights as a threat to religious freedoms, sidestepping the reality of diverse interpretations and cultural practices.[22]

In Pakistan, women's rights debates with political and religious overtones have gone back and forth for decades. The Muslim Family Laws Ordinance was passed in 1961, with provisions to discourage polygamy and protect women's rights in divorce, among others. It drew much criticism from religious leaders and had to be protected in 1963 by the Fundamental Rights Bill, the first amendment to the Constitution, which specified that the ordinance was not open to judicial review.[23] Zia-ul-Haq's military regime later imposed an 'Islamization agenda' to pacify religious factions.[24] He introduced the draconian Hudood Laws in 1979.[25] The harsh Zina Ordinance required rape victims to produce four male witnesses as evidence for the crime or face adultery charges. A bill to amend the discriminatory law was introduced in the National Assembly of Pakistan in 2004. The proposed legislation led to a split and divisions among the Assembly's members. Conservative groups felt that the law made in the 'name of Islam' should not be abolished. Liberal groups contended that customs and laws that discriminate against women must be repealed.[26] The law was finally overturned in 2006 through the Women Protection Bill.[27]

In some countries, the principle of respecting diversity, while a valid one, has been used to allow discriminatory laws grounded in religion. This argument has been used in India, where the Constitution gives equal rights to women under civil law, but Muslims, Hindus and Christians can adhere to their personal laws in marriage, divorce and other family matters. The Indian state has aimed to establish a uniform civil code, taking steps such as the Special Marriage Act of 1954, which provides that any couple can marry, irrespective of community, in a civil ceremony. Yet a uniform civil code is still not in place.

Many members of the religious hierarchy in the Pacific adopt an orthodox and patriarchal interpretation of religion that has led them to become politically engaged in fighting against legal reform benefiting women. In 2003, the Methodist Church in Fiji attempted to stop the passage of the Family Law Act, which removed systemic discrimination against women in family law, on the basis that it was un-Christian and anti-indigenous Fijian. The church was ultimately persuaded not to officially oppose the act by the ruling government party, closely aligned to the church at the time, and by various prominent individuals.[28] In Vanuatu, some Christian churches and traditional chiefs challenged the Family Protection Act 2008, designed to protect women from domestic violence. They maintained the law contradicts ni-Vanuatu custom as well as Christian and Melanesian values in the preamble of the Vanuatu Constitution.[29] The Supreme Court ruled in late November 2008 that the new law is consistent with the Constitution.

Provisions for religion in some constitutions have made it a potent legal and political force, with consequences for how women experience the justice system

The Philippines has a constitutional provision on separation of church and state,[30] but Roman Catholic beliefs are widely considered responsible for certain official policies. The Government has adopted the Catholic Church's line of opposition to contraception, with adverse impacts on the country's family planning programme.[31]

National Reforms Produce Impetus from Within

Countries in Asia-Pacific have pursued modern reforms of their legal systems for a number of reasons, including to adapt to new national priorities, eliminate outdated statutes, conform to international commitments and respond to demands from citizens. Some reforms relate to gender equality, but progress is not always consistent or straightforward. Over the years, national legal reforms have generally occurred in two ways: through legislative changes and judicial precedents.

In South Asia, Sri Lanka's Penal Code of 1883 has undergone many amendments since 1995, taking into account some criminal offences and their adverse impacts on women in particular. To curb violence against women, the Code now includes provisions on sexual harassment, grave sexual abuse, incest, sexual exploitation of children and trafficking. In addition to these new legal provisions, it also imposes stiffer sentences now. In the case of rape, for instance, the minimum sentence increased from zero to seven years.[32]

Several East Asian countries have enacted laws against violence against women in the past few years.[33] Cambodia, China and Viet Nam have reformed their land laws to confer equal rights to land titling. Viet Nam and the Philippines enacted the comprehensive 2006 Law on Gender Equality and 2009 Magna Carta of Women respectively. These laws uphold women's rights in the public and private spheres.[34] Indonesia reformed its discriminatory Citizenship Act in 2006 by conferring the right to pass on nationality to children irrespective of gender, marital status or spouse's nationality.[35]

In 2007, Nepal's Supreme Court, responding to a coalition of lesbian, gay, bisexual, transsexual and intersex groups, ordered the Government 'to formulate appropriate legislation or amend existing legislation' in order to end discrimination against these communities.[36] The following year, the first official identity card was issued describing a person as a 'third gender', instead of the usual male and female categories.[37]

Judicial precedents have advanced women's standing in Bangladesh, where the High Court gave a landmark judgment in a case in which female students of Jahangirnagar University challenged a sexual harassment inquiry set up by the university. The court ruled that the decision to exonerate the perpetrator and expel the female students was 'without lawful authority'.[38] The verdict sets a precedent that will deter future perpetrators. The court also expressed the opinion that rigid rules of corroboration are not always required to substantiate allegations of sexual harassment, highlighting an emerging progressive trend in the region.

Precedents can also have negative impacts. In 2008 the Sri Lankan Supreme Court, in a rape case, concluded that the law setting a minimum mandatory sentence for rape was tantamount to interference with judicial discretion by the legislature. The court observed that a minimum sentencing guideline conflicts with the Constitution. It maintained its right to impose a sentence that it deems appropriate.[39]

The International Community Weighs In

International agreements can be important reference points for gender equality. Countries in Asia-Pacific have proactively used them to

Countries in Asia-Pacific have pursued modern reforms of their legal systems. Some reforms relate to gender equality, but progress is not always consistent or straightforward

improve their own domestic legislation. One of the most important agreements is the 1979 Convention on the Elimination of All Forms of Discrimination against Women (CEDAW). It offers a comprehensive framework for gender equality based on the principles of equality, non-discrimination and state obligation.[40]

Out of 39 countries in Asia-Pacific, 35 states have ratified or acceded to the Convention.[41] But this signal of commitment to gender equality has not come without 'reservations'—a device that allows countries to opt out of certain parts of the Convention. The nature of reservations varies and is influenced by factors such as religion and national constitutions and laws (Figure 4.1).

Aside from the Middle East and North Africa, Asia-Pacific has the highest percentage of CEDAW States Parties with some form of reservation. It is also second only to the Middle East and North Africa in the percentage of countries that have not signed the CEDAW Optional Protocol, a complaint mechanism meant to strengthen enforcement of the Convention.[42] In the Pacific, a study of nine countries found that CEDAW compliance rates, within their *de jure* laws, ranged from 18 to 44 per cent, with Fiji having the highest ranking. [43]

Countries that have ratified CEDAW are legally bound to report in detail on their efforts to achieve gender equality to a global Committee on the Elimination of Discrimination against Women every four years.[44] In theory, governments have an obligation to follow through on the recommendations the experts make, although a variety of factors can influence this process, including levels of current political commitment and domestic resources. The recommendations can be shunted off to national women's ministries or institutions that may or may not have enough of their own power and resources to oversee far-reaching changes in laws and legal practice.[45] A number of countries in the

Figure 4.1: Too Many Reservations to CEDAW

Notes: Reservations to CEDAW in Asia-Pacific are mostly focused on social equality. Article 1 (definition of discrimination against women); article 2 (pursue all appropriate means a policy of eliminating discrimination against women); article 4 (adopt temporary special measures); article 5 (modify the social and cultural patterns of conduct of men and women); article 7 (eliminate discrimination against women in the political and public life); article 9 (confer equal rights to acquire, change or retain their nationality); article 11 (take all appropriate measures to eliminate discrimination against women in the field of employment); article 15 (ensure equality before law); article 16 (eliminate discrimination against women in all matters relating to marriage and family relations); article 29 (international arbitration over dispute related to interpretation or application of the Convention between State Parties).

Source: UN n.d.-c.

Pacific have set up women's ministries and departments to implement CEDAW, but have stopped short of passing the requisite legislation to comply with it.[46]

Some national constitutions in the Pacific allow the direct use of international conventions in domestic courts, even without ratification by national parliaments.[47] This type of provision in Fiji has encouraged courts to apply international conventions in innovative ways. In State vs. Bechu,[48] the magistrate chastised the accused during a sentencing for rape, stating: 'Women are your equal and therefore must not be discriminated against on the basis of gender. Men should be aware of … CEDAW which our country ratified.… Under the Convention the state shall ensure that all forms of discrimination against women must be eliminated at all costs. The courts shall be the watchdog of this obligation. The old school of thought – that women were inferior to men or part of their personal property, that can be discarded or treated unfairly at will – is now obsolete and should no longer be accepted by our society.'

CEDAW has been instrumental in efforts in some countries to reform civil and criminal laws. Vanuatu's 2008 Family Protection Act is the only stand-alone legislation combating domestic violence in the Pacific; it was guided by CEDAW and the Convention on the Rights of the Child 1989.[49] Viet Nam is using CEDAW in the comprehensive review of legal normative documents that has followed the adoption of its Law on Gender Equality. In Cambodia, the Ministry of Justice is spearheading a CEDAW review of legislation on domestic violence, trafficking, domestic workers and marriage.[50]

In Nepal, although marital rape is still not a criminal offence, a judgment of the Supreme Court held that an exemption from marital rape conflicts with CEDAW. The court reasoned that if an act is an offence by its very nature, it is unreasonable to say that it is not an offence merely because different categories of individuals commit it. The court ruled that marital rape is a denial of a woman's independent right to existence and self- respect.[51]

A high percentage of State Parties to CEDAW in Asia-Pacific have backed away from a full endorsement of the Convention. Through reservations to CEDAW, they have exempted themselves from commitments to defining discrimination, ending harmful traditional practices, and granting women full rights in citizenship and marriage, among others.

Apart from CEDAW, other important international conventions with implications for gender equality include the International Labour Organization's (ILO) C111 Discrimination—Employment and Occupation Convention 1958 and C143 Migrant Workers (Supplementary Provisions) Convention 1975. C143 confers upon migrant workers 'equality of treatment with nationals' in respect of guarantees of employment security. The Convention also requires Members to declare and pursue a national policy of equality of opportunity, social security, cultural rights and collective freedoms of migrant workers and their families.[52]

Shortfalls in the Substance of the Law

By themselves, laws can be weak instruments of social change. To have teeth, they must be supported by widespread acceptance of their validity and vigorous implementation. At the same time, by introducing new concepts and reforms, laws can be an essential platform for progress towards gender equality.

Looking at laws in terms of gender equality requires understanding both the overarching principles that guide legal systems—normally expressed in constitutions—and the framework of statutory provisions that then translate these principles into what most people experience as the rules that govern their lives.

Three Principles should be Enshrined in Constitutions

All legal systems draw on certain basic principles, both to create and implement laws.

Looking at laws in terms of gender equality requires understanding both the overarching principles that guide legal systems and the framework of statutory provisions that then translate these principles into what most people experience as the rules that govern their lives

CAUGHT IN BETWEEN: THE DILEMMA OF MUSLIM WOMEN IN MALAYSIA

Marina Mahathir

Malaysia is a country that can be justifiably proud of the achievements of her female citizens. Education is virtually free in government schools and most girls attend school and go on to higher education, resulting in a majority of the enrolment in universities being female. Many women work outside the home and some hold high posts in Government and the private sector, ranging from the Governor of the Central Bank to various corporate executives.

Malaysia's population is multiethnic, multicultural and multi-religious, with Muslims forming the majority faith. Historically, when it comes to family laws governing marriage, divorce, custody and inheritance, Muslims are subjected to *syariah* laws while civil laws govern the personal lives of non-Muslims. This has resulted in a disparity in the rights between the two groups, particularly for women.

For instance, civil law has outlawed polygamy for non-Muslims while it is still allowed for Muslims. However even for Muslims, polygamists had to comply with several conditions that protect existing wives before they were allowed to take additional wives. Unfortunately these laws, considered the most progressive in the world in the 1980s, have now been amended in a regressive direction, offering less protection for women than before. For instance, previously men intending to take on another wife had to obtain the written permission of his first wife but this requirement is now no longer necessary.

Although the Federal Constitution was amended in 2001 to disallow discrimination on the basis of gender, there still remain vestiges of such discrimination especially for Muslim women. For example, it is still unclear whether Muslim women can now be guardians to their own children including the right to sign legal papers for them. Previously much hardship was caused by the need to have fathers'

signatures on school registration forms, for instance.

Muslim women seeking divorces and maintenance have had to suffer an inefficient and lackadaisical *syariah* court system, often leaving them impoverished when husbands have neglected or simply refused to comply with court orders to provide for their children. Efforts to pursue these errant husbands have had some success but the majority of cases remain frustrated. As one female *syariah* lawyer ruefully remarked, 'If I can get RM300 (less than US $100) a month for my client and her kids, I would consider that a success already'.

Part of the problem is Malaysia's federal system where Muslim religious issues are controlled by the individual 13 states and Federal Territory. This has resulted in discrepancies between the Muslim Family Laws in each state which has in turn allowed men to 'shop around' to find the most suitable laws to suit them. For instance, if the conditions for polygamy proved too difficult in one state, men have gotten married in another state with more lax laws, or eloped to southern Thailand. All he needs to do upon his return to his home state is to register the marriage and it will be considered valid.

In recent years, efforts have been made to standardize these laws in all states to prevent these abuses. Unfortunately the standardization has not resulted in a better deal for women when the result has been amendments to the laws that are detrimental to them. In 2006, the Federal Territory Islamic Family Law was passed through Parliament despite strong protests by women Senators in the Upper House and by many women's groups. Amendments made to the laws in the interests of 'gender-neutrality' resulted in many women's rights being given to men without reciprocal men's rights being also given to women.

As an example, previously whatever

assets a woman brought into a marriage remained hers and were not regarded as communal property to be divided equally in the event of a divorce. With the amendments, these assets are included in communal property resulting in men being able to freeze them upon dissolution pending division. However men's rights to polygamy or to pronounce divorce by using the right of 'talak' have not been given to women.

The Federal Territory Islamic Law was not gazetted pending further discussions between the Attorney-General's Chambers, NGOs and religious bodies to amend them to make them fairer to women. The FT laws provide the template for the other states; thus it is imperative that they are improved substantially so as not to discriminate against women.

Apart from the laws, society's attitudes towards women have not changed despite the many advances that Malaysian Muslim women have enjoyed. Their roles as wife and mother still remain the primary expectation of most women, and 'failure' to play these roles 'adequately' sometimes result in violence. Despite the passing of the Domestic Violence Act in 1996, Muslim women still face obstacles ranging from husbands who believe their religion gives them the right to beat their wives, to uncooperative police when women complain. Groups like Sisters in Islam, a women's group that has been fighting for justice and equality for Muslim women for 20 years, have had some success countering these beliefs by providing alternative interpretations of the Quran. Having the Domestic Violence Act has also helped to highlight the right of women not to be abused by their husbands or other relatives.

One example of the patriarchal attitudes towards women, especially Muslim women, is the mandatory premarital HIV testing for all Muslim couples. Although it is touted as one that would help prevent women from getting infected, there has been no evidence that it has worked, nor does it empower women to protect themselves. Indeed it has not stopped women from becoming infected by their husbands later in their marriage after having had several children. A study in Kota Bharu, Kelantan state among 300 HIV-positive widows showed that many of them married drug users without knowing their vulnerability to HIV and subsequently became infected after several years of marriage. Their AIDS widowhood brought on the additional hardship of stigma and discrimination on top of poverty. Some of them remarried HIV-negative men but could not convince their new husbands to use condoms out of fear of being left once again, so great was their dependency on these men.

Efforts to prevent women, Muslim or not, from infection must hinge on an overall change in attitudes towards women. Laws that are non-discriminatory help as well as greater understanding that sexist beliefs do not have any basis in religion. Thus the work by women's groups such as Sisters in Islam is highly important in providing alternative interpretations of the Quran that reinforce the equality of women to men.

Marina Mahathir is an HIV/AIDS and women's rights activist, writer and blogger. She led the Malaysian AIDS Council for 12 years, has written several books and is a newspaper columnist and the executive producer of a TV programme for young women, 3R—Respect, Relax and Respond.

There are three main legal approaches on gender equality: traditional, protectionist and corrective. Each has repercussions for what gender equality means and how it is attained

Three principles outlined by CEDAW are particularly relevant to gender equality and have been articulated in most of Asia-Pacific constitutions: these are State obligation, the principle of equality and non-discrimination.[53]

State obligation may be legally defined but is also a matter of political commitment and philosophy. It is premised on the notion that the state should be an architect in eliminating gender discrimination, in law and legal practices, rather than leaving it solely up to free market forces, for example, or the less predictable process of social change over time.

From the standpoint of jurisprudence, there are three main legal approaches to gender equality: traditional, protectionist and corrective.[54] Each has repercussions for what gender equality means and how it is attained. The traditional approach has been one of 'treating likes alike.' This is based on the sameness principle and 'equal treatment' and ignores the gender differences between men and women. But this notion needs to be examined against the backdrop of gender discrimination—not for every issue, but for many. Women start from a different place than men facing different social, economic, political and institutional obstacles to acquiring rights and capabilities. Aside from the many instances of laws in the region that still overtly discriminate against women, women have less education to understand the law and fewer resources for expensive court battles, to cite only two obvious examples. In many cases, even with 'neutral' laws in place, courts view women through the prism of gender stereotypes and render judgments accordingly.

The protectionist approach to gender equality recognizes differences between men and women and reinforces them by sanctioning different treatment. It is based on the notion of 'likes are to be treated alike.' It takes note of biological difference, but relies on social assumptions as a standard for the roles and capacities attached to men and women. The corrective approach recognizes that women were historically disadvantaged, and that corrective measures must be taken in order to end discrimination.

In addressing wrongs, the principle of non-discrimination stresses prevention, and is thus integral to equality. It implies that legal exclusions that curtail rights and opportunities on the basis of gender must be systematically eliminated. This principle also includes indirect discrimination, which operates from assumptions that men and women already have equal opportunities, when in fact they do not.

One place for establishing these principles in national legal systems is the constitution, as the supreme law of the land and the basis for securing rights. Constitutions may also maintain discrimination (Box 4.1). Most East Asian countries prohibit discrimination on the grounds of sex and mention equality in their constitutions. South Asian countries also provide general constitutional guarantees of equality and non-discrimination for various groups, including women. With the exception of Nepal, however, they refer to the biological definition of sex, rather than the broader definition of gender, which includes socialized roles and behaviours.[55] Discrimination is not defined, and the prohibition mostly applies to the state, excluding the growing private sector. This lack of constitutional definition gives laws and court systems wide latitude in interpretation, including in ways that can perpetuate discrimination.

Lao People's Democratic Republic and Viet Nam have gone further in defining the specifics of gender equality and non-discrimination in their constitutions. Both have consequently been able to assign penalties for discriminatory acts through legal provisions.[56] In 2001, Malaysia added the word 'gender' to a constitutional provision against discrimination that includes religion, race, descent and place of birth. This seemingly simple change prompted a broad review of all legislation, including laws on domestic violence, marriage and divorce, and land ownership.[57] While there is still no clear definition of 'discrimination against women' in Malaysian law, the change has eliminated any legal argument that gender-based discrimination, unlike other forms of discrimination that had been mentioned, is permissible.

A cautionary tale related to legal principles comes from Vanuatu, reflecting some of the legal practice issues delved into later in this chapter. The Penal Code there makes unlawful discrimination a criminal offence, an unusual provision in the Pacific.[58] But no one has ever been prosecuted in Vanuatu for a breach of this section, despite the high level of sex discrimination against ni-Vanuatu women in both conventional and *kustom* law systems.

A clear example of how legal systems in

BOX 4.1

WHEN THE CONSTITUTION PERMITS DISCRIMINATION

In *Tanavalu v Tanavalu & Solomon Islands National Provident Fund*, the court maintained that the Constitution permits the use of custom law even if it discriminates against women. In this case, pension funds were paid to the father of the deceased, rather than to the deceased's widow. The father then distributed the funds at his discretion, giving nothing to the widow. The court ruled that this was in accordance with the relevant custom, where inheritance was by patrilineal succession. The widow could not object on the ground that the custom was discriminatory, as the Constitution specifically exempts custom law from the general prohibition on discriminatory laws. The result of this decision has a long-term impact on widows, whose only source of income following the death of a 'breadwinner' may be their pension funds.

Source: High Court of Solomon Islands 1998.

Asia-Pacific stray from the principles of equality and non-discrimination is in nationality rights, part of the foundation of citizenship itself. Based on the conventional idea that men are the head of the family and everything should flow through them, many Asia-Pacific governments deny female citizens the right to determine the nationality of children born to a foreign spouse. Foreign spouses of women do not have the right to obtain citizenship. Male citizens do not face similar constraints.

Pakistan has amended discriminatory laws to allow women married to foreign nationals to determine the nationality of their children.[59] In South East Asia, only Viet Nam grants mothers the right to determine the nationality of their children. Malaysia's law on citizenship states that a Malaysian woman married to a foreigner can only confer her Malaysian nationality on her child if the child is born in Malaysia. A Malaysian man married to a foreigner, however, can confer his Malaysian nationality on his child regardless of the place of birth.[60]

Gaps Entrench Inequalities

Even when well-intentioned principles provide a framework, gaps in legal systems commonly occur on issues related to women

A clear example of how legal systems in Asia-Pacific stray from the principles of equality and non-discrimination is in nationality rights

An area in Asia-
Pacific where gaps
in laws are wide
and longstanding is
violence against
women

and gender equality. These may be invisible or dismissed as insignificant. Gaps also occur when the law does not anticipate attitudes within the justice system or larger society that ensure a statute will not be fully enacted.

An area in Asia-Pacific where gaps in laws are wide and longstanding is violence against women. This is despite the mounting evidence of the prevalence of different forms of violence, including domestic abuse, rape, trafficking, harmful traditions such as honour killings, sex-selective abortions and biases in the distribution of food that cause disproportionately high rates of malnutrition among girls in some countries.

A groundbreaking 2006 global study on violence against women by the United Nations Secretary-General compared national surveys on one form of violence: the prevalence of physical assaults on women by their male partners. Prevalence rates in Papua New Guinea were among the highest in the world at 67 per cent[61]; the incidence in Bangladesh crossed 47 per cent in multiple surveys; in Viet Nam the figure was 25 per cent. The Philippines had the lowest prevalence rate in Asia-Pacific at 10 per cent.[62] The report suggests that domestic violence extracts billions of dollars from national economies each year, in part through greater burdens on health care systems. A World Bank study has estimated that five per cent of the disease burden for women aged 15 to 44 in developing countries arises comes from domestic violence and rape alone.[63]

Laws in Asia-Pacific have been slow in catching up to this reality. In South Asia, nearly half of the countries have no law on domestic violence; in the Pacific the situation is even worse, with more than 60 per cent of the countries without relevant legislation. In East Asia, meanwhile, more than three-fourths of the countries have drafted legislation on domestic abuse, some within the past few years including Indonesia, Lao

People's Democratic Republic, Republic of Korea, Thailand and Viet Nam. This testifies to a positive change there in tackling violence against women.[64]

In many instances countries lack sanctions for gender-based violence or narrowly define the circumstances under which it may take place. Lao People's Democratic Republic, for example, mentions domestic violence in its 2004 Law on the Development and Protection of Women, but stops short of suggesting it be penalized.[65] In case 'violence is not serious', the law insists upon mediation through family members, close relatives or a village mediation unit rather than prosecution of the perpetrator.[66] Its Penal Code 1990 defines rape as involving force, drugs or other means to make women unconscious for the purpose of rape.[67] This implies that a conscious woman could not be raped. Viet Nam's Penal Code considers a women's ability to defend herself—not the issue of whether or not she has given consent. Prior sexual conduct can be used to establish 'consent'.[68] Across Asia-Pacific, sexual assault laws remain focused on the limited definition of penile penetration, rather than other forms of sexual assault.

Most Asia-Pacific countries have little to offer in legislation on sexual harassment at work places, despite surveys suggesting that 30 to 40 per cent of women workers report some form of harassment – verbal, physical or sexual.[69] Cambodia, the Philippines and Thailand have laws against sexual harassment—although these provisions have limitations on their definitions of abuse. In the Philippines, supervisors, employers and managers with 'authority and influence' are penalized for acts of harassment in the workplace but the law remains silent on sexual abuses committed by co-workers.[70] Even in countries such as India where there has been a strong labour movement, unions have not taken this issue seriously. Understanding is emerging only slowly in the region, despite the growing number of women in the paid workforce.[71]

Maternity leave is another area of employment legislation where the law seems to be inadequate, including in terms of providing paternity leave for men. Most South Asian countries allow maternity leave, but the concept of paternity leave has been introduced in India only in central government employment. In East Asia, only a few countries have provisions for paternity leave. Malaysia and the Philippines grant seven days to fathers of newborns.[72] In the Pacific, most countries and territories provide for paid maternity leave in varying degrees to female civil servants, but not to women working in the private sector. None of the nine countries examined by the CEDAW legislative (*de jure*) indicators study in the Pacific met the standard of 14 weeks of paid maternity leave recommended by the Convention.[73] The ILO's C183 Maternity Protection Convention 2000 also specifies that maternity leave should be not less than 14 weeks.[74]

Some countries are making progress to bridge legal gaps that allow discrimination against women. The 2002 Acid Attacks Crime Repression Act and Acid Control Act in Bangladesh aims to stop the practice of disfiguring women by throwing acid on them; it goes so far as to provide for the death penalty for perpetrators.[75] A legal milestone in India was the 2005 Protection of Women from Domestic Violence Act. It recognizes physical abuse, mental abuse, sexual abuse and economic abuse as forms of violence, and acknowledges the concept of the shared household. Regardless of marital status or the application of different communal family laws, women can secure protective orders and file cases against defendants in the same residence.[76]

Contradictions Produce Discrimination

Contradictions in laws commonly arise when constitutions offer loosely defined promises of gender equality or non-discrimination that open the door to inconsistencies in laws and legal practices. China's Constitution stipulates that men and women should enjoy equal rights in all spheres of life but does not clearly define discrimination.[77] It lacks specific legal provisions on many issues integral to achieving gender equality, such as a guarantee of equal pay for equal work despite a persistent wage gap.[78]

In the Pacific, the principle of equality for women is not firmly embedded in most constitutions, even though some outlaw discrimination. Virtually all constitutions state that the constitution is the supreme law but recognize customary laws.[79] At the same time, it is unclear whether the constitution or the customary laws should take precedence when they conflict, and no country has standalone, comprehensive anti-discrimination legislation. Some Pacific constitutions allow exceptions to the principle of non-discrimination for customary laws.[80] This means that even though state legislation derived from the constitution may not discriminate against women, customary forms of discrimination still legally take place.

Discriminatory laws are often justified as stemming from gender differences. Sometimes this is the case with protective labour legislation that attempts to steer women away from jobs deemed unsafe for them. Certain laws may genuinely warrant this kind of thinking—maternity leave, for example, recognizes the sheer physical reality that women alone go through in giving birth and nursing. But too many others simply deprive individuals of rights, opportunities and choices based on their gender. Some are unconscious holdovers from the past; others reinforce ongoing gender stereotypes about a woman's physical or mental ability, or simply her capability to work outside the domestic sphere. A number of Pacific countries and territories restrict women's employment choices by banning them from night work and industries such as mining. In Samoa and Papua New Guinea, women are prohibited from undertaking manual work.[81]

Similar discriminatory legal provisions exist in Lao People's Democratic Republic, Mongolia, Republic of Korea and Viet Nam. Under Article 113(1) of the Labour Code in Viet Nam, an employer cannot assign a female employee to heavy or dangerous work, or work requiring contact with toxic substances that has adverse effects on her ability to bear and raise a child.[82] This legal provision limits choices and restricts rights.[83] Women in the Philippines are legally prohibited from night work.[84]

Some countries are starting to reverse discriminatory employment legislation. The Bangladesh Supreme Court, in the case of Dalia Parveen vs. Bangladesh Biman Corporation struck down a rule that allowed the travel industry to prefer young attractive women.[85] Although the Fiji Ministry for Employment still has discretion to limit the types of work that women do, it removed restrictions from legislation some years ago in response to lobbying from women's organizations.[86]

Discriminatory notions about sexuality and gender roles persist in some legal systems (Box 4.2). India's 1860 Penal Code treats adulterous acts by men and women differently. Section 497 criminalizes adultery by a man with the wife of another man 'without his consent'. But it does not penalize adultery committed by a married man with an unmarried woman, a widow or a married woman when her husband consents to it. In an example of how sexual assault laws can discriminate against men and boys, India treats non-consensual anal sex as an offence 'against the order of nature', not as rape, including when it happens to young boys.[87]

While many injustices against women in the areas of land rights and inheritance are perpetrated more as a matter of custom than law, as discussed in Chapter 2, discriminatory statutes are at work as well in some countries. In Tonga, the 1875 Constitution and 1927 Land Act established that the eldest male of the male line is preferred over others and women in inheritance. If a woman's husband dies, she does not have an automatic right to live on her husband's land. She can remain until she dies, remarries or 'fornicates'. This means that once a widow has sexual relations with another man, she loses her right to live in her home.[88]

Among indigenous peoples in the region, women are the most vulnerable and face discrimination in terms of gender, geographical remoteness and often poverty as well. Legal discrimination against them is often two-pronged: Gender biases within the customary personal laws and formal laws that marginalize women. Customary inheritance laws tend to be openly discriminatory, such as by preventing women from claiming paternal property as a matter of right; only sons can do so.[89] At times more progressive customs run into discriminatory formal laws. In Indonesia indigenous women are

While many injustices against women in the areas of land rights and inheritance are perpetrated more as a matter of custom than law, discriminatory statutes are at work in some countries

---

BOX 4.2

ERASING SOME FORMS OF DISCRIMINATION, NOT OTHERS IN THE PHILIPPINES

The Philippines provides an example of how countries can have a mixed record of both retaining and removing discriminatory statutes.

Articles 333 and 334 of the Revised Penal Code 1930 in the Philippines define sexual infidelity differently for men and women, for instance. A wife is criminally liable for adultery with a man who is not her husband. On the other hand, a husband's adulterous act with a woman not his wife is not a crime. The husband can be criminally liable for the crime of 'concubinage' only if he is caught with another woman 'under scandalous circumstances' or when he cohabits with another woman in the conjugal dwelling or in any other place. A bill is under consideration to amend articles 333 and 334 of the Philippines Penal Code.

The Philippines has moved forward in its rape laws through the 1997 Anti-Rape Act, which reclassified rape from a crime against chastity to the far more serious charge of a crime against a person. The Rape Victim Assistance and Protection Act followed the next year, mandating the establishment of a Rape Crisis Center in every province and city in the country, providing standard government services for all rape survivors, and prescribing rules to be followed in the investigation of rape cases.

Sources: Cheema 2009; Committee News 2006.

---

recognized in some customary laws as legitimate leaders. But Indonesia's Marriage Act 1974 defines the husband as the 'head' of the household and the wife as the 'housewife' effectively legitimizing the domination of men in the family and in the community. [90] Even in developed countries indigenous women may not be immune from legal discrimination.[91]

Allowances for Diversity Undercut Women's Rights

Some Asia-Pacific countries have laws that discriminate against women as a group. Others have statutes that further single out women in different communities, most prominently in South Asia. Different communities follow their own personal laws, which are mainly influenced by religion. Family, property and inheritance laws are among those most prone to following diverse legal paths. This lack of standardization explains in part why Asia has more reservations to CEDAW related to 'compatibility with traditional codes' than any other region in the world. By comparison, Central and Eastern Europe and the Commonwealth of Independent States, along with Latin America have no reservations on these grounds.[92]

In Bangladesh, India and Pakistan, marriage and divorce laws twist and turn through the requirements of Hindu, Muslim and Christian communities. In India, people from these communities may be married under their community law, under an optional civil law or under the Special Marriages Act for inter-religious marriages. One unfortunate aspect of the Act is the requirement for a one to three month notice in the office of the marriage registrar. This allows radical religious organizations to track these notices and then harass the families, particularly if the marriages involve people from different castes or religions.[93]

Divorce regulations in South Asia also vary by community. The Islamic triple *talaq,* where the divorce is complete by pronouncing the word *talaq* three times in the presence of two witnesses, is practised in Muslim communities in Afghanistan, India, Islamic Republic of Iran, Nepal and Sri Lanka.[94] Bangladesh and Pakistan have banned this procedure in favour of legal processes that stress reconciliation.[95] Because post-divorce maintenance laws for Muslims are also influenced by Islamic traditions, a woman may not be entitled to maintenance beyond the conventional three-month period of *Iddat* or, if she is pregnant, until the birth of her child (Box 4.3).

The law of divorce for Hindus in India is based on matrimonial wrongs, where the spouse who seeks divorce has to prove cruelty, adultery, desertion or other grounds listed in the statute.[96] Christian men can seek divorce on the grounds of adultery or other reasons; Christian women can only file based on adultery. Hindus in Bangladesh and Pakistan cannot obtain divorces since they are

Some Asia-Pacific countries have laws that discriminate against women as a group. Others have statutes that further single out women in different communities

> **BOX 4.3**
>
> #### SUCCUMBING TO COMMUNAL PRESSURE IN INDIA
>
> Discussions on the rights of different communities in diverse societies, while valid in principle, have often taken on political overtones that overshadow concerns about women's rights and welfare. In India, under the Code of Criminal Procedure, wives of all religions used to be entitled to maintenance as part of divorce. A Muslim husband challenged the constitutional validity of this provision, arguing that it is anti-Islamic. The Supreme Court dismissed his case, sparking communal tensions.
>
> The Government then passed the Muslim Women (Protection of Rights on Divorce) Act 1986. The Act restricted maintenance to Muslim women through the period of *Iddat*. The law stipulates that a former husband is required to give 'a reasonable and fair provision, and maintenance' to his ex-wife within the *Iddat* period.
>
> In a separate case of maintenance in 2001, the Supreme Court held that at the time of divorce, a Muslim husband is required to contemplate the future needs for the entire life of the divorced wife, and make preparatory arrangements in advance for meeting them. This judicial precedent, however, is not always followed in practice.
>
> *Note:* Iddat implies a specified period of time that must elapse before a Muslims widow or divorcee may legitimately remarry.
>
> *Sources:* Code of Criminal Procedure 1973 (CrPc): Section 125; Supreme Court of India 1985; Muslim Women (Protection of Rights on Divorce) Act 1986; section 3 (1)a; Supreme Court of India 2001.

prohibited under Sastric Hindu scriptures, which define their laws on the issue.

Malaysia follows a dual legal system of civil and *syariah* law that results in continuing discrimination against women, particularly in marriage and family relations. The restrictive interpretation of *syariah* law, including the Islamic Family Law (Federal Territories) Amendment Act 2005, adversely affects the rights of Muslim women. A lack of clarity in the legal system persists around whether civil or *syariah* law applies to marriages of non-Muslim women whose husbands convert to Islam.[97]

In Viet Nam, the 2006 Law on Gender Equality provides room for diverse customs, except those perceived as harmful under current human rights standards. It promises to protect 'the fine customs and practices of the ethnic minority people, while the backward marriage and family customs are either strictly prohibited and/or to be eradicated by mobilization'. Such harmful practices include underage and forced marriages, polygamy and snatching wives.[98]

Some countries and territories in the Pacific do not recognize customary, polygamous or religious marriages that have not been formally registered or conducted in compliance with marriage legislation, even though these were historically accepted in most parts of the sub-region until the spread of Christianity. In Fiji, some 27 per cent of Muslims enter religious marriages that are not technically legal. Women then do not have legal protections on issues such as divorce, property and custody of children.[99]

Access to Justice Depends on Gender

Globally, four billion people—most of the world's population—are excluded from the rule of law.[100] This figure covers a significant number of women in Asia-Pacific, even in countries where laws are relatively sound (Figures 4.2 and 4.3). Specific barriers, rooted in gender, prevent women from getting to court or other judicial mechanisms, or finding fair judgments once they are there. This propensity worsens when the laws themselves ignore or discriminate against women, as described in the previous section.

Effective justice systems are particularly critical when power is imbalanced, and people with a weaker voice and fewer options for recourse—like women—have limited options for redress. Women are often more vulnerable to injustice to start, and more in need of measures to protect their legal rights. Impoverished women carry an additional burden. The extra powerlessness of poverty makes them even more prone to criminal and human rights violations, and more likely to fall further into poverty through the lack of redress. They may also not be able to use justice mechanisms as tools to overcome deprivation due to the costs of litigation and their greater likelihood of being illiterate and lacking legal awareness.[101]

These tendencies, which can be found in many parts of Asia-Pacific, are bad for women. But they also weaken state accountability and erode public faith in the value of

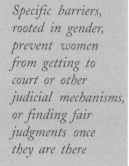

Specific barriers, rooted in gender, prevent women from getting to court or other judicial mechanisms, or finding fair judgments once they are there

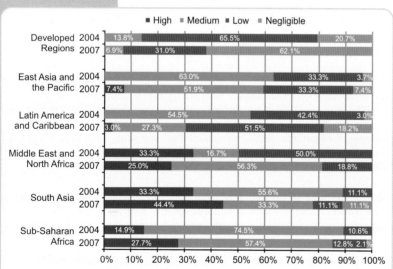

Figure 4.2: Women Face Deep Discrimination in Economic Rights

Note: The figure classifies regional groups as cited in UNIFEM 2008.
Sources: UNIFEM 2008; CIRI 2009.

public services, proven blocks to sustainable human development and the growth of democratic societies.

The lack of women's access to justice is reflected in the region's poor record on upholding women's rights. Between 2004 and 2007, discrimination against women in economic and social rights has increased in developing countries in the region. The percentage of countries with high economic or social discrimination edged upward across Asia and the Pacific (Figures 4.2 and 4.3).[102] In East Asia and the Pacific, the percentage of countries with high economic discrimination increased from zero in 2004 to over seven per cent in 2007, while the percentage of countries with medium to high levels of discrimination remained as high as 59 per cent in 2007, declining slightly from 63 per cent in 2004. In South Asia, the share of countries with high economic discrimination increased from 33 per cent to 44 per cent during the same period. A decline in medium levels of discrimination can be attributed to some countries climbing from the medium to high level of economic discrimination. Some countries have improved their position.

The social rights situation is worse—and deteriorating. The share of countries with high social discrimination has increased across the region. In South Asia, the figures jumped to 56 per cent in 2007 from 33 per cent in 2004. In East Asia and Pacific, the share of countries with medium to high discrimination rose from 52 per cent in 2004 to 62 per cent in 2007, while the portion of countries with high social discrimination increased marginally.

Getting to Court Is a Hard Road

A variety of factors come into play in reducing women's access to judicial systems. Courts may be far away, and transportation is often less available to women. Sometimes social conventions dictate that women should not

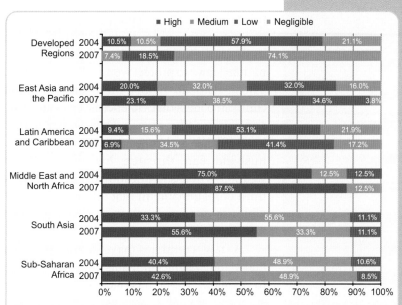

Figure 4.3: Discrimination Also Short-Changes Women's Social Rights

Note: The figure classifies regional groups as cited in UNIFEM 2008.
Sources: UNIFEM 2008; CIRI 2009.

leave their homes or travel or be active in public spheres. Women are responsible for a disproportionate share of household tasks, which means they may be less able than men to take time for complicated legal processes and repeated meetings with lawyers. If they work for wages, they will generally be paid less than men and confront poorer working conditions. This, in turn, likewise reduces the affordability and raises the risks of spending time on legal matters.

Women may face physical threats, including violence, if pursuing a legal remedy involves challenging their husbands, other family members, or the broader status quo. They may fear losing children or economic sustenance. Internalized discriminatory norms require women to suffer in silence, and define them as being less and deserving less.[103]

Information from Cambodia illustrates why many women never access justice systems. A survey carried out by the Ministry of Women's Affairs found that 22.5 per cent of married women experience violence within their homes.[104] A similar percentage of women are raped by their husbands.[105] Up to 89 per cent do nothing,[106] despite new national laws to protect women from violence. Those who do report these crimes could confront beliefs that violence is a private issue and a prerogative of men. Over 60 per cent of local officials and police tend to believe that a husband can threaten his wife with a weapon when she questions him. Nearly a third of men maintain that different forms of violence are appropriate at times in their marriages.[107]

A few countries have taken steps to make judicial mechanisms more accessible to women. India has moved forward on stopping sexual harassment by requiring workplaces that employ women to set up commissions that are at least 50 per cent female to receive and act on complaints of sexual harassment.[108] Malaysia has pioneered one-stop centres in hospitals that provide easy access to medical care, social services and specially trained police units for victims of domestic or sexual violence.[109]

Justice Systems Fail to Deliver

Women across Asia-Pacific who do find the means to turn to judicial mechanisms to resolve disputes—whether state courts, the police, lawyers or local resources—still face obstacles. Judicial practices are also subject to discriminatory social norms that do not acknowledge women's rights or concerns, or treat them seriously or fairly. For women, the lofty provisions for equality in many of the region's constitutions, while important in their own right, have little bearing on the ways in which justice is actually meted out.

Legal complexities that require onerous court proceedings represent one reason why women fail to obtain justice. Beyond the fact that men's reasons for divorce are often taken more seriously than women's, most countries

in Asia-Pacific have a fault-based divorce system. This requires a process of proving charges such as adultery, desertion for a required number of years, wilful refusal to consummate the marriage, habitual cruelty, and so on. The parties must hire lawyers, file court cases and bring witnesses to court to provide supporting evidence—a tremendous burden particularly for poor and rural women. Where courts have a duty to promote reconciliation and forgiveness, power differences related to gender can be easily overlooked. Women can confront significant financial, customary, family and community pressures to agree to circumstances that do not benefit them. If violence is taking place, it may remain shrouded by the convention that it is a private matter.

Throughout the region, the stark reality of economic inequality appears when women struggle to obtain custody of their children during divorce. Some countries follow the principle of acting in the 'best interests of the child,' often interpreted in terms of financial advantages that mostly belong to men. Women typically start out at a financial disadvantage because they have less education and access to jobs and assets, or have been economically dependent on the men they want to divorce.

These hindrances also appear in and are compounded by the unfair distribution of matrimonial property and establishment of maintenance awards. Maintenance is often based on actual financial contributions to family resources, ignoring women's long hours of unpaid household work and work in the informal cash economy. In late 2008, a court in Fiji, drawing on a new law on the more equal division of property, finally took into account domestic contributions and awarded a wife of 37 years half the marital assets.[110] In the Pacific, only Fiji specifies comprehensive guidelines on the amount of maintenance, most other court systems award grossly inadequate amounts of maintenance. Stereotypes around women's sexuality have led to some cases of reversing maintenance or child custody decisions in women's favour due to the impression of 'loose' or 'immoral' behaviour.[111]

Court systems continue to carry out procedural indignities that can leave women doubly victimized. While more countries in the region are moving to non-public trials for sensitive issues such as rape and domestic violence, women may still be expected to narrate their experiences in great detail, including to male personnel in cultures with strong taboos against public discussion of sexual acts. Many trial courts in India still insist on archaic tests for proof of rape or raise the issue of whether or not she follows a promiscuous lifestyle.[112]

Discriminatory rules for trial procedures and evidence diminish or distort women's voice in court in a number of Asia-Pacific countries. In Pakistan the value of a woman's testimony in court is considered half that of a man's in financial matters and future obligations under Qanoon-e-Shahdat Order 1984.[113] Many Pacific Island countries and territories continue to require proof of resistance in sexual assault cases and/or allow the admission of past sexual history. These requirements discourage rape victims from reporting this crime, on top of the already heavy social sanctions against speaking out against it, and a personal reluctance to possibly re-live the experience through a trial.

One of the most obvious ways in which courts fail women is when they are reluctant to uphold judgments or pursue crimes against women (Box 4.4). This tendency appears in a lack of human and financial resources for enforcement; a lack of sanctions against judicial personnel who make overtly biased decisions, including those who unnecessarily stretch or even contradict the law; and the absence of training for police and court officials on gender and the specifics of gender-

based crimes. In Fiji, before enforcement mechanisms were tightened for maintenance payments after divorce, 50 per cent of maintenance awards were not paid or enforced, a further 35 per cent of orders were enforced only intermittently and just 15 per cent of fathers paid maintenance regularly under orders.[114]

On crimes involving gender-based violence, in addition to the lack of effective legislation in Asia-Pacific, there is an unwillingness to exercise powers of arrest, file charges and pursue criminal prosecutions. Because the cases are considered low priority, less-experienced judicial personnel are assigned to them. Untrained police and court personnel may rely more on stereotypes than on current knowledge of why gender-based violence occurs and the serious damage it can inflict.

In the Pacific, non-molestation, protective orders or injunctions are generally available for people threatened by violence, but without the legislative basis for providing such protection in cases of domestic violence. The courts exercise their discretionary power sparingly and inconsistently. Only married women, and not *de facto* wives or girlfriends, may be entitled to seek orders. When these

---

Discriminatory rules for trial procedures and evidence diminish or distort women's voice in court in a number of Asia-Pacific countries

are granted and disobeyed, the police habitually do not enforce them through imprisonment, because the orders are vague and no laws set out clear guidelines. Imprisonment requires lengthy and complex contempt of court proceedings. Given that domestic violence is not high on the police list of priorities, the perpetrator is usually summoned to the police station or court, reprimanded and allowed to leave.

Pacific courts rarely award prison sentences that reflect the seriousness of domestic violence as a crime, despite the fact that it can be a repeated, habitual offence. They tend to give probationary orders that command the offender not to commit another crime for a specified period. If the offender does commit the crime again, he will be punished for the original crime. This is in effect a 'keep the peace' order. In practice, courts usually refuse to imprison a male breadwinner even when a further crime is committed.

Many examples of bias in judicial systems arise from unconscious or unquestioned assumptions, some of which can be corrected through training and stricter laws and procedures. But there are also cases of extreme judicial injustice where the legal system is deliberately used to harm women. Courts in India and Sri Lanka have also allowed the defense of 'grave and sudden provocation' to continue as a hangover from common law.[115] Such a defence mitigates the heinous nature of crimes such as murder. Despite an amendment in the Pakistan Penal Code, the mitigation of sentences for the so-called honour killings has continued unabated.[116] Running away from home is not a crime in Afghanistan. But many girls and women are in prison, some for as long as 10 years now, for having done so.[117]

Biases Remain in Customary Justice Systems

Some countries retain customary or community dispute mechanisms that operate in parallel with the national court system. These include traditional customary justice and alternate dispute resolution systems. They may function independently or be connected to the state courts (Box 4.5). They have some value in bringing justice closer to people, being less expensive and time-consuming, and in enforcing decisions quickly through community consent. The Musalihat Anjuman system in Pakistan, constituted under the 2001 Local Government Ordinance, resolves conflicts through arbitration and mediation. It encourages parties to identify issues, explore areas of compromize and generate options to resolve the dispute amicably.[118]

But unless mechanisms likes these function in communities where equality is valued and women already have a strong voice, they are prone to upholding social conventions that discriminate against women or other less powerful groups. In India, community justice mechanisms connected to caste have carried out violent sentences against members of Dalit communities for crimes such as marrying someone from another community.[119]

> Pacific courts rarely award prison sentences that reflect the seriousness of domestic violence as a crime, despite the fact that it can be a repeated, habitual offence

---

BOX 4.5

MOBILE COURTS PRODUCE INNOVATIVE LEGAL PRACTICES

Lacking enough qualified legal personnel to serve all parts of Afghanistan, the Government has introduced the concept of mobile courts as a possible solution to the problems of accessibility and security. Teams of experienced judges, prosecutors, lawyers and administrative officials make periodic visits to places that are too remote, insecure or small to have permanent staffing.

Mobile courts are also active in Bangladesh, China, India and Indonesia. In India, at least two states have founded mobile courts—buses complete with computers, records and seating that are stationed in remote towns on a rotating basis. In Indonesia, mobile courts were used in the wake of the 2004 tsunami, which destroyed the state's capacity to deal with routine tasks like land ownership claims. In China, mobile courts are increasingly being deployed to improve access to the formal justice system in rural areas

For mobile courts and other alternative dispute mechanisms to be effective on gender issues, they must be able to imaginatively resolve disputes, while being located firmly in constitutional provisions and rights. If they are used mainly because the formal system is overburdened, the focus can shift to the case disposal rate and other statistics, rather the effectiveness of justice.

Sources: Ramaseshan 2009a; UNIFEM 2008.

They commonly serve the interests of local high-caste elites, backed by community sanction, and so attempts to rein in their influence have generally not been successful.[120]

In Asia and the Pacific older men usually run local systems of justice. They may decide petty matters, such as disputes over lost livestock. But they can also weigh in on serious issues such as adultery and murder. The *jirga* system that operates in Afghanistan and parts of Pakistan, and the *shalishi* (mediation) system in rural Bangladesh are informal dispute resolution mechanisms that make decisions by consensus and impose punishments.[121] Supporters of the *jirga* emphasize that it is more accessible to women than formal systems because it allows women to remain within their communities, since venturing outside to seek formal justice can be stigmatized as immodest. But *jirga* decisions are prone to gender bias, in part because so few women participate in them. According to a sample survey in 2007 conducted by the Afghan Centre for Socio-economic and Opinion Research, women comprised only two per cent of representatives on local *jirgas*. Elderly men constituted 65 per cent of the membership. Other members included mullahs, local leaders and commanders.[122]

Not Enough Women Serve in the Justice System

Both men and women judicial officials can be advocates for gender equality within judicial systems, particularly if they have been trained to understand gender issues and how they affect the course of justice. That said, some evidence also suggests that increasing the number of women judicial officials improves women's access to justice. Women, through life experience, may be more aware of the specific problems other women face, helping them to clearly see the ways that laws and legal procedures conventionally overlook or overtly endorse gender discrimination.

In Asia and the Pacific, the level of women's representation in justice systems remains low on average. In the Philippines, about 30 per cent of the judges in High Courts and the Supreme Court are women, a relatively progressive record. But India and Pakistan have only eight per cent and three per cent, respectively, in their higher courts.[123]

Globally, gender stereotypes have impeded the progress of women in policing and played an unfortunate role in devaluing their work.[124] Women police officers comprise from 2.2 to 19.1 per cent of police forces in parts of Asia-Pacific where data is available.[125] In Bhutan, the 1980 Police Act restricts women officers to investigating cases involving women, handling female prisoners or directing traffic.[126]

In India, the state of Tamil Nadu has become a frontrunner in recruiting women for the police. In 1997, the state took advantage of a labour law requirement to ensure that 33 per cent of new recruits were women. This has increased the overall level of representation to 9.6 per cent, compared to a national average of 3.5 per cent in 2003. The introduction of 188 All-Women Police Units in the past few years, covering both rural and urban jurisdictions, has given women police more visibility. The units were set up to deal with crimes against women, including violence related to dowry problems, family disputes, marital problems, false promises of marriage, sexual assaults and rape. Increasing numbers of women now feel confident in approaching them for help with domestic disputes, and they have inspired some younger women to seek careers in policing.[127]

Police forces in Nepal, Pakistan, the Philippines and Sri Lanka have created women's units to open up opportunities for women to serve in the police, as well as to deal with the increased numbers of domestic violence cases now being reported.[128]

In Asia and the Pacific, the level of women's representation in justice systems remains low on average

Taking Action: Enforcing Rights, Correcting Wrongs

The law is meant to protect, but it can also empower, unleashing the full capacities of men and women to exercise choice and build on opportunities to achieve equality and fuel human development.

No single strategy can fix the unequal experiences that men and women have in Asia-Pacific's legal systems, because the inequalities are numerous and fed by multiple sources: the law, legal practice, political commitment and social norms. Laws that discriminate against women should be changed and gaps filled. But then they must be backed by diligent enforcement, including through the provision of sufficient knowledge and resources so that justice systems do not maintain discriminatory legal practices. Advocacy and social mobilization may also play a role in underscoring how legal inequalities in the region hold back development, and how this should be of political and broader social concern.

Achieve Inclusiveness Through Dynamic Reforms

Legal reforms aimed at gender equality can address the substance and structures of the laws—meaning the ways they are written and the judicial practices and institutions designed to uphold them—as well as the surrounding social norms that feed into them (Table 4.1). Examples of reform include changes in the law, legal literacy campaigns, judicial training, community outreach, free legal aid and childcare services that allow people with domestic responsibilities to go to court.

Reform choices are shaped by national priorities and needs, political opportunities and the demands of citizens and can be as much about advocacy and political positioning as about the technicalities of legal review.

Some typical entry points include the following:

International norms. International instruments such as CEDAW, the Beijing Declaration and Platform for Action, the ILO's Migrant Workers Convention, and the UN MDGs are useful global norms on gender equality. Many countries have used CEDAW to reform their civil and criminal laws. The effectiveness of national legal reforms, legislative and judicial, can be further enhanced by aligning state laws with international standards on gender equality.

Constitutional provisions. When the principles of gender equality, non-discrimination and state obligation are well defined and set in the constitution, they can be used to challenge any form of gender discrimination on constitutional grounds, including those in laws and legal practices.

Specific laws. Formal and customary laws and practices may be overtly discriminatory, full of gaps or contradictory. Those causing direct and immediate harm deserve priority. Gender equality laws can also be considered as part of general development strategies, such as to reduce poverty through updated employment and social protection laws. Economic barriers that limit access to justice need to be progressively removed.

Judicial practices. Because the intent behind good laws can be defeated by discriminatory judicial practices, reform measures might combine training for court personnel and police with measured guidelines for handling steps from filing cases to interpreting laws.

Progressive interpretation of religious texts. Liberal interpretation of religious texts is needed to reduce discrimination against women. Some countries are moving in the right direction. Pakistan's Council of Islamic

> Laws that discriminate against women should be changed and gaps filled. But then they must be backed by diligent enforcement

TABLE 4.1

<table>
<tr><th colspan="4" align="center">STRATEGIES TO ADDRESS LEGAL DISCRIMINATION</th></tr>
<tr>
<th>Elements of
the law</th>
<th>Direct/indirect
discrimination</th>
<th>Strategies (legislative, litigation,
specialized gender training)</th>
<th>Testimonials from the region</th>
</tr>
<tr><td colspan="4">Law and its substantive contents (formal and customary)</td></tr>
<tr>
<td>Substance</td>
<td>Discriminatory formal law</td>
<td>Amend legislation; narrow the limits of judicial discretion if possible (legislative strategy).</td>
<td>The post 1995 amendments to Sri Lanka's 1883 Penal Code includes new provisions on sexual harassment, grave sexual abuse, incest, sexual exploitation of children and trafficking. They also impose stiffer sentences for serious crimes.</td>
</tr>
<tr>
<td>Substance</td>
<td>Discriminatory customary law</td>
<td>Promulgate new laws or amend existing legislation. Test case for new positive interpretation; narrow the limits of judicial discretion if possible (legislative and litigation strategies).</td>
<td>Viet Nam's Law on Gender Equality 2006 stipulates that 'backward' marriage and family customs are either strictly prohibited and/or to be eradicated through mobilization.</td>
</tr>
<tr>
<td>Substance</td>
<td>Discriminatory act/ omission</td>
<td>File lawsuits; apply to court for issuance of writs; new legislation (litigant and legislative strategies).</td>
<td>The 2002 judgment of the Supreme Court of Nepal observed that exemption from marital rape is a denial of woman's right to self-respect and existence.</td>
</tr>
<tr>
<td>Substance</td>
<td>Discriminatory interpre-tation</td>
<td>New legislation if litigation fails; test case for new posi-tive interpretation; overall training and gender sensiti-zation of jirgas/local leaders (litigation and legislative strategies).</td>
<td>In Kiribati, the legislature enacted the 2003 Evidence Amendment Act after prosecutors failed, through a litigation strategy, to outlaw the discriminatory corroboration rule for sexual assault crimes.</td>
</tr>
<tr><td colspan="4">Access to laws (formal and customary)</td></tr>
<tr>
<td>Structure</td>
<td>Lack of access to court (remoteness and inadequacy)</td>
<td>Provide innovative methods of court access, e.g. mobile courts; obtain court orders by tele-phone or authorize trained persons to administer law in remote areas; alternate dispute resolution; jirgas.</td>
<td>Mobile courts are active in Afghanistan, Bangladesh, China, India and Indonesia.</td>
</tr>
<tr>
<td>Structure</td>
<td>Barriers to access in justice systems</td>
<td>Increased number of female law enforcement officials (judges, magistrate, police officers); counseling; safe shelters.</td>
<td>In the Indian state of Tamil Nadu, the labour law requires that 33 per cent of new police recruits are women.</td>
</tr>
<tr>
<td>Structure</td>
<td>Incapacity to enforce law/ rights owing to lack of resources or financial means</td>
<td>Provide legal representation, earmark funds for legal support;</td>
<td>Women in Need (WIN), an NGO in Sri Lanka, provides counselling and legal assistance to clients subjected to rape, domestic violence, incest, sexual abuse and sexual harassment. WIN has handled over 1,700 cases of rape, incest and domestic violence over the past two years, protecting the interests of victims, who are not in an economi-cally sound position and who would not have pursued legal remedies if not for the support given by WIN. [129]</td>
</tr>
</table>

Contd...

Contd...

Elements of the law	Direct/indirect discrimination	Strategies (legislative, litigation, specialized gender training)	Testimonials from the region
Access to laws (formal and customary)			
Culture	Discriminatory interpretation of legislation	Public interest litigation; gender training for justice agency officials; test cases and class actions;[130] amend legislation (a combination of litigation, training and legislative strategies).	India has a rich history of public interest litigation. Through this, the Supreme Court of India has issued hundreds of directives since the 1980s that provide legal redress to aggrieved parties.
Culture	Unwillingness to enforce legislation	Gender training; persuasive dialogue; advocacy through NGOs, media, etc; declaratory orders from a court; law suits for negligence/failure to act with claims for damages/compensation.	The Pacific Regional Rights Resource Team's (RRRT) lawyers, trainers and experts advise governments and civil society on promoting human rights.

Note: Three main elements of the law that determine strategies to address discrimination against women include the substance of the law (legislation, common law, customary law, legal practices, and procedures and rules); the structures that implement the law (courts, court administration and law enforcement agencies); and cultural norms that influence justice (social conditions, economic conditions and attitudes of law enforcement agencies, judges, magistrates, court officials, police and the community).

Source: Adopted from Jalal 2009.

Ideology has recommended amending the marriage form to allow women the right to divorce without going to court, a view rejected by conservative religious scholars. But if the council's view prevails, the change in the marriage form will become automatic given that the Constitution requires all national laws to accord with Islamic injunctions.[131] Indonesia's Ministry for Women's Empowerment has adopted an innovative strategy of liberal interpretation of Islamic teachings to combat battery against women.[132]

Public opinion. If people do not uphold laws because they contradict longstanding social conventions that negatively affect women, advocacy and social mobilization campaigns can persuade people of the value of thinking in new ways and complying with the law.

Because both gender equality and the law are complex, one critical aspect of building informed public opinion needs to be initial in-depth analysis. Examining the legal system requires looking within and beyond it. This might involve mapping the different elements in the law, legal practice and society that deepen or alleviate gender inequalities, and understanding how they intersect and reinforce each other and where discriminatory knots need to be untangled. Employment guarantees may be desirable, for example, but will they be minimized by the stiff competition for jobs and the pressure to work despite harsh conditions? Market forces might close wage gaps over the long term, but what if employers refuse to hire women who might take maternity leave? If these factors are in play, how can the law be constructed and implemented to counter them?

In most cases, changing legal and gender norms are long-term processes. Great tenacity, deliberation and a combination of political and people skills may be necessary, as well as strategic partnerships between people in civil society and government. Throughout, discrimination and inequality need to be understood not just in terms of what is written on paper, but what is actually happening in women's lives and what is really required for women to move forward as full citizens in their societies.

The recognition that women face different social pressures and expectations, have fewer economic resources and project a less prominent political voice can be considered in light of immediate steps for redress, such as laws for quota systems as discussed in Chapter 3. This can also be part of the ongoing process of examining and accommodating differences to maintain genuinely equal access to justice.

Some of the more dynamic legal reforms in the region have embraced the notions of inclusiveness and engagement. Malaysia's Domestic Violence Act of 1994 was an early example of understanding that domestic violence affects both men and women. It covers any member of a family subject to abuse.[133] One of the innovative features of Vanuatu's new Family Protection Act is the use of trained people in remote villages to provide temporary protection orders to women affected by violence.[134] This circumvents a longstanding issue in the Pacific of trying to extend the reach of the law to people scattered across different islands and long distances.

In Fiji women politicians and NGOs worked for 13 years, despite political instability and staunch opposition, to pass the Family Law Act 2003. Conservative churches and political actors fought the bill as threatening Fijian values with same-sex marriages and no-fault divorce. Supporters of the bill worked inside and outside the legislature to secure passage. The law has broken new ground in Fiji and the Pacific. It is based on the no-fault principle of divorce, spearheads a non-adversarial counselling system and uses a specialist Family Division of the Court, which prioritizes children's needs and parental support. It removes all forms of formal legal and financial discrimination against women in terms of their access to legal recourse under the law and grants them rights to enforceable custody and financial support.[135]

By contrast, Sri Lanka's 1995 law reform process demonstrates how reform can go awry. It resulted in more regressive legislation for people with diverse genders and sexual orientations. The text of the law criminalizing 'unnatural' sexual behaviour had been applicable only to men because it referred to 'he' throughout. A move to institute gender-neutrality in the law resulted in the word being changed from 'he' to 'person'. This made the law applicable to women as well. Consensual sexual activity between adults of the same sex remains a crime under the Penal Code.[136]

Make a Case

In Asia-Pacific countries where the law shifts not just through legislation but also through precedents, a strategy for reversing gender discrimination can be filing cases to establish new precedents. This can happen through the initiatives of lawyers and activists and the willingness of individual judges to reinterpret the law (Box 4.6).

In Fiji, a gender discriminatory rule that required corroboration for rape was outlawed in a 2004 case, *Balelala v State*.[137] The accused argued before the Supreme Court that it was dangerous to convict him on the defendant's words alone and requested that his conviction should be overturned. A requirement for corroboration in rape cases was not part of the law, but it had been a longstanding judicial practice in Fiji. The court examined its origin and said it was representative of the practice in force in England in 1944 when evidence legislation was enacted. The court ruled that the practice should be removed since it was based on an outmoded and fundamentally flawed rationale that was unfairly demeaning to women and contradicted the Fijian Constitution.

In Asia-Pacific countries where the law shifts not just through legislation but also through precedents, a strategy for reversing gender discrimination can be filing cases to establish new precedents

Issue expertise. Civil society groups have grown in number and expertise in the last decade. Some now have highly trained experts in law and gender, many of whom have benefited from the exchange of experiences and knowledge in regional and international forums. Pacific Regional Rights Resource Team (RRRT) is a widely recognized regional human rights project that covers 14 Pacific Island countries, for example. The group's lawyers, trainers and experts advise governments and civil society on promoting human rights based on Pacific constitutional provisions and international standards.

RRRT uses a unique combination of persuasive and challenging techniques and avoids the traditional 'naming, blaming and shaming' methods favoured by some human rights organizations. Over the past decade, the group has helped governments ratify CEDAW and prepare for reporting sessions. It has provided technical inputs for Fiji's Family Law Act 2003, Vanuatu's Family Protection Bill and the drafting instructions for a new Bill of Rights for Solomon Islands. Other initiatives have brought about equal citizenship rights in Fiji and equal evidence laws in rape cases in Kiribati.

Connections to women's lives. Civil society groups may work directly with the populations affected by the issue at hand, such as a discriminatory law. They may be intimately familiar with the problems that people face in a way that is outside the scope of larger, more formal public institutions. Hesitancy in reporting sexual assault crimes, for instance, might come out in one-on-one interviews with women once a relationship of trust has been built. It will not be readily picked up by a judicial system that has less time for such interactions and intervenes once a report has been made.

Flexibility and innovation. Understanding of gender discrimination and how to address it

> *Civil society organizations, particularly women's NGOs, have been the driving force behind progressive legislation for gender equality in many Asia-Pacific countries*

New precedents set in lower courts can vary and are vulnerable to being reversed by superior courts. In Kiribati, lawyers failed through litigation to outlaw the discriminatory corroboration rule for sexual assault crimes. The rule changed only when the legislature approved the Evidence Amendment Act 2003.[138]

Build on the Power of Civil Society Activism

Civil society organizations, particularly women's NGOs, have been the driving force behind progressive legislation for gender equality being passed and implemented in many Asia-Pacific countries, and the signing and ratification of international human rights conventions. While the role of civil society varies across countries, it can be valuable in legal reform efforts for several reasons:

is constantly evolving. Civil society groups work on a smaller scale and may have the capacity to try new ideas to see if they are worth institutionalizing. In Mumbai, India, men run an NGO called Men Against Violence and Abuse. Instead of focusing only on the impacts of gender-based violence on women, it seeks to change male attitudes to masculinity and provide a forum for men to oppose violence against women. The group organizes prevention programmes, public discussions on violence against women, gender sensitization programmes, and mass awareness drives using media, street plays, posters and radio. It also provides counselling and guidance to couples facing marital conflict, organizes self-defence workshops for women and publishes a men's magazine that addresses gender issues.[139]

Understanding of national context. National and sub-national civil society groups are mostly staffed by people from a given country or locality. They understand what people think and why, and how to persuade people to adopt new ways of thinking, including through rationales for more gender-balanced societies.

Political presence. Civil society groups play a prominent political role in some countries and are capable of mobilizing politicians and political constituencies around gender equality and legal reform.

Change Attitudes to Extend the Law's Reach

As has been apparent throughout this chapter, the arm of the law is only so long. Social conventions around gender form the foundations of societies, drawing deeply on human biology and adaptive social norms. Some parts of these foundations are strong and deserve to be kept, but others are weak because they are harmful to women

and men and a hindrance to human development.

It is up to each country to decide where changes need to be made and more positive norms pursued, keeping in mind commitments made internationally to basic principles such as gender equality. The law needs to be part of this endeavour—but cannot be all of it.

A look at some of the experiences with law and gender equality in the region explains why. In the Pacific, most attempts to change sexual assault laws have failed. In Fiji, draft rape laws have become embroiled in arguments about the rights of the victim over the right to due process of the accused, and about concepts perceived as too 'Western', 'feminist', radical and counter to Pacific culture. The political instability in Fiji over the last twenty years has left little space for legal reform, much less for anything seen as controversial or social threatening.

Another example can be found in the impunity for some crimes against women – which comes from judicial system failures in part, but also from the widespread beliefs, such as the notion that regardless of what the law says, men are really entitled to beat their wives. India, for example, has strict laws against dowry, child marriages and sex-selective abortion. While public awareness has grown about the harm from these practices and they even feature regularly in media reports, still all three openly take place in some communities. In Bangladesh, the minimum age of marriage for girls is 18 years, but child marriage continues to be widely practised.[140]

New ways of thinking can shift discriminatory attitudes either to produce fairer legislation and judicial practices or to achieve the standards of what already exists. This process needs to work on three fronts:

Inside the judicial system. This involves training police, judges and other judicial personnel not just on the technicalities of the law, but also about gender inequalities that

It is up to each country to decide where changes need to be made and more positive norms pursued, keeping in mind commitments made internationally to basic principles such as gender equality

disadvantage women and make legal practices discriminatory, whether or not they are intended to be so. It requires asking legal personnel to reflect on what legal neutrality really means and on the potentially positive role of judicial interpretation in moving legal systems closer to that ideal. Judicial systems cannot claim to be effective if they are missing large numbers of crimes or imposing inaccurate penalties.

Across the political arena. Many intersections exist between the judiciary and other branches of political systems. The legislature drafts and passes laws. Politicians may appoint judges. They assign budgets to courts, prisons, police and legal aid initiatives to assist the poor. Members of the executive and legislative branches who face election may also be sensitive to feedback from constituencies on whether or not the legal system meets their needs. All of these intersections provide entry points for advocating how the law and its implementation can support the achievement of gender equality, including by building on political commitments that may have been made in national forums or through international instruments such as CEDAW.

In the social sphere. Social mobilization can have any of a number of objectives, such as to convince people to use the law to protect themselves or improve their lives; to persuade them of its value so they will comply with it, even aside from the threat of punishment; and to suggest that as citizens they can call upon the judicial system to be accountable to their needs and prerogatives. This kind of advocacy needs to operate in some of the places where social norms are transmitted such as schools, the media, religious organizations and community groups.

Use the Law to Tear Down Gender Barriers

For women to have equal access to opportunities for human development, including those that come through political and economic power and voice, they must enjoy equal rights and protection under the law. Based on overall patterns in the region, it is reasonable to say that this is not currently the case in any Asia-Pacific country. Even those states that have tried to remove overtly discriminatory statutes still have gaps in laws and legal practices that fail to check gender biases. Divorce, inheritance, gender-based violence, labour rights, rules of evidence, citizenship—the list of legal issues that deserve immediate attention is long and worrisome.

Yet the gaps can be narrowed and at some point eliminated, as some countries are beginning to demonstrate. Recognizing that the law is devised by human beings and cannot claim to be fully impartial is one important step forward. Step two is to accept that the law deeply influences development in different ways and that it also shapes the outcomes of many non-legal interventions. The legal process and the law thus need to be crafted to genuinely advance gender equality.

As a third step, laws and legal practices, *de jure* and *de facto* alike, need to be designed and implemented in ways that tear down gender barriers. This does not imply a kind of legal favoritism for women and other marginalized groups. But it requires acknowledging, at the minimum, that if people cannot even get to court or will be judged mainly on their gender, then justice is not being served. Legal reform cannot be limited to fixing the laws when compliance cannot be taken for granted.

Countries in the region have made commitments to equality before the law and to banning discrimination through their constitutions, the supreme law of the land. Progressive legal initiatives, both judicial and legislative, testify to intended advances in gender equality. The promise of these milestone legal achievements should be upheld, as in the end that is what counts.

ENFORCING RIGHTS, CORRECTING WRONGS

A country's legal system influences how women and men seek opportunities and makes choices. Gender equality requires close attention to legal institutions so that both the substance of the laws and how they are upheld become powerful tools to advance equality. This calls for uncovering biases and taking corrective measures to redress past discrimination. Substantive equality in law provides legal backing for economic and political equality; political voice and economic power, in turn, influence legal systems.

An action agenda should be rooted in local circumstances while benefitting from the best international norms. It should aim to:

Achieve inclusiveness through dynamic reforms. Use international instruments to bring national laws closer to global norms on gender equality ▸ Incorporate well-defined provisions on gender equality, non-discrimination and state obligations in national constitutions ▸ Give priority to changing discriminatory and contradictory formal as well as customary laws and practices ▸ Curtail discriminatory judicial practices through training and developing capacities to advance gender equality among court personnel and police ▸ Promote progressive interpretation of religious texts to encourage acceptance of equality of all human beings and reduce discrimination against women ▸ Foster public support for upholding laws through advocacy and social mobilization campaigns ▸ Reinterpret laws and set new judicial precedents on gender equality by filing lawsuits or test cases through lawyers, activists and individual judges.

Build on the power of civil society activism. Enhance the legal expertise of civil society groups through training ▸ Support groups working with populations affected by discriminatory laws ▸ Partner with those piloting innovative ideas that may be worth scaling up and institutionalizing ▸ Work through national and sub-national civil society organizations rooted in local contexts to persuade people to adopt new ways of thinking and strive for more gender-balanced societies ▸ Build on civil society capacities to mobilize politicians and political constituencies around gender equality and legal reforms.

Change attitudes to extend the law's reach. Train police, judges and other judicial personnel inside the judicial system not just on the technicalities of the law, but also on gender inequalities that disadvantage women and make legal practices discriminatory ▸ Orient and sensitize leaders across the political arena – members of the executive and legislative branches – on how laws and their implementation can support the achievement of gender equality ▸ Mobilize people to use laws through advocacy in schools, the media, religious organizations or community groups.

5

Towards Equal Power and Voice

A Couple Stands Against Inequality

Jotiba, 1827–1890, and Savitribai, 1831–1897

In the early 19th Century in Western India, a teacher named Savitribai was pelted with stones and dirt on her way to school, braving insults just for doing her job. Her husband, Jotiba, had an idea. She could carry an extra sari to school to change into. Why stop teaching?

At a time when education for women was frowned upon, this unique husband and wife partnership welded together personal lives and public action. Jotiba Phule was one of the first founders of a school for girls in Pune, and Savitribai was one of its first teachers. In transcending traditional gender attitudes as well as caste barriers, the couple paid a serious cost. Savitribai had to justify her unorthodox activities to her own family. Jotiba faced opposition from upper castes. But both were resolute in continuing to further opportunities for girls to acquire knowledge.

Under their tutelage, a 13-year-old student named Muktabai wrote a revolutionary essay challenging the oppression of low-caste women and children, something unheard of at the time. The couple also stood by other progressive social advocates, openly supporting two women vilified by the Marathi press. Tarabai, took a public stance against women's subordination, while Ramabai, a Brahmin woman, denounced Brahmanism and its treatment of widows.

Based on an essay by Uma Chakravarthi on Jotiba Phule and a collected volume of writings on Savitribai Phule's life edited by Braj Ranjan Mani and Pamela Sardar.

Towards Equal Power and Voice

Pervasive and persistent, gender inequalities continue to overshadow even the considerable gains made by women and girls in Asia and the Pacific. But countervailing forces are also at work, at national and international levels. Institutions have improved in many countries. Catalyzing change requires establishing the priorities central to transforming the mainstream for a better balance in economic power, political voice and legal rights. To be successful, progress has to be rooted in the local context.

Many constitutions now endorse the equal worth of human beings, and modern states place great emphasis on the impartiality of economic, political and legal institutions. Citizens are not intended to be unequal. Beyond the fundamentals of these rights, gender equality is central to human development and serves the practical purpose of influencing the efficiency and sustainability of development efforts. The empowerment and participation of all people advances when gender is no longer a hindrance.

But at many points, gender discrimination creeps in. Attitudes towards gender are deeply rooted in all societies, regardless of religion, race, ethnicity, level of economic development, or type of political system. Men and women experience institutions differently, in part because attitudes are either assumed to be true and unchangeable, or because they are ignored. Imbalances in power and voice entrench these patterns, as privileged groups are able to influence institutions to secure and perpetuate their own advantages. As a result, the idea that all human beings are equally valuable and should enjoy equal opportunities and rights continues to be contested. This contrasts with increasing acceptance that there is no legitimate reason why some people should be systematically deprived of equal access to the resources, capabilities, opportunities and choices required for human development. This acceptance needs to grow as a counterweight.

Asia-Pacific finds itself at a defining moment, caught in the currents of rapid development and the global economic downturn, which is seeping into the region through job and wage losses, reduced demand, a loss of faith in the financial system and a questioning of political leadership. A number of Asia-Pacific countries are already marked by disaffection and conflict. The social exclusion of minorities and alienation of other disadvantaged groups remains prevalent, while some majorities feel like disadvantaged minorities. Inequalities intersect along the lines of gender, class, birth, religion, caste and locality. Of these, gender is the most prevalent form of inequality, cutting across levels of development. The greater parts of most populations in Asia-Pacific today face some form of exclusion, which is a threat to long term stability of the region.

In turbulent times—particularly if opportunities for improving lives seem to dim—people can revert to exalting an imagined past, an illusory golden age. This is evident in attempts to control the freedom and choices of women and girls, whether the justification is a religious statute from a thousand years ago, or the belief that women should be fired first from jobs because men are the 'real'

Gender equality is central to human development and serves the practical purpose of influencing the efficiency and sustainability of development efforts

breadwinners. These tendencies are an obvious threat to the region's attempts to achieve gender equality. And they are unfolding in an environment where countries have chased growth at the expense of equality. This means that disparities have deepened in some cases, and that the foundation for establishing equality, particularly in the current climate, is weak.

Catalyzing Change

Fortunately, countervailing forces are also at work. The contrasts within the region in male-female survival rates, education, opportunities for remunerative work and participation show that things can change, as East Asia pulls ahead of South Asia on progress towards gender equality. Many more people today are aware of the benefits of equality for individuals and societies. They are also more willing and ready to demand equality, even if that means some level of upheaval and significant revisions to existing institutions. While divisions remain among different groups, connections also are greater, as people realize that tolerance for one type of disparity in the end produces a climate that can accommodate all types.

For its part, the private sector, despite the fact that some businesses continue to use women as a cheap and easily disposable source of labour, is also recognizing that some women are becoming an economic power in and of themselves. They are consumers who make purchasing decisions. And they are professionals who add diversity to decision-making within businesses, which adds value in designing products and services, including those targeted to other women. Some countries are debating the efficacy of quotas in the private sector, voluntary or backed by law, to encourage diversity and speed up transformation. Regardless of the position on the specifics of quotas, the debate has brought the issue of equal opportunities to the forefront.

The reality too is that institutions have improved in many countries, including through greater capacity for policy-making that can make a significant difference for gender equality. More resources are available to implement policies and programmes that can be geared towards shared benefits. Political will has grown, in tandem with domestic constituencies comprising women and men who insist on progress, and flagged by international commitments to gender equality. This is obvious in the ways that gender equality has entered political campaigns through party platforms and deliberate appeals to women voters. Laws have been changed to support gender equality through people cooperating across political lines, and even in the face of vociferous and well-organized opposition.

Perhaps most significantly, ordinary people can now see the benefits of gender equality in their own lives. Women discover this when they acquire an asset or a job that allows them a much greater say in household decisions that used to be the province of men. Families have found that educated daughters are not only socially prestigious, but also a source of income and security. Some men have started to understand that gender norms can oppress them too and can be put aside in favour of new attitudes and behaviours that, for example, embrace cooperation over aggression. The intergenerational benefits of gender equality have now been clearly documented, including better health, nutrition and educational outcomes for the children of educated mothers. Greater tolerance of gender identities is being spearheaded in urban areas and public spaces, such as in the media.

While attitudes around gender can be divisive, including through resistance from influential opinion makers such as those using faith or culture as the basis for discrimination, multiple views exist that can stem from the same basic notion of the equality of all human beings. Societies are never 'finished,' with fixed institutions and attitudes—institutions influence attitudes as much as attitudes alter institutions. The region is at a turning point, with complex changes already taking place and ever more people accessing information and thinking about and interpreting it for themselves. There is increasing questioning among women and men on circumstances seen as unjust. 'Social order' has sometimes been used as an argument to justify unequal institutions and attitudes. But prioritizing 'order' over justice is costly to sustain when there is much turbulence below the surface.

It is time to catalyze change by moving beyond partial attempts. This calls for strengthening policies and programmes on women's empowerment, including by embedding gender analysis as a routine requirement for framing them. Full political and legal backing can make them central to—and transformative of—the broader mainstream.

Establishing the Priorities

Gender affects all aspects of human life and development. Its breadth and complexity must be recognized, and priorities carefully chosen in the quest for gender equality. This Report has selected three arenas—economic power, political voice and legal rights—with the potential to catalyze wider change. Each involves far-reaching systems and institutions, so that once progress takes off in some dimensions, the resulting momentum can spur rapid advancement overall. Priority interventions in all three should be chosen for their potential to transform institutions, change attitudes and strengthen assessments of gaps and progress.

Institutions require transformation because they govern patterns of exchange that determine who has power and voice. By design or functioning, institutions can set rules that enable benefits for the greater good or hold back progress. Many institutions in Asia-Pacific maintain discriminatory patterns because they are acceptable, invisible or against the interests of powerful groups. Transforming institutions goes beyond traditional gender mainstreaming exercises, which have often had little impact because they have simply treated gender as an 'add-on' to existing institutions that do not, in the end, genuinely serve the cause of gender equality.

Transformational mainstreaming implies looking at all the places where power, wealth, knowledge, capabilities, opportunities and rights intersect. It entails a commitment to aligning these with the principles of equality and justice, rather than allowing the status quo to go unchecked. This can be a challenging and time-consuming process, but it may be one that is also more sustainable and fairer in the long term. It allows societies to aim for protecting the rights and opportunities of all citizens, which has been proven as a far more efficient and effective path to development than the avenue of gross disparity.

For transformation to take place at the operational level and be sustained, attitudes must change, both within institutions and in society at large. As long as women continue to be viewed as somehow less than equal citizens, progress will be limited. Attitudes to gender must also be understood in the way that they can confine men by insisting on dominant masculinities, rather than allowing the prerogative of individual choice. Greater openness to the fluidity of gender identity is a vital part of shaping attitudes for accepting diversity. Without this acceptance, the core promise of assuring human rights to all—regardless of sex or gender identity—cannot be met.

The process of changing attitudes—and the behaviours that come out of them—requires awareness and a conscious effort to move forward. The process has to be holistic;

This Report has selected three arenas—economic power, political voice and legal rights—with the potential to catalyze wider change

awareness at the group level is important, but driven by the notion that change starts with individuals. Opportunities for learning start with education that prepares individuals to question and think for themselves. It is premised on the idea that attitudes are fluid and can change—and in fact may already be transforming, both for better or worse. These shifts are happening faster today as a result of the rapid exchange of information.

Assessing gaps and change through measurement is part of both transforming institutions and changing attitudes because it reveals what is actually taking place. Many gender equality issues have been simply obscured because they are not measured, leading people to assume that there is no problem and thus no need for a response. Careful measurement can bring gaps into clearer focus and keep attempts to close them on track through monitoring.

In each country in Asia and the Pacific, there exist practices that can restrict gender equality and also those that can support its achievement. These must be taken on board in shaping strategies to transform institutions, change attitudes and assess gaps. Progress may not always be straightforward, especially if it is perceived as producing clear winners and losers, as happening too fast or as a threat to deeply held beliefs. These concerns must be respected and managed. Gender equality is not a prescription with a single form; multiple means to achieve it are available. In this, the involvement and endorsement of people who clearly understand how gender norms operate in a given society or locality can be invaluable. To be successful, progress has to be rooted in local contexts.

An Agenda for Action

While individual Asia-Pacific countries have their own choices and needs in pursuing gender equality, some overarching strategies are common to all. Chapters 2, 3 and 4 of this Report present specific action points covering essentials for a better balance in economic power, political voice and legal rights. The following eight recommendations identify key actors and summarize proposed directions for action.

1. Make International Commitments a Reality

Countries should ratify and use international conventions that promote human rights, respect for diversity and equality for all. The range of fundamental human freedoms enshrined in the Universal Declaration of Human Rights was made specific to gender equality in CEDAW. Particular attention should be paid to removing the region's high number of reservations to CEDAW, paving the way for bringing domestic legislation in line with it. Other important international reference points include the 1995 Beijing Platform for Action and UN Security Council resolutions on women in conflict, particularly Resolutions 1325 and 1820, given the number of countries in conflict or post-conflict situations. Countries in the region have made specific commitments to achieving the MDGs by 2015, including the third goal on gender equality. Goal 3 is central to the other goals, which, in turn, are essential for achieving gender equality.

Members of parliament and the judiciary should be oriented to gender concerns, and these global instruments presented both as sources of information about gender equality and as political commitments that should be upheld. In some countries CEDAW has also become internalized in the system of national laws and used to reform criminal and civil justice systems. National laws to protect women's rights should progressively become consistent with international commitments.

International agreements, while com-

Assessing gaps and change through measurement is part of both transforming institutions and changing attitudes because it reveals what is actually taking place

posed of certain basic standards, can be viewed through the lens of respecting people's different priorities. Standards do not need to be uniformly imposed on everyone. But respect for diversity should be connected to equality of opportunity and human development, so that people as individuals can genuinely make their own choices.

Stronger South-South regional and wider international agreements should be considered to ensure women's safe migration and ease legal barriers, as single-person mobility with all the associated vulnerabilities represents a major Asia-Pacific phenomenon. Migrant work is of growing significance for females, with huge transformative potential. The risks directly linked to gender are also great—human trafficking, vulnerability to violence, HIV/AIDS, and loss of earnings, among others—and should be directly addressed.

2. Craft Economic Policies to Support Gender Equality

Too often, the gender-blind nature of economic policy-making results in choices that deny women opportunities even if they are not intended to. A more deliberate focus on gender and how it affects women's economic options is required, particularly in targeting poverty interventions to provide equal opportunities for women and men. One step may be educating economic policy makers, male and female, on how gender operates in societies and what this implies for economies. Skills required for gender analysis should be cultivated among ministries of finance and planning, as well as in others like agriculture, rural development, industry and commerce.

Governments should ensure that fiscal and monetary policies help unleash women's leadership and entrepreneurship. Monetary policy can be attuned to be more supportive of inclusive growth and human development. Directed lending to poor women for productive purposes, protection of their incomes

through micro-insurance, and the graduation of more women from microfinance to mainstream financial institutions of credit, insurance, investment and money transfer one some ways of doing so. Fiscal policy should include gender-based budgeting and the auditing of national and sub-national budgets, for both revenues and expenditures. These exercises should not be viewed as separate or discrete, but as integral to all budget categories.

Publicly funded programmes for poverty reduction, livelihoods, employment and entrepreneurship should ensure that women and single-headed households are guaranteed equal opportunities, remuneration, rights of ownership and control over assets. This will contribute to correcting past exclusions and support the relatively vulnerable through land assignments, titling, bank accounts and more independent control over their economic circumstances. Such efforts should be backed by sustained programmes for girls' education, their longer retention in formal systems, skills development to bridge knowledge gaps, and enhancing their ability to compete and negotiate for jobs and other economic resources.

Women may require specific forms of infrastructure to support their capacity to grasp economic opportunities, such as convenient childcare facilities and safe transportation networks. Policies to redistribute unpaid care work, largely seen as women's obligation, would free women to pursue other options and take better advantage of market opportunities. These need to apply to both the public and private sectors. They should include quality physical infrastructure and affordable essential care services.

Migrant workers have contributed enormously to the economies of sending and receiving locations alike. Given women's growing role in the provision of remittances and missing skills through migrant labour, safe and low-cost money transfer facilities should be available within countries and across borders.

Governments should ensure that fiscal and monetary policies help unleash women's leadership and entrepreneurship

3. Make the Content of Education and Access to It More Gender-Equal

Because education systems still perpetuate gender stereotypes, national and local governments should develop awareness of gender in school curricula and teacher training.

Civil society groups and gender experts can be brought in to guide the assessment and development of textbooks and question materials that overtly enforce stereotypes or do so by omission, such as when girls are never presented as leaders, leaving boys and girls with an impression that females do not normally lead or must be exceptional if they do so. Schools should promote female leadership and active decision-making, not only to provide positive role models for girls but also to make this perfectly normal and acceptable to boys.

Not just content but also the space where education takes place can hinder girls from participating. Safe and non-discriminatory school environments are a must, given that the lack of amenities such as transport or toilets can hold back girls from coming to school. Hostels for girls and women can help retain them longer in formal education and access quality facilities that may be far away. Recognize and remove all barriers that affect retention to help ensure that all girls complete a full cycle of schooling.

High-quality learning opportunities for women and girls, in formal systems as well as outside them, should be provided and backed by incentives as locally necessary. Some can be directly focused on market needs to add value to the time spent in remunerative work and to widen opportunities.

4. Boost Political Participation

Legislatures, political parties and political leaders should recognize the importance of women's political participation to democracy and equal citizenship. Political leaders and parties can act if they want to. Special actions to boost the number and quality of female representatives might include quotas, political party reform, gender-equality orientation and capacity development. These methods should be considered at national as well as sub-national levels. All of these measures need to be approached in the spirit of genuine change, avoiding tokenism or manipulation for political gain.

The success of quotas' in particular depends on incentives for compliance and sanctions for the lack of compliance. Quotas have a proven track record in many countries but may not automatically be the best mechanism for raising women's participation, though they do have the potential to quicken the process. Consideration should be given to timelines and exit strategies, as well as to advocacy to explain the value of women's political participation and counter impressions that quotas are mainly about women taking seats from men. There may be scope to adopt minimum quotas for both women and men, thus underscoring the principles of balanced representation and fairness.

As elections grow more expensive, campaign finance reform is important in opening doors to women as politicians, especially new candidates. Women on average start from a financial disadvantage, with fewer of their own resources and more limited access to political networks that can provide them. One approach is to limit the sums spent by parties or candidates in the course of a single election. Other options include the equitable distribution of airtime on public television and radio stations, and political party commitments to channel resources into the campaigns of women candidates.

Several countries in Asia and the Pacific face crises or are emerging from them. National and sub-national political leaders should assure better gender balance in leadership across all aspects of crisis management, whether involving natural disasters, conflicts or a sustained economic downturn. A token female politician will not be adequate for all voices to be heard and the particularities of gender addressed (such as female segregation, restricted mobility, sexual violence, invisibility of female ex-combatants, male vulnerability to recruitment, sudden job losses in export-oriented sectors, and HIV/AIDS). Highly unbalanced leadership may result in partial understanding, selective priorities and incomplete solutions in situations where these can do the most damage, including by destabilizing the prospects for full and rapid recovery.

5. Pursue Gender-Equitable Laws

Parliaments should reform gender discriminatory laws and make new ones where needed. This should include ironing out discrepancies between customary and formal laws that perpetuate discrimination as well as gaps between laws and constitutional principles. Countries should have specific constitutional provisions on equality and non-discrimination by gender. This will narrow the wide latitude of interpretation enjoyed by courts and law enforcement agencies. Harmful traditional and customary practices, under current human rights standards, should be banned. Many countries in the region have already set precedents to outlaw such practices.

Where applicable, a process of building social consensus and buy-in should surround the adoption of new and/or improved legal statutes. This may include reaching out to faith-based organizations as important agents for change.

Legal systems should be subjected to an overall gender equality review of national legislation, as some countries have done, including for CEDAW compliance. This Report has also identified a few categories of laws with extra urgency. To boost women's economic options, states should change discriminatory inheritance legislation, given the enormous disparities faced by women in establishing control and ownership over assets. Joint land titling can be an important step to counteract land inheritance practices guided by patrilineal succession, but it should be coupled with strategies to ensure that women are doing more than just signing their names to a deed.

Legislation on gender-friendly employment standards should be in place, along with mechanisms to ensure implementation. Key provisions comprise equal employment opportunities; equal pay for equal work; protection from sexual harassment supported by accessible complaint systems; paid maternity leave for 14 weeks; and basic rights for migrant women, including those who are short-term seasonal workers.

Marriage, divorce and maintenance laws continue to underscore women's second-class status and should be revised to support gender equality. A major legal gap in the region, while lessening, is in addressing gender-based violence. Laws need to be adopted and implemented effectively to reduce widespread impunity. They should not provide space for mediation. Offenders should be automatically prosecuted so that women and their families are not pressured into backing away from cases.

In general, women should enjoy all legal rights independently from men and their marital status. Special vulnerabilities among widows, young girls and single women may dictate additional forms of protection.

6. Address Legal Discrimination and Close Gaps Between Laws and Legal Practice

The justice system should ensure that legal practices are consistent with laws on the books and that access to justice is broadly available, whether that means taking justice to people through mobile courts or providing free legal aid to those with few resources.

Countries should have specific constitutional provisions on equality and non-discrimination by gender; States should change discriminatory inheritance legislation

Members of the judiciary as well as the police should be sensitized to the reality that, regardless of what the law says, men and women experience the justice system differently. This occurs due to issues such as affordability, stigmas faced by women and gender stereotyping by the judiciary, unconscious or otherwise. Professional training for lawyers, judges, magistrates and police should include an orientation around the needs of marginalized groups, with women being the largest of these categories. This may need to initially draw upon existing provisions in the national legal system that will be familiar to judicial professionals, before moving into the terrain of gender equality and social norms.

Crimes against women should not be treated lightly, whether they involve harassment in the streets (also known as Eve-teasing) or honour killings and female infanticide, euphemistically called 'social deaths'. These terms reflect disrespect and an affront to dignity that translate in turn into the reception women find in the legal system. Judges should set judicial precedents to uphold women's dignity and strengthen their security. They should not treat domestic violence as a 'private affair'. Prevention and response systems should be broadly available to survivors of violence so they can access all legal, administrative and social options available to press charges.

More female judges and police officers should be recruited. All officials in the justice system should receive training on gender issues. Male police officials should also be trained to take seriously and to act upon reported cases of crimes against women through proper investigation and charges against offenders. Legal education and training in general should include gender analysis and orientation.

7. Collect Better Data and Strengthen Capacity for Gender Analysis

National statistical systems should streng-then capacities to collect, report and analyze sex-disaggregated data, especially in overlooked areas such as for tracking the prevalence of gender-based violence and male-female gaps in asset ownership. Systematic and ongoing assessments should feed into policy efforts to close disparities, with information readily available on changes over time. All relevant line ministries should be engaged in monitoring, in addition to women's affairs, such as agriculture, commerce, education, finance, health, industry, infrastructure, labour and others. Both official statistical systems and administrative data should ensure gender-based assessments that serve as monitoring cross-checks.

Measuring women's unpaid work can incorporate instruments such as time-use surveys, in recognition that many women's activities take place in the home or the informal sector, outside of conventional data gathering systems. To better understand patterns of female migration, data collection and sharing should improve between origin and destination countries and sub-national regions.

While sex-disaggregated data is a necessary tool, it is not sufficient. Strengthen technical capacities in gender analysis across all ministries, without taking such skills for granted. This will ensure that differences in male-female experiences and the barriers and opportunities they face are clearly understood and taken into account much more fully, systematically and on an ongoing basis, based on agreed frameworks. Locally relevant gender analysis frameworks should be developed to help raise critical questions and analyse information through a gender 'lens,' which can feed into strengthening policies and programmes across the board.

8. Foster New Attitudes

Civil society, the media, academic institutions, religious organizations, businesses and other groups involved in shaping social attitudes should be enlisted in influencing those attitudes to support gender equality.

Concrete advocacy tools can be developed around international conventions, national laws and initiatives, the principles of religious faiths or customs, mechanisms for gender analysis and gender-budgeting. New channels

---

BOX 5.1

LOOK WITHIN TO FURTHER GENDER EQUALITY

Advancing gender equality is a joint responsibility of everyone, just as the benefits of more fulfilled lives and fairer societies are for all people to enjoy. As the analysis in this Report underscores, institutions, attitudes and assessments simultaneously need to be part of a transformative process of change. Much takes place in people's daily lives that, one way or another, impinges on how institutions work and attitudes emerge. Much depends on how individuals—men, women and people with other gender identities—think and act in public and private, sometimes quite unwittingly. Examining these attitudes and adjusting behaviours accordingly not only affects current gender dynamics, but also has demonstration and transmission effects that influence the next generation. To transmit more positive attitudes, make institutions work better and support change that is just, individuals can:

Be self-aware and informed. Understand your rights as human beings—does gender interfere with them unfairly? Learn about your national laws and avenues for justice and protection. Recognize stereotypes when confronted by them, in the media or elsewhere. Knowledge is power: It can help you challenge harmful social practices and communicate the need for change to others. Have you ever been tempted to interfere with someone's rights based on gender because you could get away with it? Understand and respect diversity. This learning is important for yourself, as well as to help other people who may confront discrimination.

Stop gender-based violence. Have you observed violence and harassment linked to gender, on the street, at home, at the workplace, at the train or bus station, or in an institution? Have you been a party to gender-based violence, perhaps unknowingly? Realize that gender-based violence is an extreme violation of human decency and dignity—harmful for the victim and unwholesome for the perpetrator. Don't stay silent in the face of gender-based violence in your own home or elsewhere. Assist the victim. Approach local authorities and support agencies to expose, punish and deter offenders. Perpetrators may also need help through information and rehabilitation to avoid recurrence.

Share responsibilities and respect rights at home. Is unpaid household work largely the 'default' responsibility of women in your home? If so, why? Joint sharing of household work and family decisions can create a healthy home environment and allow a better work-leisure balance for all. Mutual respect

for spouse, sons, daughters and parents can strengthen voluntary bonds (as against those enforced through material dependence). Respect the right of spouses to control their earnings. As parents and grandparents, treat sons (and sons-in-law) and daughters (and daughters-in-law) equally. Provide equal access to opportunities for education. Encourage boys and girls to handle their own personal work and share common household responsibilities. As daughters and sons, don't give up your inheritance rights. Equally, support your family—take away the stereotype that only sons care for parents in old age.

Treat girls and boys equally in and out of the classroom and on the playground. As an educator, mentor or coach for young people from early childhood to adulthood, have you ensured that girls and boys receive equal attention? Encourage all students to explore a range of subjects. Ensure that girls are not guided towards stereotypes or kept on the sidelines during sports and extra-curricular activities. Options should be guided by aptitude and ability rather than gender. This builds confidence and skills for both girls and boys.

Break gender stereotypes in the workplace. Is there respect for colleagues of all genders at work? Ensure that there is a well-documented and publicized policy on sexual harassment at work and that new recruits are made aware of the policy as part of normal orientation. Watch out for gender-based prejudices and stereotypes that might guide professional decisions. If you are a manager, remember that gender-sensitive actions can signal to employees core principles of equality and a harassment-free workplace.

Nurture leadership potential of both males and females in the family and in the community. Are women and girls in your family and neighbourhood encouraged to aspire to leadership positions? Encourage women to explore their entrepreneurial and professional talents. Support them to reach their full potential through education, jobs, entrepreneurship and other opportunities. Support and join women's collectives, such as self-help groups, to bolster women's voices and decision-making.

Cast your vote for candidates who promote gender issues. As a citizen have you petitioned your local representative to put 'gender equality' on the agenda? You can also support women candidates for local and national elections, and campaign for making elections affordable and safe.

---

of advocacy and communication should be explored in areas where new technology is widespread. Businesses can be brought on board through practices within their own firms as well as in advertising. In countries where businesses conduct market surveys to design products and advertisements, they may also be a ready source of information on how attitudes are changing and which advocacy messages can build on these.

Enlisting people in changing mindsets to support gender equality may need to start with the development of capacities to understand how gender operates in societies and what benefits can come from addressing inequalities and embracing diversity – both for particular groups and society as a whole. There is much that individuals of all genders can do in their daily lives (Box 5.1).

Fostering new attitudes should include advocacy for addressing the needs of men and boys that arise from male gender norms

Fostering new attitudes should include advocacy for addressing the needs of men and boys that arise from male gender norms. Working with men and boys requires intensive efforts to promote examining roles and defining the benefits of new ideas. Dominant masculinities can be questioned, opening space to explore diverse interpretations of what it means to be a man. In general, there should be a strong push behind the inclusion of men in the understanding of gender equality and steps to achieve it, recognizing their transformative role.

A particular area of focus needs to be in making societies more alert to gender-based violence, more so in crisis situations when normal social bonds may have broken down. The diagnosis and recognition of violent acts should extend to those that may be less visible, such as forced marriages. Male family members need to realize that domestic violence is an extreme affront to the dignity of a woman in denying her control over her own being.

A Turning Point for Gender Equality

Across all eight areas in this Agenda for Action, piecemeal implementation will not be adequate. Boundaries need to be pushed so that changes take root and begin to generate their own momentum. The region is at a turning point. The agenda needs to be put in place simultaneously on the economic, legal and political fronts, given connections among the three, and maintained over time.

The overarching goal of human development is that people at large should be able to make choices and have access to capabilities and opportunities for fulfilling lives. These should never be taken away or diminished on the basis of gender. Inclusive development rests on the principles of equality and participation. It is the only route forward that is efficient, empowering and sustainable – and extends justice to all.

Definitions of Technical Terms

Adolescent fertility rate Number of births per 1,000 women aged 15-19.

Adult literacy rate (% aged 15 and older) Percentage of people aged 15 and above who can, with understanding, read and write a short, simple statement on their everyday life.

Bapakism 'Rule by the father' in the Bahasa language in Indonesia.

Biwi Hindustani for 'wife'; also used in Urdu.

Body mass index (BMI) A simple index of weight-for-height that is commonly used to classify underweight, overweight and obese adults. It is defined as the weight in kilograms divided by the square of the height in meters (kg/m^2). (BMI $<$ 18.5 = underweight; BMI $\geq$ 25.0 = overweight; and BMI $\geq$ 30.0 = obesity.)

Common law The body of law derived from judicial decisions, rather than from statutes or constitutions.

Countercyclical policy Government policy aimed at reducing or neutralizing the effects of economic cycles. Such policies normally encourage spending during downturns, and tighten credit during upturns, particularly when inflation becomes a serious threat to economic stability.

Customary law Law consisting of customs that are accepted as legal requirements or obligatory rules of conduct; practices and beliefs that are so vital and intrinsic a part of social and economic system that they are treated as if they are laws. Customary law is also referred as informal law.

Decent work The idea is captured in four strategic objectives: fundamental principles and rights at work and international labour standards; employment and income opportunities; social protection and social security; and social dialogue and tripartism. These objectives hold for all workers—women and men—in both formal and informal economies; in wage employment or working on their own account; in the fields, factories and offices; in their home or in the community.

De facto A Latin word for 'in point of fact'; actual; existing in fact.

De jure A Latin word for 'as a matter of law'; existing by right or according to law.

De facto marriage A marriage in which a couple lives together without being legally married. It is also used for a marriage that is defective for some reason, even if the parties live as husband and wife. A related term is a 'common law marriage' where persons who live together as man and wife for a sufficient time and with the intent of having an exclusive relationship akin to a marriage are allowed to have the legal rights of formally married persons.

Domestic violence Any act of violence or abuse of a family member by another family member or someone who is in a close relationship to the victim. It includes, physical, sexual, psychological and economic abuse.

Domicile The place at which a person has been physically present and regards as home.

Economic assets Those from which economic benefits may be derived by their owners by holding or using them, over a period of time.

Electoral quotas Quotas entail a requirement that identified minority or under-represented groups, such as women, constitute a certain number or percentage of the members of a body, whether it is a candidate list, a parliamentary assembly, a committee or a government. The quota system places the burden of recruitment not on the individual, but on those who control the recruitment process. The core idea behind quotas for women is to recruit women into political positions and to ensure that women are not isolated in political life. Electoral quotas for women may be constitutional, legislative or set by political parties.

Electoral systems How the votes cast in an election are converted into offices/seats won by parties and candidates. The key variables are the electoral formula used (i.e. whether a plurality/majority, proportional, mixed or other system is used, and what mathematical formula is used to calculate the seat allocation), the ballot structure (i.e. whether the voter votes for a candidate or a party, and whether the voter makes a single choice or expresses a series of preferences) and the district magnitude (not how many voters live in a district, but how many representatives to the legislature that district elects).

Fa'aaloalo Samoan for 'respect'.

Gender parity index (GPI) Ratio of female-to-male values (or male to female, in certain cases) of a given indicator. A GPI of 1 indicates parity between sexes; a GPI above or below 1 indicates a disparity in favour of one sex over the other.

Gender wage gaps The difference between female and male wages for similar work. It is often expressed in terms of female wages as a percentage of male wages.

Gender-based violence Any act that results in, or is likely to result in, physical, sexual or psychological harm linked to a person's gender. It includes violent acts such as rape, torture, mutilation, sexual slavery, forced impregnation and murder. Threats of these acts are also forms of violence.

Gross tertiary school enrolment ratio The ratio of total tertiary enrolment, regardless of age, to the population of the age group that officially corresponds to this level of education. Tertiary education, whether or not to an advanced research qualification, normally requires, as a minimum condition of admission, the successful completion of education at the secondary level.

Iddah or iddat A specified period of time that must elapse before a Muslim widow or divorcee may legitimately remarry.

Informal sector A group of household enterprises or unincorporated enterprises owned by households that includes informal own-account enterprises, which may employ contributing family workers and employees on an occasional basis; and enterprises of informal employers, which employ one or more employees on a continuous basis. The enterprise of informal employers must fulfill one or both of the following criteria: size of unit below a specified level of employment, and non-registration of the enterprise or its employees.

Jirga A local institution of dispute settlement that incorporates prevalent local customary laws, institutionalized rituals, and a body of selected village elders whose ruling about the settlement of a dispute (or local problem) is binding on the parties involved.

Labor force participation rate (% of female/male population aged 15 +) Proportion of the population (female/male) aged 15 and older that is economically active: all people who supply labour for the production of goods and services (for paid work) during a specified period.

Legislative assembly The name given in some countries to either a legislature, or to one of its chambers.

Life expectancy at birth The number of years a newborn infant could expect to live if prevailing patterns of mortality at the time of its birth were to stay the same throughout its life.

Majoritarian/majority electoral system A voting system based on a 'winner takes all' or 'first past the post' principle. This is in contrast to the proportional representation family of electoral systems, which split the mandates in rough proportion with votes gained by each party.

Malnutrition prevalence—height for age (% children under 5) Percentage of children under five whose height for age is more than two standard deviations below the median for the international reference, as established by the World Health Organization, population aged 0 to 59 months.

Malnutrition prevalence—weight for age (% children under 5) Percentage of children under five whose weight for age is more than two standard deviations below the median reference standard for their age, as established by the World Health Organization.

Masculinity Features, physical or otherwise, traditionally considered to be characteristic of males.

Matai Samoan for 'chief'.

Maternal mortality ratio (per 100,000 live births) The number of women who die during pregnancy (before a child is born) and childbirth, per 100,000 live births.

Matrilineal inheritance The inheritance of property or titles through the mother or the female line only.

Microfinance The provision of a broad range of financial services, such as deposits, loans, payment services, money transfers and insurance, to poor and low-income households, and to their microenterprises. It usually involves small amounts for which formal financial institutions consider the transaction costs too high or the clients too risky.

Missing women Those females who have died as a result of discriminatory treatment in access to health and nutrition also due to selective abortion and information.

Mixed representation electoral system Two electoral systems using different formulae run alongside each other. Voters cast votes to elect representatives under both systems. Mixed systems typically combine a plurality/majority system (or occasionally another system) that is usually a single-member district system with a list proportional representation system.

Nazim Elected heads of local councils in Pakistan.

Net primary school enrolment ratio The ratio of school age children enrolled in primary school compared to the total population of corresponding school age children.

Net secondary school enrolment ratio
The ratio of school age children enrolled in secondary school compared to the total population of school age children.

Panchayats or gram panchayats Forms of local governments at the village or small town level in India. The *gram panchayat* is the foundation of the *panchayat* political system. A *gram panchayat* can be set up in villages with a minimum population of 500. Sometimes two or more villages are clubbed together to form group-*gram panchayats*, such as when the populations of individual villages are less than 500.

Patrilineal inheritance The inheritance of property or titles through the father or through the male line only.

Penal code A compilation of criminal laws, defining and categorizing the offences and setting forth their respective punishments.

Primary completion rate (% of relevant age group) The percentage of students completing the last year of primary school. It is calculated by taking the total number of students in the last grade of primary school minus the number of repeaters in that grade. The resulting figure is then divided by the total number of children of official graduation age.

Proportion of seats held by women in national parliaments (%) The number of seats held by women members in single or lower chambers of national parliaments, expressed as a percentage of all occupied seats.

Proportional representation electoral systems Sometimes referred to as full representation, it is a category of electoral system aimed at a close match between the percentage of votes that groups of candidates (grouped by a certain measure) obtain in elections and the percentage of seats they receive (usually in legislative assemblies).

Public interest litigation Litigation filed in a court of law, for the protection of the 'public interest', typically related to issues such as pollution, terrorism, road safety, constructional hazards, etc.

Qanoon-e-shahdat The law of evidence in Pakistan.

Ratio of female-to-male enrolments in tertiary education (% of female to male) Percentage of women enrolled at the tertiary level in public and private schools compared to the percentage of men.

Ratio of female-to-male primary enrolment rate (% of female to male) Percentage of girls enrolled at the primary level in public and private schools compared to the percentage of boys.

Ratio of female-to-male secondary enrolment rate (% of female to male) Percentage of girls enrolled at the secondary level in public and private schools compared to the percentage of boys.

Reservations A unilateral statement, however phrased or named, made by a State when signing, ratifying, accepting, approving or acceding to a treaty, whereby it purports to exclude or to modify the legal effect of certain provisions of the treaty in their application to that State.

Sarpanch A democratically elected head of a village level statutory institution of local self-government called the *gram panchayat* in India and Pakistan. The *sarpanch* is the focal point of contact between government officers and the village community. It is an elected position.

Scheduled castes (SC) and scheduled tribes (ST) Indian population groupings that are explicitly recognized by the Constitution of India. They are historically marginalized 'social groups' and they together comprise about a quarter of India's total population.

Sex ratio at birth The number of boys born alive per 100 girls born alive.

Share of women employed in the non-agricultural sector (percentage of total non-agricultural employment) The total number of women employed in the non-agricultural sector (industry and services) expressed as a percentage of total employment in the non-agricultural sector.

Shia Muslims The second largest denomination in Islam.

Subsistence agriculture A form of agriculture where almost all production is consumed by the household; often characterized by low inputs mostly provided by the household itself.

Sunni Muslims The largest denomination in Islam.

Talaq An Islamic term. The dissolution of a valid marriage contract forthwith or at a latter date by the husband, his agent or his wife duly authorized to do so, using the word 'Talaq', or a derivative or a synonymy thereof.

Tehsil An administrative division of some countries of South Asia. Generally, a *tehsil* consists of a city or town that serves as its headquarters, possibly additional towns and a number of villages. As an entity of local government, it exercises certain fiscal and administrative powers over the villages and municipalities within its jurisdiction. It is the ultimate executive agency for land records and related administrative matters.

Time use survey A detailed portrait of how individuals spend their time during a given period, illustrating the types of activities in which people engage and for how long.

Ultra vires Unauthorized; beyond the scope of power allowed or granted by a corporate charter or by law.

Unemployment The share of the labour force that is without work but available for, and actively seeking, employment.

Usufruct rights Legal right to use and enjoy the advantages or profits deriving from another person's property.

Notes

Chapter 1

1. Overall, Nordic countries come closest in terms of equal opportunities.
2. Universal Declaration of Human Rights 1948.
3. UNIFEM South Asia Regional Office and Partners for Law in Development 2004.
4. UNIFEM South Asia Regional Office and Partners for Law in Development 2004.
5. World Bank 2009b.
6. See later in this chapter, 'Where the Region Stands: A Snapshot'.
7. HDRU estimates based on Klasen and Wink (2002), who gave the latest and perhaps the most refined estimates of missing women for selected developing countries, including Bangladesh, China, India, the Islamic Republic of Iran, Republic of Korea, Nepal and Pakistan. They estimated the number and per cent of missing women for countries with suspiciously high sex ratios or other evidence of female disadvantage using the most recent population census data. Sri Lanka does not have any missing women.
8. World Bank 2009b.
9. Based on World Bank 2009b.
10. World Bank 2009b.
11. Based on World Bank 2009b.
12. Chen and Ravallion 2008.
13. FAO n.d.-b.
14. The labour force participation rate is the proportion of the population aged 15 and older that is economically active, including those who are actually working and those who are actively seeking employment. People are pushed out of the labour force due to cultural and social factors, long-term illness or because they have given up finding a job. The participation rate is usually less than 100 per cent – considerably less so in some countries (see Table 11 in the Statistical Annex).
15. World Bank 2009b.
16. World Bank 2009b.
17. IPU 2009; World Bank 2009b.
18. Commission on Legal Empowerment of the Poor 2008.
19. World Bank 2009b.
20. Srivastava 2009a.
21. In the Yogyakarta Principles on the Application of international Human Rights Law in relation to sexual orientation and gender identity, sexual orientation is understood to refer to each person's capacity for profound emotional, affectional and sexual attraction to, and intimate and sexual relations with, individuals of a different gender or the same gender or more than one gender. Gender Identity is understood to refer to each person's deeply felt internal and individual experience of gender, which may or may not correspond with the sex assigned at birth, including the personal sense of the body (which may involve, if freely chosen, modification of bodily appearance or function by medical, surgical or other means) and other expressions of gender, including dress, speech and mannerisms. (Yogyakarta Principles 2007).
22. Abeysekera 2009.
23. Gampat 2009b.
24. Klasen and Lamanna 2008.
25. Education is one of the three pillars of the Human Development Index, which is a measure of human development. As will become clear in the discussion, most of the empirical work on gender equality has focused on education.
26. Caselli et al. 1996; Dollar and Gatti 1999; Forbes 2000; Hill and King 1993; Klasen 1999; Knowles et al. 2002.
27. Blau 1986; Ketkar 1978; World Bank 2001.
28. Blau 1986; Behrman and Deolalikar 1988.
29. Blau 1986; Bach et al. 1985; King et al. 2008.
30. Blecker and Seguino 2002; Esteve-Volart 2004.
31. Stotsky 2006.
32. World Bank 2009b.
33. Evans 2009.

34. Gampat 2009a.
35. Constable 2009.
36. Burgonio 2009.
37. World Bank 2009a.
38. UN 2005c.
39. UNDP 1995.
40. Wax and Sen 2009.
41. UN 1996.
42. ECOSOC conclusions 1997/2, cited in UN n.d.-b.
43. Daly 2005.
44. UN 2005d.
45. Menon-Sen 2009.
46. Rees 2002, cited in Lahiri-Dutt 2009.
47. UN 1996.
48. Chakraborty 2009.
49. Sinha and Adam 2006, cited in Sinha 2009.
50. Regional aggregates are taken from the World Bank's World Development Indicators database (World Bank 2009b). As per the Bank's definition, aggregates for East Asia and the Pacific, Europe and Central Asia, Latin America and the Caribbean, and the Middle East and North Africa do not include high-income economies. In South Asia and sub-Saharan Africa, there are no economies classified as high income (see 'Notes' in World Development Indicators online, World Bank 2009b). For the Bank's classification of regions, see http://go. worldbank.org/D7SN0B8YU0.
51. The term 'missing women', a phrase coined by Nobel Prize-winning economist Amartya Sen, refers to the number of females who have died as a result of discriminatory treatment in access to health and nutrition (Sen 1990a; 1990b). Sen's estimate is based on the actual population sex ratio (the number of males divided by the number of females) against an 'expected' population sex ratio, given equal treatment of the sexes in the distribution of survival-related goods and services. If the actual ratio exceeds the expected, the excess constitutes the number of 'missing women' at that point in time. A subsequent debate refined Sen's estimates by using different demographic techniques, particularly with regard to the critical assumption about the expected sex ratio (Coale 1991; Klasen 1994).

The latest and perhaps the most refined estimates of missing women for selected developing countries were given by Klasen and Wink (2002). They estimated the number and per cent of missing women for several countries (those with suspiciously high sex ratios or other evidence of female disadvantage), using the most recent population census data. Based on Klasen and Wink's percentage figures for missing women (column 2, Appendix Table 1.2), the present Report updates those estimates for the countries in the Asia-Pacific region where updated population figures for 2007 were available. The new estimates for 2007 are shown in column 4 of the table. It is interesting to note that Sri Lanka does not have any missing women. The critical assumption underlying these new estimates is that the percentage used in 2001 is still applicable to 2007. In other words, the presumption is that preferences for sons and other factors that prejudice the survival of females remain unchanged.

52. Klasen and Wink 2002.
53. This result holds true so long as the value of the aversion to inequality parameter is greater than zero. If it is equal to zero, then GDI = HDI. Incidentally, the correlation coefficient between the two is very high—in 2007 it was 0.99 for Asia-Pacific countries, as well as 0.99 for the 155 countries in the world for which data is available. This close association between the two indicates GDI and HDI move together.
54. Some exceptions are starting to emerge. For example, recent national statistics for Nepal show that GEM is showing higher values than the GDI, indicating potential for gains in opportunities even at lower levels of income (UNDP Nepal 2009).

Chapter 2

1. Economist 2006.
2. UNESCAP 2007a.
3. This estimate includes developed countries. See UNESCAP 2007a.
4. The sub-regional estimates are based on the countries for which data are available for the time period. For example, East Asia and the Pacific sub-region includes China, Fiji, Hong Kong, China (SAR), Indonesia, Macao, China (SAR), Malaysia, Papua New Guinea, the Philippines, Singapore, the Republic of Korea, Taiwan, Province of

China and Thailand. See Klasen and Lamanna 2008.

5. Klasen and Lamanna 2008.

6. See Ford Foundation 2002; Doss et al. 2008.

7. See Agarwal 1994; Agarwal 1997; World Bank 2001; Quisumbing 2003; Deere and Doss 2006.

8. UN Millennium Project 2005.

9. Narayan 2001.

10. Mason and Carlsson 2004, cited in ICRW and Millennium Project 2005.

11. Malla 2000, cited in Doss et al. 2008.

12. Out of a sample of 93 national agricultural censuses conducted worldwide from 1989 to 1999, only 53 contained information on female headed holdings (FAO n.d.-b).

13. ILO 2009a.

14. Unni 1999.

15. AusAID 2008.

16. Stege et al. 2008.

17. U.S. Department of State 2009.

18. Agarwal 1994.

19. Allen et al. 2008.

20. Ito 2007.

21. Hirayama 2006, cited in Ito 2007.

22. Parts of some countries follow other systems that could be advantageous to women, such as Bhutan, Cook Islands, India, Indonesia, Lao People's Democratic Republic, Papua New Guinea, the Philippines, Sri Lanka and Thailand. Ten per cent of the population of the Pacific traditionally follows matrilineal transmission of land rights (Crocombe 1994, cited in Smiley 2006). However, even in matrilineal systems women's personal autonomy was limited. The senior male of the household had substantial control over property. In the contemporary context, in Kerala, for instance, '...reforms and the consolidation of marriage as the dominant framework of women's property rights speak directly to women's contemporary disadvantage in property rights through the "thinning" of parental inheritance and the growing importance of dowry and spousal inheritance' (Government of Kerala 2006).

23. Agarwal 1994.

24. Both the *Mitakshara* and *Dayabhaga* were two main schools of inheritance in Hindu law. The Hindu Succession Act of 1956 unified the system of inheritance following broadly a *Mitakshara* pattern.

25. Agarwal 2005.

26. Ramaseshan 2009a.

27. Bowen 1998. As per Article 176: An only daughter's share is half the entire value of the inheritance; if there is more than one daughter, the daughters collectively receive two-thirds of the entire value of the inheritance; and if there is one daughter and one son, the inheritance ratio is one to two.

28. The Asia Foundation et al. 2006.

29. Agarwal 1994.

30. Grace 2005.

31. Debroux n.d.

32. Agarwal 1994; Agarwal 2003.

33. There is a substantial literature on this. For references, see Agarwal 2003; Quisumbing and Maluccio 2003; Duraisamy 1992, among others.

34. See Rahman and Menken 1990; Swaminathan et al. 2007; and also references in Agarwal 1994.

35. Agarwal and Panda 2007.

36. Computed from NSSO (2006) and population projections from the 2001 Census (Government of India 2006).

37. FAO Statistics (http:/faostat.fao.org). Figures relate to 2006 (FAO n.d.-a).

38. FAO Statistics (http:/faostat.fao.org). Figures relate to 2006 (FAO n.d.-a).

39. See Government of Nepal 2001.

40. Agarwal 1994. There is no comprehensive data for ownership holdings, but figures in the Agricultural Census 1995-1996 indicate that women held only 9.5 per cent of all operational land holding (Government of India 1995-96).

41. Li 2003.

42. Agarwal 1994.

43. Agarwal 2005.

44. See Agarwal 1994 for India, Pakistan, Bangladesh, Nepal, and Sri Lanka; Estudillo et al. 2001 for the Philippines; and also see the reports of States Parties to UN Committee on CEDAW.

45. FAO n.d.-a.

46. Agarwal 1994.

47. Agarwal 2003.

48. Burra 2004.

49. Wood and Palmer-Jones 1991.

50. IFAD 2009.

51. Agarwal 2008.

52. Agarwal 2008.

53. Agarwal 2002a.

54. Agarwal 2002b; Kelkar and Nathan 2005.
55. See Mason 1998; Agarwal 1998; Allendorf 2007, cited in Doss et al. 2008.
56. Upadhay 2003, cited in Rustagi and Menon 2009.
57. See Doss 1996; Quisumbing and Hallman 2006, cited in Doss et al. 2008.
58. Global Entrepreneurship Monitor (GEM) provides comparable data for a cross-national assessment of entrepreneurial activity in 41 countries whose economies represent more than 70 per cent of the world's population and 93 per cent of global GDP in 2007 (Allen et al. 2008).
59. Allen et al. 2008; Allen et al. 2007.
60. Debroux n.d.
61. FAO 2009.
62. Norwegian Agency for International Development et al. 1987.
63. Moser and Dani 2008, cited in Rustagi and Menon 2009.
64. ADB et al. 2008.
65. Chandra and Lewai 2005, cited in ADB 2006.
66. ADB and World Bank 2005.
67. World Savings Banks Institute 2008.
68. Pitt et al. 2006.
69. Hossain 1988.
70. PARWAZ n.d.
71. Shylendra 2006.
72. FAO and SIDA 1987.
73. FAO 2008.
74. Yunus 2006.
75. Grameen Bank 2009a.
76. The Microcredit Summit Campaign 2009.
77. Yunus 2006.
78. Mayoux 2000.
79. Pitt and Khandker 1998; Johnson n.d.
80. Grameen Bank 2009a.
81. See Yunus 2006.
82. Pitt and Khandker 1996; Montgomery et al. 1996.
83. Grameen Bank 2009b.
84. Kabeer 2005.
85. Murthy et al. n.d.
86. Snodgrass and Sebstad 2002.
87. Pitt and Khandker 1998.
88. Sarangi 2007.
89. See Figures 1.7 and 1.8 in Chapter 1, and Table 5 in the Statistical Annex of this Report.
90. WHO 2008.
91. Murthy 2009.
92. Du et al. 2008, cited in Murthy 2009.
93. See also Smith et al. 2004.
94. WHO 2000.
95. Pandey 1997.
96. Chand 2006.
97. Commission on AIDS in Asia 2008.
98. UNESCO 2009b.
99. Commission on AIDS in Asia 2008.
100. Decker et al. 2009.
101. Swaminathan et al. 2007.
102. Pradhan and Sundar 2006.
103. ARROW 2008, cited in Murthy 2009; see Law No. 23 of 1992 (CEDAW 2005a).
104. Larson et al. 2006.
105. Li et al. 2008, cited in Murthy 2009.
106. Nussbaum and Glover 1995, cited in Mitra 2009.
107. Kabeer 2000; Blomqvist 2004, cited in Nazneen 2009.
108. Kabeer 2008.
109. Ahmad 1998, cited in Sonpar and Kapur 2003.
110. Mitra 2009.
111. ILO 2009a.
112. ILO 2009a. Figures for 2008 are preliminary estimates.
113. ILO 1999.
114. Time use surveys also show that women earn less than men on average. Even the country with lowest gap between female and male estimated income, such as Mongolia, time use data in 2008 show that working men earn 38 per cent more than the working women on average. See National Statistical Office of Mongolia and UNDP Mongolia 2009.
115. Mitra 2009, based on data from Key Indicators of the Labour Market, ILO 2007.
116. ILO 2009a.
117. CEDAW 1997.
118. The limitations of the indicator are: (1) there might be people that carry a high economic risk despite the fact that they have a wage and salary job, and the latter should not be equated to decent work; (2) unemployed people are not covered even though they are vulnerable; (3) there can be people in the two vulnerable status groups who do not carry a high economic risk, especially in developed economies. Despite these limitations, vulnerable employent shares are indicative for informal economy employment, particularly for the less developed economies and regions (ILO 2009a).

119. ILO 2009a.
120. Mitra 2009.
121. UNIFEM 2008; Kabeer 2007, cited in Nazneen 2009.
122. Elson 1999; Kabeer 2007, cited in Nazneen 2009.
123. For Taiwan, Province of China, for example, see Hsiang-Lin n.d.
124. ITUC-CSI-IGB 2007.
125. Ghosh 2008.
126. Ghosh 2008.
127. Emmet 2009.
128. World Bank 2004, cited in Mitra 2009.
129. Chen n.d.
130. Mitra 2009.
131. Chen n.d.
132. Joshi 1996, cited in Mitra 2009.
133. Bullock 1994 and ILO 1998b, cited in Mitra 2009.
134. Mitra 2005.
135. Lu 2001, cited in Mitra 2009.
136. Lu 2001, cited in Mitra 2009.
137. World Bank 2007.
138. World Bank 2007.
139. World Bank et al. 2009.
140. Resurreccion and Sajor 2008.
141. Jackson and Rao 2004, cited in Nazneen 2009.
142. Gill 2001, cited in Nazneen 2009.
143. UNESCAP 2004.
144. Narsey 2007.
145. See Chakraborty 2009.
146. UNESCAP 2007a.
147. See Klasen and Lamanna 2008.
148. See Klasen 1999; Lagerlöf 2003; Klasen and Lamanna 2008 among others.
149. Dollar and Gatti 1999.
150. World Bank 2009b.
151. World Bank 2009b.
152. UNESCO 2009a.
153. Law and Chan 2004.
154. Raynor 2005.
155. UNGEI 2008.
156. UNGEI 2008.
157. World Bank 2009b.
158. World Bank 2009b.
159. Mehran 2003.
160. World Bank 2009b.
161. Yamanaka and Piper (2005) identify six types of cross-border migration of women in Asia: domestic workers; entertainers and/or sex workers; unauthorised workers; immigrant wives; skilled workers; and workers who share an ethnic heritage with that of the host population (such as Japanese-Brazilians in Japan and Korean-Chinese in the Republic of Korea).
162. **North East Asia**: Cambodia, China, Hong Kong, China (SAR), Macao, China (SAR), Democratic People's Republic of Korea, Japan, Republic of Korea, Lao People's Democratic Republic, Mongolia, Viet Nam; **South East Asia**: Brunei Darussalam, Indonesia, Malaysia, Myanmar, the Philippines, Singapore, Thailand, Timor-Leste; **South & West Asia**: Afghanistan, Bangladesh, Bhutan, India, Islamic Republic of Iran, Maldives, Nepal, Pakistan, Sri Lanka; **Pacific**: Australia, Cook Islands, Fiji, Kiribati, Marshall Islands, Federated States of Micronesia, Nauru, New Zealand, Niue, Palau, Papua New Guinea, Samoa, Solomon Islands, Tokelau, Tonga, Tuvalu, Vanuatu.
163. Asis 2003.
164. National Commission on the Role of Filipino Women 2009.
165. Kundu 2009.
166. Gender and Development Research Institute 2006, cited in Resurreccion 2009.
167. Sward and Skeldon 2009.
168. Sirimanne 2009.
169. Foreman and Cao 2009.
170. Hugo 2005.
171. UN 2003.
172. Phetsiriseng 2007.
173. Lorenzo et al. 2007.
174. World Bank 2006.
175. Van Eyck 2003; Van Eyck 2005, cited in Resurreccion 2009.
176. ILO 1998a.
177. UN 2003.
178. Inglis 2003.
179. Kawar n.d.; Piper 2005.
180. UNDP et al. 2008.
181. De Haan and Rogaly 2002.
182. Resurreccion and Van Khanh 2007.
183. Shamim and Salahuddin 1995, cited in UNDESA 2001.
184. See Indira Awas Yojana (Government of India 2008).
185. Shefali 2004.
186. Murthy et al. 2008.
187. Todd 1996, cited in ILO 1998b; Hunt and Kasynathan 2002.
188. See ILO n.d.-a. ILO's concept of 'decent work' is based on four strategic objectives: fundamental principles and rights at work and international labour standards; emp-

loyment and income opportunities; social protection and social security; and social dialogue and tripartism. In 2008, the concept was formally confirmed with the adoption of the ILO 'Declaration on Social Justice For a Fair Globalization' by acclamation of member States, workers and employers attending the 97th International Labour Conference meeting in Geneva.

189. Cited in Song 2009.
190. See Integrated Child Development Services (ICDS) Scheme (Government of India n.d.).
191. UN 2009b.
192. UNDP 2008c.
193. Some important conventions on rights include ILO Convention No. 87 on 'Freedom of Association and Protection of the Right to Organise Convention, 1948' and ILO Convention No. 98 on 'Right to Organise and Collective Bargaining Convention, 1949'. See ILO n.d.-b.
194. Phetsiriseng 2007.

Chapter 3

1. International IDEA 2003.
2. IPU 2009.
3. IPU 2009.
4. IPU 2009.
5. UNDP 2008a.
6. IPU 2009.
7. IPU 2009.
8. Independent Election Commission Secretariat 2009.
9. IPU 2009.
10. Shameem 2008.
11. IPU 2009.
12. Jolly and Macintyre 1989.
13. Halapua 2003.
14. Crocombe 2001.
15. CEDAW 2008b.
16. Robinson 2000.
17. Anderson 1990.
18. Sen 2002; Robinson 2004.
19. Prokop 2009.
20. Independent Election Commission Secretariat n.d.
21. International IDEA 2005.
22. Women's Environment and Development Organization n.d.
23. To the best of our knowledge, these indicators are not available in any readily accessible publication. They have been compiled by the HDRU based on extensive internet research. Samoa is an exception and has achieved gender purity in university heads (Reference: Statistical annex, Table 17, in this Report).
24. Soin 1994.
25. Shvedova 2005.
26. Soin 1994.
27. Anandhi 2002.
28. International IDEA 2005.
29. Basu 2003.
30. Grey 2001.
31. Lithgow 2000.
32. Vickers 2005
33. Mohanty 2001.
34. U.S. Department of State 2002; Center for Asia-Pacific Women in Politics 2009.
35. Constitution of the Republic of Maldives 2008, Article 109 (Hussain 2008).
36. Jalal 2009.
37. Constitution of the Independent State of Western Samoa 1960: Article 15.
38. CEDAW 2003a.
39. IPU 2009.
40. International IDEA 2003.
41. Basu 2005.
42. IPU 2009.
43. International IDEA 2003.
44. International IDEA 2003.
45. IPU 2008.
46. UNIFEM 2008.
47. International IDEA and Stockholm University n.d.-b.
48. International IDEA and Stockholm University n.d.-b.
49. Torres 2009.
50. Burgonio 2009.
51. Republic Act No. 9710, 2009.
52. International IDEA and Stockholm University n.d.-b.
53. The Constitution of India 1949: Article 243D.
54. The term panchayat used here is a creation of the Constitution and should not be confused with caste *panchayats*.
55. International IDEA and Stockholm University n.d.-b; IPU 2009.
56. Fraenkel 2006.
57. International IDEA and Stockholm University n.d.-a.
58. International IDEA and Stockholm University n.d.-b.
59. Torres 2009.
60. Torres 2009.
61. International IDEA and Stockholm University n.d.-a.

62. International IDEA and Stockholm University n.d.-b.
63. International IDEA 2003.
64. UN Millennium Project 2005.
65. IPU 2009.
66. International IDEA 2003.
67. International IDEA 2003.
68. Undarya 2008.
69. United Nations Country Team Mongolia 2009.
70. Media Center of the General Elections Commission (KPU) 2009. In IPU 2009, this number is 16.6 per cent.
71. International IDEA and Stockholm University n.d.-a.
72. Reyes 2002; Raman 2002; Tambiah 2003.
73. UNDP n.d.
74. International IDEA 2003.
75. Jahan 2009.
76. IPU 2009.
77. iKNOW Politics 2009.
78. Clark 2009.
79. Basu 2005.
80. Lowe-Lee 2006.
81. The Asia Foundation 2008.
82. Basu 2005. In Bangladesh, the jump in women voters' participation in parliamentary elections has been remarkable since 1996, due in part to women's groups organizing protests against the Hussain Ershad regime and organizing large-scale voter turnout for the poll that year.
83. Yadav 2009.
84. IPU 2008; UNIFEM 2008.
85. IPU 2008.
86. IPU 2009.
87. Jalal 2009; Torres 2009.
88. International IDEA 2005.
89. Equivalent to about US $8,328.00 at the time of publication.
90. Soin 1994.
91. UNDEF 2009.
92. Rajivan and Senarathne 2009.
93. ICRC 2003; Bennett and Bannon 2004.
94. Clavé-Çelik 2008; Bennett and Bannon 2004.
95. Keairns 2002; Brett 2002.
96. Bouta et al. 2005.
97. UNDP Nepal facilitated the collection of data on registered female combatants in the country in 2009 and places this number at around 19 per cent.
98. Manoharan 2003; Bennett and Bannon 2004.
99. Manoharan 2003.
100. More recent UN Resolutions 1820 (2008), 1888 and 1889 (2009) have also renewed 1325's measures to improve women's participation in peace processes, reaffirming the key role women can play in rebuilding war-torn societies and condemned continuing sexual violence against women in conflict and post-conflict situations.
101. UN 2005b.
102. Clavé-Çelik 2008.
103. UN 2005b.
104. International IDEA 2005.
105. International IDEA 2003.
106. International IDEA and Stockholm University n.d.-b.
107. Jahan 2009.
108. IPU 2008.
109. Grey 2001.
110. Grey 2001.
111. Elson 2006.
112. Heerah 2006.
113. Neumayer and Plümper 2007.
114. BBC News 2009.
115. Wordsworth 2007.
116. Narayanaswamy and Sever 2004.
117. Drage 2001.
118. Khan and Mohsin 2009.
119. UNDEF 2008.
120. International IDEA 2003.
121. Heerah 2006.
122. Press Information Bureau 2009.
123. Sehgal 2008.
124. Fiji Women's Rights Movement et al. 2007.
125. Jalal 2009.
126. Hanh and Dung n.d.
127. International IDEA 2005.
128. Heerah 2006.
129. Naripokkho 2006; Bangladesh Women's Health Coalition 2006, cited in Murthy 2007.
130. Nagar 2000.
131. Nagar 2000.
132. Nagar 2000.
133. Pande 2000.

Chapter 4

1. Kapur 2007.
2. CIRI (Cingranelli-Richards) 2009.
3. Al Jazeera 2009.
4. Reid 2009.
5. Rajivan and Sarangi 2009.
6. Ramaseshan 2009a.

7. De Schweinitz 1983.
8. Dhagamwar 1992.
9. Stege et al. 2008.
10. Civil Law of the Republic of Afghanistan (Civil Code) 1977: Article 2.
11. U.S. Department of State 2009.
12. Cheema 2009.
13. Ministry of Planning and Investment 2008.
14. Lee 2006.
15. Jahangir 2004.
16. Ahmed 2009.
17. Jalal 2009.
18. Jalal 2009.
19. Kapur 2007.
20. Cheema 2009.
21. Cheema 2009.
22. Kapur 2007.
23. Roy 1996.
24. Ihsan and Zaidi 2006.
25. Hudood is plural for hadd that implies limit. Hudood laws constitute five criminal statutes of Pakistan: Property Ordinance deals with theft and robbery; Zina Ordinance stipulates legal provisions on rape, adultery, fornication and abduction; Prohibition Order deals with alcohol and narcotics related offences; Qazf Ordinance deals with offence of false accusation of zina; and the Execution of the Punishment of Whipping Ordinance specifies the mode of whipping for those convicted under the Hudood Ordinances.
26. Abbas 2004.
27. Cheema 2009.
28. Jalal 2009.
29. Radio New Zealand International 2008.
30. The 1987 Constitution of the Republic of the Philippines: Section 6.
31. CEDAW 2004b.
32. Cheema 2009.
33. See Table 19 on legal indicators on domestic violence in the Statistical Annex.
34. Manuel 2009; Republic Act No. 9710, 2009.
35. Law of the Republic of Indonesia No. 12 on Citizenship of the Republic of Indonesia 2006: Article 4.
36. Baudh 2008.
37. Hindustan Times 2008.
38. Women Living Under Muslim Laws 2009.
39. Cheema 2009.
40. UNIFEM South Asia Regional Office and Partners for Law in Development 2004.
41. UN n.d.-c.
42. UNIFEM 2008.
43. Jivan and Forster 2007.
44. UN n.d.-a.
45. Jalal 2006.
46. Jalal 2007.
47. Fiji Islands Constitution Amendment Act 1997: Section 43(2); The Constitution of Tuvalu 1978, section 15(5)(c); Constitution of the Independent State of Papua New Guinea 1975: Section 39(3).
48. Magistrates Court of Fiji 1999.
49. Jalal 2009.
50. Manuel 2009.
51. Supreme Court of Nepal 2002.
52. C143 Migrant Workers (Supplementary Provisions) Convention 1975: Article 8(2) and article 10.
53. UNIFEM South Asia Regional Office and Partners for Law in Development 2004.
54. Ramaseshan 2009a.
55. Interim Constitution of Nepal (2063) 2007: Preamble.
56. CEDAW 2008a; Law on Gender Equality 2006.
57. CEDAW 2004c.
58. Penal Code (Cap 135) 1981: Section 150.
59. CEDAW 2005b.
60. Constitution of Malaysia 1957: Article 15(3).
61. Victimisation through sexual assault and rape ranged as high as 89 per cent in Southern Highlands Province to 60 per cent in the National Capital District (Haley 2005).
62. Firm estimates are difficult and figures may vary. The survey responses have been used to arrive at the conclusion. Data on violence in Viet Nam is unreliable. Estimates vary widely.
63. UN 2006.
64. See Table 19 on legal indicators on domestic violence in the Statistical Annex.
65. Decree of the President of the Lao People's Democratic Republic on the Promulgation of the Law on Development and Protection of Women 2004: Section 29.
66. Decree of the President of the Lao People's Democratic Republic on the Promulgation of the Law on Development and Protection of Women 2004: Section 35.
67. CEDAW 2008a.
68. Chiongson 2009.
69. UN 2006.

70. Anti-Sexual Harassment Act 1995: Section 3.
71. Rameseshan 2009b.
72. CEDAW 2004 (c and b).
73. Jivan and Forster 2007.
74. C183 Maternity Protection Convention 2000: Article 4(1).
75. CEDAW 2003b.
76. The Protection of Women From Domestic Violence Act 2005: Section 5.
77. Constitution of the People's Republic of China 2004: Article 48(1).
78. CEDAW 2006a.
79. Jalal 2009.
80. The Constitution of Solomon Islands 1978 No. 783: Section 15(5)(d).
81. Labour and Employment Act 1972: Section 33(2); Employment Act 1978: Section 98 (b). In case of Samoa the draft Labour and Employment Bill 2009 shall remove the limitation on manual work.
82. Labour Code of Socialist Republic of Vietnam 1994: Article 113(1).
83. Chiongson 2009.
84. Labor Code of the Philippines 1974: Article 130.
85. Hon Mr Justice A.M. Mahmudur Rahman 2001.
86. Fiji Employment (Amendment) Act No. 6 of 1996: Section 3.
87. Indian Penal Code 1860: Article 377.
88. Jalal 1998.
89. Roy 2004.
90. Asian Indigenous Women's Network et al. 2007.
91. Roy 2004. In Norway the promulgation of Reindeer Herding Act 1978 created a system of herding licenses. In the past reindeer herds belonged to the family but legislation removed the herds as family asset and made it the asset of the license holder only. The license holders, with very few exceptions, were generally men. This led to the alienation of women from this traditional activity, with very few women holding licenses under their own names even though they continue to do the same work as before.
92. UNIFEM 2008.
93. Chakravarti 2005.
94. Ramaseshan 2009a.
95. Muslim Family Laws Ordinance 1961: Section 7(4).
96. The Hindu Marriage Act of 1955: Section 13.
97. CEDAW 2006b.
98. Chiongson 2009.
99. Jalal 1998.
100. Commission on Legal Empowerment of the Poor 2008.
101. UNDP 2005.
102. UNIFEM 2008.
103. Partners for Law in Development 2006.
104. UN 2005a.
105. MoWA et al. 2005.
106. MoWA et al. 2005.
107. MoWA et al. 2005.
108. Supreme Court of India 1997.
109. CEDAW 2004c.
110. High Court of Fiji 2008.
111. Jalal 1998.
112. Ramaseshan 2009a.
113. Qanun-e-Shahadat Order 1984: Article 17.
114. Jalal 2009.
115. Indian Penal Code 1860: Section 300(d) exception 1; Penal Code 1883 (for Sri Lanka): Section 325. The Penal Codes of both countries allow the discriminatory legal provision of 'grave and sudden provocation' to be used as defence by accused in murder cases. For instance under Indian Penal Code 1860: Section 300 (on murder) sub section (d) exception 1 stipulates 'Culpable homicide is not murder if the offender, whilst deprived of the power of self-control by grave and sudden provocation, causes the death of the person who gave the provocation or causes the death of any other person by mistake or accident'.
116. Jilani and Ahmed 2004.
117. Kabul Center for Strategic Studies 2008.
118. Government of Pakistan 2008.
119. Ramaseshan 2009a.
120. Ramaseshan 2009a.
121. There is no bar on the parties to the dispute to approach and seek justice through formal courts.
122. Wardak 2009.
123. See Table 17 on inequalities: Influencing decision (judges in higher judiciary) in the Statistical Annex.
124. Natarajan 2005b.
125. Natarajan 2005a.
126. CEDAW 2007. The law is under review and expected to be replaced by Police Act 2009.

127. Natarajan 2005a.

128. Natarajan 2005b.

129. Women in Need 2004.

130. Class action is a lawsuit filed by one or more people on behalf of themselves and a larger group of people 'who are similarly situated'. Examples might include: all women who have suffered from defective contraceptive devices or all those over-charged by a public utility during a parti-cular period, etc.

131. Gondal 2008.

132. UNESCAP 2007b.

133. Manuel 2009.

134. The Family Protection Act 2008: Section 17.

135. Family Law Act 2003.

136. Penal Code 1883: Section 365 A.

137. The Supreme Court of Fiji 2004.

138. Evidence Act 2003: Section 11.

139. Men Against Violence and Abuse n.d.

140. CEDAW 2004a. Traditional religious and customary practices have not taken strong position against child marriage.

Bibliography

Abbas, Zaffar. 2004. 'Women's bill splits Pakistani MPs'. *BBC*. 31 March.

Abeysekera, Sunila. 2009. 'Unequal power and voice: Discrimination against people who challenge normative sexualities in the Asia Pacific region'. Note for the Asia-Pacific Human Development Report *Power, voice and rights: A turning point for gender equality in Asia and the Pacific*. Unpublished.

ADB (Asian Development Bank). 2006. *Republic of the Fiji Islands: Country gender assessment*. Pacific Regional Department and Regional and Sustainable Development Department. Manila: ADB.

ADB (Asian Development Bank), Canadian International Development Agency, European Commission, National Commission on the Role of Filipino Women, United Nations Children's Fund, United Nations Development Fund for Women, and United Nations Population Fund. 2008. *Paradox and promise in the Philippines: A joint country gender assessment*. Manila: Asian Development Bank.

ADB (Asian Development Bank), and World Bank. 2005. *Mongolia: Country gender assessment*. Manila: Asian Development Bank and World Bank.

Agarwal, Bina. 2008. *Rethinking collectivities: Institutional innovations in group farming, community forestry and strategic alliances*. Occasional Paper. B.N. Ganguli Memorial Lecture. New Delhi: Centre for the Study of Developing Societies.

———. 2005. 'Landmark step to gender equality'. *The Hindu*, Sunday Magazine. 25 September.

———. 2003. 'Gender and land rights revisited: Exploring new prospects via the state, family and market'. *Journal of Agrarian Change* 3 (1-2): 184-224.

———. 2002a. *Are we not peasants too? Land rights and women's claims in India*. Seeds. Number 21. New York: Population Council.

———. 2002b. 'The hidden side of group behaviour: A gender analysis of community forestry in South Asia'. In Judith Heyer, Frances Stewart, and Rosemary Thorp, eds. *Group behaviour and development: Is the market destroying cooperation?* UNU/WIDER Studies in Development Economics, Queen Elizabeth House Series in Development Studies. New York: Oxford University Press.

———. 1998. 'Widows versus daughters or widows as daughters? Property, land and economic security in rural India'. In Martha Alter Chen, ed. *Widows in India: Social neglect and public action*. New Delhi: Sage Publications.

———. 1997. '"Bargaining" and gender relations: Within and beyond the household'. *Feminist Economics* 3 (1): 1-51.

———. 1994. *A field of one's own: Gender and land rights in South Asia*. Cambridge: Cambridge University Press.

Agarwal, Bina, and Pradeep Panda. 2007. 'Toward freedom from domestic violence: The neglected obvious'. *Journal of Human Development and Capabilities* 8 (3): 359-388.

Ahmad, K. 1998. *Report on the other gender: A seminar on men's issues*. Gender Unit. Islamabad: UNDP.

Ahmed, Saeed. 2009. 'Woman suspected of witchcraft burned alive'. *CNN.com/Asia*. 8 January.

Al Jazeera. 2009. 'Afghans rally against women's law'. 16 April.

Allen, Elaine, Amanda Elam, Nan Langowitz, and Monica Dean. 2008. *Global entrepreneurship monitor: 2007 Report on women and entrepreneurship*. Wellesley, Massachusetts: The Center for Women's Leadership at Babson College.

Allen, Elaine, Nan Langowitz, and Maria Minniti. 2007. *Global entrepreneurship monitor: 2006 Report on women and entrepreneurship*. Wellesley, Massachusetts and London: The Center for Women's Leadership at Babson College and London Business School.

Allendorf, Keera. 2007. 'Do women's land rights promote empowerment and child health in Nepal?'. *World Development* 35 (11): 1975-1988.

An Act to Amend Some Nepal Acts for Maintaining Gender Equality, 2063. 2006. Unofficial translation. [http://www.iwraw-ap.org/resources/laws.htm]. Last accessed on 26 September 2009.

Anandhi, S. 2002. 'Interlocking patriarchies and women in governance: A Case study of Panchayati Raj institutions in Tamil Nadu'. In Karin Kapadia, ed. *The violence of develop-*

ment: *The politics of identity, gender and social inequalities in India.* New Delhi: Kali for Women.

Anderson, Benedict R. O'G. 1990. *Language and power: Exploring political cultures in Indonesia.* New York: Cornell University Press.

Anti-Sexual Harassment Act 1995. Republic Act No. 7877. [http://www.chanrobles.com/legal4antisexualharassmentact.htm#REPUBLIC%20ACT%20NO.%207877]. Last accessed on 21 October 2009.

ARROW (Asia-Pacific Resource and Research Centre for Women). 2008. *Advocating accountability: Status report on maternal health and young people's sexual and reproductive health and rights in South Asia.* Kuala Lumpur: ARROW.

Asian Indigenous Women's Network (AIWN), Aliansi Masyarakat Adat Nusantara (AMAN), and Rights and Democracy. 2007. *Portrait of the indigenous women of Asia.* Baguio City, Philippines: AIWN, AMAN, and Rights and Democracy.

Asis, Maruja M.B. 2003. 'Asian women migrants: Going the distance, but not far enough'. Feature Story. Migration Information Source. Washington, DC: Migration Policy Institute.

AusAID (Australian Agency for International Development). 2008. *Making land work: Reconciling customary land and development in the Pacific.* Volume I. Canberra: Australian Agency for International Development.

Bach, Rebecca, Saad Gadalla, Hind Abu Seoud Khattab, and John Gulick. 1985. 'Mothers' influence on daughters' orientations toward education: An Egyptian case study'. *Comparative Education Review* 29 (3): 375-384.

Bangladesh Women's Health Coalition (BWHC). 2006. *Women's health and rights advocacy partnership completion report: 2003-2006.* Internal document. Dhaka: BWHC.

Basu, Amrita. 2005. *Women, political parties and social movements in South Asia.* Occasional Paper No. 5. Geneva: United Nations Research Institute for Social Development.

———. **2003.** 'Gender and governance: Concepts and contexts'. In Martha Nussbaum, Amrita Basu, Yasmin Tambiah, and Niraja Gopal Jayal. *Essays on gender and governance.* Human Development Resource Centre. New Delhi: UNDP.

Baudh, Sumit. 2008. *Human rights and the criminalisation of consensual same-sex sexual acts in the Commonwealth, South and Southeast Asia.* Working paper. New Delhi: The South and Southeast Asia Resource Centre on Sexuality, Tarshi.

BBC News. 2009. 'Afghan "anti-woman law changed"'. 8 July. [http://news.bbc.co.uk/2/hi/south_asia/8141420.stm]. Last accessed on 23 October 2009.

Behrman, Jere Richard, and Anil B. Deolalikar. 1988. 'Health and nutrition'. In Hollis Chenery, and T.N. Srinivasan, eds. *Handbook of development economics.* Volume 1. Amsterdam: North Holland.

Bennett, Lynn, and Ian Bannon. 2004. 'Social change in conflict-affected areas of Nepal'. Social Development Notes. Conflict Prevention and Reconstruction (CPR). No. 15. Social Development Department. Washington, DC: World Bank.

Blau, David M. 1986. 'Fertility, child nutrition, and child mortality in Nicaragua: An economic analysis of interrelationships'. *Journal of Developing Areas* 20 (2): 185-201.

Blecker, Robert A., and Stephanie Seguino. 2002. 'Macroeconomic effects of reducing gender wage inequality in an export-oriented, semi-industrialized economy'. *Review of Development Economics* 6 (1): 103-119.

Blomqvist, Gunilla. 2004. 'Gender discourses at work: Export industry workers and construction workers in Chennai, Tamil Nadu, India'. PhD thesis. Göteborg University.

Bouta, Tsjeard, Georg Frerks, and Ian Bannon. 2005. *Gender, conflict, and development.* Washington, DC: World Bank.

Bowen, R. John. 1998. '"You may not give it away": How social norms shape Islamic law in contemporary Indonesian jurisprudence'. *Islamic law and society* 5(3): 382-408.

Brett, Rachel. 2002. 'Juvenile justice, counter-terrorism and children'. *Disarmament forum (Children and security)* 3: 29-36.

Brown, Oli, and Alec Crawford. 2006. *Addressing land ownership after natural disasters: An agency survey.* Winnipeg, Manitoba: International Institute for Sustainable Development.

Bullock, Susan. 1994. *Women and work.* London: Zed Books.

Burgonio, T.J. 2009. 'Magna Carta of women finally a law'. *Phillipine Daily Inquirer.* 15 August.

Burra, Neera. 2004. 'Empowering women for household food security: UNDP's experience'. New Delhi: United Nations Development Programme.

C143 Migrant Workers (Supplementary Provisions) Convention 1975. International Labour Organization. [http://www.ilo.org/ilolex/cgi-lex/convde.pl?C143]. Last accessed on 14 October 2009.

C183 Maternity Protection Convention. 2000. International Labour Organization. [http://www.ilo.org/ilolex/cgi-lex/convde.pl?C183]. Last accessed on 14 October 2009.

Caselli, Francesco, Gerardo Esquivel, and Fernando Lefort. 1996. 'Reopening the convergence debate: A new look at cross-country growth empirics'. *Journal of Economic Growth* 1 (3): 363-389.

CEDAW. 2008a. *Consideration of reports submitted by States parties under article 18 of the Convention on the Elimination of All Forms of Discrimination against Women. Combined sixth and seventh periodic report of States parties: Lao People's Democratic Republic.* Committee on the Elimination of Discrimination against Women. CEDAW/C/LAO/7.

_____. **2008b.** *Consideration of reports submitted by States parties under article 18 of the Convention on the Elimination of All Forms of Discrimination against Women. Initial periodic report of States parties: Timor-Leste.* Committee on the Elimination of Discrimination against Women. CEDAW/C/TLS/1.

_____. **2007.** *Consideration of reports submitted by States parties under article 18 of the Convention on the Elimination of All Forms of Discrimination against Women. Seventh periodic report of States parties: Bhutan.* Committee on the Elimination of Discrimination against Women. CEDAW/C/BTN/7.

_____. **2006a.** *Concluding comments of the Committee on the Elimination of Discrimination against Women: China.* Committee on the Elimination of Discrimination against Women. Thirty-sixth session, 7-25 August 2006. CEDAW/C/CHN/CO/6.

_____. **2006b.** *Concluding comments of the Committee on the Elimination of Discrimination against Women: Malaysia.* Committee on the Elimination of Discrimination against Women. Thirty-fifth session, 15 May-2 June 2006. CEDAW/C/MYS/CO/2.

_____. **2005a.** *Consideration of reports submitted by States parties under article 18 of the Convention on the Elimination of All Forms of Discrimination against Women. Combined fourth and fifth periodic reports of States parties: Indonesia.* Committee on the Elimination of Discrimination against Women. CEDAW/C/IDN/4-5.

_____. **2005b.** *Consideration of reports submitted by States parties under article 18 of the Convention on the Elimination of All Forms of Discrimination against Women. Combined initial, second and third periodic reports of States parties: Pakistan.* Committee on the Elimination of Discrimination against Women. CEDAW/C/PAK/1-3.

_____. **2004a.** *Concluding observations adopted at the 31st session. Fifth periodic reports: Bangladesh.* CEDAW/C/BGD/CO/.

_____. **2004b.** *Consideration of reports submitted by States parties under article 18 of the Convention on the Elimination of All Forms of Discrimination against Women. Combined fifth and sixth periodic reports of States parties: Philippines.* Committee on the Elimination of Discrimination against Women. CEDAW/C/PHI/5-6.

_____. **2004c.** *Consideration of reports submitted by States parties under article 18 of the Convention on the Elimination of All Forms of Discrimination against Women. Combined initial and second periodic reports of States parties: Malaysia.* Committee on the Elimination of Discrimination against Women. CEDAW/C/MYS/1-2.

_____. **2003a.** *Consideration of reports submitted by States parties under article 18 of the Convention on the Elimination of All Forms of Discrimination against Women. Combined initial, second and third periodic report of States parties: Samoa.* Committee on the Elimination of Discrimination against Women. CEDAW/C/WSM/1-3.

_____. **2003b.** *Consideration of reports submitted by States parties under article 18 of the Convention on the Elimination of All Forms of Discrimination against Women. Fifth periodic report of States parties: Bangladesh.* Committee on the Elimination of Discrimination against Women. CEDAW/C/BGD/5.

_____. **1997.** *Consideration of reports submitted by States parties under article 18 of the Convention on the Elimination of all Forms of Discrimination Against Women. Third and fourth periodic reports of States parties: China.* Committee on the Elimination of Discrimination against Women. CEDAW/C/CHN/3-4.

Center for Asia-Pacific Women in Politics. 2009. 'Statistics'. Asia Pacific online network of women in politics, governance and transformative leadership. Updated in April 2009. [http://www.onlinewomeninpolitics.org/Statistics.htm]. Last accessed on 26 January 2010.

Chakraborty, Lehka. 2009. 'Gender sensitive fiscal policies: Experience of ex-post and ex-ante gender budgets in Asia Pacific'. Technical background paper for the Asia-Pacific Human Development Report *Power, voice and rights: A turning point for gender equality in Asia and the Pacific.* Unpublished.

Chakravarti, Uma. 2005. 'From fathers to husbands: Of love, death and marriage in North India'. In Lynn Welchman, and Sara Hossain, eds. *'Honour': Crimes, paradigms and violence against women.* London: Zed Books.

———. **2003.** 'Reconceptualising gender: Phule, brahmanism and brahmanical patriarchy'. In Anupama Rao ed. *Gender and caste.* Series Issues in Contemporary Feminism, New Delhi: Kali for Women.

Chand, Anand. 2006. 'Physical and psychological health problems of garment workers in the Fiji'. *Pacific Health Dialog* 13 (2): 65-70.

Chandra, Dharma, and Vasemaca Lewai. 2005. *Women and men of Fiji Islands: Gender statistics and trends.* Demographic Report No. 10. Suva: Population Studies, University of the South Pacific.

Cheema, Hasna. 2009. 'Benchmarking legislation (*dejure*) on gender equality: Findings from Indonesia, Pakistan, the Philippines, Sri Lanka and Viet Nam'. HDRU Brief No. 3 for the Asia-Pacific Human Development Report *Power, voice and rights: A turning point for gender equality in Asia and the Pacific.* Unpublished.

Chen, Martha Alter. n.d. 'Women in the informal sector: A global picture, the global movement'. [http://info.worldbank.org/etools/docs/library/76309/dc2002/proceedings/pdfpaper/module6mc.pdf]. Last accessed on 10 November 2009.

Chen, Martha Alter, Joann Vanek, and Marilyn Carr. 2004. *Mainstreaming informal employment and gender in poverty reduction. A handbook for policy-makers and other stakeholders.* London and Ottawa: Commonwealth Secretariat and International Development Research Centre.

Chen, Shaohua, and Martin Ravallion. 2008. *The developing world is poorer than we thought, but no less successful in the fight against poverty.* World Bank Policy Research Working Paper No. 4703. Washington, DC: World Bank.

Chiongson, Rea Abada. 2009. *CEDAW and the law: A gendered and rights-based review of Vietnamese legal documents through the lens of CEDAW.* Report edited by Matthew Coghlan and Vu Ngoc Binh. Hanoi: UNIFEM.

CIRI (The Cingranelli-Richards). 2009. 'CIRI human rights data project'. The Cingranelli-Richards (CIRI) Human Rights Dataset. [http://ciri.binghamton.edu/myciri/my_ciri_login.asp]. Last accessed on 21 October 2009.

Civil Law of the Republic of Afghanistan (Civil Code). 1977. Official Gazette No. 353, published 1977/01/05 (1355/10/15 A.P.). Asian Legal Information Institute. [http://www.asianlii.org/af/legis/laws/clotroacogn353p1977010513551015a650/]. Last accessed on 21 October 2009.

Civil-Military Fusion Centre. 2009. 'CFC weekly Afghanistan newsletter'. 22 July.

Clark, Lesley. 2009. 'Increasing gender balance in Australian Parliaments: The implementation of voluntary gender quotas by the Australian Labor Party'. [http://www.iknowpolitics.org/en/node/10701]. Last accessed on 28 October 2009.

Clavé-Çelik, Elsa. 2008. 'Images of the past and realities of the present: Aceh's *Inong Balee*'. *IIAS Newsletter*, No. 48.

Coale, Ansley J. 1991. 'Excess female mortality and the balance of the sexes in the population: An estimate of the number of "missing females"'. *Population and Development Review* 17 (3): 517-523.

Code of Criminal Procedure. 1973. Indian legislation. Commonwealth Legal Information Institute. [http://www.commonlii.org/in/legis/num_act/cocp1973209/]. Last accessed on 21 October 2009.

Commission on AIDS in Asia. 2008. *Redefining AIDS in Asia: Crafting an effective response.* Report of the Commission on AIDS in Asia. New Delhi: Oxford University Press.

Commission on Legal Empowerment of the Poor. 2008. *Making the law work for everyone. Volume 1. Report of the Commission on Legal Empowerment of the Poor.* New York: Commission on Legal Empowerment of the Poor and UNDP.

Committee News. 2006. 'Committee okays bills amending Family Code, Revised Penal Code'. *Committee News* 13 (108). 15 May.

Constable, Pamela. 2009. 'Karzai's challengers face daunting odds'. *Washington Post.* 6 July.

Constitution of Malaysia. 1957. Part III: Citizenship. Commonwealth Legal Information Institute. [http://www.commonlii.org/my/legis/const/1957/3.html]. Last accessed on 21 October 2009.

Constitution of the Independent State of Papua New Guinea. 1975. Papua New Guinea consolidated legislation. Pacific Islands Legal Information Institute. [http://www.paclii.org/pg/legis/consol_act/cotisopng534/]. Last accessed on 21 October 2009.

Constitution of the Independent State of Western Samoa 1960. Samoa consolidated legislation. Pacific Islands Legal Information Institute. [http://www.paclii.org/ws/legis/consol_act/cotisows1960535/]. Last accessed on 23 October 2009.

Constitution of the People's Republic of China. 2004. Asian Legal Information Institute. [http://www.asianlii.org/cn/legis/const/2004/1.html]. Last accessed on 21 October 2009.

Crocombe, Ron. 2001. *The South Pacific.* Suva: University of the South Pacific.

_____. **1994.** 'Trends and issues in Pacific land tenure'. In Ron Crocombe, and Malama Meleisea, eds. *Land issues in the Pacific.* Christchurch and Suva: Macmillan Brown Centre for Pacific Studies, University of Canterbury, and Institute of Pacific Studies, University of the South Pacific.

Dalby, Liza. 2000. *The tale of Murasaki.* New York: Anchor Books.

Daly, Mary. 2005. 'Gender mainstreaming in theory and practice'. *Social Politics: International Studies in Gender, State & Society* 12 (3): 433-450.

Das, Arpita. 2009. 'Understanding gender: Expanding the discourse'. In UNDP (United Nations Development Programme). *E-discussion: Gender – Overcoming unequal power, unequal voice.* Asia Pacific Human Development Network. Colombo: UNDP Regional Centre for Asia Pacific.

De Haan, Arjan, and Ben Rogaly. 2002. 'Introduction: Migrant workers and their role in rural change'. *Journal of Development Studies* 38 (5): 1-14.

De Schweinitz, Karl Jr. 1983. *The rise and fall of British India: Imperialism as inequality.* New York: Methuen.

Debroux, Philippe. n.d. 'Women entrepreneurship in Asia: The cases of Japan, South-Korea, Malaysia and Vietnam: Context, assessment of the current situation and prospects'. [http://www.solvay.edu/FR/Research/Bernheim/documents/AbstractSolvay271108.pdf]. Last accessed on 29 October 2009.

Decker, Michele R., George R. Seage, David Hemenway, Anita Raj, Niranjan Saggurti, Donta Balaiah, and Jay G. Silverman. 2009. 'Intimate partner violence as both a risk marker and risk factor for women's HIV infection: Findings from Indian husband-wife dyads'. *Journal of Acquired Immune Deficiency Syndromes* 51 (5): 593-600.

Decree of the President of the Lao People's Democratic Republic on the Promulgation of the Law on Development and Protection of Women. 2004. [http://www.mfa.gov.sg/vientiane/Laws/Women%20and%20Children%20Law%20&%20Decree%20FINAL.pdf]. Last accessed on 16 November 2009.

Deere, Carmen Diana, and Cheryl R. Doss. 2006. 'The gender asset gap: What do we know and why does it matter?'. *Feminist Economics* 12 (1-2): 1-50.

Dhagamwar, Vasudha. 1992. *Law power and justice: The protection of personal rights in the Indian Penal Code.* New Delhi: Sage.

Diamond Sutra Recitation Group, eds. 2007. *Chung Hyo Ye: Tales of filial devotion, loyalty, respect and benevolence from the history and folklore of Korea.* Korean Spirit and Culture Series III. Pohang, Republic of Korea: Yong Hwa Publications.

Dollar, David, and Roberta Gatti. 1999. *Gender inequality, income, and growth: Are good times good for women?* Policy Research Report on Gender and Development. Working Paper Series No. 1. Washington, DC: World Bank Development Research Group/Poverty Reduction and Economic Management Network.

Doss, Cheryl R. 1996. 'Testing among models of intrahousehold resource allocation'. *World Development* 24 (10): 1597-1609.

Doss, Cheryl, Caren Grown, and Carmen Diana Deere. 2008. *Gender and asset ownership: A guide to collecting individual-level data.* Policy Research Working Paper No. 4704. Washington, DC: World Bank.

Drage, Jean. 2001. 'Women in local government in Asia and the Pacific: A comparative analysis of thirteen countries'. Paper presented to the Asia-Pacific Summit of Women Mayors and Councillors: 18-22 June, Phitsanulok, Thailand.

Du, Lili, Ziqing Zhuang, Hongyu Guan, Jingcai Xing, Xianzhi Tang, Limin Wang, Zhenglun Wang, Haijiao Wang, Yuewei Liu, Wenjin Su, Stacey Benson, Sean Gallagher, Dennis Viscusi, and Weihong Chen. 2008. 'Head-and-face anthropometric survey of Chinese workers'. *Annals of Occupational Hygiene* 52 (8): 773-782.

Duraisamy, P. 1992. *Gender, intrafamily allocation of resources and child schooling in South India.* Economic Growth Center Discussion Paper No. 667. New Haven, CT: Yale University.

Economist. 2006. 'A guide to womenomics'. *The Economist.* 12 April.

Elson, Diane. 2006. *Budgeting for women's rights: Monitoring government budgets for compliance to CEDAW.* New York: UNIFEM.

_____. **1999.** 'Labour markets as gendered institutions: Equality, efficiency and empowerment issues'. *World Development* 27 (3): 611-627.

Emmett, Bethan. 2009. *Paying the price for the economic crisis.* Oxfam International Discussion Paper. Oxford: Oxfam International.

Employment Act. 1978. Papua New Guinea consolidated legislation. Pacific Islands Legal Information Institute. [http://www.paclii.org/

pg/legis/consol_act/ea1978149/]. Last accessed on 21 October 2009.

Esteve-Volart, Berta. 2004. *Gender discrimination and growth: Theory and evidence from India.* STICERD Development Economics Paper DEDPS42. London: London School of Economics and Political Science.

Estudillo, Jonna P., Agnes R. Quisumbing, and Keijiro Otsuka. 2001. 'Gender differences in land inheritance and schooling investments in the rural Philippines'. *Land Economics* 77 (1): 130-143.

European Union Election Observation Mission (EU EOM). 2009. *Preliminary statement: Afghan elections take place in a reasonably well-organised manner, amid widespread violence and intimidation.* Islamic Republic of Afghanistan – Presidential and Provincial Council Elections 2009. 22 August.

Evans, Kevin. 2009. 'Addressing corruption in special development situations from a human development perspective: Lessons from the Asia-Pacific region'. In Anuradha K. Rajivan, and Ramesh Gampat, eds. *Perspectives on corruption and human development.* New Delhi: Macmillan.

Evidence Act. 2003. Kiribati sessional legislation. Pacific Islands Legal Information Institute. [http://www.paclii.org/ki/legis/num_act/ea200380/]. Last accessed on 21 October 2009.

Family Law Act. 2003. Fiji sessional legislation. Pacific Islands Legal Information Institute. [http://www.paclii.org/fj/legis/num_act/fla2003114/]. Last accessed on 16 November 2009.

FAO (Food and Agriculture Organization of the United Nations). 2009. *The state of world fisheries and aquaculture 2008.* Rome: FAO.

———. **2008.** 'Non-wood forest products'. [http://www.fao.org/forestry/6388/en/]. Last accessed on 29 October 2009.

———. **n.d.-a.** 'FAO statistics'. [http://faostat.fao.org]. Last accessed on 28 September 2009.

———. **n.d.-b.** *Women, agriculture and food security.* Rome: FAO.

FAO (Food and Agriculture Organization of the United Nations), and SIDA (Swedish International Development Authority). 1987. *Restoring the balance: Women and forest resources.* Produced by FAO Forestry Department, with assistance from the Swedish International Development Authority. Rome: FAO. [http://www.fao.org/DOCREP/006/S5500E/S5500E00.HTM]. Last accessed on 13 May 2009.

Fiji Employment (Amendment) Act No. 6 of 1996. Fiji sessional legislation. Pacific Islands Legal Information Institute [http://www.paclii.org/fj/legis/num_act/ea1996229/]. Last accessed on 21 October 2009.

Fiji Islands Constitution Amendment Act. 1997. Fiji sessional legislation. Pacific Islands Legal Information Institute. [http://www.paclii.org/fj/legis/num_act/ca1997268/]. Last accessed on 21 October 2009.

Fiji Women's Rights Movement (FWRM), Pacific Regional Rights Resource Team (RRRT), and United Nations Development Programme (UNDP). 2007. *An analysis of influencing Fiji's Family Law: A case study of legislative advocacy and campaigning in Fiji.* Towards inclusive governance: Promoting participation of disadvantaged groups in Asia Pacific. Bangkok: UNDP Regional Centre.

Forbes, Kristin J. 2000. 'A reassessment of the relationship between inequality and growth'. *The American Economic Review* 90 (4): 869-887.

Ford Foundation. 2002. *Building assets to reduce poverty and injustice.* New York: Ford Foundation.

Foreman, William, and Bonnie Cao. 2009. 'Chinese professional women work as nannies, maids'. *AP News.* Bay Ledger News Zone. February 19.

Fraenkel, Jon. 2006. 'The impact of electoral systems on women's representation in Pacific parliaments'. Report No. 2. In Elise Huffer, Jon Fraenkel, Alamanda Lauti, Ofa Guttenbeil-Likiliki, Susie Saitala Kofe, and Fakavae Taomia. *A woman's place is in the house – The house of parliament. Research to advance women's political representation in Forum Island Countries. A regional study presented in five reports.* Suva: Pacific Islands Forum Secretariat.

Gampat, Ramesh. 2009a. 'Gender equality: Opportunities or outcomes?'. HDRU brief No. 1 for the Asia-Pacific Human Development Report *Power, voice and rights: A turning point for gender equality in Asia and the Pacific.* Unpublished.

———. **2009b.** 'Sex and gender: Beyond culture and socialization'. Technical background paper for the Asia-Pacific Human Development Report *Power, voice and rights: A turning point for gender equality in Asia and the Pacific.* Unpublished.

Gender and Development Research Institute. 2006. *Status of women in Thailand: An overview.* Bangkok: Gender and Development Research Institute.

Ghosh, Jayati. 2008. 'The crisis of home-based work'. Macroscan. 17 May.

Gill, K.K. 2001. 'Diversification of agriculture and women's employment in Punjab'. *The Indian Journal of Labour Economics* 44 (2): 259-267.

Gondal, Ziaullah. 2008. 'CII for changes in wedding, divorce laws'. *Pakistan Observer*. 16 November.

Government of India. 2008. *Annual report 2007-2008: Bharat Nirman through rural development*. Ministry of Rural Development. New Delhi: Government of India.

_____. 2006. *Census of India 2001: Population projections for India and States 2001-2026*. Report of the technical group on population projections, National Commission on Population, Office of the Registrar General, & Census Commissioner. New Delhi: Government of India.

_____. 1995-96. *Agricultural Census of India*. Ministry of Agriculture. New Delhi: Government of India.

_____. n.d. 'Integrated Child Development Services (ICDS) scheme'. Ministry of Women and Child Development. [http://wcd.nic.in/]. Last accessed on 29 October 2009.

Government of Kerala. 2006. *Human development report 2005*. Report prepared by the Centre for Development Studies for the Government of Kerala. Thiruvananthapuram: State Planning Board, Government of Kerala.

Government of Nepal. 2001. *Census of Nepal, 2001*. National Planning Commission, CBS and GoN. Kathmandu: Government of Nepal.

Government of Pakistan. 2008. 'Gender justice'. Ministry of Local Government and Rural Development. [http://www.pakistan.gov.pk/divisions/ContentInfo.jsp?DivID=45&cPath=618_621&ContentID=3273]. Last accessed on 21 October 2009.

Grace, Jo. 2005. *Who owns the farm? Rural women's access to land and livestock*. Working Paper. Kabul: The Afghanistan Research and Evaluation Unit.

Grameen Bank. 2009a. 'Grameen Bank at a glance'. May. [http://www.grameen-info.org/index.php?option=com_content&task=view&id=26&Itemid=175]. Last accessed on 9 July 2009.

_____. 2009b. 'Grameen Bank monthly update in US$: May, 2009'. [http://www.grameen-info.org/index.php?option=com_content&task=view&id=453&Itemid=527]. Last accessed on 9 July 2009.

Grey, Sandra. 2001. 'Women and parliamentary politics: Does size matter? Critical mass and women MPs in the New Zealand House of Representatives'. Paper presented at the 51st Political Studies Association Conference: 10-12 April, Manchester.

Halapua, Winston. 2003. *Tradition, lotu and militarism in Fiji*. Lautoka: Fiji Institute of Applied Studies.

Haley, Nicole. 2005. *PNG armed violence assessment*. Final report submitted to UNDP.

Hampel-Milagrosa, Aimée. 2008. *Gender differentiated impact of investment climate reforms: A critical review of the doing business report*. DIE Research Project on 'Improving the Investment Climate in Developing Countries'. Discussion Paper No. 16/2008. Bonn: German Development Institute.

Hanh, Vuong Thi, and Doan Thuy Dung. n.d. 'Women in politics in Vietnam'. [http://www.wedo.org/wp-content/uploads/vietnam.doc]. Last accessed on 22 October 2009.

Hausmann, Ricardo, Laura D. Tyson, and Saadia Zahidi. 2009. *The global gender gap report 2009*. Geneva: World Economic Forum.

Hawken, Angela, and Gerardo L. Munck. 2009. 'Cross-national indices with gender-differentiated data: What do they measure? How valid are they?'. Technical background paper for the Asia-Pacific Human Development Report *Power, voice and rights: A turning point for gender equality in Asia and the Pacific*. Unpublished.

Hayes, Kirsty. 2009. 'Addressing crisis and gender in Asia and the Pacific'. Technical background paper for the Asia-Pacific Human Development Report *Power, voice and rights: A turning point for gender equality in Asia and the Pacific*. Unpublished.

Heerah, Shirini. 2006. *Creating spaces for change: Women's empowerment and the case of Panchayati Raj in India*. Santo Domingo: United Nations International Research and Training Institute for the Advancement of Women (INSTRAW).

High Court of Fiji. 2008. *Khan v Nisha*. Court Appeal No. 06/Suv/0021.

High Court of Solomon Islands. 1998. *Tanavalu v Tanavalu and Solomon Islands National Provident Fund Board*. Civil Case No. 185 of 1995 (12 January 1998). [http://www.paclii.org/sb/cases/SBHC/1998/4.html]. Last accessed on 21 October 2009.

Hill, M. Anne, and Elizabeth M. King. 1993. 'Women's education in developing countries: An overview'. In Elizabeth M. King, and M. Anne Hill, eds. *Women's education in developing countries: Barriers, benefits, and policies*. Published for the World Bank. Baltimore and London: The Johns Hopkins University Press.

Hindustan Times. 2008. 'Nepal gives formal recognition to third gender'. 18 September.

Hirayama, Yosuke. 2006. *Josei to jutaku shisan* (Women and residential assets), *josei no raifu kosu to jutaku shoyu* (The life courses of women and home ownership). Tokyo: The Institute for Research on Household Economics.

Hon Mr Justice A.M. Mahmudur Rahman. 2001. 'Domestic application of international human rights norms and access to justice: The Bangladesh experience'. In Commonwealth Secretariat. *Developing human rights jurisprudence, volume 8. Eighth judicial colloquium on the domestic application of international human rights norms. Bangalore, India, 27-30 December 1998.* London: Commonwealth Secretariat and Interights.

Hossain, Mahabub. 1988. *Credit for alleviation of rural poverty: The Grameen Bank in Bangladesh.* Research Report No. 65. International Food Policy Research Institute in collaboration with the Bangladesh Institute of Development Studies. Washington, DC: International Food Policy Research Institute.

Hossain, Rokeya Sakhawat. 1905. 'Sultana's dream'. *The Indian Ladies' Magazine.* Madras.

———. 1988. *Sultana's dream – A feminist utopia and selections from the secluded ones.* Edited and translated by Roushan Jahan. New York: The Feminist Press.

Hsiang-Lin, Lai. n.d. 'Taiwan country report: Based on the conference presentations'. [http://actrav.itcilo.org/actrav-english/telearn/global/ilo/frame/epztaiw.htm]. Last accessed on 29 October 2009.

Hugo, Graeme. 2005. *Migration in the Asia-Pacific region.* A paper prepared for the Policy Analysis and Research Programme of the Global Commission on International Migration. Geneva: Global Commission on International Migration.

Hunt, Juliet, and Nalini Kasynathan. 2002. 'Reflections on microfinance and women's empowerment'. *Development Bulletin* 57: 71-75.

Hussain, Dheena. 2008. *Functional translation of the Constitution of the Republic of Maldives 2008.* At the request of Ministry of Legal Reform, Information and Arts. [http://www.maldivesinfo.gov.mv/home/upload/downloads/Compilation.pdf]. Last accessed on 22 October 2009.

ICRC (International Committee of the Red Cross). 2003. *Women and war: Special report.* Geneva: ICRC.

ICRW (International Center for Research on Women). 2006. *Property ownership and inheritance rights of women for social protection: The South Asia experience. Synthesis report of three studies.* New Delhi: International Center for Research on Women.

ICRW (International Center for Research on Women), and Millennium Project. 2005. *Property ownership for women enriches, empowers and protects: Toward achieving the third Millennium Development Goal to promote gender equality and empower women.* ICRW Millennium Development Goals Series. Washington, DC: International Center for Research on Women.

IFAD (International Fund for Agricultural Development of the United Nations). 2009. 'Evaluation: Bangladesh'. [http://www.ifad.org/evaluation/public_html/ eksyst/doc/country/pi/bangladesh/cesba94e_3.htm]. Last accessed on 14 September 2009.

———. 2003. *IFAD rural poverty reduction project in Prey Veng and Svay Rieng.* Design Document. Draft Working Paper 2. Gender Analysis and Gender Mainstreaming. Phnom Penh.

Ihsan, Fatiman, and Yasmin Zaidi. 2006. 'The interplay of CEDAW, national laws and customary practices in Pakistan: A literature review'. In Shaheen Sardar Ali, ed. *Conceptualising Islamic law, CEDAW and women's human rights in plural legal settings: A comparative analysis of application of CEDAW in Bangladesh, India and Pakistan.* Delhi: UNIFEM South Asia Regional Office.

IIPS (International Institute for Population Sciences), and Macro International. 2008. *National family health survey (NFHS-3), India, 2005-06: Kerala.* Mumbai: IIPS.

iKNOW Politics. 2009. 'Consolidated response on best practices used by political parties to promote women in politics'. [http://www.iknowpolitics.org/files/consolidated_resposne_iKP_women_political_Parties_ENG.pdf]. Last accessed on 22 October 2009.

ILO (International Labour Organization). 2009a. *Global employment trends for women.* Geneva: ILO.

———. 2009b. *Key indicators of the labour market (KILM).* Sixth edition. Geneva: ILO.

———. 2007. *Key indicators of the labour market (KILM). 5th edition.* Geneva: ILO.

———. 1999. *Towards full employment. Technical report for discussion at the Asian Regional Consultation on Follow-up to the World Summit for Social Development (Bangkok, 13-15 January 1999).* Bangkok: ILO Regional Centre for Asia and the Pacific. [http://www.ilo.org/public/

english/region/asro/bangkok/feature/f-emp00.htm]. Last accessed on 29 October 2009.

———. **1998a.** 'Sex industry assuming massive proportions in Southeast Asia'. Press Release. ILO/98/31. 19 August.

———. **1998b.** 'Women in the informal sector and their access to microfinance'. Paper prepared for the Inter-Parliamentary Union (IPU) Annual Conference: 2-11 April, Windhoek, Namibia.

———. **n.d.-a.** 'Decent work for all'. [http://www.ilo.org/global/About_the_ILO/Mainpillars/WhatisDecentWork/lang—en/index.htm]. Last accessed on 29 October 2009.

———. **n.d.-b.** *ILOLEX database of international labour standards.* [http://www.ilo.org/ilolex/english/newratframeE.htm]. Last accessed on 6 November 2009.

Independent Election Commission Secretariat. 2009. 'Final figures of candidates for presidential and provincial council elections 2009'. Press release. 9 May. Kabul: Independent Election Commission.

———. **n.d.** 'The contents of the declaration by Afghan clerics in relation to elections from the Islamic perspective and the women participation in the electoral process'. IEC Fact Sheet No. 11. [http://www.iec.org.af/assets/PDF/FactSheet/eng/fs11E.pdf]. Last accessed on 22 October 2009.

Indian Penal Code 1860. Act No. 45. Indian legislation. Commonwealth Legal Information Institute. [http://www.commonlii.org/in/legis/num_act/ipc1860111/]. Last accessed on 27 October 2009.

Inglis, Christine. 2003. 'Mothers, wives, and workers: Australia's migrant women'. *In the News*. Migration Information Source. Washington, DC: Migration Policy Institute.

Interim Constitution of Nepal (2063) 2007. [http://www.worldstatesmen.org/Nepal_Interim_Constitution2007.pdf]. Last accessed on 27 October 2009.

International Gay and Lesbian Human Rights Commission. 2009. 'Nepal: Lesbian visibility increases after the Government recognizes LGBT rights'. 21 May. [http://www.iglhrc.org/cgi-bin/iowa/article/takeaction/resourcecenter/906.html]. Last accessed on 17 November 2009.

International IDEA (Institute for Democracy and Electoral Assistance). 2005. *Women in Parliament: Beyond numbers.* A revised edition. Edited by Juke Ballington and Azza Karam. Stockholm: International Institute for Democracy and Electoral Assistance.

———. **2003.** *The implementation of quotas: Asian experiences.* Quota Workshops Report Series. Stockholm: International Institute for Democracy and Electoral Assistance.

International IDEA (Institute for Democracy and Electoral Assistance), and Stockholm University. n.d.-a. 'Global database of quotas for women: About quotas'. [http://www.quotaproject.org/aboutQuotas.cfm]. Last accessed on 22 July 2009.

———. **n.d.-b.** 'Global database of quotas for women: Country overview'. [http://www.quotaproject.org/country.cfm]. Last accessed on 27 July 2009.

IPU (Inter-Parliamentary Union). 2009. 'Women in national parliaments'. Situations as of 30 June. [http://www.ipu.org/wmn-e/classif.htm]. Last accessed on 22 July 2009.

———. **2008.** *Equality in politics: A survey of women and men in parliaments.* Reports and Documents No. 54. Geneva: IPU.

Ireland, Doug. 2008. 'Nepal's first gay MP speaks: Nation's two largest political parties embrace LGBT rights'. Direland. May 8.

Ito, Yukiko. 2007. *Home purchases increasing among women in their thirties.* JCER Staff Report. 20 July. Tokyo: Japan Center for Economic Research.

ITUC-CSI-IGB. 2007. '2007 Annual survey of violations of trade union rights: Asia and the Pacific'. [http://survey07.ituc-csi.org/getcontinent.php?IDContinent=3&IDLang=EN]. Last accessed on 2 November 2009.

Jackson, Cecile, and Nitya Rao. 2004. *Understanding gender and agrarian change under liberalisation: The case of India.* Geneva: UNRISD.

Jahan, Rounaq. 2009. Keynote presentation made at the dialogue on 'Women's Political Representation: Lessons from Global Experiences for Bangladesh' organised by the Centre for Policy Dialogue: 18 August, Dhaka.

Jahangir, Asma. 2004. 'Mukhtar Mai: Challenging a tribal code of honor'. *Timeasia*. 4 October.

Jalal, Imrana P. 2009. 'Gender equity in justice systems of the Pacific Island Countries and Territories: Implications for human development'. Technical background paper for the Asia-Pacific Human Development Report *Power, voice and rights: A turning point for gender equality in Asia and the Pacific.* Unpublished.

———. **2007.** 'Progress on CEDAW ratification, implementation and reporting since 2004: An overview'. Paper presented at the 10th Triennial Conference of Pacific Women: 27-31 May, Noumea, New Caledonia.

_____. **2006.** *Pacific culture and human rights: Why Pacific Island Countries should ratify international human rights treaties.* [http://www.rrrt.org/assets/Pacific%20Culture%20and%20Human%20Rights.pdf]. Last accessed on 27 October 2009.

_____. **1998.** *Law for Pacific women: A legal rights handbook.* Suva: Fiji Women's Rights Movement.

Jilani, Hina, and Eman M. Ahmed. 2004. 'Violence against women: The legal system and institutional responses in Pakistan'. In Savitri Goonesekere, ed. *Violence, law and women's rights in South Asia.* New Delhi: Sage.

Jivan, Vedna, and Christine Forster. 2007. *Translating CEDAW into law: CEDAW legislative compliance in nine Pacific Island countries.* Suva: UNDP Pacific Centre and UNIFEM Pacific Regional Office.

Johnson, Susan. n.d. 'Gender and microfinance: Guidelines for good practice'. [http://www.gdrc.org/icm/wind/gendersjonson.html]. Last accessed on 2 November 2009.

Jolly, Margaret, and Martha Macintyre. 1989. 'Introduction'. In Margaret Jolly, and Martha Macintyre, eds. *Family and gender in the Pacific: Domestic contradictions and the colonial impact.* Cambridge: Cambridge University Press.

Joshi, Gopal. 1996. 'The urban informal sector: Lessons learned and the way forward'. Paper presented at the National Workshop on Gearing up for the Challenges and Opportunity in the Urban Informal Sector: September, Manila.

Kabeer, Naila. 2008. *Paid work, women's empowerment and gender justice: Critical pathways of social change.* Working Paper No 3. Pathways of Women's Empowerment. University of Sussex. [http://www.pathwaysofempowerment.org/PathwaysWP3-website.pdf]. Last accessed on 29 July 2009.

_____. **2007.** *Marriage, motherhood, masculinity in the global economy: Reconfiguration of personal and economic life.* IDS Working Paper No. 290. Brighton: IDS.

_____. **2005.** 'Is microfinance a 'magic bullet' for women's empowerment? Analysis of findings from South Asia'. *Economic and Political Weekly.* 29 October.

_____. **2000.** *The power to choose: Bangladeshi women workers and labour market decisions in London and Dhaka.* London: Verso.

Kabul Center for Strategic Studies. 2008. 'Afghanistan's women's status after the Taliban: Shukria Barekzai explains'. *Kabul Direct* 2 (3): 12-15.

Kapur, Ratna. 2007. 'Challenging the liberal subject: Law and gender justice in South Asia'. In Maitrayee Mukhopadhyay, and Navsharan Singh, eds. *Gender justice, citizenship, and development.* New Delhi and Ottawa: Zubaan and International Development Research Centre (IDRC).

Kawar, Mary. n.d. 'Gender and migration: Why are women more vulnerable?'. [http://www.antigone.gr/en/library/files/selected_publications/international/070603.pdf]. Last accessed on 11 November 2009.

Keairns, Yvonne E. 2002. *The voices of girl child soldiers: Summary.* New York, Geneva and London: Quaker United Nations Office and Coalition to Stop the Use of Child Soldiers.

Kelkar, Govind, and Dev Nathan. 2005. 'Gender, livelihood and resources in South Asia'. Paper presented at the Fifth South Asia Regional Ministerial Conference Celebrating Beijing Plus Ten: 3-5 May, Islamabad.

Ketkar, Suhas L. 1978. 'Female education and fertility: Some evidence from Sierra Leone'. *The Journal of Developing Areas* 13 (1): 22-33.

Khan, Zarina Rahman, and Amena Mohsin. 2009. 'Women's empowerment through local governance: Emerging issues and debates in Bangladesh'. Paper presented at the Pathways mid-term review conference: 20-24 January, Cairo.

Khanal, Rameshore P. 2009. 'Highlights of budget 2010'. Presentation made at the local donor's meeting (7 August) by the Finance Secretary, Government of Nepal.

King, Elizabeth M., Stephan Klasen, and Maria Porter. 2008. *Women and development.* Copenhagen Consensus 2008. Women and Development. Frederiksberg: Copenhagen Consensus Center.

Kiribati Court of Appeal 2006. *Toakarawa v The Republic of Kiribati.* Criminal Appeal 04.

Klasen, Stephan. 1999. *Does gender inequality reduce growth and development? Evidence from cross-country regressions.* Policy Research Report on Gender and Development. Working Paper Series No. 7. Washington, DC: World Bank Development Research Group/Poverty Reduction and Economic Management Network.

_____. **1994.** '"Missing women" reconsidered'. *World Development* 22 (7): 1061-1071.

Klasen, Stephan, and Francesca Lamanna. 2008. *The impact of gender inequality in education and employment on economic growth in developing countries: Updates and extensions.* Discussion Paper No. 175. Ibero-America Institute for Economic Research. Goettingen: Georg-August-Universität Göttingen.

Klasen, Stephen, and Claudia Wink. 2002. *Missing women: A review of the debates and an analysis of recent trends.* [http://papers.ssrn.com/sol3/papers.cfm?abstract_id= 321861]. Last accessed 12 October 2009.

Knowles, Stephen, Paula K. Lorgelly, and P. Dorian Owen. 2002. 'Are educational gender gaps a brake on economic development? Some cross-country empirical evidence'. *Oxford Economic Papers* 54 (1): 118-149.

Kundu, Amitabh. 2009. *Urbanisation and migration: An analysis of trend, pattern and polices in Asia.* Human Development Reports Research Paper 2009/16. New York: United Nations Development Programme.

Kusakabe, Kyoko. 2004. 'Women's work and market hierarchies along the border of Lao PDR'. *Gender, Place and Culture* 11 (4): 581-594.

Labor Code of the Philippines 1974. Presidential Decree No. 442, as amended. [http://www. dole.gov.ph/laborcode/PRESIDENTIAL_DECREE_NO_442.pdf]. Last accessed on 27 October 2009.

Labour and Employment Act 1972. Samoa consolidated legislation. Pacific Islands Legal Information Institute. [http://www.paclii.org/ws/legis/consol_act/laea1972228/]. Last accessed on 20 October 2009.

Labour Code of Socialist Republic of Vietnam 1994. (As amended 2 April 2002, effective from 1 January 2003). [http://www.global-standards.com/Resources/VNLaborCode1994-2002.pdf]. Last accessed on 27 October 2009.

Lagerlöf, Nils-Petter. 2003. 'Gender equality and long-run growth'. *Journal of Economic Growth* 8 (4): 403-426.

Lahiri-Dutt, Kuntala. 2009. 'On gender mainstreaming'. In UNDP (United Nations Development Programme). *E-discussion: Gender – Overcoming unequal power, unequal voice.* Asia Pacific Human Development Network. Colombo: UNDP Regional Centre for Asia Pacific.

Larson, Charles P., Unnati Rani Saha, Rafiqul Islam, and Nikhil Roy. 2006. 'Childhood diarrhoea management practices in Bangladesh: Private sector dominance and continued inequities in care'. *International Journal of Epidemiology* 35 (6): 1430-1439.

Larssen, Amila de Saram. 2008. 'Sunil Pant: From computer engineer to the first openly gay member of Nepal's Constituent Assembly'. [http://bistandsaktuelt.typepad.com/blade/2008/11/sunil-pant-from-computer-engineer-to-the-first-openly-gay-member-of-nepals-constituent-assembly.html]. Last accessed on 22 October 2009.

Law, Kenneth W.K., and Annie H.N. Chan. 2004. 'Gender role stereotyping in Hong Kong's primary school Chinese language subject textbooks'. *Asian Journal of Women's Studies* 10 (1): 49-69.

Law of the Republic of Indonesia No. 12 on Citizenship of the Republic of Indonesia. 2006. [http://www.unhcr.org/refworld/country,LEGAL,,,IDN,,4538aae64,0.html]. Last accessed on 16 November 2009.

Law on Gender Equality. 2006. Socialist Republic of Vietnam. Law No. 73/2006/QH11. [http://www.wcwonline.org/pdf/lawcompilation/VIETNAMLawGenderEquality.pdf]. Last accessed on 27 October 2009.

Lee, Sunhwa. 2006. 'A gender analysis of the 2004 Viet Nam Household Living Standard Survey'. Mimeo.

Legal Aid and Consultancy Center. n.d. 'Eleventh Amendment of Country Code (Muluki Ain) on women's rights, 2002'. [http://www.laccnepal.com/eleventh_amendment.html]. Last accessed on 9 July 2009.

Li, Zhijian, Cui Hao, Liu Ping, Zhang Liqiong, Yang Hongbin, and Zhang Lu. 2008. 'Prevalence and causes of blindness and visual impairment among the elderly in rural Southern Harbin, China'. *Ophthalmic Epidemiology* 15 (5): 334-338.

Li, Zongmin. 2003. 'Women's land tenure rights in rural China: A Synthesis'. Mimeo. Beijing: Ford Foundation.

Lithgow, Lynette. 2000. *A question of relativity: The role of the news media in shaping the view of women in Asian political dynasties.* Working Paper Series. Working Paper No. 2000-13. Cambridge: The Joan Shorenstein Center and John F. Kennedy School of Government, Harvard University.

Lorenzo, Fely Marilyn E., Jaime Galvez-Tan, Kriselle Icamina, and Lara Javier. 2007. 'Nurse migration from a source country perspective: Philippine country case study'. *Health Services Research* 42 (3): 1406-1418.

Lowe-Lee, Florence. 2006. 'Korean women: You have come a long way'. *Korea Insight* 8 (5): 1-2.

Lu, Yu-Hsia. 2001. 'The "boss's wife" and Taiwanese small family business'. In Mary C. Brinton, ed. *Women's working lives in East Asia.* Stanford: Stanford University Press.

Magistrates Court of Fiji. 1999. *State vs. Bechu.* Criminal Case No. 79/94.

Malla, S.P. 2000. *Baseline study on inheritance right of women: A report.* Kathmandu: Forum for Women, Law and Development.

Mani, Braj Ranjan and Pamela Sardar, eds. 2008. *A forgotten liberator: The life and struggle of Savitribai Phule.* New Delhi: Mountain Peak.

Manoharan, N. 2003. 'Tigresses of Lanka: From girls to guerillas'. Article No. 1001. 21 March. New Delhi: Institute of Peace and Conflict Studies.

Manuel, Marlon. 2009. 'Gender equity in justice systems of East Asia: Implications for human development'. Technical background paper for the Asia-Pacific Human Development Report *Power, voice and rights: A turning point for gender equality in Asia and the Pacific.* Unpublished.

Mason, Karen Oppenheim. 1998. 'Wives' economic decision-making power in the family: Five Asian countries'. In Karen Oppenheim Mason, Noriko O. Tsuya, and Minja Kim Choe, eds. *The changing family in comparative perspective: Asia and the United States.* Honolulu: East-West Center.

Mason, K., and H. Carlsson. 2004. 'The impact of gender equality in land rights on development'. Paper presented at the 'Human Rights and Development: Towards Mutual Reinforcement' Conference: 1 March, New York.

Mayoux, Linda. 2000. *Micro-finance and the empowerment of women: A review of the key issues.* Geneva: ILO.

Media Center of the General Elections Commission (KPU). 2009. 'Keterwakilan Perempuan di dpr ri – Periode 2009-2014 (Women representation in the House of Representatives – Period 2009-2014)'. Media Center. [http://mediacenter.kpu.go.id/images/mediacenter/DATA_OLAHAN/juni/perempuan_dpr_ terpilih_3.pdf]. Last accessed on 24 August 2009.

Mehran, Golnar. 2003. *Gender and education in Iran.* Background paper prepared for the Education for All Global Monitoring Report 2003/4, The Leap to Equality. 2004/ED/EFA/MRT/PI/50. Paris: UNESCO.

Mehrvar, Mehrak, Chhay Kim Sore, and My Sambath. 2008. *Women's perspectives: A case study of systematic land registration – Cambodia.* Phnom Penh: Gender and Development for Cambodia and Heinrich Böll Stiftung Cambodia.

Men Against Violence and Abuse (MAVA). n.d. 'About MAVA'. [http://www.mavaindia.org/AboutUs.html]. Last accessed on 27 October 2009.

Menon-Sen, Kalyani. 2009. 'Gender mainstreaming: A road well-travelled, but miles to go for equality'. Technical background paper for the Asia-Pacific Human Development Report *Power, voice and rights: A turning point for gender equality in Asia and the Pacific.* Unpublished.

Mernissi, Fatema. 2001. *Scheherazade goes west: Different cultures, different harems.* New York: Washington Square Press.

Ministry of Planning and Investment. 2008. *Viet Nam continues to achieve the millennium development goals.* Hanoi: Ministry of Planning and Investment.

Mitra, Arup. 2009. 'Women employment in Asia Pacific region'. Technical background paper for the Asia-Pacific Human Development Report *Power, voice and rights: A turning point for gender equality in Asia and the Pacific.* Unpublished.

————. 2005. 'Women in the urban informal sector: Perpetuation of meagre earnings'. *Development and Change* 36 (2): 291-316.

Mohanty, Bidyut. 2001. *Women and political empowerment 1999. Women's political empowerment day celebrations on Panchayats, women and family welfare.* New Delhi: Institution of Social Sciences.

Montgomery, R., D. Bhattacharya, and D. Hulme. 1996. 'Credit for the poor in Bangladesh: The BRAC rural development programme and the government Thana resource development and employment programme'. In David Hulme, and Paul Mosley, eds. *Finance against poverty (II).* London: Routledge.

Moser, Caroline, and Anis A. Dani, eds. 2008. *Assets, livelihoods and social policy.* Washington, DC: World Bank.

MoWA (Ministry of Women's Affairs), GTZ (German Technical Assistance), EWMI (East West Management Institute), and UNIFEM (United Nations Development Fund for Women) 2005. *Violence against women: A baseline survey.* Final Report Cambodia 2005. Phnom Penh: MoWA, GTZ, EWMI and UNIFEM.

Murthy, Ranjani K. 2009. 'Reversing gender inequities in health and economy in Asia-Pacific: Options for the future'. Technical background paper for the Asia-Pacific Human Development Report *Power, voice and rights: A turning point for gender equality in Asia and the Pacific.* Unpublished.

————. 2007. *Accountability to citizens on gender and health.* Background paper prepared for the Women and Gender Equity Knowledge Network of the WHO Commission on Social Determinants of Health. [http://www.who.int/

social_determinants/resources/account-ability_to_citizens_wgkn_2007.pdf]. Last accessed on 22 October 2009.

Murthy, Ranjani K., K. Raju, and Amitha Kamath. n.d. *Towards women's empowerment and poverty reduction: Lessons from the participatory impact assessment of South Asian Poverty Alleviation Programme in Andhra Pradesh, India*. [http://siteresources.worldbank.org/INTEMPOWERMENT/Resources/13338_murthy_etal.pdf]. Last accessed on 3 November 2009.

Murthy, Ranjani K., Josephine Sagayam, Rengalakshmi, and Sudha Nair. 2008. 'Gender, efficiency, poverty reduction and empowerment: Reflections from an agriculture and credit programme in Tamil Nadu, India'. *Gender and Development* 16 (1): 101-116.

Muslim Family Laws Ordinance 1961. [http://www.vakilno1.com/saarclaw/pakistan/muslim_family_laws_ordinance.htm]. Last accessed on 27 October 2009.

Muslim Women (Protection of Rights on Divorce) Act. 1986. Indian legislation. Commonwealth Legal Information Institute. [http://www.commonlii.org/in/legis/num_act/mworoda1986482/]. Last accessed on 27 October 2009.

Nagar, Richa. 2000. 'Mujhe jawab do! (Answer me!): Women's grass-roots activism and social spaces in Chitrakoot (India)'. *Gender, Place and Culture: A Journal of Feminist Geography* 7 (4): 341-362.

Narayan, Deepa. 2001. '"Consultations with the poor" from a health perspective'. *Development: Health and Poverty in a Social Context* 44 (1): 15-21.

Narayanaswamy, Lata, and Charlie Sever. 2004. 'Security and gender-based violence: What is the significance for development interventions?'. Document prepared for DfID. November. Brighton: BRIDGE Development and Gender.

Narsey, Wadan. 2007. *Gender issues in employment, underemployment and incomes in Fiji*. Suva, Fiji: Vanuavou Publications.

Naripokkho. 2006. *Women's health and rights advocacy partnership completion report: 2003-2006. Internal document.* Dhaka: Naripokko.

Natarajan, Mangai. 2005a. 'Status of women police in Asia: An agenda for future research'. Paper presented at the Fourth Australasian Women and Policing Conference on 'Improving policing for women in the Asia Pacific region': 21-24 August, Darwin.

Natarajan, Mangai, ed. 2005b. *Women police.* Aldershot, UK: Ashgate.

National Commission on the Role of Filipino Women. 2009. *Statistics on Filipino women overseas employment*. San Miguel Manila: National Commission on the Role of Filipino Women. [http://www.ncrfw.gov.ph/index.php/statistics-on-filipino-women/14-factsheets-on-filipino-women/71-statistics-fs-filipino-women-overseas-employment]. Last accessed on 11 September 2009.

National Statistical Office of Mongolia, and UNDP (United Nations Development Programme) Mongolia. 2009. *Report of time use survey 2007*. Ulaanbaatar, Mongolia: National Statistical Office.

Nazneen, Sohela. 2009. 'Rural livelihoods and gender'. Technical background paper for the Asia-Pacific Human Development Report *Power, voice and rights: A turning point for gender equality in Asia and the Pacific*. Unpublished.

Neumayer, Eric, and Thomas Plümper. 2007. 'The gendered nature of natural disasters: The impact of catastrophic events on the gender gap in life expectancy, 1981–2002'. *Annals of the Association of American Geographers* 97 (3): 551–566.

Nishikiori, Nobuyuki, Tomoko Abe, Dehiwala G.M. Costa, Samath D. Dharmaratne, Osamu Kunii, and Kazuhiko Moji. 2006. 'Who died as a result of the tsunami? Risk factors of mortality among internally displaced persons in Sri Lanka: A retrospective cohort analysis'. *BMC Public Health* 6: 73.

Norwegian Agency for International Development, UNDP (United Nations Development Programme), and FAO (Food and Agriculture Organization of the United Nations). 1987. *Women in aquaculture*. Proceedings of the ADCP/NORAD workshop on women in aquaculture: 13-16 April, Rome. Edited by Colin E. Nash, Carole R. Engle, and Donatella Crosetti. Rome: FAO.

NSSO (National Sample Survey Organisation). 2006. *Employment and unemployment situation in India (July 2004–June 2005). NSS 61st Round*. New Delhi: NSSO, Government of India.

Nussbaum, Martha, and Jonathan Glover, eds. 1995. *Women, culture and development: A study of human capabilities*. New York: Oxford University Press.

Office of Women's Affairs and Family Development, and UNDP (United Nations Development Programme) Thailand. 2008. *Report on Thailand gender-disaggregated statistics 2008*. Bangkok: UNDP.

Panda, Pradeep. 2006. 'Domestic violence and women's property ownership: Delving deeper into the linkages in Kerala'. In ICRW (International Center for Research on Women). *Property ownership and inheritance rights of women for social protection: The South Asia experience. Synthesis report of three studies.* New Delhi: International Center for Research on Women.

Panda, Pradeep, and Bina Agarwal. 2005. 'Marital violence, human development and women's property status in India'. *World Development* 33 (5): 823-850.

Pande, R. 2000. 'From anti-arrack to total prohibition: The women's movement in Andhra Pradesh, India'. *Gender, Technology and Development* 4 (1): 131-144.

Pandey, M.R. 1997. 'Women, wood energy and health'. *Wood Energy News* 12 (1): 3-5. December 1996/April 1997. Issued by the Regional Wood Energy Development Programme in Asia (GCP/RAS/154/NET).

Partners for Law in Development (PLD). 2006. *National conference on women and access to justice: A report.* New Delhi: Partners for Law in Development.

PARWAZ. n.d. 'Impact'. PARWAZ-Microfinance Institution: Empowering Afghan women. Kabul. [http://www.parwaz.org/whoserve.html]. Last accessed on 4 November 2009.

Penal Code 1883. (Sri Lanka). Commonwealth Legal Information Institute. [http://www.commonlii.org/lk/legis/consol_act/pc25130.pdf]. Last accessed on 27 October 2009.

Penal Code (Cap 135) 1981. Vanuatu consolidated legislation 2006. Pacific Islands Legal Information Institute. [http://www.paclii.org/vu/legis/consol_act/pc66/]. Last accessed on 27 October 2009.

Phetsiriseng, Inthasone. 2007. *Gender concerns in migration in Lao PDR – Migration mapping study: A review of trends, policy and programme initiatives.* A study conducted for UNIFEM, Lao PDR. [http://apmrn.anu.edu.au/conferences/8thAPMRNconference/17.Gender%20Concerns%20in%20Migration%20in%20Lao%20PDR.pdf]. Last accessed on 27 August 2009.

Piper, Nicola. 2005. *Gender and migration.* Paper prepared for the Policy Analysis and Research Programme of the Global Commission on International Migration. Geneva: Global Commission on International Migration.

Pitt, Mark M., and Shahidur R. Khandker. 1998. 'The impact of group-based credit programs on poor households in Bangladesh: Does the gender of participants matter?'. *Journal of Political Economy* 106 (5): 958-996.

———. **1996.** *Household and intrahousehold impact of the Grameen Bank and similar targeted programs in Bangladesh.* World Bank Discussion Paper No. 320. Washington, DC: World Bank.

Pitt, Mark M., Shahidur R. Khandker, and Jennifer Cartwright. 2006. 'Empowering women with micro finance: Evidence from Bangladesh'. *Economic Development and Cultural Change* 54 (4): 791-831.

Pradhan, Basanta K., and Ramamani Sundar. 2006. *Gender impact of HIV and AIDS in India.* NACO (National AIDS Control Organisation), NCAER (National Council of Applied Economic Research), and UNDP (United Nations Development Programme) India. New Delhi: UNDP.

Press Information Bureau. 2009. 'Women partnership in Panchayati Raj system'. Press release. 10 July. Government of India. [http://pib.nic.in/release/release.asp?relid=50131]. Last accessed on 22 October 2009.

Prokop, Michaela A. 2009. 'Gender and socio-cultural factors in Afghanistan: Barriers and opportunities in promoting equality'. Note prepared for the Asia-Pacific Human Development Report *Power, voice and rights: A turning point for gender equality in Asia and the Pacific.* Unpublished.

Qanun-e-Shahadat Order 1984. P.O. No. 10 of 1984. [http://www.jamilandjamil.com/publications/pub_litigation_laws/qanuneshahadat1984.htm]. Last accessed on 27 October 2009.

Quisumbing, Agnes R., ed. 2003. *Household decisions, gender, and development: A synthesis of recent research.* Washington, DC: IFPRI.

Quisumbing, Agnes R., and Kelly Hallman. 2006. 'Marriage in transition: Evidence on age, education, and assets from six developing countries'. In Cynthia B. Lloyd, Jere R. Behrman, Nelly P. Stromquist, and Barney Cohen, eds. *The changing transitions to adulthood in developing countries: Selected studies.* Washington, DC: The National Academies Press.

Quisumbing, Agnes R., and John A. Maluccio. 2003. 'Resources at marriage and intrahousehold allocation: Evidence from Bangladesh, Ethiopia, Indonesia, and South Africa'. *Oxford Bulletin of Economics and Statistics* 65 (3): 283-327.

Radio New Zealand International. 2008. 'Vanuatu watchdog queries delay on new domestic violence bill'. *Radio New Zealand International.* 7 July.

Rahman, Omar M., and Jane Menken. 1990. *The impact of marital status and living* *arrangements on old age female mortality in rural Bangladesh*. Paper No. 1. Department of Epidemiology, Harvard School of Public Health, and Population Studies Center. Philadelphia: University of Pennsylvania.

Rajivan, Anuradha K. 2009. 'A young woman saves Kabul society'. In UNDP (United Nations Development Programme). *E-discussion: Gender – Overcoming unequal power, unequal voice.* Asia Pacific Human Development Network. Colombo: UNDP Regional Centre for Asia Pacific.

Rajivan, Anuradha K., and Niranjan Sarangi. 2009. 'Equality, equity and gender'. HDRU Brief No. 2 for the Asia-Pacific Human Development Report *Power, voice and rights: A turning point for gender equality in Asia and the Pacific*. Unpublished.

Rajivan, Anuradha K., and Ruwanthi Senarathne. 2009. 'Women in armed conflicts: Inclusion and exclusion'. HDRU Brief No. 4 prepared for the Asia-Pacific Human Development Report *Power, voice and rights: A turning point for gender equality in Asia and the Pacific*. Unpublished.

Raman, Vasanthi. 2002. 'The implementation of quotas for women: The Indian experience'. Paper presented at the workshop on 'The implementation of quotas: Asian experiences' hosted by International IDEA: 25 September, Jakarta.

Ramaseshan, Geeta. 2009a. 'Gender equity in justice systems of South Asia: Implications for human development'. Technical background paper for the Asia-Pacific Human Development Report *Power, voice and rights: A turning point for gender equality in Asia and the Pacific*. Unpublished.

————. **2009b.** 'Sexual harassment in the workplace: A case for legal intervention'. In UNDP (United Nations Development Programme). *E-discussion: Gender – Overcoming unequal power, unequal voice.* Asia Pacific Human Development Network. Colombo: UNDP Regional Centre for Asia Pacific.

Ramirez-Machado, José Maria. 2003. *Domestic work, conditions of work and employment: A legal perspective.* Conditions of Work and Employment Series No. 7. Geneva: ILO.

Raynor, Janet. 2005. 'Educating girls in Bangladesh: Watering a neighbour's tree?'. In Oxfam. *Beyond access: Transforming policy and practice for gender equality in education.* Edited by Sheila Aikman and Elaine Unterhalter. Oxford: Oxfam GB.

Rees, Teresa. 2002. 'The politics of "mainstreaming" gender equality'. In Esther Breitenbach, Alice Brown, Fiona Mackay, and Janette Webb, eds. *The changing politics of gender equality in Britain.* Basingstoke and New York: Palgrave.

Reid, Rachel. 2009. 'For Afghan women, rights again at risk'. *The Washington Post.* 18 August.

Republic Act No. 9710. 2009. An act providing for the Magna Carta of Women. Republic of the Philippines. [http://www.congress.gov.ph/download/ra_14/RA09710.pdf]. Last accessed on 23 November 2009.

Resurreccion, Bernadette P. 2009. 'Gender and migration'. Technical background paper for the Asia-Pacific Human Development Report *Power, voice and rights: A turning point for gender equality in Asia and the Pacific.* Unpublished.

Resurreccion, Bernadette P., and Edsel E. Sajor. 2008. *Gender dimensions of the adoption of the System of Rice Intensification (SRI) in Cambodia.* [http://ciifad.cornell.edu/sri/countries/cambodia/cambOxfamSRIGenderEval08.pdf]. Last accessed on 4 November 2009.

Resurreccion, Bernadette, and Ha Thi Van Khanh. 2007. 'Able to come and go: Reproducing gender in female rural-urban migration in the Red River Delta'. *Population, Space & Place* 13 (3): 211-224.

Reyes, Socorro L. 2002. 'Quotas for women for legislative seats at the local level in Pakistan'. [http://www.idea.int/publications/wip/upload/CS_Pakistan_Reynes.pdf]. Last accessed on 22 October 2009.

Robinson, Kathryn. 2004. 'Islam, gender, and politics in Indonesia'. In Virginia Hooker, and Amin Saikal, eds. *Islamic perspectives on the new millennium.* Singapore: ISEAS.

————. **2000.** 'Indonesian women: From *Orde Baru* to *Reformasi*'. In Louise Edwards, and Mina Roces, eds. *Women in Asia: Tradition, modernity and globalisation.* Sydney: Allen & Unwin.

Roy, Asim. 1996. *Islam in South Asia: A regional perspective.* New Delhi: South Asian Publishers.

Roy, K. Chandra. 2004. *Indigenous women: A gender perspective.* Guovdageaidnu-Kautokeino, Norway: Resource Centre for the Rights of Indigenous Peoples.

Rustagi, Preet, and Rajini Menon. 2009. 'Women's command over assets: Addressing gender inequalities'. Technical background paper for the Asia-Pacific Human Development Report *Power, voice and rights: A turning point for gender equality in Asia and the Pacific.* Unpublished.

Sachs, Carolyn E. 2007. 'Going public: Net-working globally and locally'. *Rural Sociology* 72 (1): 2–24.

Sarangi, Niranjan. 2007. 'Microfinance and the rural poor. A study of group-based credit pro-grammes in Madhya Pradesh, India'. *Doctoral Thesis.* Submitted to Jawaharlal Nehru University, New Delhi, India.

Sehgal, Rashme. 2008. 'Panchayat women no longer need sarpanch patis'. *InfoChange Women.* InfoChange News and Features. March.

Sen, Amartya. 1990a. 'Gender and cooperative conflicts'. In Irene Tinker, ed. *Persistent inequalities: Women and world development.* New York: Oxford University Press.

——. 1990b. 'More than 100 million women are missing'. *The New York Review of Books* 37 (20): 61-66.

Sen, Krishna. 2002. 'Gendered citizens in the new Indonesian democracy'. *Review of Indonesian and Malaysian Affairs* 36 (1): 51-65.

Shameem, Nazhat. 2008. 'Concepts of equality'. *Fiji Sun.* 15 September. [http://solivakasama.wordpress.com/2008/09/15/in-her-own-words/]. Last accessed on 22 October 2009.

Shamim, Ishrat, and Khaleda Salahuddin. 1995. *Widows in rural Bangladesh: Issues and concerns.* Dhaka: Centre for Women and Children Studies.

Shefali, Mashuda Khatun. 2004. 'Women's housing needs and rights'. *The Daily Star.* 27 May.

Shvedova, Nedezhda. 2005. 'Obstacles to women's participation in parliament'. In International IDEA. *Women in parliament: Beyond numbers.* A Revised Edition. Edited by Julie Ballington, and Azza Karam. Stockholm: International Institute for Democracy and Electoral Assistance.

Shylendra, H.S. 2006. 'Microfinance institutions in Andhra Pradesh: Crisis and diagnosis'. *Economic and Political Weekly.* 20 May.

Silvey, Rachel M. 2000. 'Stigmatized spaces: Gender and mobility under crisis in South Sulawesi, Indonesia'. *Gender, Place and Culture* 7 (2): 143-161.

Sinha, Anushree. 2009. 'Gender integration in macro analysis for better policy'. In UNDP (United Nations Development Programme). *E-discussion: Gender – Overcoming unequal power, unequal voice.* Asia Pacific Human Develop-ment Network. Colombo: UNDP Regional Centre for Asia Pacific.

Sinha, Anushree, and Christopher Adam. 2006. 'Trade reforms and informalization: Getting behind jobless growth in India'. In Basudeb Guha–Khasnobis, and Ravi Kanbur, eds. *Informal labour markets and development.* New York: Palgrave Macmillan.

Sirimanne, Shamika. 2009. 'Emerging issue: The gender perspectives of the financial crisis'. Interactive expert panel. Written statement. Commission on the Status of Women, Fifty-third session: 2-13 March, New York. New York: United Nations.

Sky News. 2008. 'Thai schools' transgender toilets'. *SkyNews.* 30 July.

Smiley, David. 2006. 'Land tenure in Pacific island countries'. *Development Bulletin* 70: 84-86.

Smith, Kirk R., Sumi Mehta, and Mirjam Maeusezahl-Feuz. 2004. 'Indoor air pollution from household use of solid fuels'. In Majid Ezzati, Alan D. Lopez, Anthony Rodgers, and Christopher J.L. Murray, eds. *Comparative quantification of health risks: Global and regional burden of disease attributable to selected major risk factors.* Volume 2. Geneva: WHO.

Snodgrass, Donald R., and Jennefer Sebstad. 2002. *Clients in context: The impacts of microfinance in three countries. Synthesis report.* Management Systems International. Washington, DC: Assessing the Impact of Microenterprise Services (AIMS).

Soin, Kanwaljit. 1994. 'Why women, what politics'. Paper presented at the First Asia-Pacific Congress of Women in Politics: 21-23 June, Manila.

Song, Hyunjoo. 2009. 'Gender and education'. Technical background paper for the Asia-Pacific Human Development Report *Power, voice and rights: A turning point for gender equality in Asia and the Pacific.* Unpublished.

Sonpar, Shobna, and Ravi Kapur. 2003. 'Non-conventional indicators of gender disparities under structural reforms'. In Swapna Mukhopadhyay, and Ratna M. Sudarshan, eds. *Tracking gender equity under economic reforms: Continuity and change in South Asia.* New Delhi and Ottawa: Kali for Women and Inter-national Development Research Centre.

South Asia Citizen's Web. 2006. 'Towards a politics of justice: Affirming diversities; resist-ing divisiveness'. Declaration of the National Co-ordination Committee of the Seventh National Conference of Autonomous Women's Movements in India: 9-12 September, Kolkata. [http://www.sacw.net/Wmov/TowardsaPoliticsofJustice.html]. Last accessed on 17 November 2009.

Srivastava, Sanjay. 2009a. 'Gender identities, histories and norms'. Technical background paper for the Asia-Pacific Human Development Report *Power, voice and rights: A turning point for gender equality in Asia and the Pacific.* Unpublished.

———. **2009b.** 'Gender, work and the world: Liberal economies and restrictive norms'. In UNDP (United Nations Development Programme). *E-discussion: Gender – Overcoming unequal power, unequal voice.* Asia Pacific Human Development Network. Colombo: UNDP Regional Centre for Asia Pacific.

Stege, Kristina E., Ruth Maetala, Anna Naupa, and Joel Simo. 2008. *Land and women: The matrilineal factor. The cases of the Republic of the Marshall Islands, Solomon Islands and Vanuatu.* Edited by Elise Huffer. Suva, Fiji: Pacific Islands Forum Secretariat.

Stotsky, Janet G. 2006. *Gender and its relevance to macroeconomic policy: A survey.* IMF Working Paper No. WP/06/233. Washington, DC: International Monetary Fund.

Supreme Court of India. 2001. *Daniel Latifi v. Union of India.* AIR SCC 740.

———. **1997.** *Vishaka and others v. State of Rajasthan and others.* AIR 1997 SC 3011.

———. **1985.** *Mohd. Ahmed Khan v Shah Bano Begum and Ors.* AIR 945 1985. [http://www.cscsarchive.org/dataarchive/textfiles/textfile.2008-07-22.2150472804/file]. Last accessed on 20 October 2009.

Supreme Court of Nepal. 2002. *Forum for women, law and development (FWLD) vs. His Majesty's Government/Nepal (HMG/N).* Writ no 55/048. 2 May.

Swaminathan, Hema, Nandita Bhatla, and Swati Chakraborty. 2007. *Women's property rights as an AIDS response: Emerging efforts in South Asia.* A publication in partnership with UNDP Regional Centre in Colombo, and The Global Coalition on Women and AIDS. New Delhi: International Center for Research on Women (ICRW).

Sward, Jon, and Ron Skeldon. 2009. *Migration and the financial crisis: How will the economic downturn affect migrants?* Briefing No. 17. Development Research Centre on Migration, Globalisation and Poverty. Brighton: University of Sussex.

Tambiah, Yasmin. 2003. 'The impact of gender inequality on governance'. In Nussbaum, Martha, Amrita Basu, Yasmin Tambiah, and Niraja Gopal Jayal. *Essays on gender and governance.* Human Development Resource Centre. New Delhi: UNDP.

The 1987 Constitution of the Republic of the Philippines. [http://www.chanrobles.com/philsupremelaw2.html]. Last accessed on 27 October 2009.

The Asia Foundation. 2008. *State building, security, and social change in Afghanistan: Reflections on a survey of the Afghan people.* Kabul: The Asia Foundation.

The Asia Foundation, Asian Development Bank (ADB), Canadian International Development Agency (CIDA), National Democratic Institute (NDI), and World Bank. 2006. *Indonesia: Country gender assessment.* Southeast Asia Regional Department, Regional and Sustainable Development Department, Asian Development Bank. Manila: ADB.

The Constitution of India 1949. (As modified up to the 1st December 2007). Ministry of Law and Justice. Government of India. [http://lawmin.nic.in/coi/coiason29july08.pdf]. Last access date 23 October 2009.

The Constitution of Solomon Islands 1978. No 783. Solomon Islands consolidated legislation. Pacific Islands Legal Information Institute. [http://www.paclii.org/sb/legis/consol_act/c1978167/]. Last accessed on 27 October 2009.

The Constitution of Tuvalu 1978. Tuvalu consolidated legislation. Pacific Islands Legal Information Institute. [http://www.paclii.org/tv/legis/consol_act/cot277/]. Last accessed on 27 October 2009.

The Family Protection Act 2008. No 28. Republic of Vanuatu. Vanuatu sessional legislation. Pacific Islands Legal Information Institute. [http://www.paclii.org/vu/legis/num_act/fpa2008206/]. Last accessed on 27 October 2009.

The Hindu Marriage Act 1955. Indian legislation. Commonwealth Legal Information Institute. [http://www.commonlii.org/in/legis/num_act/hma1955136/]. Last accessed on 20 October 2009.

The Microcredit Summit Campaign. 2009. 'More than 100 million of world's poorest benefit from microcredit'. Press releases. 26 January. [http://www.microcreditsummit.org/press_releases/more_than_100_million_of_worlds_poorest_benefit_%20from_microcredit/]. Last accessed on 3 November 2009.

The Protection of Women From Domestic Violence Act 2005. Indian legislation. Commonwealth Legal Information Institute. [http://www.commonlii.org/in/legis/num_act/powfdva2005435/]. Last accessed on 27 October 2009.

The Supreme Court of Fiji. 2004. *Balelala v State.* Criminal appeal No. AAU0003.

Todd, Helen. 1996. *Women at the center: Grameen Bank borrowers after one decade.* Boulder: Westview Press.

Tonguthai, Pawadee. 2009. 'Development case for gender equality'. Technical background paper for the Asia-Pacific Human Development Report *Power, voice and rights: A turning point for gender equality in Asia and the Pacific.* Unpublished.

Torres, Amaryllis T. 2009. 'Claiming spaces for political participation, crossing the gender divide'. Technical background paper for the Asia-Pacific Human Development Report *Power, voice and rights: A turning point for gender equality in Asia and the Pacific.* Unpublished.

UN (United Nations). 2009a. 'Trends in international migrant stock: The 2008 revision'. CD-ROM Documentation. POP/DB/MIG/Stock/Rev.2008. Department of Economic and Social Affairs, Population Division. New York: United Nations.

_____. 2009b. *World population prospects, the 2008 revision.* United Nations Population Division. UNdata: A world of information. United Nations Statistics Division. [http://data.un.org/Browse.aspx?d = PopDiv]. Last accessed between 2-16 July 2009.

_____. 2006. *In-depth study on all forms of violence against women. Report of the Secretary-General.* Sixty-first session. A/61/122/Add.1.

_____. 2005a. *Baseline survey representative of the Cambodian population on violence against women.* The UN Secretary-General's Database on Violence Against Women. [http://web-apps01.un.org/vawdatabase/searchDetail.action?measureId = 4762&baseHREF = country&baseHREFId = 297]. Last accessed on 25 July 2009.

_____. 2005b. *Facts and figures on women, peace and security.* October. New York: United Nations Department of Public Information. [http://www.unifem.org/news_events/currents/documents/currents200510_WPS_Facts.pdf]. Last accessed on 22 October 2009.

_____. 2005c. *In larger freedom: Towards development, security and human rights for all. Report of the Secretary-General.* Fifty-ninth session, Agenda items 45 and 55. Integrated and coordinated implementation of and follow-up to the outcomes of the major United Nations conferences and summits in the economic, social and related fields. Follow-up to the outcome of the Millennium Summit. A/59/2005. [http://www.un.org/largerfreedom/contents.htm]. Last accessed 12 October 2009.

_____. 2005d. *Mainstreaming a gender perspective into national policies and programmes.* Commission on the Status of Women. Forty-ninth session (28 February-11 March 2005). Follow-up to the Fourth World Conference on Women and to the special session of the General Assembly entitled 'Women 2000: Gender equality, development and peace for the twenty-first century'. E/CN.6/2005/L.5/Rev.1. [http://www.unescap.org/esid/GAD/Issues/Beijing % 2B10/Draft % 20resolution % 20Gender % 20mainstreaming.pdf]. Last accessed on 12 October 2009.

_____. 2003. *Levels and trends of international migration to selected countries in Asia.* New York: United Nations Department of Economic and Social Affairs.

_____. 1996. *Report of the fourth world conference on women.* A/CONF.177/20/Rev.1. New York: United Nations. [http://www.un.org/womenwatch/daw/beijing/pdf/Beijing % 20full % 20report % 20E.pdf]. Last accessed on 12 October 2009.

_____. n.d.-a. 'Convention on the elimination of all forms of discrimination against women: Overview of the convention'. Division for the Advancement of Women (DAW). [http://www.un.org/womenwatch/daw/cedaw/]. Last accessed on 21 October 2009.

_____. n.d.-b. 'Institutional mechanisms for the advancement of women'. In UN. *Beijing at ten and beyond.* [http://www.un.org/womenwatch/daw/beijing/beijingat10/H. % 20Institutional % 20mechanisms % 20for % 20the % 20advancement % 20of % 20women.pdf]. Last accessed on 12 October 2009.

_____. n.d.-c. 'Treaty collection. Chapter IV: Human rights. Convention on the elimination of all forms of discrimination against women'. Status as at 24 July 2009. [http://treaties.un.org/Pages/ViewDetails.aspx?src = TREATY&mtdsg_no = IV-8&chapter = 4&lang = en#36]. Last accessed on 24 July 2009.

UN (United Nations) Country Team Mongolia. 2009. *Mongolia: Common country assessment update.* Draft (June).

UN Millennium Project. 2005. *Taking action: Achieving gender equality and empowering women.* Task Force on Education and Gender Equality. London: Earthscan.

UNAMA (United Nations Assistance Mission in Afghanistan), and OHCHR (Office of the United Nations High Commissioner for Human Rights). 2009. *Silence is violence: End the abuse of women in Afghanistan.* [http://unama.unmissions.org/Portals/UNAMA/vaw-english.pdf]. Last accessed on 12 October 2009.

Undarya, Tumursukh. 2008. 'Women's efforts vs. politicians' power'. 28 January. [http://www.iknowpolitics.org/en/node/4492]. Last accessed on 22 October 2009.

UNDEF (The United Nations Democracy Fund). 2009. 'Deepening democracy: Women's participation in politics and peace.' Final project narrative report. First round. Internal document.

———. **2008.** 'Promoting women in democratic decision-making in Cambodia'. Final project narrative report. First round. Internal document.

Underhill-Sem, Yvonne. 2009. 'Gender, culture and the Pacific context'. Technical background paper for the Asia-Pacific Human Development Report *Power, voice and rights: A turning point for gender equality in Asia and the Pacific.* Unpublished.

UNDESA (United Nations Department of Economic and Social Affairs). 2001. *Women 2000 – Widowhood: Invisible women, secluded or excluded.* Division for the Advancement of Women. New York: UNDESA.

UNDP (United Nations Development Programme). 2009. *Human development report 2009 – Overcoming barriers: Human mobility and development.* Published for UNDP. New York: Palgrave Macmillan.

———. **2008a.** *Asia-Pacific human development report – Tackling corruption, transforming lives: Accelerating human development in Asia and the Pacific.* UNDP Regional Centre in Colombo. New Delhi: Macmillan.

———. **2008b.** *Capacity development: Empowering people and institutions – Annual report 2008.* New York: United Nations Development Programme.

———. **2008c.** *Voices and visions: The Asia Pacific Court of women on HIV, inheritance and property rights.* Regional HIV and Development Programme for Asia and the Pacific. Colombo: UNDP Regional Centre in Colombo.

———. **2005.** *Programming for justice: Access for all. A practitioner's guide to a human rights-based approach to access to justice.* Bangkok: UNDP Regional Centre.

———. **1995.** *Human development report 1995.* New York: Oxford University Press.

———. **n.d.** *Governing systems and executive-legislative relations (Presidential, parliamentary and hybrid system).* [http://www.undp.org/governance/docs/Parl-Pub-govern.htm]. Last accessed on 22 October 2009.

UNDP (United Nations Development Programme) Indonesia. 2009. 'Where legislative quotas stumble, public awareness steps in: Real strides in women's political representation in Indonesia'. Box prepared for the Asia-Pacific Human Development Report *Power, voice and rights: A turning point for gender equality in Asia and the Pacific.* Unpublished.

UNDP (United Nations Development Programme) Nepal. 2009. *Nepal human development report 2009 – State transformation and human development.* Kathmandu: United Nations Development Programme.

UNDP (United Nations Development Programme) Pacific Centre. 2009. 'Women and peace in Bougainville'. Note prepared for the Asia-Pacific Human Development Report *Power, voice and rights: A turning point for gender equality in Asia and the Pacific.* Unpublished.

UNDP (United Nations Development Programme), CARAM Asia (Coordination of Action Research for AIDS and Mobility in Asia), Caritas Lebanon Migrant Center, UNAIDS, IOM (International Organization for Migration), and UNIFEM (United Nations Development Fund for Women). 2008. *HIV vulnerabilities of migrant women: From Asia to the Arab States. Shifting from silence, stigma and shame to safe mobility with dignity, equity and justice.* Colombo: UNDP Regional Centre in Colombo.

UNDP (United Nations Development Programme), and Women for Democratic Development Foundation. 2006. *Women's right to a political voice in Thailand – Millennium development goal 3: Promote gender equality and empower women.* Bangkok: UNDP.

UNESCAP (United Nations Economic and Social Commission for Asia and the Pacific). 2007a. *Economic and social survey of Asia and the Pacific 2007: Surging ahead in uncertain times.* Bangkok: UNESCAP.

———. **2007b.** *Violence against women: Harmful traditional and cultural practices in the Asian and Pacific region.* Gender Equality and Empowerment Section, Social Development Division, Economic and Social Commission for Asia and the Pacific. Bangkok: UNESCAP.

———. **2004.** 'Integrating unpaid work into national policies: Information for statisticians'. *Information Brief.* 3 March. Statistics Division. Bangkok: UNESCAP.

UNESCO (United Nations Educational, Scientific and Cultural Organization). 2009a. *EFA global monitoring report 2009. Overcoming inequality: Why governance matters.* Paris and Oxford: UNESCO and Oxford University Press.

_____. **2009b.** 'HIV/AIDS and STI's'. HIV Coordination, Adolescent Reproductive and School Health. Bangkok: UNESCO. [http://www.unescobkk.org/education/hivaids/projects/adolescent-reproductive-sexual-healtharsh/information-resources-publications/hivaids-and-stds/]. Last accessed on 27 October 2009.

_____. **2004.** *Role of men and boys in promoting gender equality.* Advocacy Brief. Bangkok: UNESCO Asia and Pacific Regional Bureau for Education.

UNGEI (United Nations Girls' Education Initiative). 2008. *Making education work: The gender dimension of the school to work transition.* Bangkok: East Asia and Pacific Regional UNGEI.

UN-HABITAT (United Nations Human Settlements Programme). 2007. *Policy makers guide to women's land, property and housing rights across the world.* Nairobi: UN-HABITAT.

UNIFEM (United Nations Development Fund for Women). 2008. *Progress of the world's women 2008/2009: Who answers to women? Gender and accountability.* New York: UNIFEM.

UNIFEM (United Nations Development Fund for Women), World Bank, ADB (Asian Development Bank), UNDP (United Nations Development Programme), and DFID/UK (Department for International Development of the United Kingdom). 2004. *A fair share for women: Cambodia gender assessment.* Phnom Penh: UNIFEM, World Bank, ADB, UNDP, and DFID/UK.

UNIFEM (United Nations Development Fund for Women) South Asia Regional Office, and Partners for Law in Development (PLD). 2004. *CEDAW: Restoring rights for women.* New Delhi: Partners for Law in Development.

Universal Declaration of Human Rights 1948. G.A. Res. 217A (III), U.N. Doc. A/810 at 71 (1948).

Unni, Jeemol. 1999. 'Property rights for women: Case for joint titles to agricultural land and urban housing'. *Economic and Political Weekly.* 22 May.

Upadhay, Bhawana. 2003. 'Gender issues in Nepalese livestock production'. *Asian Journal of Women's Studies* 9 (1): 80-98.

U.S. Department of State. 2009. *2008 human rights report: Bhutan.* 2008 Country reports on human rights practices: Bhutan. Bureau of Democracy, Human Rights, and Labor. [http://www.state.gov/g/drl/rls/hrrpt/2008/sca/119133.htm]. Last accessed on 29 October 2009.

_____. **2002.** *Brunei: 2001 Country reports on human rights practices.* 4 March. Bureau of Democracy, Human Rights, and Labor. [http://www.state.gov/g/drl/rls/hrrpt/2001/eap/8255.htm]. Last accessed on 22 October 2009.

Van Eyck, Kim, ed. 2005. *Who cares? Women health workers in the global labour market.* Ferney-Voltaire Cedex and London: Public Services International and Unison.

Van Eyck, Kim. 2003. *Women and international migration in the health sector. Final report of Public Services International's participatory action research 2003.* Ferney-Voltaire Cedex: Public Services International.

Vickers, Adrian. 2005. *A history of modern Indonesia.* Cambridge: University of Cambridge Press.

Wardak, Ali. 2009. 'Gender, customary law and dispute settlement in Afghanistan: Barriers and opportunities in promoting equality'. Note prepared for the Asia-Pacific Human Development Report *Power, voice and rights: A turning point for gender equality in Asia and the Pacific.* Unpublished.

Wax, Emily, and Ria Sen. 2009. 'New Delhi lifts colonial-era ban on gay sex'. *Washington Post.* 3 July.

WHO (World Health Organization). 2008. *Health situation in the South-East Asia region 2001-2007.* New Delhi: WHO Regional Office for South-East Asia.

_____. **2002.** *Gender and health in disasters.* Gender and Health. July. Geneva: WHO.

_____. **2000.** *Women of South East Asia: A profile.* New Delhi: WHO Regional Office for South-East Asia.

Williamson, Oliver E. 2000. 'The new institutional economics: Taking stock, looking ahead'. *Journal of Economic Literature* 38 (3): 595 613.

Women In Need. 2004. 'Legal support to victims of violence/counselling'. [http://www.winsl.org/html/Activities.php#Legal]. Last accessed on 27 October 2009.

Women Living Under Muslim Laws (WLUML). 2009. 'Bangladesh: University students' victory in sexual harassment case'. 2 June. [http://www.wluml.org/english/newsfulltxt.shtml?cmd%5B157%5D=x-157-564621]. Last accessed on 27 October 2009.

Women's Environment and Development Organization (WEDO). n.d. 'Getting the balance right in national cabinets'. [http://www.wedo.org/wp-content/uploads/5050_cabinets-factsheet021.pdf]. Last accessed on 22 October 2009.

Wood, Geoffrey D., and Richard Palmer-Jones. 1991. *The water sellers: A cooperative* *venture by the rural poor.* West Hartford, Connecticut: Kumarian Press.

Wordsworth, Anna. 2007. *A matter of interests: Gender and the politics of presence in Afghanistan's Wolesi Jirga.* Issues Paper Series. Kabul: Afghanistan Research and Evaluation Unit.

World Bank. 2009a. *Global development finance: Charting a global recovery – I: Review, analysis and outlook.* Washington, DC: World Bank.

———. **2009b.** *World development indicators online 2009.* [https://publications.worldbank. org/register/WDI?return%5furl=%2fextop%2fsubscriptions%2fWDI%2f]. Last accessed between 2-16 July 2009.

———. **2007.** *World development report 2008: Agriculture for development.* Washington, DC: World Bank.

———. **2006.** *At home and away: Expanding job opportunities for Pacific Islanders through labour mobility.* Washington, DC: World Bank.

———. **2004.** *World development report 2005: A better investment climate for everyone.* Washington, DC, and New York: World Bank and Oxford University Press.

———. **2001.** *Engendering development: Through gender equality in rights, resources, and voice.* A World Bank Policy Research Report. Washington, DC and New York: World Bank and Oxford University Press.

World Bank, FAO (Food and Agriculture Organization of the United Nations) and IFAD (International Fund for Agricultural Development). 2009. *Gender in agriculture source book.* Washington, DC: World Bank.

World Savings Banks Institute. 2008. *Overview of microfinance in Asia/Pacific and selected experiences from WSBI members.* Brussels: WSBI.

Yadav, Yogendra. 2009. 'Six myths about Indian elections'. *BBC News.* 3 April.

Yamanaka, Keiko, and Nicola Piper. 2005. *Feminized migration in East and Southeast Asia: Policies, actions and empowerment.* Occasional Paper No. 11. Geneva: United Nations Research Institute for Social Development.

Yogyakarta Principles. 2007. *The Yogyakarta Principles: Principles on the application of international human rights law in relation to sexual orientation and gender identity.* [http://www.yogyakartaprinciples.org/principles_en_principles.htm]. Last accessed on 7 September 2009.

Yunus, Muhammad. 2006. 'The Nobel Peace Prize 2006: Nobel lecture'. 10 December. Oslo. [http://nobelprize.org/nobel_prizes/peace/laureates/2006/yunus-lecture-en.html]. Last accessed on 26 October 2009.

Indicators

A Woman's Tale Lasts a Thousand Years

Murasaki Shikibu, circa 11th Century

Long before the era of printing presses, a meticulously crafted novel, running into volumes written by a woman made waves in the Japanese court. No statistics were kept on the number of copies or versions circulating then, yet the novel had become very popular. The author, a little known noblewoman, had been brought up by her father and given an education that few people, let alone girls, commonly received in the 11th century. Her 'Tale of Genji' revolves around a sensitive male hero, unusual for the time.

The author's observations on contemporary life and ideal male-female relationships resonated widely; many versions of the Tale circulated through handwritten copies. Even the Empress and the Regent were not immune. They promoted the author to a formal position within the court, a rare honour for a woman of that era.

Today, history has obscured her real name, so she is known as Murasaki, after one of her characters. Her Tale lives on, even a thousand years after it was written, undiminished as a literary masterpiece, and loved around the world.

Based on 'The Tale of Murasaki' by Liza Dalby.

Readers' Guide and Notes to Tables

The following tables contain data on gender equality and human development in countries in the Asia-Pacific region, including UNDP programme countries. The data are grouped into 11 dimensions that attempts to capture different aspects of gender inequality, including in human development and the macroeconomy, demography, health and mortality, education, assets and income, paid and unpaid work, political voice, influencing decisions, international conventions, legal instruments and gender measures. The most popular are composite indices of gender inequality are also presented. Data and indicators that track the relevant Millennium Development Goals (MDGs) are also included in the tables.

Data Coverage

For this Report, countries have been grouped into three categories: East Asia, South and West Asia, and the Pacific. The total number of countries is 39: 16 from **East Asia** (Brunei Darussalam, Cambodia, China, Democratic People's Republic of Korea, Indonesia, Japan, Lao Peoples' Democratic Republic, Malaysia, Mongolia, Myanmar, the Philippines, the Republic of Korea, Singapore, Thailand, Timor-Leste, Viet Nam); nine from **South and West Asia** (Afghanistan, Bangladesh, Bhutan, India, Islamic Republic of Iran, Maldives, Nepal, Pakistan, Sri Lanka); and 14 from the **Pacific** (Australia, Federated States of Micronesia, Fiji, Kiribati, Marshall Islands, Nauru, New Zealand, Palau, Papua New Guinea, Samoa, Solomon Islands, Tonga, Tuvalu, Vanuatu). Within sub-regions, countries are arranged according to

HDI value (2007) in descending order. Countries that do not have an HDI ranking are placed at the end of the sub-sections in the tables.

Data Sources and Inconsistencies

For the production of the Asia-Pacific Human Development Reports, the Regional Human Development Report Unit is a user of data, not a producer. As such, it uses data produced by international institutions with the resources and expertise to do so. Data sources are given in abbreviated form at the end of each table, while the full citations are available in the statistical reference. These sources include online databases, reports of international institutions, the official websites of governments, public universities and websites showing national legislation. The databases include the United Nations Statistics Division, United Nations Treaty Collection, UNESCO Institute for Statistics, World Development Indicators online and GenderStats online of The World Bank, ILOLEX Database of International Labour Standards of ILO, the Institutions and Development Database (GID-DB) of OECD, and the Inter Parliamentary Union (IPU). Reports include UNDP's global Human Development Report 2009 and 2007/2008, UNDP's Human Development Indices: A Statistical Update 2008, UNIFEM's Report on the Progress of the World's Women 2008/2009, the UNDP Pacific Centre and UNIFEM Pacific Regional Office Report on Translating CEDAW into Law 2007, reports of State Parties to the UN Committee on CEDAW, the World Economic Forum's Global Gender Gap

Report 2009, and the 2008 Social Watch Report. URLs of online sources may change over time, which explains why the date of access of a given website is mentioned for all online sources.

Because international sources often rely on data supplied by national authorities, there can be inconsistencies between the data reported by these two sources. There are several reasons for this. International data agencies often apply international standards and harmonization procedures to improve comparability across countries. Missing data points for a country may be produced by an estimate based on various methodologies, even a small national survey. Because of the difficulties in coordination between national and international data agencies, international data series may not incorporate the most recent data, which often explains the time lag in data from international sources. All these factors can lead to inconsistencies between national and international estimates.

A note of caution: since international agencies continually improve their data series, some indicators may not be comparable across countries or even temporally.

Time Period

This Report uses the most recent information available at the time the material went to print. Data are presented at different points in time in order to capture trends, starting from 1990. For most indicators, data are reported at ten-year intervals (i.e. 1990, 2000) and the latest year for which data are available. For example, the latest Gender Gap Index of the World Economic Forum refers to 2009, while the latest year for most socio-economic indicators is 2007. In cases where data for all three reference points (1990, 2000 and the latest year) are not available, data for the year nearest the reference points are used.

NOTES ON SELECTED INDICATORS

Acceptance of polygamy within society. Produced by the OECD, this indicator sheds light on the acceptance of polygamy (where a person has more than one spouse). The indicator scale varies between 0 = no and 1 = complete acceptance (OECD n.d.-a.).

Adult literacy rate (% aged 15 and older). See definitions of technical terms.

Contributing family workers (% of employed). A contributing family worker is defined according to the 1993 International Classification by Status in Employment (ICSE) as a person who works without pay in an economic enterprise operated by a related person living in the same household (UNDP 2007). The indicator shows the percentage of contributing family workers (female/male) to total employed (female/male).

Early marriage (women). Produced by OECD, this indicator refers to the number of girls between 15 and 19 years of age who are currently married, divorced or widowed as a percentage of all persons in that age group. These percentages are derived from census data classified by current marital status, sex and age group (OECD n.d.-a.).

Expected years of schooling. Expected years of schooling is the number of years a child of school entrance age is expected to spend at school or university, including years spent repeating one or more classes (World Bank 2009b).

Female legislators, senior officials and managers (% of total). Women's share of positions is defined according to the International Standard Classification of Occupations, including legislators, senior government officials, traditional chiefs and heads of villages, senior officials of special-interest organizations, corporate manages, directors and chief executives, production and operations department managers, and other department and general managers (UNDP 2007).

Gross (tertiary) school enrolment (%). Gross enrolment rate is the total enrolment, regardless of age, as a percentage of the population of the age group that officially corresponds to the level of education (World Bank 2009a). It is thus possible that gross tertiary enrolment rate will exceed 100 per cent.

Labour force participation rate (% of female/ male population aged 15+). See definitions of technical terms.

Life expectancy at birth. See definitions of technical terms.

Market activities (% of total work time). This encompasses time spent on activities such as employment in establishments, primary production not in establishments, services for income and other production of goods not in establishments, as defined according to the 1993 revised UN System of National Accounts (UNDP 2007).

Maternal mortality ratio (per 100,000 live births). See definitions of technical terms.

Missing women. Amartya Sen coined the term 'missing women' to refer to those who have died as a result of discriminatory treatment in access to health and nutrition (Sen 1990a, 1990b). There are several estimates of 'missing women' based on different methodologies. The latest and most robust estimate was given by Klasen and Wink (2002).

Mortality rate under age five (per 1,000 live births). This is the probability that a newborn baby will die before reaching age five, if subject to current age-specific mortality rates (WHO 2008).

Net (primary/secondary) school enrolment (%). Net enrolment rate indicates children of official school age (based on the International Standard Classification of Education 1997) who are enrolled in school as a percentage of the population of the corresponding official school age (World Bank 2009a).

Non market activities (% of total work time). This comprises time spent on activities such as household maintenance (cleaning, laundry, meal preparation and clean up), management and shopping for own household; care for children, the sick, the elderly and the disabled in own household; and community services, as defined according to the 1993 revised UN System of National Accounts (UNDP 2007).

Population aged 15-19 ever married (%). This refers to the percentage of women and men in that age group who are currently married, and those who had been married in the past but are currently divorced or widowed. In general, these percentages are derived from census or survey data on the population classified by their current marital status, sex and age group. The indicator is a useful measure of the prevalence of marriage at young ages (UN 2008b).

Prevalence of HIV (% people aged 15-49). Refers to people in the age group of 15-49 years who are infected with HIV as a percentage of total persons in that age group (World Bank 2009a).

Primary completion rate (% of relevant age group). Primary completion rate is the percentage of students completing the last year of primary school. It is calculated by taking the total number of students in the last grade of primary school, minus the number of repeaters in that grade, divided by the total number of children of official graduation age (World Bank 2009a).

Progression to secondary school (%). Progression to secondary school refers to the number of new entrants to the first grade of secondary school in a given year as a percentage of the number of students enrolled in the final grade of primary school in the previous year (World Bank 2009a).

Share of women employed in the non-agricultural sector (% of total nonagricultural employment). See definitions of technical terms.

Singulate mean age at marriage. This indicator is an estimate of the average number of years lived prior to first marriage, if people marry before age 50 (UN 2008b).

Unemployment (% of female/male labour force). See definitions of technical terms.

Wage equality for similar work (female-over-male ratio). This ratio refers to female wage over male wage for similar work. It is based on data in the World Economic Forum's Executive Opinion Survey 2009 (Hausmann et al. 2009).

Women's access to bank loans. Produced by OECD, women's access to bank loans is measured on a scale from 0 = full to 1 = impossible. Variations between 0 and 1 indicate the extent of restrictions or the size of the female population for which the restrictions are relevant. One signifies complete discrimination against women (Jütting et al. 2006).

Women's access to land. Produced by OECD,

women's access to land ownership indicates the quality of women's ownership rights. It is measured by a scale from 0 = full to 1 = impossible. Variations between 0 and 1 indicate the extent of restrictions or the size of the female population for which the restrictions are relevant. One signifies complete discrimination against women (Jütting et al. 2006).

Women's access to property other than land. Produced by OECD, women's access to property other than land indicates the quality of women's ownership rights. It is measured by a scale from 0 = full to 1 = impossible. Variations between 0 and 1 indicate the extent of restrictions or the size of the female population for which the restrictions are relevant. One signifies complete discrimination against women (Jütting et al. 2006).

New Indicators Compiled by HDRU [1]

Ambassadors (% female). This indicator shows the share of female ambassadors as a percentage of total ambassadors appointed by a country, as per data compiled during June 2009. The HDRU used the following methodology for the calculation of this indicator: *First*, the list of embassies of the country was obtained from the official ministry website. *Second*, from each embassy website the name of the ambassador (ambassadors are named as high commissioners in commonwealth member states) was obtained. *Third*, all ambassadors of a country were disaggregated by male and female. *Finally*, the percentage of female ambassadors was calculated. Data was compiled for the following Asia-Pacific countries: Bangladesh, Brunei Darussalam, Cambodia, Fiji, India, Indonesia, Malaysia,

---

[1] To the best of our knowledge, these indicators are not available in any readily accessible publication. They have been compiled by the Human Development Report Unit (HDRU) based on extensive Internet research.

Maldives, Myanmar, New Zealand, Pakistan, the Philippines, Samoa, Sri Lanka, Timor-Leste and Viet Nam. This indicator was not compiled for other countries in the region because some countries do not have an official website listing ambassadors, some official websites do not provide full information about ambassadors, and some official websites do not provide information in English.

Heads of universities (% female). This shows the proportion of female university heads (vice-chancellors and faculty heads) as a percentage of total university heads in a country, as per data compiled during June 2009. The HDRU used the following methodology for the calculation of this indicator: *First*, a list of public universities was obtained from official ministry of education websites in each country. *Second*, a list of female and male university heads (vice-chancellors and faculty heads) was obtained from each public university website and the numbers were summed up. In some universities faculty heads are not mentioned. In such cases deprtment heads were counted as faculty heads. *Finally,* the percentage of female heads was calculated. Universities that do not have official web sites and universities with inadequate information were left out. This constraint, together with those of time and resources, allowed for the compilation of this indicator for a small sample of countries covering all the sub-regions: Cambodia, Malaysia, the Philippines, Singapore and Viet Nam from East Asia; New Zealand and Samoa from the Pacific; and Bangladesh, India, Maldives, Nepal and Sri Lanka from South Asia.

Judges in higher judiciary (% female). This indicator shows the percentage of female judges in the higher judiciary of a country, as per data compiled during June 2009. Higher judiciary refers to high and supreme courts (or their equivalent). The HDRU used the following methodology for the calculation of

this indicator: *First*, a list of judges was collected from the official websites of the supreme and high courts in a country. *Second,* the total number of judges was disaggregated by males and females. *Finally*, female judges were calculated as a percentage of the total number. Issues in compiling this indicator included: the absence of official websites, availability of data for only Supreme Court judges (Nepal and Mongolia), and availability of data for only High court judges (Bhutan). These limitations, together with those of time and resources, allowed for the compilation of this indicator for only a small sample of countries covering all the sub-regions: Japan, Malaysia, Mongolia and the Philippines from East Asia; Australia and Papua New Guinea from the Pacific; and Bhutan, India, Nepal, Pakistan and Sri Lanka from South Asia. The Court of Appeal in the Philippines is equivalent to a high court, the Federal Court in Malaysia is equivalent to a supreme court, and the National Court in Papua New Guinea is equivalent to a high court.

In addition to above three indicators, the HDRU compiled information on the legal status of women vis-à-vis men in terms of seven indicators vital to the three main sub-themes of the Report. The indicators include inheritance laws, marital property rights in case of divorce, nationality laws, gender based violence (three indicators) and paternity laws; they are not available in any database. They are, in effect, an innovative attempt to show gender inequality in legislation in Asia-Pacific countries.

The main sources for compiling these indicators were reports of States Parties to the UN Committee on the Elimination of Discrimination against Women (CEDAW). National legislation is used for countries where no information is available from these reports on specific indicators, or where laws have been changed and new laws have been promulgated since the last report to CEDAW.

For Pacific countries, the UNDP Pacific Centre and UNIFEM Pacific Regional Office Report 2007 is used. This joint study (Jivan and Forster 2007) assesses *de jure* national legislation in terms of its compliance with CEDAW for nine Pacific countries. Since only a few Pacific countries have submitted reports to the committee, the study is a useful source of information.

A detailed discussion of each indicator of legal status and its sources follows.

Inheritance law (land and property). This indicator assesses the legal status of women's inheritance rights vis-à-vis those of men. The assessment criterion is *equal* or *unequal* rights. The sources used include:

- Reports of States Parties to the UN Committee on CEDAW: Bangladesh, Bhutan, Cambodia, China, Democratic People's Republic of Korea, India, Lao Peoples' Democratic Republic, Malaysia, Mongolia, Myanmar, Nepal, New Zealand, the Philippines, the Republic of Korea, Thailand, Timor-Leste and Viet Nam.
- National legislation: Afghanistan, Australia, Indonesia, Islamic Republic of Iran, Maldives, Pakistan and Sri Lanka. Indonesia has a codified law on inheritance (Presidential Instruction No. 1 of 1991 on The Compilation of Islamic Law) that is not referred to in its 2005 report to CEDAW.
- UNDP Pacific Centre and UNIFEM Pacific Regional Office Report 2007: Federated States of Micronesia, Fiji, Kiribati, Marshall Islands, Papua New Guinea, Samoa, Solomon Islands, Tuvalu and Vanuatu.

Marital property rights in case of divorce. This indicator assesses the legal status of women vis-à-vis that of men with regard to the right to marital property after divorce. The

assessment criterion is *equal* or *unequal* rights. The sources include:

- Reports of States Parties to the UN Committee on CEDAW: Australia, Bangladesh, Bhutan, Cambodia, China, Democratic People's Republic of Korea, Indonesia, Lao Peoples' Democratic Republic, Malaysia, Mongolia, Myanmar, Nepal, New Zealand, Pakistan, the Philippines, the Republic of Korea, Singapore, Thailand, Timor-Leste and Viet Nam.
- National legislation: Maldives and Sri Lanka.
- UNDP Pacific Centre and UNIFEM Pacific Regional Office Report 2007: Federated States of Micronesia, Fiji, Kiribati, Marshall Islands, Papua New Guinea, Samoa, Solomon Islands, Tuvalu and Vanuatu.

Nationality law on marriage to foreign national. The indicator assesses the legal status of a female spouse vis-à-vis that of a male to retain, change or acquire nationality in case of marriage to a foreign national. The assessment criterion is *equal* or *unequal* rights. The sources include:

- Reports of States Parties to the UN Committee on CEDAW: Australia, Bangladesh, Bhutan, Cambodia, China, Democratic People's Republic of Korea, India, Lao Peoples' Democratic Republic, Malaysia, Maldives, Myanmar, New Zealand, Pakistan, the Philippines, the Republic of Korea, Singapore, Thailand, Timor-Leste and Viet Nam.
- National legislation: Indonesia, Mongolia, Nepal and Sri Lanka. Indonesia, for instance, amended its nationality law (Act No 12, 2006 concerning citizenship), but this is not referred to in its 2004 report to CEDAW.
- UNDP Pacific Centre and UNIFEM

Pacific Regional Office Report 2007: Federated States of Micronesia, Fiji, Kiribati, Marshall Islands, Papua New Guinea, Samoa, Solomon Islands, Tuvalu and Vanuatu.

Existence of legislation against gender-based violence (domestic violence). The indicator shows the existence or non-existence of laws on domestic violence. The indicator assigns 'yes' if legislation exists or 'no' if legislation is non-existent. The sources include:

- Reports of States Parties to the UN Committee on CEDAW: Australia, Bhutan, Cambodia, China, India, Japan, Lao Peoples' Democratic Republic, Malaysia, Maldives, Mongolia, Myanmar, New Zealand, the Philippines, the Republic of Korea, Singapore and Timor-Leste.
- National legislation: Indonesia, Nepal, Pakistan, Sri Lanka, Thailand and Viet Nam. Nepal, for instance, passed law on domestic violence in 2009, but the last report to CEDAW was submitted in 2003.
- UNDP Pacific Centre and UNIFEM Pacific Regional Office Report 2007: Federated States of Micronesia, Fiji, Kiribati, Marshall Islands, Papua New Guinea, Samoa, Solomon Islands, Tuvalu and Vanuatu.

Existence of legislation against gender-based violence (sexual assault/rape). The indicator shows the existence or non-existence of laws on rape/sexual assault. The indicator assigns 'yes' if legislation exists or 'no' if legislation is non-existent. The sources include:

- Reports of States Parties to the UN Committee on CEDAW: Australia, Bangladesh, Democratic People's Republic of Korea, India, Japan, Lao Peoples' Democratic Republic, Malaysia, Mongolia, Myanmar, Nepal, New Zealand, Pakistan, the Philippines, the

Republic of Korea, Singapore, Sri Lanka, Thailand and Timor-Leste.
- National legislation: China, Indonesia and Viet Nam. Viet Nam, for instance, does not mention the rape provision in its 2005 report to CEDAW.
- UNDP Pacific Centre and UNIFEM Pacific Regional Office Report 2007: Federated States of Micronesia, Fiji, Kiribati, Marshall Islands, Papua New Guinea, Samoa, Solomon Islands, Tuvalu and Vanuatu.

Existence of legislation against gender-based violence (sexual harassment in work places): The indicator shows the existence or non-existence of laws on sexual harassment in work places. The indicator assigns 'yes' if legislation exists or 'no' if legislation is non-existent. The sources include:

- Reports of States Parties to the UN Committee on CEDAW: Australia, Bangladesh, Bhutan, Cambodia, India, Indonesia, Japan, Lao Peoples' Democratic Republic, Malaysia, Maldives, Mongolia, Myanmar, Nepal, New Zealand, Pakistan, the Philippines, the Republic of Korea, Singapore, Thailand, Timor-Leste and Viet Nam.
- National legislation: Sri Lanka.
- UNDP Pacific Centre and UNIFEM Pacific Regional Office Report 2007: Federated States of Micronesia, Fiji, Kiribati, Marshall Islands, Papua New Guinea, Samoa, Solomon Islands, Tuvalu and Vanuatu.

Paternity law. This indicator shows the existence or non-existence of paternity laws. The indicator assigns 'yes' if legislation exists or 'no' if legislation is non-existent. The sources include:

- Reports of States Parties to the UN Committee on CEDAW: Australia,

Bhutan, India, Japan, Malaysia, New Zealand, the Philippines and Singapore.
- National legislation: Mongolia.
- UNDP Pacific Centre and UNIFEM Pacific Regional Office Report 2007: Federated States of Micronesia, Fiji, Kiribati, Marshall Islands, Papua New Guinea, Samoa, Solomon Islands, Tuvalu and Vanuatu.

Gender Measures

As is now well known, UNDP introduced two new composite indices in its 1995 Human Development Report. The Gender-related Development Index (GDI) assesses the impact of gender inequality on human development. It adjusts the Human Development Index (HDI) by imposing a welfare penalty on gender gaps in the HDI's three components. The Gender Empowerment Measure (GEM) measures the extent to which there is gender equity in economic and political power. It reflects gender equity in participation in governmental and managerial decision-making and professional roles, and economic activity.

Since 1995, there have been several other attempts to construct indices based on gender-disaggregated data. This Report presents the five most popular indices that aggregate gender-differentiated data on most countries of the world (Hawken and Munck 2009). Besides the GDI and GEM, these include Social Watch's Gender Equity Index (GEI), the World Economic Forum's Global Gender Gap Index (GGI) and the OECD's Social Institutions and Gender Index (SIGI). These are briefly introduced here.

I. UNDP's Gender-related Development Index (GDI)

While the HDI measures average achievement in basic human development capabilities, the GDI adjusts this to reflect the inequalities between men and women in three dimensions: a long and healthy life, knowledge and a decent standard of living (UNDP 2007). The GDI covered 155 countries/areas in 2007, varying between 0 (minimum) and 1 (maximum). Higher values indicate greater gender equality.

Dimensions and Indicators

1. *A long and healthy life is based on one indicator*
   Life expectancy at birth.
2. *Knowledge is based on two indicators*
   Adult literacy rate; and
   Combined primary, secondary and tertiary gross enrolment ratios.
3. *A decent standard of living is based on one indicator*
   Estimated earned income (PPP US $).

II. UNDP's Gender Empowerment Measure (GEM)

Focusing on women's opportunities rather than their capabilities, the GEM captures gender inequality in three key areas: political participation and decision-making power, economic participation and decision-making power, and power over economic resources (UNDP 2007). The GEM covered 109 countries/areas in 2007, ranging between 0 (minimum) and 1 (maximum). Higher values indicate greater gender equality.

Dimensions and Indicators

1. *Political participation and decision-making power is measured by one indicator*
   Women's and men's percentage shares of parliamentary seats.
2. *Economic participation and decision-making power is measured by two indicators*
   Women's and men's percentage shares of positions as legislators, senior officials and managers; and
   Women's and men's percentage shares of professional and technical positions.

3. *Power over economic resources is measured by one indicator*
   Women's and men's estimated earned income (PPP US $).

III. *The World Economic Forum's Gender Gap Index (GGI)*

The GGI captures gender gaps by drawing on 14 indicators, grouped into four dimensions: economic participation and opportunity, educational attainment, health and survival and political empowerment (Hausmann et al. 2009). The GGI covered 134 countries/areas in 2009, varying between 0 and 1. Higher values indicate greater gender equality (or a lower gender gap).

Dimensions and Indicators

1. *Economic participation and opportunity comprises five indicators*
   Ratio of female labour force participation over male value;
   Wage equality between women and men for similar work (female-over-male ratio);
   Ratio of estimated female earned income over male value;
   Ratio of female legislators, senior officials and managers over male value; and
   Ratio of female professional and technical workers over male value.
2. *Educational attainment comprises four indicators*
   Ratio of female literacy rate over male value;
   Ratio of female net primary level enrolment over male value;
   Ratio of female net secondary level enrolment over male value; and
   Ratio of female gross tertiary enrolment over male value.
3. *Health and survival comprises two indicators*
   Ratio of female healthy life expectancy over male value; and

Sex ratio at birth (converted to female-over-male ratio).
4. *Political empowerment comprises three indicators*
   Ratio of women with seats in parliament over male value;
   Ratio of women at ministerial level over male value; and
   Ratio of number of years of a female head of state (last 50 years) over male value.

IV. *Social Watch's Gender Equity Index (GEI)*

This index captures gender inequity by drawing upon 10 indicators in three different dimensions: empowerment, economic activity and education (Social Watch n.d.). In 2008, the GEI covered 157 countries, ranging between 0 per cent (maximum gender gap) to 100 per cent (no gender gap).

Dimensions and Indicators

1. *The empowerment dimension comprises four indicators*
   Percentage of women in technical positions;
   Percentage of women in management and government positions;
   Percentage of women in parliaments; and
   Percentage of women in ministerial posts.
2. *The economic activity dimension comprises two indicators*
   Estimated earned income (PPP, US $, female and male); and
   Labour force participation rate (female and male).
3. *The education dimension comprises four indicators*
   Literacy rate (for youth ages 15-24, female and male);
   Primary school enrolment rate (net, female and male);
   Secondary school enrolment rate (net, female and male); and

Tertiary education enrolment rate (gross, female and male).

V. OECD's Social Institutions and Gender Index (SIGI)

The SIGI draws on 12 innovative indicators on social institutions, which are grouped into five dimensions: family code, physical integrity, son preference, civil liberties and ownership rights (OECD n.d.-a.). The SIGI 2009 covers 102 non-OECD countries, varying between 0 and 1. As opposed to the above four indices, higher values of the SIGI show higher gender inequality.

Dimensions and Indicators

1. *The family code dimension refers to institutions that influence the decision-making power of women in the household. It comprises four indicators*

   Early marriage measures the percentage of girls between the ages of 15 and 19 who are married, divorced or widowed, providing an indication of forced or arranged marriages;

   Polygamy measures the acceptance within a society of men having multiple wives. Women in polygamous relationships are frequently prevented from pursuing a pro-fessional or academic career and are generally much younger than their husband;

   Parental authority measures whether women have the same right to be a legal guardian of a child during marriage, and whether women have custody rights over a child after divorce;

   Inheritance measures whether widows and daughters have equal rights as heirs. In many countries, inheritance is the only way in which women can obtain ownership of land, for example.

2. *Physical integrity comprises two indicators*

   Violence against women measures the existence of women's legal protection against violent attacks such as rape, assault and sexual harassment;

   Female genital mutilation measures the share of women who have been subjected to any type of female genital cutting.

3. *Son preference reflects the economic valuation of women. It is based on one indicator*

   Missing women measures gender bias in mortality due to sex selective abortions or insufficient care given to baby girls.

4. *Civil liberties comprises two indicators*

   Freedom of movement measures the level of restrictions women face in moving freely outside of their own household, for example by being able to go shopping or visit friends without being escorted by male members of the family;

   Freedom of dress measures the extent to which women are obliged to follow a certain dress code in public; for example, in some countries, women may be required to cover their face or body when leaving the house.

5. *Ownership rights cover women's rights and de facto access to several types of property. It includes three indicators*

   Women's access to land measures women's rights and de facto access to agricultural land;

   Women access to property other than land measures women's rights and de facto access to other types of property, especially immovable property;

   Women's access to credit measures women's rights and de facto access to bank loans. Even though women generally have the legal right to obtain credit, they frequently face restrictions, as when banks ask for the written permission of a woman's husband or require land as collateral, an asset women frequently don't have.

HDI AND MACROECONOMY

TABLE 1

		HDI TRENDS			
		HDI trends			
By HDI rank (2007)		*1990*	*1995*	*2000*	*2007*
East Asia					
10	Japan	0.918	0.931	0.943	0.960
23	Singapore	0.851	0.884	..	0.944
26	Korea (Republic of)	0.802	0.837	0.869	0.937
30	Brunei Darussalam	0.876	0.889	0.905	0.920
66	Malaysia	0.737	0.767	0.797	0.829
87	Thailand	0.706	0.727	0.753	0.783
92	China	0.608	0.657	0.719	0.772
105	Philippines	0.697	0.713	0.726	0.751
111	Indonesia	0.624	0.658	0.673	0.734
115	Mongolia	..	..	0.676	0.727
116	Viet Nam	0.599	0.647	0.690	0.725
133	Lao People's Democratic Republic	..	0.518	0.566	0.619
137	Cambodia	..	..	0.515	0.593
138	Myanmar	0.487	0.506	..	0.586
162	Timor-Leste	..	..	..	0.489
	Korea (Democratic People's Republic of)	..	..	..	..
South and West Asia					
88	Iran (Islamic Republic of)	0.672	0.712	0.738	0.782
95	Maldives	..	0.683	0.730	0.771
102	Sri Lanka	0.683	0.696	0.729	0.759
132	Bhutan	..	..	..	0.619
134	India	0.489	0.511	0.556	0.612
141	Pakistan	0.449	0.469	..	0.572
144	Nepal	0.407	0.436	0.500	0.553
146	Bangladesh	0.389	0.415	0.493	0.543
181	Afghanistan	..	..	..	0.352
Pacific					
2	Australia	0.902	0.938	0.954	0.970
20	New Zealand	0.884	0.911	0.930	0.950
94	Samoa	0.697	0.716	0.742	0.771
99	Tonga	..	..	0.759	0.768
108	Fiji	..	..	..	0.741
126	Vanuatu	..	..	0.663	0.693
135	Solomon Islands	..	..	..	0.610
148	Papua New Guinea	0.432	0.461	..	0.541
	Kiribati	..	..	..	..
	Marshall Islands	..	..	..	..
	Micronesia (Federated States of)	..	..	..	..
	Nauru	..	..	..	..
	Palau	..	..	..	..
	Tuvalu	..	..	..	..

Notes: Countries without HDI rankings in this statistical annex do not have HDI values. In such cases, these countries are placed at the end of the sub-sections in the table. All tables follow this arrangement of countries.
.. implies data not available (valid for all tables).
Source: UNDP 2009.

TABLE 2

MACROECONOMIC INDICATORS

By HDI rank (2007)	GDP per capita (constant 2000 US$)[a]			Real GDP growth (annual %)[a]			Inequality: Ratio of expenditure shares of richest 20% to poorest 20%[b]	MDG Population below income poverty line (%)[c]	
								$1.25 per day (PPP)	$2 per day (PPP)
	1990	2000	2007	1990	2000	2007	1990–2004	2000–2006	2000–2006
East Asia									
10 Japan	33369	36789	40745	5.2	2.9	2.1	3.4	..	..
23 Singapore	14658	23019	28964	9.2	10.1	7.7	9.7	..	..
26 Korea (Republic of)	6615	10884	14563	9.2	8.5	5.0	4.7	..	..
30 Brunei Darussalam	18713	17996	17944	1.1	2.8	0.6	..	..	..
66 Malaysia	2608	4030	5009	9.0	8.9	6.3	12.4	< 2	7.8
87 Thailand	1462	2023	2713	11.2	4.8	4.8	7.7	< 2	11.5
92 China	392	949	1811	3.8	8.4	13.0	12.2	15.9	36.3
105 Philippines	918	996	1215	3.0	6.0	7.2	9.3	22.6	45.0
111 Indonesia	612	800	1034	9.0	4.9	6.3	5.2	21.4	53.8
115 Mongolia	522	454	684	–2.5	0.5	10.2	5.4	22.4	49.0
116 Viet Nam	227	402	617	5.1	6.8	8.5	4.9	21.5	48.4
133 Lao People's Democratic Republic	231	332	468	5.6	5.8	7.9	5.4	44.0	76.8
137 Cambodia	..	293	495	..	8.8	10.2	7.3	40.2	68.2
138 Myanmar	..	..	..	2.8	9.8	..	..	..	..
162 Timor-Leste	..	406	301	..	13.7	7.8	..	52.9	77.5
Korea (Democratic People's Republic of)	..	..	..	..	..	..	..	..	..
South and West Asia									
88 Iran (Islamic Republic of)	1292	1584	2137	13.7	5.1	7.8	9.7	< 2	8.0
95 Maldives	..	2287	3244	..	4.8	6.6	..	..	..
102 Sri Lanka	574	873	1140	6.4	6.0	6.8	6.9	14.0	39.7
132 Bhutan	504	801	1277	10.7	7.2	19.1	..	26.2	49.5
134 India	318	453	686	5.5	4.0	9.1	5.6	41.6	75.6
141 Pakistan	465	536	654	4.5	4.3	6.0	4.3	22.6	60.3
144 Nepal	177	225	246	4.6	6.2	3.2	9.1	55.1	77.6
146 Bangladesh	261	338	439	5.9	5.9	6.4	4.9	49.6	81.3
181 Afghanistan	..	..	..	..	..	..	..	..	..
Pacific									
2 Australia	17147	21151	23936	3.9	4.0	3.3	7.0	..	..
20 New Zealand	11106	13193	15178	0.0	2.4	3.0	6.8	..	..
94 Samoa	1124	1339	1713	–4.4	7.0	6.1	..	..	..
99 Tonga	1256	1557	1666	–2.0	3.6	–0.3	..	..	..
108 Fiji	1807	2108	2202	3.6	–1.7	–6.6	..	..	..
126 Vanuatu	1252	1289	1275	11.7	2.7	5.0	..	..	..
135 Solomon Islands	748	721	764	1.8	–14.3	10.2	..	..	..
148 Papua New Guinea	571	654	656	–3.0	–2.5	6.2	12.6	..	..
Kiribati	411	556	487	2.1	–0.1	1.7	..	..	..
Marshall Islands	2639	2097	2282	7.0	0.9	3.5	..	..	..
Micronesia (Federated States of)	1970	2028	1851	1.9	4.7	–3.2	..	..	..
Nauru	..	..	..	..	..	..	..	..	..
Palau	..	6266	6702	..	0.3	2.5	..	..	..
Tuvalu	..	..	..	..	..	..	..	..	..

Sources: (a) World Bank 2009a; (b) UNDP 2007; (c) UNDP 2008.

DEMOGRAPHY

TABLE 3																
	DEMOGRAPHIC TRENDS															
By HDI rank (2007)	Total population (millions)[a]			Female population (% total population)[a]			Male-female sex ratio at birth[b]		Male-female sex ratio by age group 1997–2006[c]				Total fertility rate[b]		
	1990	2000	2007	1990	2000	2007	1990-1995	2000-2005	0-4 years	5–14 years	15–49 years	60+ years	1990-1995	1995-2000	2000-2005
East Asia															
10 Japan	123.5	126.9	127.8	50.9	51.1	50.7	1.06	1.06	1.05	1.05	1.02	0.78	1.5	1.4	1.3
23 Singapore	3.0	4.0	4.6	49.7	49.6	49.5	1.07	1.07	1.06	1.06	0.98	0.85	1.8	1.6	1.4
26 Korea (Republic of)	42.9	47.0	48.5	49.7	49.9	49.9	1.10	1.10	1.08	1.11	1.04	0.73	1.7	1.5	1.2
30 Brunei Darussalam	0.3	0.3	0.4	47.1	47.9	48.2	1.06	1.06	..	1.09	1.01	0.96	3.1	2.7	2.3
66 Malaysia	18.1	23.3	26.5	49.3	49.1	49.1	1.06	1.06	1.07	1.06	1.03	0.91	3.5	3.1	2.9
87 Thailand	54.3	60.7	63.8	50.4	50.9	51.2	1.05	1.05	1.04	1.05	0.97	0.81	2.1	1.9	1.8
92 China	1135.2	1262.6	1318.3	48.4	48.3	48.2	1.15	1.21	1.20	1.12	1.05	0.95	2.0	1.8	1.8
105 Philippines	61.2	76.2	87.9	49.6	49.6	49.6	1.06	1.06	1.05	1.05	1.01	0.88	4.1	3.7	3.3
111 Indonesia	178.2	206.3	225.6	49.9	50.0	50.0	1.05	1.05	1.04	1.06	0.99	0.94	2.9	2.6	2.4
115 Mongolia	2.1	2.4	2.6	50.1	50.0	50.1	1.05	1.05	1.02	1.01	0.99	0.79	3.5	2.4	2.1
116 Viet Nam	66.2	77.6	85.2	50.2	50.0	49.9	1.05	1.05	1.06	1.05	0.97	0.70	3.3	2.5	2.3
133 Lao People's Democratic Republic	4.1	5.2	5.9	49.9	50.0	50.1	1.05	1.05	1.01	1.03	0.99	0.89	5.8	5.2	3.9
137 Cambodia	9.7	12.8	14.4	52.4	51.5	51.2	1.05	1.05	1.04	1.05	0.88	0.72	5.5	4.5	3.4
138 Myanmar	40.1	45.9	48.8	50.2	50.3	50.4	1.03	1.03	1.02	1.01	1.01	0.84	3.1	2.7	2.4
162 Timor-Leste	0.7	0.8	1.1	48.5	48.9	49.2	1.05	1.05	..	..	..	..	5.7	7.0	7.0
Korea (Democratic Peoples Republic of)	20.1	22.9	23.8	51.0	50.9	50.6	1.05	1.05	..	..	..	..	2.4	2.1	1.9
South and West Asia															
88 Iran (Islamic Republic of)	54.4	63.9	71.0	48.8	49.2	49.2	1.05	1.05	1.05	1.08	1.02	1.06	4.0	2.5	2.1
95 Maldives	0.2	0.3	0.3	48.7	48.7	48.7	1.04	1.04	1.04	1.06	0.97	1.20	5.3	3.4	2.4
102 Sri Lanka	17.1	18.7	20.0	49.5	50.1	50.5	1.04	1.04	1.03	1.03	0.97	0.89	2.5	2.2	2.3
132 Bhutan	0.5	0.6	0.7	48.7	49.3	47.2	1.04	1.04	1.01	1.02	1.17	1.07	5.4	4.2	3.4
134 India	849.5	1015.9	1124.8	48.0	48.1	48.2	1.08	1.08	1.07	1.10	1.07	0.97	3.9	3.5	3.1
141 Pakistan	108.0	138.1	162.5	48.4	48.5	48.5	1.05	1.05	1.04	1.08	1.04	1.25	5.7	5.0	4.4
144 Nepal	19.1	24.4	28.1	49.6	50.3	50.4	1.05	1.05	1.03	1.05	0.95	1.02	4.9	4.4	3.6
146 Bangladesh	113.0	139.4	158.6	48.5	48.7	48.8	1.04	1.04	..	..	..	..	4.0	3.3	2.8
181 Afghanistan	..	..	..	..	..	..	1.06	1.06	..	..	..	..	8.0	8.0	7.3

Contd...

Contd...

By HDI rank (2007)	Total population (millions)[a]			Female population (% total population)[a]			Male-female sex ratio at birth[b]		Male-female sex ratio by age group 1997–2006[c]				Total fertility rate[b]		
	1990	*2000*	*2007*	*1990*	*2000*	*2007*	*1990-1995*	*2000-2005*	*0-4 years*	*5–14 years*	*15–49 years*	*60+ years*	*1990-1995*	*1995-2000*	*2000-2005*
Pacific															
2 Australia	17.1	19.2	21.0	50.1	50.4	49.9	1.05	1.05	1.06	1.05	1.01	0.87	1.9	1.8	1.8
20 New Zealand	3.4	3.9	4.2	50.7	50.9	50.4	1.06	1.06	..	1.05	..	..	2.1	2.0	1.9
94 Samoa	0.2	0.2	0.2	47.5	48.0	47.9	1.08	1.08	1.10	1.09	1.12	0.90	4.7	4.5	4.5
99 Tonga	0.1	0.1	0.1	49.6	49.2	48.9	1.05	1.05	1.07	1.11	1.03	1.00	4.5	4.2	4.2
108 Fiji	0.7	0.8	0.8	49.2	49.2	49.2	1.06	1.06	..	..	..	..	3.4	3.2	3.0
126 Vanuatu	0.1	0.2	0.2	48.5	48.8	48.9	1.07	1.07	1.06	1.08	1.01	1.10	4.8	4.6	4.3
135 Solomon Islands	0.3	0.4	0.5	48.2	48.2	48.2	1.09	1.09	..	..	..	..	5.5	4.9	4.4
148 Papua New Guinea	4.1	5.4	6.3	48.2	49.0	49.2	1.08	1.08	1.08	1.12	1.04	1.23	4.7	4.6	4.4
Kiribati	0.1	0.1	0.1	..	..	..	..	..	1.06	1.05	0.96	0.71	..	..	..
Marshall Islands	0.0	0.1	0.1	..	..	..	..	..	1.05	1.06	1.04	0.98	..	..	..
Micronesia (Federated States of)	0.1	0.1	0.1	48.9	49.4	49.0	1.07	1.07	1.05	1.09	1.01	0.86	4.8	4.5	4.1
Nauru	..	..	..	..	..	..	..	..	..	..	..	..	..	..	..
Palau	0.0	0.0	0.0	..	..	..	..	..	1.01	1.06	1.29	0.78	..	..	..
Tuvalu	..	..	..	..	..	..	..	..	1.11	1.12	0.96	0.75	..	..	..

Sources: (a) World Bank 2009a; (b) UN 2009; (c) Calculated based on data from UN 2008a.

TABLE 4

Social Trends

By HDI rank (2007)	Missing women (million)[a]	Early marriage (women)[b]	Poly-gamy[b]	Population aged 15-19 ever married or in union (%)[c]			Singulate mean age at marriage[c]		
	2007			Year	Female	Male	Year	Female	Male
East Asia									
10 Japan	..	1.0	0.0	2000	0.9	0.5	2000	29	31
23 Singapore	..	1.0	..	2000	1.0	0.1	2001	27	30
26 Korea (Republic of)	0.2	..	..	2000	0.7	0.3	1995	26	29
30 Brunei Darussalam	..	..	..	2001	6.6	1.1	1991	25	27
66 Malaysia	..	5.0	0.7	2000	4.9	1.1	2000	25	29
87 Thailand	..	15.0	0.0	2000	11.1	3.4	1990	24	26
92 China	42.6	1.0	0.0	2000	1.2	0.3	1999	23	25
105 Philippines	..	10.0	0.0	1995	9.6	3.3	1995	24	27
111 Indonesia	..	13.0	0.5	2000	13.3	3.1	2000	23	26
115 Mongolia	..	6.0	..	2000	5.6	1.3	2000	24	26
116 Viet Nam	..	8.0	0.0	..	..	..	1997	22	..
133 Lao People's Democratic Republic	..	27.0	..	1995	19.7	6.4	2000	21	..
137 Cambodia	..	12.0	..	2004	10.5	1.6	1998	23	24
138 Myanmar	..	11.0	0.0	1991	10.7	3.3	1991	25	26
162 Timor-Leste	..	..	..	..	..	..	..	..	..
Korea (Democratic People's Republic of)	..	..	..	..	..	..	..	..	..
South and West Asia									
88 Iran (Islamic Republic of)	1.3	18.0	1.0	1996	17.7	2.5	1996	22	25
95 Maldives	..	..	..	2000	12.0	1.3	2000	22	26
102 Sri Lanka	0.0	7.0	0.5	..	..	..	1993	25	..
132 Bhutan	..	27.0	..	..	..	..	1990	21	24
134 India	42.7	30.0	0.2	1991	35.7	9.5	1999	20	25
141 Pakistan	6.1	21.0	1.0	2003	13.4	2.6	1998	21	26
144 Nepal	0.1	40.0	0.1	2001	33.6	11.9	2001	19	23
146 Bangladesh	3.2	48.0	1.0	1991	51.3	5.0	2000	19	..
181 Afghanistan	..	..	..	..	..	..	..	..	..
Pacific									
2 Australia	..	1.0	0.0	2001	1.0	0.4	2000	29	31
20 New Zealand	..	7.0	0.0	1991	1.1	0.4	1996	25	27
94 Samoa	..	..	..	..	..	..	1999	24	27
99 Tonga	..	..	..	1996	5.0	1.7	1996	26	28
108 Fiji	..	10.0	0.0	1986	13.3	2.4	1996	23	26
126 Vanuatu	..	..	..	1989	11.8	2.3	..	..	..
135 Solomon Islands	..	..	..	..	..	..	..	..	..
148 Papua New Guinea	..	21.0	..	..	..	..	1996	21	..
Kiribati	..	..	..	..	..	..	..	..	..
Marshall Islands	..	..	..	1999	14.2	7.6	..	..	..
Micronesia (Federated States of)	..	..	..	1994	10.2	4.2	..	..	..
Nauru	..	..	..	..	..	..	..	..	..
Palau	..	..	..	1995	8.9	2.0	..	..	..
Tuvalu	..	..	..	2002	10.7	2.0	..	..	..

Notes: Missing women: 'Missing women' refers to those who have died as a result of discriminatory treatment in access to health and nutrition. The figures here are calculated by applying 2007 female population on estimate of percentage of missing women by Klasen and Wink 2002.
Early marriage (women): Number of girls between 15 and 19 years of age who are currently married, divorced or widowed in a particular age group as a percentage of all persons in that age group (OECD n.d.-a.).
Polygamy: Acceptance of polygamy (i.e. the practice of marriage in which a person has more than one spouse) within a society (between 0 = no and 1 = complete acceptance) (OECD n.d.-a.).
Sources: (a) Data are estimates based on Klasen and Wink 2002 and World Bank 2000a; (b) OECD n.d.-a.; (c) UN 2008b.

HEALTH AND MORTALITY

TABLE 5						
INEQUALITIES: LIFE EXAPECTANCY						
By HDI rank (2007)	Life expectancy at birth					
	Female			Male		
	1990	2000	2006	1990	2000	2006
East Asia						
10 Japan	81.9	84.6	85.8	75.9	77.7	79.0
23 Singapore	76.9	80.1	82.6	71.9	76.1	77.8
26 Korea (Republic of)	75.5	79.6	82.4	67.3	72.3	75.7
30 Brunei Darussalam	76.4	78.6	79.5	72.1	73.9	74.8
66 Malaysia	72.5	75.1	76.5	68.2	70.3	71.8
87 Thailand	70.6	73.5	74.8	63.6	63.3	65.9
92 China	69.7	73.0	..	66.9	69.9	..
105 Philippines	67.8	71.8	73.6	63.6	67.5	69.2
111 Indonesia	63.5	69.4	..	60.0	65.7	..
115 Mongolia	62.7	67.6	..	59.0	61.6	..
116 Viet Nam	67.7	73.9	..	64.1	70.3	..
133 Lao People's Democratic Republic	55.8	62.1	65.3	53.4	59.7	62.5
137 Cambodia	56.6	59.1	61.4	53.3	54.0	56.6
138 Myanmar	61.1	63.2	64.9	57.0	57.1	58.6
162 Timor-Leste	47.7	57.5	..	46.1	56.0	..
Korea (Democratic People's Republic of)	73.6	69.7	69.2	66.5	64.1	64.9
South and West Asia						
88 Iran (Islamic Republic of)	66.0	70.0	72.0	64.0	68.0	69.0
95 Maldives	59.2	64.4	68.7	61.8	65.1	67.2
102 Sri Lanka	73.5	74.7	..	66.9	67.0	..
132 Bhutan	54.7	63.4	67.0	51.6	60.0	63.6
134 India	60.0	63.6	..	59.3	61.4	..
141 Pakistan	60.1	63.2	..	59.7	62.6	..
144 Nepal	54.2	60.8	63.7	54.7	60.2	62.8
146 Bangladesh	55.1	61.6	64.6	54.5	60.3	62.8
181 Afghanistan	41.3	41.9	43.5	41.4	42.0	43.5
Pacific						
2 Australia	80.2	82.0	83.5	74.0	76.6	78.7
20 New Zealand	78.4	81.3	82.0	72.5	76.1	78.0
94 Samoa	68.7	72.9	74.6	62.1	66.4	68.2
99 Tonga	71.1	72.8	74.1	68.6	70.8	72.1
108 Fiji	68.8	69.7	70.9	64.6	65.4	66.4
126 Vanuatu	65.0	69.5	71.8	62.0	66.0	68.0
135 Solomon Islands	57.8	62.3	64.2	57.0	61.1	62.5
148 Papua New Guinea	57.8	59.7	60.3	52.3	53.9	54.5
Kiribati	59.1	62.2	..	54.6	57.0	..
Marshall Islands	73.3	67.8	..	68.8	62.8	..
Micronesia (Federated States of)	66.8	68.0	69.1	65.7	66.8	67.6
Nauru	..	..	..	..	..	..
Palau	75.0	74.5	..	63.4	66.6	..
Tuvalu	..	..	..	..	..	..

Source: World Bank 2009a.

TABLE 6

INEQUALITIES: CHILD, ADULT AND MATERNAL HEALTH

By HDI rank (2007)	Infant mortality rate (per 1000 live births)[a] — MDG						Mortality rate under age 5 (per 1000 live births)[a] — MDG						Adult (15+ population) mortality rate (per 1000 adults)[b]						Maternal mortality ratio (per 100,000 live births)[b] — MDG
	Female			Male			Female			Male			Female			Male			2005
	1990	2000	2006	1990	2000	2006	1990	2000	2006	1990	2000	2006	1990	2000	2006	1990	2000	2006	
East Asia																			
10 Japan	4.0	3.0	3.0	5.0	4.0	3.0	6.0	4.0	3.0	7.0	5.0	4.0	53.5	47.6	44.3	108.8	98.3	89.7	6
23 Singapore	7.0	2.0	2.0	8.0	3.0	3.0	8.0	4.0	3.0	10.0	4.0	3.0	80.0	55.4	47.1	138.0	97.9	83.0	14
26 Korea (Republic of)	8.0	5.0	4.0	8.0	5.0	5.0	..	..	..	9.0	6.0	5.0	116.6	58.6	46.8	239.1	150.8	114.3	14
30 Brunei Darussalam	9.0	7.0	7.0	11.0	9.0	9.0	10.0	8.0	..	12.0	10.0	10.0	98.2	71.7	64.6	148.6	102.0	89.4	13
66 Malaysia	14.0	10.0	9.0	18.0	12.0	11.0	20.0	13.0	11.0	24.0	15.0	13.0	125.0	102.3	89.1	198.0	179.5	155.5	62
87 Thailand	22.0	10.0	7.0	30.0	13.0	8.0	26.0	11.0	7.0	36.0	14.0	8.0	123.0	174.2	161.6	206.9	325.6	276.0	110
92 China	43.0	36.0	24.0	31.0	25.0	17.0	52.0	42.0	27.0	40.0	32.0	21.0	135.0	106.1	92.1	160.0	164.9	153.1	45
105 Philippines	34.0	25.0	20.0	47.0	34.0	28.0	51.0	33.0	26.0	72.0	47.0	37.0	207.6	128.1	107.0	273.4	181.6	160.8	230
111 Indonesia	56.0	34.0	25.0	64.0	38.0	28.0	85.0	45.0	31.0	97.0	51.0	36.0	219.4	153.2	123.0	275.4	202.3	172.3	420
115 Mongolia	71.0	43.0	31.0	88.0	54.0	38.0	98.0	55.0	38.0	118.0	66.0	46.0	211.4	202.6	174.7	250.8	298.1	267.9	46
116 Viet Nam	38.0	23.0	15.0	38.0	23.0	14.0	51.0	29.0	16.0	55.0	31.0	17.0	153.1	112.3	93.1	215.0	158.1	139.2	150
133 Lao People's Democratic Republic	104.0	67.0	51.0	135.0	87.0	67.0	154.0	95.0	70.0	172.0	107.0	79.0	..	227.3	195.6	..	269.4	237.9	660
137 Cambodia	76.0	70.0	58.0	93.0	86.0	71.0	106.0	95.0	75.0	125.0	113.0	89.0	318.8	266.2	248.0	391.6	386.7	359.0	540
138 Myanmar	78.0	67.0	64.0	102.0	87.0	83.0	113.0	96.0	91.0	143.0	121.0	114.0	..	202.2	192.4	..	312.3	303.8	380
162 Timor-Leste	117.0	74.0	41.0	150.0	95.0	53.0	153.0	92.0	48.0	201.0	123.0	63.0	..	274.3	236.9	..	310.2	271.5	380
Korea (Democratic People's Republic of)	41.0	41.0	41.0	43.0	43.0	43.0	53.0	53.0	53.0	53.0	..	..	116.4	120.8	128.3	223.2	197.3	182.4	370
South and West Asia																			
88 Iran (Islamic Republic of)	46.0	31.0	26.0	62.0	41.0	34.0	69.0	42.0	33.0	75.0	46.0	36.0	174.3	122.5	103.9	169.7	172.0	155.3	140
95 Maldives	75.0	42.0	23.0	81.0	43.0	29.0	109.0	52.0	27.0	113.0	56.0	34.0	284.2	204.4	160.9	207.8	210.0	185.7	120
102 Sri Lanka	20.0	12.0	9.0	31.0	20.0	14.0	26.0	16.0	11.0	38.0	23.0	15.0	122.0	114.1	101.6	182.0	268.4	240.9	58
132 Bhutan	98.0	71.0	58.0	116.0	83.0	68.0	154.0	93.0	65.0	178.0	107.0	75.0	..	207.0	174.4	..	257.9	223.4	440
134 India	83.0	67.0	58.0	81.0	65.0	57.0	122.0	95.0	81.0	108.0	84.0	72.0	241.4	186.8	167.8	236.5	267.3	259.7	450
141 Pakistan	91.0	77.0	71.0	109.0	92.0	85.0	128.0	107.0	96.0	132.0	109.0	98.0	230.0	162.7	145.2	232.3	197.0	176.9	320
144 Nepal	99.0	64.0	46.0	98.0	63.0	46.0	140.0	85.0	59.0	144.0	87.0	60.0	375.7	240.6	211.3	349.8	263.3	235.4	830
146 Bangladesh	89.0	59.0	46.0	111.0	73.0	57.0	140.0	87.0	65.0	157.0	97.0	73.0	308.2	232.3	202.6	321.7	262.0	235.1	570
181 Afghanistan	156.0	154.0	154.0	179.0	176.0	176.0	257.0	254.0	254.0	263.0	260.0	260.0	476.0	434.9	418.0	486.0	462.0	444.7	1800

Contd...

Contd...

By HDI rank (2007)	MDG Infant mortality rate (per 1000 live births)[a]						MDG Mortality rate under age 5 (per 1000 live births)[a]						Adult (15+ population) mortality rate (per 1000 adults)[b]						MDG Maternal mortality ratio (per 100,000 live births)[b]
	Female			Male			Female			Male			Female			Male			
	1990	2000	2006	1990	2000	2006	1990	2000	2006	1990	2000	2006	1990	2000	2006	1990	2000	2006	2005
Pacific																			
2 Australia	7.0	5.0	4.0	9.0	6.0	6.0	8.0	6.0	5.0	10.0	7.0	6.0	67.0	55.4	47.8	125.4	96.6	84.0	4
20 New Zealand	7.0	6.0	4.0	10.0	7.0	6.0	9.0	7.0	6.0	13.0	9.0	7.0	93.1	67.1	58.8	142.9	104.2	91.7	9
94 Samoa	38.0	10.0	9.0	42.0	44.0	37.0	49.0	19.0	15.0	51.0	48.0	40.0	201.6	131.3	112.2	261.5	228.2	199.8	..
99 Tonga	30.0	25.0	22.0	24.0	20.0	18.0	35.0	29.0	25.0	30.0	25.0	22.0	193.8	131.6	117.8	260.1	161.2	143.8	..
108 Fiji	17.0	15.0	14.0	21.0	18.0	17.0	19.0	17.0	17.0	25.0	19.0	19.0	161.0	170.2	154.2	220.0	249.7	232.9	210
126 Vanuatu	46.0	37.0	28.0	48.0	38.0	30.0	58.0	45.0	34.0	62.0	48.0	36.0	241.2	152.3	128.1	288.0	198.8	176.4	..
135 Solomon Islands	84.0	64.0	54.0	86.0	65.0	55.0	123.0	89.0	74.0	118.0	86.0	71.0	..	225.5	206.6	253.8	237.9		220
148 Papua New Guinea	66.0	55.0	51.0	72.0	63.0	58.0	90.0	76.0	69.0	97.0	85.0	77.0	385.8	304.9	305.5	424.8	422.5	422.1	470
Kiribati	62.0	48.0	44.0	68.0	56.0	51.0	83.0	69.0	63.0	92.0	71.0	65.0	..	208.0	..	..	269.0	..	..
Marshall Islands	55.0	48.0	44.0	70.0	62.0	56.0	81.0	60.0	50.0	102.0	76.0	62.0	..	230.0	..	..	302.0	..	..
Micronesia (Federated States of)	45.0	37.0	33.0	45.0	37.0	33.0	57.0	46.0	41.0	58.0	47.0	41.0	255.9	168.4	156.6	315.7	191.1	181.3	..
Nauru	28.0	28.0	28.0	22.0	23.0	23.0	33.0	32.0	32.0	28.0	28.0	28.0	..	..	..	..	..	..	..
Palau	13.0	14.0	11.0	22.0	11.0	9.0	16.0	16.0	12.0	24.0	13.0	10.0	..	..	..	..	..	..	..
Tuvalu	38.0	28.0	32.0	46.0	40.0	30.0	48.0	40.0	38.0	58.0	45.0	37.0	..	..	..	..	..	..	..

Sources: (a) WHO 2008; (b) World Bank 2009a.

TABLE 7

	VULNERABILITY TO HIV			
	MGD			
By HDI rank (2007)	Prevalence of HIV (% people aged 15-49)		Adult females with HIV (% of HIV population aged 15 and above)	
	2000	2007	2001	2007
East Asia				
10 Japan	..	..	22.2	24.0
23 Singapore	0.1	0.2	34.5	29.3
26 Korea (Republic of)	..	0.1	26.5	27.7
30 Brunei Darussalam	..	..	..	..
66 Malaysia	0.3	0.5	23.3	26.6
87 Thailand	1.8	1.4	36.9	41.7
92 China	0.1	0.1	25.5	29.0
105 Philippines	..	..	50.0	26.8
111 Indonesia	0.1	0.2	10.8	20.0
115 Mongolia	..	0.1	..	20.0
116 Viet Nam	0.3	0.5	24.7	27.1
133 Lao People's Democratic Republic	0.1	0.2	45.5	24.1
137 Cambodia	1.6	0.8	25.8	28.6
138 Myanmar	0.9	0.7	33.4	41.7
162 Timor-Leste	..	..	..	..
Korea (Democratic People's Republic of)	..	..	..	..
South and West Asia				
88 Iran (Islamic Republic of)	0.1	0.2	26.7	28.2
95 Maldives	..	..	..	..
102 Sri Lanka	..	..	33.3	37.8
132 Bhutan	..	0.1	..	20.0
134 India	0.5	0.3	38.5	38.3
141 Pakistan	0.1	0.1	26.0	28.7
144 Nepal	0.5	0.5	21.8	25.0
146 Bangladesh	..	..	1.3	16.7
181 Afghanistan	..	..	..	..
Pacific				
2 Australia	0.1	0.2	7.1	6.7
20 New Zealand	0.1	0.1	16.7	35.7
94 Samoa	..	..	..	..
99 Tonga	..	..	..	..
108 Fiji	0.1	0.1	..	..
126 Vanuatu	..	..	..	..
135 Solomon Islands	..	..	..	..
148 Papua New Guinea	0.3	1.5	34.7	39.6
Kiribati	..	..	..	..
Marshall Islands	..	..	..	..
Micronesia (Federated States of)	..	..	..	..
Nauru	..	..	..	..
Palau	..	..	..	..
Tuvalu	..	..	..	..

Source: World Bank 2009a.

EDUCATION

TABLE 8

	INEQUALITIES: SCHOOL ENROLMENT												
	MDG						MDG						
By HDI rank (2007)	Net primary school enrolment (%)						Net secondary school enrolment (%)				Gross tertiary school enrolment (%)		
	Female			Male			Female		Male		Female		Male	
	1991	2000	2006	1991	2000	2006	2000	2006	2000	2006	2000	2006	2000	2006
East Asia														
10 Japan	99.9	..	..	99.6	..	..	100.0	98.9	98.9	98.5	43.6	53.5	51.0	60.9
23 Singapore	..	..	..	..	..	..	..	..	..	..	..	..	..	..
26 Korea (Republic of)	99.3	99.8	..	99.3	99.8	..	91.3	93.2	90.7	98.7	57.5	72.4	98.2	111.2
30 Brunei Darussalam	91.2	..	93.9	92.8	..	93.7	..	92.4	..	87.9	16.8	20.1	9.0	10.1
66 Malaysia	92.6	96.9	..	93.4	96.7	..	67.5	..	62.2	..	26.7	..	25.2	..
87 Thailand	87.4	..	93.9	88.1	..	94.5	..	74.7	..	67.5	38.4	47.5	32.0	44.4
92 China	96.1	..	..	99.7	..	..	..	..	..	..	..	21.3	..	21.8
105 Philippines	95.9	..	92.5	96.8	..	90.5	..	66.2	..	54.8	..	31.6	..	25.5
111 Indonesia	94.5	90.9	93.7	98.2	94.1	97.1	47.0	60.5	49.4	60.2	..	..	..	..
115 Mongolia	90.9	91.5	92.5	89.4	88.4	90.4	66.1	86.5	53.6	76.6	37.1	57.8	20.7	36.8
116 Viet Nam	86.4	..	..	94.2	..	..	..	..	..	..	7.9	..	11.0	..
133 Lao People's Democratic Republic	57.3	73.9	81.2	66.7	80.5	86.1	24.6	32.3	31.4	37.5	1.9	7.3	3.6	10.8
137 Cambodia	65.7	83.4	89.0	78.2	90.9	90.9	11.6	28.3	20.7	33.0	1.0	3.0	3.1	6.0
138 Myanmar	..	..	..	..	..	..	..	..	..	..	..	..	..	..
162 Timor-Leste	..	..	..	..	..	..	..	..	..	..	..	..	..	..
Korea (Democratic People's Republic of)	..	..	..	..	..	..	..	..	..	..	..	..	..	..
South and West Asia														
88 Iran (Islamic Republic of)	88.7	79.2	..	95.9	81.1	..	..	..	..	..	17.7	28.3	20.4	25.4
95 Maldives	86.7	98.7	97.4	86.8	97.8	97.4	42.7	70.0	36.9	64.5	..	..	..	..
102 Sri Lanka	82.3	..	..	86.2	..	..	..	..	..	..	..	..	..	..
132 Bhutan	..	55.7	79.2	..	61.9	78.9	19.2	38.7	19.2	38.3	2.1	4.0	4.1	6.8
134 India	..	72.3	86.8	..	85.4	90.4	..	..	..	..	7.6	9.9	11.5	13.6
141 Pakistan	..	..	57.3	..	..	73.5	16.8	25.8	24.2	33.3	..	4.2	..	4.9
144 Nepal	41.5	63.4	..	83.1	77.1	..	..	..	..	..	2.3	..	5.9	..
146 Bangladesh	70.8	83.9	..	81.4	83.0	..	44.0	..	42.2	..	3.6	4.9	7.1	8.6
181 Afghanistan	17.4	..	..	31.4	..	..	..	..	..	..	..	..	..	..
Pacific														
2 Australia	99.6	94.9	96.8	99.2	94.4	96.1	91.2	88.0	89.2	86.5	72.4	81.8	58.9	64.0
20 New Zealand	97.9	98.8	99.4	98.2	98.6	99.3	..	..	..	..	78.8	96.3	54.2	63.9
94 Samoa	..	90.7	..	..	89.5	..	68.6	..	60.0	..	7.1	..	7.7	..
99 Tonga	95.1	..	..	97.9	..	..	76.2	67.5	69.0	54.0	6.0	..	3.7	..
108 Fiji	..	97.5	91.1	..	97.6	91.4	79.7	82.8	72.7	75.6	..	..	..	..
126 Vanuatu	71.2	93.3	87.4	70.1	94.5	88.2	34.9	..	30.6	..	..	..	..	..
135 Solomon Islands	77.1	..	..	89.5	..	..	16.5	..	20.1	..	..	..	..	..
148 Papua New Guinea	60.8	..	..	71.0	..	..	..	..	..	..	..	..	..	..
Kiribati	..	..	..	..	..	..	..	..	..	..	..	..	..	..
Marshall Islands	..	..	..	..	..	..	..	..	..	..	..	..	..	..
Micronesia (Federated States of)	100.0	..	..	96.5	..	..	..	..	..	..	..	..	..	..
Nauru	..	..	..	..	..	..	..	..	..	..	..	..	..	..
Palau	..	94.5	..	..	98.3	..	..	..	..	..	57.7	..	24.5	..
Tuvalu	..	..	..	..	..	..	..	..	..	..	..	..	..	..

Note: Secondary and tertiary enrolment data are not available for most countries for the year 1991.
Source: World Bank 2009a.

TABLE 9

INEQUALITIES: EDUCATIONAL ATTAINMENT

By HDI rank (2007)	Adult literacy (% aged 15 and above)[a]		MDG Primary completion rate (% of relevant age group)[b]				MDG Progression to secondary school (%)[b]				Expected years of schooling[c]					
	Female	Male	Female		Male		Female		Male		Female			Male		
	1999–2007		2000	2006	2000	2006	2000	2006	2000	2006	1991	2000	2006	1991	2000	2006
East Asia																
10 Japan	..	..	..	..	..	..	..	..	..	..	13.0	14.4	14.8	13.5	14.7	15.1
23 Singapore	91.6	97.3	..	..	..	..	..	..	..	..	11.5	..	..	12.4	..	..
26 Korea (Republic of)	..	..	98.2	95.1	97.8	105.9	99.3	..	99.4	..	12.9	14.2	15.4	14.3	16.7	17.8
30 Brunei Darussalam	93.1	96.5	121.3	108.7	122.0	105.2	..	94.5	..	91.7	12.6	13.7	14.4	12.5	13.1	13.7
66 Malaysia	89.6	94.2	..	..	..	..	..	..	..	..	10.0	12.1	..	10.0	11.6	..
87 Thailand	92.6	95.9	..	..	..	..	..	88.8	..	84.9	9.6	..	13.9	9.9	..	13.2
92 China	90.0	96.5	..	..	..	..	..	..	..	..	8.7	..	11.2	10.0	..	11.2
105 Philippines	93.7	93.1	..	97.5	..	90.3	..	..	..	..	11.1	..	12.1	10.6	..	11.5
111 Indonesia	88.8	95.2	..	98.9	..	98.7	..	..	..	..	9.5	..	..	10.5	..	..
115 Mongolia	97.7	96.8	90.5	110.0	84.0	107.6	98.3	97.4	95.3	95.2	10.0	10.1	13.8	8.8	8.3	12.0
116 Viet Nam	86.9	93.9	93.5	..	98.3	..	92.0	..	94.0	..	7.2	..	..	7.9	10.7	..
133 Lao People's Democratic Republic	63.2	82.5	62.5	69.8	74.1	80.1	70.9	75.9	75.9	79.3	5.8	7.2	8.4	7.8	9.1	10.1
137 Cambodia	67.7	85.8	41.2	86.1	53.0	87.1	70.4	77.8	80.8	80.6	5.4	6.6	9.2	7.9	8.3	10.5
138 Myanmar	86.4	93.9	..	..	..	..	65.2	70.1	66.8	75.2	7.1	..	..	7.3	..	..
162 Timor-Leste	..	..	..	..	..	..	..	..	..	..	..	..	..	..	..	..
Korea (Democratic People's Republic of)	..	..	..	..	..	..	..	..	..	..	..	..	..	..	..	..
South and West Asia																
88 Iran (Islamic Republic of)	77.2	87.3	88.5	107.8	91.7	94.7	90.4	77.5	89.6	89.3	8.6	10.9	..	10.6	12.0	..
95 Maldives	97.1	97.0	..	127.0	..	130.7	..	85.4	..	76.5	..	12.6	12.3	..	12.4	12.2
102 Sri Lanka	89.1	92.7	..	106.8	..	105.6	..	..	..	..	11.7	..	..	11.6	..	..
132 Bhutan	38.7	65.0	48.6	73.1	56.2	73.3	82.6	..	82.3	..	3.6	7.1	10.0	5.3	8.5	10.6
134 India	54.5	76.9	64.3	83.1	79.7	88.0	84.5	..	88.1	..	6.3	7.3	9.4	9.1	9.4	10.6
141 Pakistan	39.6	67.7	..	52.9	..	70.2	..	..	..	..	3.1	..	5.7	5.8	..	7.3
144 Nepal	43.6	70.3	56.8	72.3	73.9	79.6	72.6	..	70.9	..	5.4	7.5	..	9.4	9.9	..
146 Bangladesh	48.0	58.7	80.0	..	74.9	..	89.1	..	79.2	..	4.7	8.5	..	6.5	8.6	..
181 Afghanistan	12.6	43.1	..	..	..	..	..	..	..	..	1.9	..	..	3.6	..	..
Pacific																
2 Australia	..	..	..	..	..	..	..	..	..	..	13.7	20.6	20.7	13.2	20.2	20.3
20 New Zealand	..	..	..	..	..	..	..	..	..	..	14.8	18.3	20.4	14.5	16.8	18.6
94 Samoa	98.4	98.9	96.1	..	93.5	..	99.4	..	95.7	..	12.2	12.4	..	10.5	11.8	..
99 Tonga	99.3	99.2	..	102.4	..	97.7	87.1	..	83.6	..	..	..	..	..	..	..
108 Fiji	..	..	99.5	97.8	101.3	98.4	96.6	..	100.0	..	8.5	..	..	8.8	..	..
126 Vanuatu	76.1	80.0	88.1	..	84.4	..	43.4	65.3	42.0	63.0	..	..	..	..	..	..
135 Solomon Islands	..	..	..	..	..	..	55.0	..	56.6	..	..	6.3	..	..	7.1	..
148 Papua New Guinea	53.4	62.1	..	..	..	..	..	..	..	..	4.2	..	..	5.3	..	..
Kiribati	..	..	95.0	..	102.5	..	..	..	..	..	..	14.2	..	..	11.4	..
Marshall Islands	..	..	..	..	..	..	..	..	..	..	..	..	..	..	..	..
Micronesia (Federated States of)	..	..	..	..	..	..	..	..	..	..	17.1	..	..	17.5	..	..
Nauru	..	..	..	..	..	..	..	..	..	..	..	..	..	..	..	..
Palau	90.5*	93.3	90.4	..	106.7	..	..	..	..	..	..	15.4	..	..	13.7	..
Tuvalu	..	..	..	..			..	..	..	..	..	..	..	..	..	..

Note: *Data refer to an earlier year than that specified.

Sources: (a) UNDP 2009; (b) World Bank 2009a; (c) World Bank 2009b.

ASSETS AND INCOME

TABLE 10

INIQUALITIES: ACCESS TO ASSETS AND INCOME

By HDI rank (2007)	Women's access to land *a	Women's access to bank loans *a	Women's access to property other than land *a	Technicians [b]			Researchers [b]			Estimated earned income (PPP US $) – 2007 [c]	
				Year	Total	Female (%)	Year	Total	Female (%)	Female	Male
East Asia											
10 Japan	0.0	0.0	0.0	2007	93841	32.0	2007	883386	13.0	21143	46706
23 Singapore	..	..	..	2007	3224	39.7	2007	31657	27.4	34554	64656
26 Korea (Republic of)	0.0	0.0	0.0	2007	94319	30.5	2007	289098	14.9	16931	32668
30 Brunei Darussalam	..	..	..	..	..	..	2004	244	40.6	36838	62631
66 Malaysia	0.0	0.2	0.0	..	..	..	2006	19021	37.7	7972	18886
87 Thailand	0.0	0.0	0.0	1996	4913	43.3	2005	34084	50.3	6341	10018
92 China	0.2	0.2	0.2	..	..	..	..	..	..	4323	6375
105 Philippines	0.0	0.0	0.0	..	..	..	2005	10690	52.0	2506	4293
111 Indonesia	0.2	0.2	0.2	..	..	..	2005	35564	30.6	2263	5163
115 Mongolia	..	..	..	2000	294	51.0	2007	1740	48.1	3019	3454
116 Viet Nam	0.5	0.3	0.3	..	..	..	2002	41117	42.8	2131	3069
133 Lao People's Democratic Republic	..	..	..	..	..	..	2002	209	23.0	1877	2455
137 Cambodia	..	..	..	..	..	..	2002	744	20.7	1465	2158
138 Myanmar	0.0	0.0	0.0	..	..	..	2002	4725	85.5	640	1043
162 Timor-Leste	..	..	..	..	..	..	..	..	..	493	934
Korea (Democratic People's Republic of)	..	..	..	..	..	..	..	..	..	..	..
South and West Asia											
88 Iran (Islamic Republic of)	0.0	0.0	0.0	..	..	..	2006	67795	23.0	5304	16449
95 Maldives	..	..	..	..	..	..	..	..	..	3597	6714
102 Sri Lanka	0.5	0.0	0.0	..	..	..	2006	4520	41.5	3064	5450
132 Bhutan	..	..	..	..	..	..	..	..	..	2636	6817
134 India	0.5	0.5	0.5	..	..	..	..	..	..	1304	4102
141 Pakistan	0.8	0.7	0.5	..	..	..	2007	53729	27.3	760	4135
144 Nepal	1.0	0.7	0.6	..	..	..	2002	3000	15.0	794	1309
146 Bangladesh	0.8	0.3	0.5	..	..	..	..	..	..	830	1633
181 Afghanistan	..	..	..	..	..	..	..	..	..	442	1845
Pacific											
2 Australia	..	..	..	..	..	..	..	..	..	28759	41153
20 New Zealand	..	..	..	2001	4200	38.5	2001	22045	39.3	22456	32375
94 Samoa	..	..	..	..	..	..	..	..	..	2525	6258
99 Tonga	..	..	..	..	..	..	..	..	..	2705	4752
108 Fiji	0.5	0.5	0.0	..	..	..	..	..	..	2349	6200
126 Vanuatu	..	..	..	..	..	..	..	..	..	2970	4332
135 Solomon Islands	..	..	..	..	..	..	..	..	..	1146	2264
148 Papua New Guinea	..	..	..	..	..	..	..	..	..	1775	2383
Kiribati	..	..	..	..	..	..	..	..	..	..	..
Marshall Islands	..	..	..	..	..	..	..	..	..	..	..
Micronesia (Federated States of)	..	..	..	..	..	..	..	..	..	..	..
Nauru	..	..	..	..	..	..	2003	19	15.8	..	..
Palau	..	..	..	..	..	..	..	..	..	..	..
Tuvalu	..	..	..	..	..	..	..	..	..	..	..

Note: * The values vary between 0 and 1 (0 = full and 1 = impossible).

Sources: (a) OECD n.d.-a.; (b) UNESCO 2009; (c) UNDP 2009.

WORK: PAID AND UNPAID

TABLE 11

INEQUALITIES: LABOUR FORCE PARTICIAPTION AND UNEMPLOYMENT											
	Labour force participation						Unemployment				
By HDI rank (2007)	Female (% of female population aged 15 +)			Male (% of male population aged 15 +)			Female (% of female labor force)			Male (% of male labor force)		
	1990	*2000*	*2007*	*1990*	*2000*	*2007*	*1990*	*2000*	*2007*	*1990*	*2000*	*2007*
East Asia												
10 Japan	50.1	49.3	48.0	77.4	76.4	72.1	2.2	4.5	3.7	2.0	5.0	4.0
23 Singapore	50.7	52.3	53.6	79.3	78.7	76.3	..	6.6	4.3	..	5.6	3.7
26 Korea (Republic of)	47.0	48.8	49.3	73.4	73.3	72.7	1.8	3.6	2.6	2.9	5.0	3.7
30 Brunei Darussalam	45.0	55.2	58.3	82.6	78.9	74.8	..	..	..	..	..	..
66 Malaysia	42.9	44.3	44.7	80.6	81.0	80.2	..	3.1	3.4	..	2.9	3.2
87 Thailand	75.6	66.6	65.7	87.4	81.2	80.5	2.4	2.3	1.1	2.0	2.4	1.3
92 China	73.2	72.7	70.6	85.1	82.6	79.5	..	..	..	..	..	..
105 Philippines	47.4	48.6	49.8	82.5	81.5	80.4	9.8	9.9	6.0	7.1	10.3	6.4
111 Indonesia	50.3	50.2	49.6	81.4	85.0	86.1	..	6.7	10.8	..	5.7	8.1
115 Mongolia	54.8	57.6	58.3	65.2	66.2	61.2	..	16.6	..	..	18.2	..
116 Viet Nam	74.0	70.3	69.3	81.4	77.1	76.0	..	2.1	..	..	2.4	..
133 Lao People's Democratic Republic	80.3	80.0	79.0	83.4	81.6	79.5	..	..	..	..	..	..
137 Cambodia	77.4	75.4	74.9	84.6	84.5	86.6	..	2.8	..	..	2.2	..
138 Myanmar	68.9	68.8	69.2	87.6	86.7	86.3	8.8	..	..	4.7	..	..
162 Timor-Leste	52.0	54.8	57.8	81.1	80.3	83.1	..	..	..	..	..	..
Korea (Democratic People's Republic of)	50.6	53.2	58.3	83.4	81.6	79.5	..	..	..	..	..	..
South and West Asia												
88 Iran (Islamic Republic of)	21.5	28.3	31.8	80.8	73.4	74.7	..	..	15.7	..	..	9.3
95 Maldives	20.3	37.5	54.3	77.5	72.4	76.2	..	2.7	..	..	1.6	..
102 Sri Lanka	45.5	38.4	42.8	79.2	77.9	75.2	23.6	11.1	9.0	9.1	5.8	4.3
132 Bhutan	25.2	23.9	43.2	83.7	82.3	79.8	..	..	..	..	..	..
134 India	35.1	34.3	34.2	84.7	82.6	81.5	..	4.1	..	..	4.4	..
141 Pakistan	11.2	16.1	20.8	86.1	84.1	84.9	0.7	15.8	8.4	2.8	5.5	4.5
144 Nepal	48.1	52.7	59.0	80.4	77.2	76.2	..	..	..	..	..	..
146 Bangladesh	62.0	54.8	57.2	89.1	86.8	84.5	..	3.3	..	..	3.2	..
181 Afghanistan	28.3	27.0	28.3	87.1	87.5	88.6	..	..	..	..	..	..
Pacific												
2 Australia	52.2	54.7	57.4	75.8	72.4	71.5	7.2	6.1	4.8	6.7	6.5	4.0
20 New Zealand	53.5	57.0	60.7	74.3	73.6	74.5	7.3	5.8	3.9	8.1	6.1	3.3
94 Samoa	39.7	41.6	40.9	76.5	77.8	76.0	..	..	..	..	..	..
99 Tonga	27.7	47.2	52.9	72.8	73.5	70.8	..	..	..	..	..	..
108 Fiji	29.1	39.1	39.2	83.6	79.1	78.8	..	..	..	..	..	..
126 Vanuatu	79.5	78.9	79.4	88.9	87.5	88.2	..	..	..	..	..	..
135 Solomon Islands	58.6	56.2	54.0	82.0	81.9	80.8	..	..	..	..	..	..
148 Papua New Guinea	71.3	71.3	71.3	74.8	73.7	73.4	5.9	1.3	..	9.0	4.3	..
Kiribati	..	..	..	..	..	..	..	..	..	..	..	..
Marshall Islands	..	..	..	..	..	..	..	..	..	..	..	..
Micronesia (Federated States of)	..	..	..	..	..	..	..	..	..	..	..	..
Nauru	..	..	..	..	..	..	..	..	..	..	..	..
Palau	..	..	..	..	..	..	..	..	..	..	..	..
Tuvalu	..	..	..	..	..	..	..	..	..	..	..	..

Source: World Bank 2009b.

TABLE 12

INEQUALITIES: EMPLOYMENT STATUS

By HDI rank (2007)	Self-employed				Wage and salaried workers					
	Female (% of females employed)		Male (% of males employed)		Female (% of females employed)			Male (% of males employed)		
	2000	2007	2000	2007	1990	2000	2007	1990	2000	2007
East Asia										
10 Japan	7.8	5.8	13.8	12.5	72.3	81.4	86.4	80.8	84.2	86.0
23 Singapore	5.1	8.8	13.3	18.8	..	94.2	89.9	..	86.5	80.8
26 Korea (Republic of)	19.2	18.5	33.8	31.1	56.8	61.5	68.8	63.1	64.3	67.7
30 Brunei Darussalam	..	..	..	..	..	..	..	..	..	..
66 Malaysia	12.5	13.9	24.3	24.7	..	76.4	77.3	..	73.0	72.5
87 Thailand	21.4	27.7	43.3	41.4	25.6	38.8	42.4	31.0	40.2	44.6
92 China	..	..	..	..	..	..	..	..	..	..
105 Philippines	33.3	31.0	40.5	39.9	..	49.5	51.0	..	50.0	51.1
111 Indonesia	..	35.8	..	56.3	..	..	30.7	..	..	35.9
115 Mongolia	17.6	..	46.1	..	..	43.6	..	..	39.3	..
116 Viet Nam	30.3	..	56.0	..	..	15.1	..	..	21.7	..
133 Lao People's Democratic Republic	..	..	..	..	..	..	..	..	..	..
137 Cambodia	28.9	..	54.6	..	..	12.1	..	..	18.6	..
138 Myanmar	..	..	..	..	..	..	..	..	..	..
162 Timor-Leste	..	..	..	..	..	..	..	..	..	..
Korea (Democratic People's Republic of)	..	..	..	..	..	..	..	..	..	..
South and West Asia										
88 Iran (Islamic Republic of)	..	24.3	..	40.8	..	..	42.2	..	..	53.4
95 Maldives	37.4	..	69.4	..	37.1	28.8	..	48.9	21.3	..
102 Sri Lanka	18.0	23.2	36.9	38.4	..	55.5	55.1	..	56.6	57.2
132 Bhutan	..	..	..	..	..	..	..	..	..	..
134 India	..	..	..	..	..	..	..	..	..	..
141 Pakistan	16.8	13.5	47.3	40.8	..	33.1	24.6	..	36.0	40.6
144 Nepal	..	..	..	..	..	..	..	..	..	..
146 Bangladesh	11.0	..	49.8	..	..	8.3	..	..	15.2	..
181 Afghanistan	..	..	..	..	..	..	..	..	..	..
Pacific										
2 Australia	9.6	8.7	16.1	14.3	87.8	89.3	91.0	82.8	83.3	85.5
20 New Zealand	13.4	11.2	25.2	20.4	86.5	85.1	87.2	75.1	74.0	78.7
94 Samoa	..	..	..	..	..	..	..	..	..	..
99 Tonga	..	..	..	..	..	..	..	..	..	..
108 Fiji	..	..	..	..	..	..	..	..	..	..
126 Vanuatu	..	..	..	..	..	..	..	..	..	..
135 Solomon Islands	..	..	..	..	..	..	..	..	..	..
148 Papua New Guinea	..	..	..	..	..	..	..	..	..	..
Kiribati	..	..	..	..	..	..	..	..	..	..
Marshall Islands	..	..	..	..	..	..	..	..	..	..
Micronesia (Federated States of)	..	..	..	..	..	..	..	..	..	..
Nauru	..	..	..	..	..	..	..	..	..	..
Palau	..	..	..	..	..	..	..	..	..	..
Tuvalu	..	..	..	..	..	..	..	..	..	..

Source: World Bank 2009b.

TABLE 13

INEQUALITIES: WAGES AND MATERNAL BENEFITS

By HDI rank (2007)	Wage equality for similar work (ratio of female over male)[a]	Number of weeks of maternity leave[b]		Maternal leave benefits (% of wages paid in covered period)[b]	
	2009	1990	2004	1990	2004
East Asia					
10 Japan	0.59	14	14	60	60
23 Singapore	0.79	8	8	100	100
26 Korea (Republic of)	0.55	..	13	..	100
30 Brunei Darussalam	0.74	..	..	..	..
66 Malaysia	0.73	8	9	100	100
87 Thailand	0.76	12	13	100	100
92 China	0.71	8	13	100	100
105 Philippines	0.74	14	9	100	100
111 Indonesia	0.72	12	12	100	100
115 Mongolia	0.80	14	17	..	70
116 Viet Nam	0.74	..	20	100	100
133 Lao People's Democratic Republic	..	12	12	100	70
137 Cambodia	0.73	12	13	100	50
138 Myanmar	..	..	12	..	67
162 Timor-Leste	..	..	..	..	..
Korea (Democratic People's Republic of)	..	..	..	..	..
South and West Asia					
88 Iran (Islamic Republic of)	..	12	13	67	67
95 Maldives	..	..	..	..	..
102 Sri Lanka	0.72	12	12	100	100
132 Bhutan	..	..	..	..	..
134 India	0.66	12	12	100	100
141 Pakistan	0.58	12	12	100	100
144 Nepal	0.57	7	7	100	100
146 Bangladesh	0.50	12	12	100	100
181 Afghanistan	..	..	..	100	100
Pacific					
2 Australia	0.68	12	52	..	0
20 New Zealand	0.77	14	14	0	100
94 Samoa	..	..	..	..	..
99 Tonga	..	..	..	..	..
108 Fiji	..	12	12	..	..
126 Vanuatu	..	..	12	..	50
135 Solomon Islands	..	12	12	25	25
148 Papua New Guinea	..	6	6	0	0
Kiribati	..	..	12	..	25
Marshall Islands	..	..	..	..	..
Micronesia (Federated States of)	..	..	..	..	..
Nauru	..	..	..	..	..
Palau	..	..	..	..	..
Tuvalu	..	..	..	..	..

Note: In some countries, maternity leaves are given in terms of days. These are rounded and converted to weeks.

Sources: (a) Hausmann et al. 2009; (b) World Bank 2009b.

TABLE 14

INEQUALITIES: SECTORAL SHARE OF EMPLOYMENT

By HDI rank (2007)	Employment in agriculture						Employment in industry						Employment in services						MDG Share of women employment in the non-agricultural sector (% of total non-agricultural employment)		
	Female (% of female employment)			Male (% of male employment)			Female (% of female employment)			Male (% of male employment)			Female (% of female employment)			Male (% of male employment)					
	1990	2000	2005	1990	2000	2005	1990	2000	2005	1990	2000	2005	1990	2000	2005	1990	2000	2005	1990	2000	2005
East Asia																					
10 Japan	8.5	5.5	4.5	6.3	4.7	4.4	27.4	21.5	17.6	38.6	38.0	35.3	63.6	72.4	76.8	54.5	56.7	59.1	38.0	40.0	41.3
23 Singapore	..	0.0	0.0	..	0.0	0.0	..	20.9	20.5	..	42.2	36.0	..	78.8	79.1	..	..	..	..	..	..
26 Korea (Republic of)	20.3	12.2	8.9	16.3	9.5	7.2	30.2	19.2	16.6	39.0	34.5	34.1	49.6	68.6	74.4	44.7	55.9	58.5	38.1	40.1	41.8
30 Brunei Darussalam	..	..	..	..	..	..	..	..	..	..	..	..	..	..	..	..	..	..	..	30.3	..
66 Malaysia	25.3	14.0	..	26.4	20.7	..	28.0	28.9	..	27.3	33.9	..	46.8	57.0	..	46.3	45.4	..	37.8	36.7	..
87 Thailand	65.0	47.5	40.7	63.1	49.8	44.2	12.3	17.3	18.7	15.5	20.4	21.6	22.7	35.2	40.5	21.3	29.7	34.1	45.3	46.1	47.9
92 China	..	..	..	..	..	..	..	..	..	..	..	..	..	..	..	..	..	..	37.8	37.8	..
105 Philippines	31.3	24.5	24.8	53.1	45.3	44.7	12.8	13.2	11.7	16.3	17.7	16.9	55.8	62.3	63.5	30.5	37.0	38.5	40.3	41.1	41.9
111 Indonesia	56.3	46.6	45.2	55.6	44.2	43.4	12.4	14.9	14.7	14.6	19.1	19.8	31.1	38.5	40.1	29.7	36.6	36.8	29.2	31.7	29.6
115 Mongolia	..	46.5	36.8	..	50.6	43.0	..	11.3	14.8	..	16.8	18.9	..	42.2	48.4	..	32.6	38.1	..	50.4	53.1
116 Viet Nam	..	66.3	..	..	64.2	..	..	10.1	..	..	14.7	..	..	23.6	..	..	21.0	..	..	48.2	..
133 Lao People's Democratic Republic	..	..	..	..	..	..	..	..	..	..	..	..	..	..	..	..	..	..	..	..	50.2
137 Cambodia	..	74.9	..	..	72.4	..	..	9.6	..	..	7.1	..	..	15.4	..	..	20.2	..	..	51.9	..
138 Myanmar	..	..	..	..	..	..	..	..	..	..	..	..	..	15.4	..	..	..	..	40.6	..	..
162 Timor-Leste	..	..	..	..	..	..	..	..	..	..	..	..	..	..	..	..	..	..	..	..	..
Korea (Democratic People's Republic of)	..	..	..	..	..	..	..	..	..	..	..	..	..	..	..	..	..	..	40.7	..	..
South and West Asia																					
88 Iran (Islamic Republic of)	..	..	34.2	..	..	22.8	..	..	28.4	..	..	30.9	..	..	37.4	..	..	46.3	..	13.6	..
95 Maldives	..	5.4	..	..	17.9	..	..	24.1	..	..	16.4	..	..	39.0	..	..	55.8	..	..	36.7	..

Contd...

By HDI rank (2007)	Employment in agriculture						Employment in industry						Employment in services						MDG
	Female (% of female employment)			Male (% of male employment)			Female (% of female employment)			Male (% of male employment)			Female (% of female employment)			Male (% of male employment)			Share of women employment in the non-agricultural sector (% of total non-agricultural employment)		
	1990	2000	2005	1990	2000	2005	1990	2000	2005	1990	2000	2005	1990	2000	2005	1990	2000	2005	1990	2000	2005
South and West Asia																					
102 Sri Lanka	..	..	..	..	..	..	..	..	..	..	..	..	..	..	..	..	..	..	39.1	46.0	39.8
132 Bhutan	..	..	..	..	..	..	..	..	..	..	..	..	..	..	..	..	..	..	..	..	..
134 India	..	..	..	..	..	..	..	..	..	..	..	..	..	..	..	..	..	..	12.7	16.6	18.1
141 Pakistan	72.2	72.9	67.3	48.4	44.4	38.1	14.1	9.0	15.0	20.6	19.5	21.4	13.5	18.1	17.6	30.9	36.1	40.5	6.6	7.4	9.7
144 Nepal	..	..	..	..	..	..	..	..	..	..	..	..	..	..	..	..	..	..	..	..	..
146 Bangladesh	84.9	76.9	..	54.4	53.3	..	8.8	9.0	..	15.7	11.0	..	2.1	12.1	..	25.3	30.3	..	..	22.9	..
181 Afghanistan	..	..	..	..	..	..	..	..	..	..	..	..	..	..	..	..	..	..	17.8	..	..
Pacific																					
2 Australia	4.0	3.5	2.5	6.7	6.1	4.6	12.7	10.5	9.4	33.9	30.6	30.6	83.3	86.0	87.9	59.4	63.2	64.5	44.6	48.1	48.9
20 New Zealand	7.8	5.8	5.0	12.8	11.0	8.9	14.2	12.2	10.5	32.6	32.3	31.9	77.7	81.4	84.3	54.2	56.3	58.9	44.9	46.3	47.1
94 Samoa	..	..	..	..	..	..	..	..	..	..	..	..	..	..	..	..	..	..	..	30.2	..
99 Tonga	..	..	..	..	..	..	..	..	..	..	..	..	..	..	..	..	..	..	..	..	..
108 Fiji	..	..	..	..	..	..	..	..	..	..	..	..	..	..	..	..	..	..	29.9	33.2	30.6
126 Vanuatu	..	..	..	..	..	..	..	..	..	..	..	..	..	..	..	..	..	..	..	..	..
135 Solomon Islands	..	..	..	..	..	..	..	..	..	..	..	..	..	..	..	..	..	..	..	..	..
148 Papua New Guinea	..	..	..	..	..	..	..	..	..	..	..	..	..	..	..	..	..	..	..	..	..
Kiribati	..	..	..	..	..	..	..	..	..	..	..	..	..	..	..	..	..	..	27.9	32.1	..
Marshall Islands	..	..	..	..	..	..	..	..	..	..	..	..	..	..	..	..	..	..	..	37.5	..
Micronesia (Federated States of)	..	..	..	..	..	..	..	..	..	..	..	..	..	..	..	..	..	..	..	..	33.2
Nauru	..	..	..	..	..	..	..	..	..	..	..	..	..	..	..	..	..	..	..	..	..
Palau	..	..	..	..	..	..	..	..	..	..	..	..	..	..	..	..	..	..	..	..	..
Tuvalu	..	..	..	..	..	..	..	..	..	..	..	..	..	..	..	..	..	..	..	..	..

Source: (a) World Bank 2009a.

TABLE 15

INEQUALITIES: MARKET AND NON-MARKET ACTIVITIES

By HDI rank (2007)	Contributing family workers[a]						Market activities (% of total work time)[b]			Non-market activities (% of total work time)[b]		
	Female (% of females employed)			Male (% of males employed)			Year	Women	Men	Year	Women	Men
	1990	2000	2007	1990	2000	2007						
East Asia												
10 Japan	16.7	10.6	7.3	2.5	1.7	1.1	1996	43	93	1996	57	7
23 Singapore	..	0.6	1.3	..	0.2	0.4	..	..	..	..	..	..
26 Korea (Republic of)	24.5	19.2	12.7	2.5	2.0	1.2	2004	40	86	2004	60	14
30 Brunei Darussalam	..	..	..	..	..	..	..	..	..	..	..	..
66 Malaysia	..	11.1	8.8	..	2.7	2.7	..	..	..	..	..	..
87 Thailand	56.1	39.8	29.9	27.0	16.4	14.0	..	..	..	..	..	..
92 China	..	..	..	..	..	..	..	..	..	..	..	..
105 Philippines	..	17.2	18.0	..	9.6	9.0	..	..	..	..	..	..
111 Indonesia	..	..	33.6	..	..	7.8	..	..	..	..	..	..
115 Mongolia	..	38.6	..	..	14.0	..	2000	49	76	2000	51	24
116 Viet Nam	..	53.1	..	..	21.2	..	..	..	..	..	..	..
133 Lao People's Democratic Republic	..	..	..	..	..	..	..	..	..	..	..	..
137 Cambodia	..	59.0	..	..	26.6	..	..	..	..	..	..	..
138 Myanmar	..	..	..	..	..	..	..	..	..	..	..	..
162 Timor-Leste	..	..	..	..	..	..	..	..	..	..	..	..
Korea (Democratic People's Republic of)	..	..	..	..	..	..	..	..	..	..	..	..
South and West Asia												
88 Iran (Islamic Republic of)	..	..	32.7	..	..	5.4	..	..	..	..	..	..
95 Maldives	6.6	3.4	..	4.0	1.3	..	..	..	..	..	..	..
102 Sri Lanka	..	26.5	21.7	..	6.5	4.4	..	..	..	..	..	..
132 Bhutan	..	..	..	..	..	..	..	..	..	..	..	..
134 India	..	..	..	..	..	..	2000	35	92	2000	65	8
141 Pakistan	..	50.1	61.9	..	16.7	18.6	..	..	..	..	..	..
144 Nepal	..	..	..	..	..	..	..	..	..	..	..	..
146 Bangladesh	..	73.2	..	..	10.1	..	..	..	..	..	..	..
Pacific												
2 Australia	1.2	1.1	0.4	0.5	0.6	0.2	1997	30	62	1997	70	38
20 New Zealand	1.9	1.3	1.5	0.7	0.5	0.8	1999	32	60	1999	68	40
94 Samoa	..	..	..	..	..	..	..	..	..	..	..	..
99 Tonga	..	..	..	..	..	..	..	..	..	..	..	..
108 Fiji	..	..	..	..	..	..	..	..	..	..	..	..
126 Vanuatu	..	..	..	..	..	..	..	..	..	..	..	..

Contd...

Contd...

By HDI rank (2007)	Contributing family workers[a]						Market activities (% of total work time)[b]			Non-market activities (% of total work time)[b]		
	Female (% of females employed)			Male (% of males employed)			Year	Women	Men	Year	Women	Men
	1990	2000	2007	1990	2000	2007						
Pacific												
135 Solomon Islands	..	..	..	..	..	..	..	..	..	..	..	..
148 Papua New Guinea	..	..	..	..	..	..	..	..	..	..	..	..
Kiribati	..	..	..	..	..	..	..	..	..	..	..	..
Marshall Islands	..	..	..	..	..	..	..	..	..	..	..	..
Micronesia (Federated States of)	..	..	..	..	..	..	..	..	..	..	..	..
Nauru	..	..	..	..	..	..	..	..	..	..	..	..
Palau	..	..	..	..	..	..	..	..	..	..	..	..
Tuvalu	..	..	..	..	..	..	..	..	..	..	..	..

Notes: Contributing family workers: Contributing family worker is defined according to the 1993 International Classification by Status in Employment (ICSE) as a person who works without pay in an economic enterprise operated by a related person living in the same household (UNDP 2007). The indicator shows the percentage of contributing family workers (female/male) to total employed (female/male).

Market activities: Time spent on activities such as employment in establishments, primary production not in establishments, services for income and other production of goods not in establishments as defined according to the 1993 revised UN System of National Accounts (UNDP 2007).

Non-market activities: Time spent on activities such as household maintenance (cleaning, laundry, meal preparation and clean up), management and shopping for own household; care for children, the sick, the elderly and the disabled in own household; and community services, as defined according to the 1993 revised UN System of National Accounts (UNDP 2007).

Sources: (a) World Bank 2009b; (b) UNDP 2007.

POLITICAL VOICE

TABLE 16										
INEQUALITIES: POLITICAL VOICE										
	MDG									
By HDI rank (2007)	*Seats in parliament held by women (% of total)[a]*		*Women in ministerial positions (% of total)[b]*	*Year women received right to vote*[b]	*Year women received right to stand for election*[b]	*Year first woman (E) elected or (A) appointed to parliament[c]*	*Existence of quotas for women's political representation**[d]*			
	2000	*2009#*	*2008##*				*Type 1*	*Type 2*	*Type 3*	*Type 4*
East Asia										
10 Japan	10.7	12.3	12	1945, 1947	1945, 1947	1946 E	..	..	..	..
23 Singapore	4.3	24.5	0	1947	1947	1963 E	..	..	..	..
26 Korea (Republic of)	5.9	13.7	5	1948	1948	1948 E		yes	yes	yes
30 Brunei Darussalam	..	..	7	NA	NA	NA	..	..	..	..
66 Malaysia	14.5	15.4	9	1957	1957	1959 E	..	..	..	..
87 Thailand	6.8	12.7	10	1932	1932	1948 A	..	..	..	yes
92 China	21.8	21.3	9	1949	1949	1954 E	..	yes	..	..
105 Philippines	11.8	20.2	9	1937	1937	1941 E	..	yes	yes	yes
111 Indonesia	8.0	16.6	11	1945, 2003	1945	1950 A	..	yes	..	..
115 Mongolia	10.5	4.0	20	1924	1924	1951 E	..	..	..	..
116 Viet Nam	26.0	25.8	4	1946	1946	1976 E	..	..	..	..
133 Lao People's Democratic Republic	21.2	25.2	11	1958	1958	1958 E	..	..	..	..
137 Cambodia	9.3	15.8	7	1955	1955	1958 E	..	..	..	..
138 Myanmar	..	..	0	1935	1946	1947 E	..	..	..	..
162 Timor-Leste	..	29.2	25	..	..	..	..	..	..	..
Korea (Democratic People's Republic of)	20.1	15.6	0	1946	1946	1948 E	..	yes	..	..
South and West Asia										
88 Iran (Islamic Republic of)	3.4	2.8	3	1963	1963	1963 E + A	..	..	..	..
95 Maldives	6.0	6.5	14	1932	1932	1979 E	..	..	..	..
102 Sri Lanka	..	5.8	6	1931	1931	1947 E	..	..	..	..
132 Bhutan	9.3	13.9	0	1953	1953	1975 E	..	..	..	..
134 India	..	10.3	10	1935, 1950	1935, 1950	1952 E	..	..	yes	yes
141 Pakistan	..	21.2	4	1956	1956	1973 E	..	yes	yes	..
144 Nepal	7.9	33.2	20	1951	1951	1952 A	yes	yes	yes	..
146 Bangladesh	9.1	18.6	8	1935, 1972	1935, 1972	1973 E	yes	..	yes	..
181 Afghanistan	..	25.9	4	1963	1963	1965 E	yes	yes	..	..
										Contd...

Contd...

By HDI rank (2007)	MDG						Existence of quotas for women's political representation **d			
	Seats in parliament held by women (% of total)[a]		Women in ministerial positions (% of total)[b]	Year women received right to vote *[b]	Year women received right to stand for election *[b]	Year first woman (E) elected or (A) appointed to parliament[c]				
	2000	2009[#]	2008[##]				Type 1	Type 2	Type 3	Type 4
Pacific										
2 Australia	25.0	29.6	24	1902, 1962	1902, 1962	1943 E	..	..	..	yes
20 New Zealand	30.8	33.6	32	1893	1919	1933 E	..	..	..	..
94 Samoa	8.2	8.2	23	1948, 1990	1948, 1990	1976 A	..	..	..	..
99 Tonga	0.0	3.1	..	1960	1960	1993 E	..	..	..	..
108 Fiji	..	..	8	1963	1963	1970 A	..	..	..	..
126 Vanuatu	0.0	3.8	8	1975, 1980	1975, 1980	1987 E	..	..	..	..
135 Solomon Islands	2.0	0.0	0	1974	1974	1993 E	..	..	..	..
148 Papua New Guinea	1.8	0.9	4	1964	1963	1977 E	..	..	..	..
Kiribati	4.9	4.3	8	1967	1967	1990 E	..	..	..	..
Marshall Islands	3.0	3.0	10	1979	1979	1991 E	..	..	..	..
Micronesia (Federated States of)	0.0	0.0	14	1979	1979	..	..	..	..	..
Nauru	..	0.0	0	1968	1968	1986 E	..	..	..	..
Palau	3.3	6.9	0	1979	1979	..	..	..	..	..
Tuvalu	0.0	0.0	0	1967	1967	1989 E	..	..	..	..

Notes: # Data are as of 31 July 2009 where there are lower and upper houses, data refer to combined share of women's seats in both houses.

Data are as of January 2008. The total includes deputy prime ministers and ministers. Prime ministers were also included when they held ministerial portfolios. Vice-presidents and heads of governmental or public agencies are not included.

* Data refer to the year in which the right to vote or stand for national election on a universal and equal basis was recognized. Where two years are shown, the first refers to the first partial recognition of the right to vote or stand for election. In some countries, women were granted the right to vote or stand at local elections before obtaining these rights for national elections. Data on local election rights are not included in this table.

** Quota systems are put in place to promote gender balance within political positions. They ensure a 'critical minority' which varies from 20 to 40 per cent (UNIFEM 2008). Sometimes quotas ensure minimum representation for women; sometimes they ensure minimum representation of either sex (usually 40 per cent in this case). For more information on quotas, including definitions, see IDEA's Global Database of Quotas for Women (http://www.quotaproject.org/).

Type 1: Constitutional Quota for National Parliaments.

Type 2: Sanctions (enforceable measures) are legally mandated and applied when mandated quotas in national parliaments are not met; applicable only to Quota Type 2.

Type 3: Constitutional or Legislative Quota at Sub-national Level.

Type 4: Political Party Quota for Electoral Candidates.

NA: Not applicable.

Sources: (a) IPU 2009; (b) UNDP 2009; (c) UNDP 2007; (d) UNIFEM 2008.

INFLUENCING DECISIONS

TABLE 17

INEQUALITIES: INFLUENCING DECISIONS

By HDI rank (2007)	Female legislators, senior officials and managers (% of total)[a]	Proportion of administrative and managerial positions held by women (%)[b]	Ambassadors (% female)[c]	Judges in higher judiciary (% female)[c]	Heads of universities (% female)[d]
	1999-2007	2005			
East Asia					
10 Japan	9	12.5	2.8	6.3	..
23 Singapore	31	0.0	8.1	..	4.4
26 Korea (Republic of)	9	5.6	..	..	..
30 Brunei Darussalam	35	..	14.7	..	..
66 Malaysia	23	9.1	11.6	24.5	15.7
87 Thailand	30	7.7	11.9	..	..
92 China	17	6.3	..	..	..
105 Philippines	57	25.0	30.7	30.4	45.5
111 Indonesia	14	10.8	7.1	..	..
115 Mongolia	48	5.9	..	41.2	..
116 Viet Nam	22	11.5	..	..	17.8
133 Lao People's Democratic Republic	..	0.0	..	..	..
137 Cambodia	14	7.1	15.4	..	13.3
138 Myanmar	..	..	3.7	..	..
162 Timor-Leste	..	22.2	16.7	..	..
Korea (Democratic People's Republic of)	..	..	..	..	..
South and West Asia					
88 Iran (Islamic Republic of)	13	6.7	..	..	..
95 Maldives	14	11.8	10.0	..	14.3
102 Sri Lanka	24	10.3	7.1	12.5	21.8
132 Bhutan	..	0.0	..	0.0	..
134 India	..	3.4	10.9	7.7	19.6
141 Pakistan	3	5.6	10.8	2.8	..
144 Nepal	14	7.4	0.0	9.5	0.0
146 Bangladesh	10	8.3	7.9	..	6.4
181 Afghanistan	..	10.0	..	..	..
Pacific					
2 Australia	37	20.0	29.2	19.5	..
20 New Zealand	40	23.1	22.2	..	16.4
94 Samoa	29	7.7	0.0	..	66.7
99 Tonga	27	..	..	..	..
108 Fiji	51	9.1	0.0	..	..
126 Vanuatu	..	8.3	..	..	..
135 Solomon Islands	..	0.0	..	..	..
148 Papua New Guinea	..	..	..	7.3	..
Kiribati	27	0.0	..	..	..
Marshall Islands	19	0.0	..	..	..
Micronesia (Federated States of)	..	..	..	..	..
Nauru	..	..	..	..	..
Palau	36	12.5	..	..	..
Tuvalu	25	..	..	..	..

Notes: Judges in higher judiciary (% female): Data refers to Supreme Court and High Courts. But for some countries data available for one court, such as Nepal and Mongolia – only Supreme Court; Bhutan – Only High Court. The name of High Court and Supreme Court is different in some countries, such as the Philippines – Court of Appeal is equivalent of High Court; Malaysia – Federal Court is equivalent of Supreme Court; Papua New Guinea – National Court is equivalent of High Court.

Data on ambassadors, judges in higher judiciary and heads of universities (including vice-chancellors and faculty heads) were compiled using the relevant official websites of each country during June 2009. See Readers' guide in the Report for detail explanation.

Sources: (a) UNDP 2009; (b) World Bank 2009b; (c) Data compiled from government official websites (as of June 2009); (d) Data compiled from public university websites (as of June 2009).

INTERNATIONAL CONVENTIONS

TABLE 18

RATIFICATION/ACCESSION/SUCCESSION YEAR OF INTERNATIONAL HUMAN RIGHTS INSTRUMENTS AND LABOUR RIGHTS CONVENTIONS

By HDI rank (2007)	Equal Remuneration Convention 1951[a]	Discrimination (Employment and Occupation) Convention 1958[a]	Civil and political rights[b]		Economic, social and cultural rights[b]		Discrimination against women[b]		International Convention on the Protection of the Rights of All Migrant Workers and Members of their Families (ICRMW) 1990[b]
			International Covenant on Civil and Political Rights (ICCPR) 1966	ICCPR Optional Protocol 1966	International Covenant on Economic, Social and Cultural Rights (ICESCR) 1966	ICESCR Optional Protocol 2008	Convention on the Elimination of All Forms of Discrimination against Women (CEDAW) 1979	CEDAW optional protocol 1999	
East Asia									
10 Japan	1967	..	1979	–	1979	–	1985	–	–
23 Singapore	2002	..	–	–	–	–	1995	–	–
26 Korea (Republic of)	1997	1998	1990	1990	1990	–	1984	2006	–
30 Brunei Darussalam	..	..	–	–	–	–	2006	–	–
66 Malaysia	1997	..	–	–	–	–	1995	–	–
87 Thailand	1999	..	1996	–	1999	–	1985	2000	–
92 China	1990	2006	S	S	2001	–	1980	–	S
105 Philippines	1953	1960	1986	1989	1974	–	1981	2003	1995
111 Indonesia	1958	1999	2006	–	2006	–	1984	S	S
115 Mongolia	1969	1969	1974	1991	1974	–	1981	2002	–
116 Viet Nam	1997	1997	1982	–	1982	–	1982	–	–
133 Lao People's Democratic Republic	2008	2008	2009	–	2007	–	1981	–	–
137 Cambodia	1999	1999	1992	S	1992	–	1992	S	S
138 Myanmar	..	..	–	–	–	–	1997	–	–
162 Timor-Leste	..	..	2003	–	2003	S	2003	2003	2004
Korea (Democratic People's Republic of)	..	..	1981	–	1981	–	2001	–	–
South and West Asia									
88 Iran (Islamic Republic of)	1972	1964	1975	–	1975	–	–	–	–
95 Maldives	..	..	2006	2006	2006	–	1993	2006	–
102 Sri Lanka	1993	1998	1980	1997	1980	–	1981	2002	1996
132 Bhutan	..	..	–	–	–	–	1981	–	–
134 India	1958	1960	1979	–	1979	–	1993	–	–
141 Pakistan	2001	1961	S	–	2008	–	1996	–	–
144 Nepal	1976	1974	1991	1991	1991	–	1991	2007	–
146 Bangladesh	1998	1972	2000	–	1998	–	1984	2000	S
181 Afghanistan	1969	1969	1983	–	1983	–	2003	–	–
Pacific									
2 Australia	1974	1973	1980	1991	1975	–	1983	2008	–
20 New Zealand	1983	1983	1978	1989	1978	–	1985	2000	–
94 Samoa	2008	2008	2008	–	–	–	1992	–	–
99 Tonga	..	..	–	–	–	–	–	–	–
108 Fiji	2002	2002	–	–	–	–	1995	–	–
126 Vanuatu	2006	2006	2008	–	–	–	1995	2007	–
135 Solomon Islands	..	..	–	–	1982	S	2002	2002	–
148 Papua New Guinea	2000	2000	2008	–	2008	–	1995	–	–
Kiribati	2009	2009	–	–	–	–	2004	–	–
Marshall Islands	..	..	–	–	–	–	2006	–	–
Micronesia (Federated States of)	..	..	–	–	–	–	2004	–	–
Nauru	..	..	–	S	–	–	..	–	–
Palau	..	..	–	–	–	–	..	–	–
Tuvalu	..	..	–	–	–	–	1999	–	–

Notes: '–' implies not signed, not ratified; 'S' implies signed only.
Sources: (a) ILO n.d.; (b) UN n.d.

LEGAL INSTRUMENTS

	TABLE 19							
	LEGAL INSTRUMENTS							
By HDI Rank (2007)	Inheritance laws (Land/ Property)	Marital property rights in case of divorce	Nationality law in respect with marriage to foreign national	Existence of legislation against gender based violence			Paternity Law
	Legal status: Women vis-à-vis men	Legal status: Women vis-à-vis men	Legal status: Women vis-à-vis men	Domestic violence	Sexual assault/ rape	Sexual harassment at workplaces	
East Asia							
10 Japan	..	..	..	Yes	Yes	Yes	Yes
23 Singapore	..	Equal rights	Equal rights	Yes	Yes	No	Yes
26 Korea (Republic of)	Equal rights	Equal rights	Equal rights	Yes	Yes	Yes	..
30 Brunei Darussalam	(..)	(..)	(..)	(..)	(..)	(..)	(..)
66 Malaysia	Unequal rights (as applicable to majority)	Equal rights	Unequal rights	Yes	Yes	No	Yes
87 Thailand	Equal rights	Equal rights	Unequal rights	Yes *(h)*	Yes	Yes	..
92 China	Equal rights	Equal rights	Equal rights	Yes	Yes *(j)*	..	..
105 Philippines	Equal rights	Equal rights	Equal rights	Yes	Yes	Yes	Yes
111 Indonesia	Unequal rights *(a)*	Equal rights	Unequal rights *(a1)*	Yes *(a2)*	Yes	No	..
115 Mongolia	Unequal rights	Equal rights	Equal rights *(f)*	Yes	Yes	No	Yes *(f1)*
116 Viet Nam	Equal rights	Equal rights	Equal rights	Yes *(i)*	Yes *(i1)*	No	..
133 Lao People's Democratic Republic	Equal rights	Equal rights	Equal rights	Yes	Yes	..	..
137 Cambodia	Equal rights	Equal rights	Equal rights	Yes	Yes	Yes	..
138 Myanmar	Equal rights	Equal rights	Equal rights	No	Yes	..	..
162 Timor-Leste	Unequal rights	Unequal rights	Equal rights	No	Yes	Yes	..
Korea (Democratic People's Republic of)	Equal rights	Equal rights	Equal rights	..	Yes	..	..

Contd...

Contd...

By HDI Rank (2007)	Inheritance laws (Land/ Property)	Marital property rights in case of divorce	Nationality law in respect with marriage to foreign national	Existence of legislation against gender based violence			Paternity Law
	Legal status: Women vis-à-vis men	Legal status: Women vis-à-vis men	Legal status: Women vis-à-vis men	Domestic violence	Sexual assault/ rape	Sexual harassment at workplaces	
South and West Asia							
88 Iran (Islamic Republic of)	Unequal rights (b)	—	—	—	—	—	—
95 Maldives	*Unequal rights (as applicable to majority)	Unequal rights (e)	Equal rights	No	..	No	..
102 Sri Lanka	Equal rights as applicable to majo-rity (c)	Equal rights as applicable to majo-rity (c1)	Equal rights (c2)	Yes (c3)	Yes	Yes (c4)	..
132 Bhutan	Equal rights	Equal rights	Equal rights	No	Yes	Yes	Yes
134 India	Equal rights (as applicable to majority)	..	Equal rights	Yes	Yes	No	Yes
141 Pakistan	*Unequal rights	Unequal rights	Unequal rights	Yes (j)	Yes	Yes	..
144 Nepal	Equal rights	Equal rights	Unequal rights (g)	Yes (g1)	Yes	No	..
146 Bangladesh	Unequal rights	Unequal rights	Unequal rights	No (k)	Yes	Yes	..
181 Afghanistan	*Unequal rights	(..)	(..)	(..)	(..)	(..)	(..)
Pacific							
2 Australia	Equal rights (d)	Equal rights	Equal rights	Yes	Yes	Yes	Yes
20 New Zealand	Equal rights	Equal rights	Equal rights	Yes	Yes	Yes	Yes
94 Samoa	Equal rights	Unequal rights	Equal rights	No	Yes	Yes	..
99 Tonga	—	—	—	—	—	—	—
108 Fiji	Unequal rights	Equal rights	Equal rights	Yes (l)	Yes	No	..

Contd...

Contd...

By HDI Rank (2007)	Inheritance laws (Land/Property)	Marital property rights in case of divorce	Nationality law in respect with marriage to foreign national	Existence of legislation against gender based violence			Paternity Law
	Legal status: Women vis-à-vis men	Legal status: Women vis-à-vis men	Legal status: Women vis-à-vis men	Domestic violence	Sexual assault/rape	Sexual harassment at workplaces	
Pacific							
126 Vanuatu	Unequal rights	Unequal rights	Unequal rights	Yes	Yes	No	..
135 Solomon Islands	Unequal rights	Unequal rights	Unequal rights	No	Yes	No	..
148 Papua New Guinea	Unequal rights	Equal rights	Equal rights	No	Yes	No	..
Kiribati	Unequal rights	No Legislation	Unequal rights	No	Yes	No	..
Marshall Islands	Unequal rights	Equal rights	Equal rights	No	Yes	No	..
Micronesia (Federated States of)	No legislation	Equal rights	Equal rights	No	No	No	..
Nauru	—	—	—	—	—	—	—
Palau	—	—	—	—	—	—	—
Tuvalu	Unequal rights	Unequal rights	Unequal rights	No	Yes	No	..

Notes: (..) implies Reports of States Parties to UN Committee on CEDAW not submitted.

— Refers to no data available as countries are not signatories to CEDAW.

* No information on inheritance rights is available from Reports of States Parties to UN Committee on CEDAW. However, these countries follow Islamic Principles of inheritance. The female's inheritance share is half of male's share. See Ihsan and Zaidi 2006; OECD n.d.-b.; Committee on the Elimination of Discrimination against Women 2001.

Sources: States Parties reports to UN Committee on CEDAW (listed in the Statistical References); National legislation (in case where laws enacted/changed/amended); UNDP Pacific Centre and UNIFEM Pacific Regional Office Report 2007 (Jivan and Forster 2007).

(a) Sriro 2006.

(a1) http://www.unhcr.org/refworld/country,LEGAL,,,IDN,,4538aae64,0.html. Last accessed on 30 July 2009.

(a2) http://webapps01.un.org/vawdatabase/countryInd.action?countryId=640. last accessed on 30 July 2009.

(b) http://www.alaviandassociates.com/documents/civilcode.pdf. Last accessed on 30 July 2009.

(c) http://www.commonlii.org/lk/legis/consol_act/mrai69364.pdf . Last accessed on 30 July 2009.

(c1) http://www.commonlii.org/lk/legis/consol_act/cpc105233.pdf. Last accessed on 30 July 2009.

(c2) http://www.commonlii.org/lk/legis/consol_act/c248191.pdf. Last accessed on 30 July 2009.

(c3) http://www.apwld.org/pdf/srilanka_domestic_violence_bill2002.pdf. Last accessed on 30 July 2009.

(c4) http://www.commonlii.org/lk/legis/consol_act/pc25130.pdf. Last accessed on 30 July 2009.

(d) http://www.comlaw.gov.au/ComLaw/Legislation/ActCompilation1.nsf/0/884E588EC5056075CA2575F5000BB872/$file Sex Discrimination 8 4_WD02.pdf). Last accessed on 30 July 2009.

(e) http://www.agoffice.gov.mv/pdf/sublawe/238.pdf. Last accessed on 30 July 2009.

(f) http://www.mn.emb-japan.go.jp/jp/ryouji/immig_laws/on_citizenship.pdf. Last accessed on 30 July 2009.

(f1) http://www.asianlii.org/mn/legis/laws/lol1999123/. Last accessed on 30 July 2009.

(g) http://www.unmin.org.np/downloads/keydocs/Interim.Constitution.Bilingual.UNDP.pdf. Last accessed on 30 July 2009.

(g1) http://www.loc.gov/lawweb/servlet/lloc_news?disp3_1237_text. Last accessed on 22 September 2009.

(h) http://www.lawreform.go.th. Last accessed on 30 July 2009.

(i) http://www.iknowpolitics.org/files/law_domestic_violence_viet_nam.pdf. Last accessed on 19 August 2009.

(i1) http://www.worldlii.org/vn/legis/pc66.txt. Last accessed on 30 July 2009.

(j) http://www.dailytimes.com.pk/default.asp?page=2009%5C08%5C05%5Cstory_5-8-2009_pg7_4. Last accessed on 19 August 2009.

(k) http://www.wluml.org/english/newsfulltxt.shtml?cmd%5B157%5D=x-157-541056. Last accessed on 24 August 2009.

(l) http://www.fiji.gov.fj/publish/page_15612.shtml. Last accessed on 20 August 2009.

GENDER MEASURES

<table>
<tr><td colspan="6">TABLE 20</td></tr>
<tr><td colspan="6" align="center">POPULAR MEASURES OF GENDER EQUALITY</td></tr>
<tr>
<td>By HDI rank (2007)</td>
<td>Gender-related Development Index (GDI)[a]</td>
<td>Gender Empowerment Measure (GEM)[a]</td>
<td>Global Gender Gap Index (GGI)[b]</td>
<td>Gender Equity Index (GEI)[c]</td>
<td>Social Insitutions and Gender Index (SIGI)[d]</td>
</tr>
<tr>
<td></td>
<td>2007</td>
<td>2007</td>
<td>2009</td>
<td>2008</td>
<td>2009</td>
</tr>
<tr><td colspan="6">East Asia</td></tr>
<tr><td>10 Japan</td><td>0.945</td><td>0.567</td><td>0.677</td><td>61</td><td>..</td></tr>
<tr><td>23 Singapore</td><td>..</td><td>0.786</td><td>0.666</td><td>66</td><td>0.015</td></tr>
<tr><td>26 Korea (Republic of)</td><td>0.926</td><td>0.554</td><td>0.615</td><td>54</td><td>..</td></tr>
<tr><td>30 Brunei Darussalam</td><td>0.906</td><td>..</td><td>0.652</td><td>63</td><td>..</td></tr>
<tr><td>66 Malaysia</td><td>0.823</td><td>0.542</td><td>0.647</td><td>58</td><td>..</td></tr>
<tr><td>87 Thailand</td><td>0.782</td><td>0.514</td><td>0.691</td><td>70</td><td>0.011</td></tr>
<tr><td>92 China</td><td>0.770</td><td>0.533</td><td>0.691</td><td>69</td><td>0.218</td></tr>
<tr><td>105 Philippines</td><td>0.748</td><td>0.560</td><td>0.758</td><td>76</td><td>0.008</td></tr>
<tr><td>111 Indonesia</td><td>0.726</td><td>0.408</td><td>0.658</td><td>52</td><td>0.128</td></tr>
<tr><td>115 Mongolia</td><td>0.727</td><td>0.410</td><td>0.722</td><td>70</td><td>0.039</td></tr>
<tr><td>116 Viet Nam</td><td>0.723</td><td>0.554</td><td>0.680</td><td>71</td><td>0.030</td></tr>
<tr><td>133 Lao People's Democratic Republic</td><td>0.614</td><td>..</td><td>..</td><td>..</td><td>0.036</td></tr>
<tr><td>137 Cambodia</td><td>0.588</td><td>0.427</td><td>0.641</td><td>60</td><td>0.022</td></tr>
<tr><td>138 Myanmar</td><td>..</td><td>..</td><td>..</td><td>..</td><td>0.046</td></tr>
<tr><td>162 Timor-Leste</td><td>..</td><td>..</td><td>..</td><td>55</td><td>..</td></tr>
<tr><td>Korea (Democratic People's Republic of)</td><td>..</td><td>..</td><td>..</td><td>..</td><td>..</td></tr>
<tr><td colspan="6">South and West Asia</td></tr>
<tr><td>88 Iran (Islamic Republic of)</td><td>0.770</td><td>0.331</td><td>0.584</td><td>54</td><td>0.304</td></tr>
<tr><td>95 Maldives</td><td>0.767</td><td>0.429</td><td>0.648</td><td>62</td><td>..</td></tr>
<tr><td>102 Sri Lanka</td><td>0.756</td><td>0.389</td><td>0.740</td><td>53</td><td>0.059</td></tr>
<tr><td>132 Bhutan</td><td>0.605</td><td>..</td><td>..</td><td>..</td><td>0.163</td></tr>
<tr><td>134 India</td><td>0.594</td><td>..</td><td>0.615</td><td>40</td><td>0.318</td></tr>
<tr><td>141 Pakistan</td><td>0.532</td><td>0.386</td><td>0.546</td><td>42</td><td>0.283</td></tr>
<tr><td>144 Nepal</td><td>0.545</td><td>0.486</td><td>0.621</td><td>44</td><td>0.167</td></tr>
<tr><td>146 Bangladesh</td><td>0.536</td><td>0.264</td><td>0.653</td><td>51</td><td>0.245</td></tr>
<tr><td>181 Afghanistan</td><td>0.310</td><td>..</td><td>..</td><td>..</td><td>0.582</td></tr>
<tr><td colspan="6">Pacific</td></tr>
<tr><td>2 Australia</td><td>0.966</td><td>0.870</td><td>0.728</td><td>76</td><td>..</td></tr>
<tr><td>20 New Zealand</td><td>0.943</td><td>0.841</td><td>0.788</td><td>78</td><td>..</td></tr>
<tr><td>94 Samoa</td><td>0.763</td><td>0.431</td><td>..</td><td>50</td><td>..</td></tr>
<tr><td>99 Tonga</td><td>0.765</td><td>0.363</td><td>..</td><td>..</td><td>..</td></tr>
<tr><td>108 Fiji</td><td>0.732</td><td>..</td><td>0.641</td><td>..</td><td>0.055</td></tr>
<tr><td>126 Vanuatu</td><td>0.692</td><td>..</td><td>..</td><td>56</td><td>..</td></tr>
<tr><td>135 Solomon Islands</td><td>..</td><td>..</td><td>..</td><td>..</td><td>..</td></tr>
<tr><td>148 Papua New Guinea</td><td>..</td><td>..</td><td>..</td><td>..</td><td>0.209</td></tr>
<tr><td>Kiribati</td><td>..</td><td>..</td><td>..</td><td>..</td><td>..</td></tr>
<tr><td>Marshall Islands</td><td>..</td><td>..</td><td>..</td><td>..</td><td>..</td></tr>
<tr><td>Micronesia (Federated States of)</td><td>..</td><td>..</td><td>..</td><td>..</td><td>..</td></tr>
<tr><td>Nauru</td><td>..</td><td>..</td><td>..</td><td>..</td><td>..</td></tr>
<tr><td>Palau</td><td>..</td><td>..</td><td>..</td><td>..</td><td>..</td></tr>
<tr><td>Tuvalu</td><td>..</td><td>..</td><td>..</td><td>..</td><td>..</td></tr>
</table>

Notes: The GDI ranges between 0 (minimum) and 1 (maximum). Higher values indicate greater gender equality (UNDP 2007). The GEM ranges between 0 (minimum) and 1 (maximum). Higher values indicate greater gender equality (UNDP 2007). The GGI varies between 0 and 1. Higher values indicate greater gender equality (Hausmann et al. 2009). The GEI ranges between 0% (maximum gender gap) and 100% (no gender gap) (Social Watch n.d.). The SIGI varies between 0 (no or very low inequality) and 1 (high inequality) (OECD n.d.-a). Higher values indicate high inequality.

Sources: (a) UNDP 2009; (b) Hausmann et al. 2009; (c) Social Watch n.d.; (d) OECD n.d.-a.

MILLENNIUM DEVELOPMENT GOALS, TARGETS AND INDICATORS

Goals and Targets#	Indicators for monitoring progress#
Goal 1: Eradicate extreme poverty and hunger	
Target 1.A: Halve, between 1990 and 2015, the proportion of people whose income is less than one dollar a day	1.1 Proportion of population below $1 (PPP) per day [a] 1.2 Poverty gap ratio 1.3 Share of poorest quintile in national consumption
Target 1.B: Achieve full and productive employment and decent work for all, including women and young people	1.4 Growth rate of GDP per person employed 1.5 Employment-to-population ratio 1.6 Proportion of employed people living below $1 (PPP) per day 1.7 Proportion of own-account and contributing family workers in total employment
Target 1.C: Halve, between 1990 and 2015, the proportion of people who suffer from hunger	1.8 Prevalence of underweight children under-five years of age 1.9 Proportion of population below minimum level of dietary energy consumption
Goal 2: Achieve universal primary education	
Target 2.A: Ensure that, by 2015, children everywhere, boys and girls alike, will be able to complete a full course of primary schooling	2.1 Net enrolment ratio in primary education 2.2 Proportion of pupils starting grade 1 who reach last grade of primary 2.3 Literacy rate of 15-24 year-olds, women and men
Goal 3: Promote gender equality and empower women	
Target 3.A: Eliminate gender disparity in primary and secondary education, preferably by 2005, and in all levels of education no later than 2015	3.1 Ratios of girls to boys in primary, secondary and tertiary education 3.2 Share of women in wage employment in the non-agricultural sector 3.3 Proportion of seats held by women in national parliament
Goal 4: Reduce child mortality	
Target 4.A: Reduce by two-thirds, between 1990 and 2015, the under-five mortality rate	4.1 Under-five mortality rate 4.2 Infant mortality rate 4.3 Proportion of 1 year-old children immunised against measles
Goal 5: Improve maternal health	
Target 5.A: Reduce by three quarters, between 1990 and 2015, the maternal mortality ratio	5.1 Maternal mortality ratio 5.2 Proportion of births attended by skilled health personnel
Target 5.B: Achieve, by 2015, universal access to reproductive health	5.3 Contraceptive prevalence rate 5.4 Adolescent birth rate 5.5 Antenatal care coverage (at least one visit and at least four visits) 5.6 Unmet need for family planning
Goal 6: Combat HIV/AIDS, malaria and other diseases	
Target 6.A: Have halted by 2015 and begun to reverse the spread of HIV/AIDS	6.1 HIV prevalence among population aged 15-24 years 6.2 Condom use at last high-risk sex 6.3 Proportion of population aged 15-24 years with comprehensive correct knowledge of HIV/AIDS 6.4 Ratio of school attendance of orphans to school attendance of non-orphans aged 10-14 years
Target 6.B: Achieve, by 2010, universal access to treatment for HIV/AIDS for all those who need it	6.5 Proportion of population with advanced HIV infection with access to antiretroviral drugs

Contd...

Contd...

Goals and Targets[#]	Indicators for monitoring progress[#]
Target 6.C: Have halted by 2015 and begun to reverse the incidence of malaria and other major diseases	6.6 Incidence and death rates associated with malaria 6.7 Proportion of children under 5 sleeping under insecticide-treated bednets 6.8 Proportion of children under 5 with fever who are treated with appropriate anti-malarial drugs 6.9 Incidence, prevalence and death rates associated with tuberculosis 6.10 Proportion of tuberculosis cases detected and cured under directly observed treatment short course

Goal 7: Ensure environmental sustainability

Target 7.A: Integrate the principles of sustainable development into country policies and programmes and reverse the loss of environmental resources	7.1 Proportion of land area covered by forest 7.2 CO_2 emissions, total, per capita and per \$1 GDP (PPP) 7.3 Consumption of ozone-depleting substances 7.4 Proportion of fish stocks within safe biological limits 7.5 Proportion of total water resources used
Target 7.B: Reduce biodiversity loss, achieving, by 2010, a significant reduction in the rate of loss	7.6 Proportion of terrestrial and marine areas protected 7.7 Proportion of species threatened with extinction
Target 7.C: Halve, by 2015, the proportion of people without sustainable access to safe drinking water and basic sanitation	7.8 Proportion of population using an improved drinking water source 7.9 Proportion of population using an improved sanitation facility
Target 7.D: By 2020, to have achieved a significant improvement in the lives of at least 100 million slum dwellers	7.10 Proportion of urban population living in slums [b]

Goal 8: Develop a global partnership for development

Target 8.A: Develop further an open, rule-based, predictable, non-discriminatory trading and financial system Includes a commitment to good governance, development and poverty reduction – both nationally and internationally **Target 8.B:** Address the special needs of the least developed countries Includes: tariff and quota free access for the least developed countries' exports; enhanced programme of debt relief for heavily indebted poor countries (HIPC) and cancellation of official bilateral debt; and more generous ODA for countries committed to poverty reduction **Target 8.C:** Address the special needs of landlocked developing countries and small island developing States (through the Programme of Action for the Sustainable Development of Small Island Developing States and the outcome of the twenty-second special session of the General Assembly)	*Some of the indicators listed below are monitored separately for the least developed countries (LDCs), Africa, landlocked developing countries and small island developing States.* Official development assistance (ODA) 8.1 Net ODA, total and to the least developed countries, as percentage of OECD/DAC donors' gross national income 8.2 Proportion of total bilateral, sector-allocable ODA of OECD/DAC donors to basic social services (basic education, primary health care, nutrition, safe water and sanitation) 8.3 Proportion of bilateral official development assistance of OECD/DAC donors that is untied 8.4 ODA received in landlocked developing countries as a proportion of their gross national incomes 8.5 ODA received in small island developing States as a proportion of their gross national incomes Market access 8.6 Proportion of total developed country imports (by value and excluding arms) from developing countries and least developed countries, admitted free of duty 8.7 Average tariffs imposed by developed countries on agricultural products and textiles and clothing from developing countries 8.8 Agricultural support estimate for OECD countries as a percentage of their gross domestic product 8.9 Proportion of ODA provided to help build trade capacity

Contd...

Contd...

Goals and Targets#	Indicators for monitoring progress#
Target 8.D: Deal comprehensively with the debt problems of developing countries through national and international measures in order to make debt sustainable in the long term	<u>Debt sustainability</u> 8.10 Total number of countries that have reached their HIPC decision points and number that have reached their HIPC completion points (cumulative) 8.11 Debt relief committed under HIPC and MDRI Initiatives 8.12 Debt service as a percentage of exports of goods and services
Target 8.E: In cooperation with pharmaceutical companies, provide access to affordable essential drugs in developing countries	8.13 Proportion of population with access to affordable essential drugs on a sustainable basis
Target 8.F: In cooperation with the private sector, make available the benefits of new technologies, especially information and communications	8.14 Telephone lines per 100 population 8.15 Cellular subscribers per 100 population 8.16 Internet users per 100 population

Notes: The Millennium Development Goals and targets come from the Millennium Declaration, signed by 189 countries, including 147 heads of State and Government, in September 2000 (http://www.un.org/millennium/declaration/ares552e.htm) and from further agreement by member states at the 2005 World Summit (Resolution adopted by the General Assembly – A/RES/60/1, (http://www.un.org/Docs/journal/asp/ws.asp?m=A/RES/60/1). The goals and targets are interrelated and should be seen as a whole. They represent a partnership between the developed countries and the developing countries "to create an environment – at the national and global levels alike – which is conducive to development and the elimination of poverty".

Effective 15 January 2008.

a For monitoring country poverty trends, indicators based on national poverty lines should be used, where available.

b The actual proportion of people living in slums is measured by a proxy, represented by the urban population living in households with at least one of the four characteristics: (a) lack of access to improved water supply; (b) lack of access to improved sanitation; (c) overcrowding (3 or more persons per room); and (d) dwellings made of non-durable material.

Source: http://mdgs.un.org/unsd/mdg/Host.aspx?Content=Indicators/OfficialList.htm. Last accessed on 30 September 2009.

Statistical References

Committee on the Elimination of Discrimination against Women. 2001. 'Monitoring committee for women's anti discrimination Convention consider report of Maldives'. 498th and 499th Meetings. UN Press Release. WOM/1255. [http://www.un.org/News/Press/docs/2001/wom1255.doc.html]. Last accessed on 5 January 2009.

Hausmann, Ricardo, Laura D. Tyson, and Saadia Zahidi. 2009. *The global gender gap report 2009.* Geneva: World Economic Forum.

Hawken, Angela, and Gerardo L. Munck. 2009. 'Cross-national indices with gender-differentiated data: What do they measure? How valid are they?' Technical background paper for the Asia-Pacific Human Development Report *Power, voice and rights: A turning point for gender equality in Asia and the Pacific.* Unpublished.

Ihsan, Fatiman, and Yasmin Zaidi. 2006. 'The interplay of CEDAW, national laws and customary practices in Pakistan: A literature review'. In Shaheen Sardar Ali, ed. *Conceptualising Islamic law, CEDAW and women's human rights in plural legal settings: A comparative analysis of application of CEDAW in Bangladesh, India and Pakistan.* Delhi: UNIFEM South Asia Regional Office.

ILO (International Labour Organization). n.d. *ILOLEX database of international labour standards.* [http://www.ilo.org/ilolex/english/newratframeE.html]. Last accessed on 6 November 2009.

IPU (Inter-Parliamentary Union). 2009. 'Women in national parliaments'. Situation as of 31 July. [http://www. ipu.org/wmn-e/classif.html]. Last accessed on 18 September 2009.

Jivan, Vedna, and Christine Forstcr. 2007. *Translating CEDAW into law: CEDAW legislative compliance in nine Pacific Island countries.* Suva: UNDP Pacific Centre and UNIFEM Pacific Regional Office.

Jütting, Johannes P., Christian Morrisson, Jeff Dayton-Johnson, and Denis Drechsler. 2006. *Measuring gender (in)equality: Introducing the gender, institutions and development data base (GID).* OECD Development Centre Working Paper No. 247. Paris: OECD.

Klasen, Stephen, and Claudia Wink. 2002. *Missing women: A review of the debates and an analysis of recent trends.* [http://papers.ssrn.com/sol3/papers.cfm?abstract_id=321861]. Last accessed on 16 July 2009.

OECD (Organization for Economic Co-operation and Development). n.d.-a. Gender, institutions and development data base 2009 (GID-DB). [http://stats.oecd.org/index. aspx]. Last accessed on 2 July 2009.

OECD (Organization for Economic Co-operation and Development). n.d.-b. Gender equality and social institutions in Afghanistan. [http://genderindex.org/country/afghanistan]. Last accessed on 5 January 2009.

Sen, Amartya. 1990a. 'Gender and cooperative conflicts'. In Irene Tinker, ed. *Persistent inequalities: Women and world development.* New York: Oxford University Press.

Sen, Amartya. 1990b. 'More than 100 million women are missing'. *The New York Review of Books* 37 (20): 61-66.

Social Watch. n.d. Gender equity index 2008. [http://www.socialwatch.org/node/9269]. Last accessed on 2 July 2009.

Sriro, Andrew I. 2006. *Sriro's desk reference of Indonesian law.* Jakarta: Equinox Publishing.

UN (United Nations). 2009. *World population prospects: The 2008 revision.* United Nations Population Division. UNdata: A world of information. United Nations Statistics Division. [http://data.un.org/Browse.aspx?d = PopDiv]. Last accessed on 17 November 2009.

UN (United Nations). 2008a. *Demographic yearbook.* UNdata: A world of information. United Nations Statistics Division. [http://unstats.un.org/unsd/demographic/products/dyb/dyb2006.htm]. Last accessed on 2 July 2009.

UN (United Nations). 2008b. *Gender info 2007.* UNdata: A world of information. United Nations Statistics Division. [http://data.un.org/Browse.aspx?d = 16]. Last accessed on 17 November 2009.

UN (United Nations). n.d. *United Nations treaty collection.* [http://treaties.un.org/Pages Treaties.aspx?id = 4&subid = A&lang = en]. Last accessed on 1 October 2009.

UNDP (United Nations Development Programme). 2009. *Human development report 2009 – Overcoming barriers: Human mobility and development.* New York: Palgrave Macmillan.

UNDP (United Nations Development Programme). 2008. *Human development indices: A statistical update 2008.* New York: United Nations Development Programme.

UNDP (United Nations Development Programme). 2007. *Human development report 2007/2008 – Fighting climate change: Human solidarity in a divided world.* New York: Palgrave Macmillan.

UNESCO (United Nations Educational, Scientific and Cultural Organization). 2009. *Data Centre.* UNESCO Institute for Statistics. [http://stats.uis.unesco.org/unesco/Table Viewer/document.aspx?ReportId = 143&IF_ Language = eng]. Last accessed on 17 November 2009.

UNIFEM (United Nations Development Fund for Women). 2008. *Progress of the world's women 2008/2009: Who answers to women? Gender and accountability.* New York: UNIFEM.

WHO (World Health Organization). 2008. *WHO data: Mortality and burden of disease.* UNdata: A world of information. United Nations Statistics Division. [http://data.un.org/Browse.aspx?d = WHO&f = inID % 3a MBD07]. Last accessed on 17 November 2009.

World Bank. 2009a. *World development indicators online 2009.* [https://publications.worldbank. org/register/WDI?return % 5furl = % 2fextop % 2fsubscriptions % 2fWDI % 2f]. Last accessed on 2 July 2009.

World Bank. 2009b. *Gender stats online 2009.* [http://ddp-ext.worldbank.org/ext/DDPQQ/member.do?method = getMembers&userid = 1&queryId = 182]. Last accessed on 2 July 2009.

Reports of States Parties to UN Committee on CEDAW

CEDAW. 2009. *Consideration of reports submitted by States Parties under article 18 of the Convention on the Elimination of All Forms of Discrimination against Women. Fourth periodic report of States Parties: Singapore.* Committee on the Elimination of Discrimination against Women. CEDAW/C/SGP/4.

CEDAW. 2008a. *Consideration of reports submitted by States Parties under article 18 of the Convention on the Elimination of All Forms of Discrimination against Women. Initial periodic report of States Parties: Timor-Leste.* Committee on the Elimination of Discrimination against Women. CEDAW/C/TLS/1.

CEDAW. 2008b. *Consideration of reports submitted by States Parties under article 18 of the Convention on the Elimination of All Forms of Discrimination against Women. Sixth periodic report of States Parties: Japan.* Committee on the Elimination of Discrimination against Women. CEDAW/C/JPN/6.

CEDAW. 2007a. *Consideration of reports submitted by States Parties under article 18 of the Convention on the Elimination of All Forms of Discrimination against Women. Seventh periodic report of States Parties: Bhutan.* Committee on the Elimination of Discrimination against Women.CEDAW/C/BTN/7.

CEDAW. 2007b. *Consideration of reports submitted by States Parties under article 18 of the Convention on the Elimination of All*

Forms of Discrimination against Women. Combined fifth, sixth and seventh periodic reports of States Parties: Mongolia. Committee on the Elimination of Discrimination against Women. CEDAW/C/MNG/7.

CEDAW. **2007c.** *Consideration of reports submitted by States Parties under article 18 of the Convention on the Elimination of All Forms of Discrimination against Women. Combined second and third periodic reports of States Parties: Myanmar.* Committee on the Elimination of Discrimination against Women. CEDAW/C/MMR/3.

CEDAW. **2007d.** *Consideration of report submitted by States Parties under article 18 of the Convention on the Elimination of All Forms of Discrimination against Women. Sixth periodic report of States Parties: Republic of Korea.* Committee on the Elimination of Discrimination against Women. CEDAW/C/KOR/6.

CEDAW. **2005a.** *Consideration of reports submitted by States Parties under article 18 of the Convention on the Elimination of All Forms of Discrimination against Women. Combined second and third periodic reports of States Parties: India.* Committee on the Elimination of Discrimination against Women. CEDAW/C/IND/2-3.

CEDAW. **2005b.** *Consideration of reports submitted by States Parties under article 18 of the Convention on the Elimination of All Forms of Discrimination against Women. Combined fourth and fifth periodic reports of States Parties: Indonesia.* Committee on the Elimination of Discrimination against Women. CEDAW/C/IDN/4-5.

CEDAW. **2005c.** *Consideration of reports submitted by States Parties under article 18 of the Convention on the Elimination of All Forms of Discrimination against Women. Combined second and third periodic reports of States Parties: Maldives.* Committee on the Elimination of Discrimination against Women. CEDAW/C/MDV/2-3.

CEDAW. **2005d.** *Consideration of reports submitted by States Parties under article 18 of the Convention on the Elimination of All Forms of Discrimination against Women. Combined initial, second and third periodic reports of States Parties: Pakistan.* Committee on the Elimination of Discrimination against Women. CEDAW/C/PAK/1-3.

CEDAW. **2005e.** *Consideration of reports submitted by States Parties under article 18 of the Convention on the Elimination of All Forms of Discrimination against Women. Combined fifth and sixth periodic reports of States Parties: Viet Nam.* Committee on the Elimination of Discrimination against Women. CEDAW/C/VNM/5-6.

CEDAW. **2004a.** *Consideration of reports submitted by States Parties under article 18 of the Convention on the Elimination of All Forms of Discrimination against Women. Combined initial, second and third periodic reports of States Parties: Cambodia.* Committee on the Elimination of Discrimination against Women. CEDAW/C/KHM/1-3.

CEDAW. **2004b.** *Consideration of reports submitted by States Parties under article 18 of the Convention on the Elimination of All Forms of Discrimination against Women. Combined fifth and sixth periodic report of States Parties: China.* Committee on the Elimination of Discrimination against Women. CEDAW/C/CHN/5-6.

CEDAW. **2004c.** *Consideration of reports submitted by States Parties under article 18 of the Convention on the Elimination of All Forms of Discrimination against Women. Combined initial and second periodic reports of States Parties: Malaysia.* Committee on the Elimination of Discrimination against Women. CEDAW/C/MYS/1-2.

CEDAW. **2004d.** *Consideration of reports submitted by States Parties under article 18 of the Convention on the Elimination of All Forms of Discrimination against Women. Combined fifth and sixth periodic reports of States Parties: Philippines.* Committee on the Elimination of Discrimination against Women. CEDAW/C/PHI/5-6.

CEDAW. **2004e.** *Consideration of reports submitted by States Parties under article 18 of the Convention on the Elimination of All Forms of Discrimination against Women. Combined fourth and fifth periodic report of States Parties: Thailand.* Committee on the Elimination of Discrimination against Women. CEDAW/C/THA/4-5.

CEDAW. 2003a. *Consideration of reports submitted by States Parties under article 18 of the Convention on the Elimination of All Forms of Discrimination against Women. Fifth periodic report of States Parties: Bangladesh.* Committee on the Elimination of Discrimination against Women. CEDAW/C/BGD/5.

CEDAW. 2003b. *Consideration of reports submitted by States Parties under article 18 of the Convention on the Elimination of All Forms of Discrimination against Women. Combined initial, second, third, fourth and fifth periodic reports of States Parties: Lao People's Democratic Republic.* Committee on the Elimination of Discrimination against Women. CEDAW/C/LAO/1-5.

CEDAW. 2003c. *Consideration of reports submitted by States Parties under article 18 of the Convention on the Elimination of All Forms of Discrimination against Women. Combined second and third periodic report of States Parties: Nepal.* Committee on the Elimination of Discrimination against Women. CEDAW/C/NPL/2-3.

CEDAW. 2002. *Consideration of reports submitted by States Parties under article 18 of the Convention on the Elimination of All Forms of Discrimination against Women. Initial report of States Parties: Democratic People's Republic of Korea.* Committee on the Elimination of Discrimination against Women. CEDAW/C/PRK/1.

CEDAW. 1999. *Consideration of reports submitted by States Parties under article 18 of the Convention on the Elimination of All Forms of Discrimination against Women. Third and fourth reports of States Parties: Sri Lanka.* Committee on the Elimination of Discrimination against Women. CEDAW/C/LKA/3-4.